The Cambridge Introduction to
Early English Theatre

This introduction offers an overview of early English theatre from the earliest recorded vernacular texts in the late medieval period to the closing of the theatres in 1642. Where most existing studies focus on one side or the other of an imaginary boundary between 'medieval' and 'early modern' or 'Renaissance' drama, this book examines the theatre of nearly three centuries in a way that highlights continuities as well as divisions. The study is organised into five subject-based chapters: Places of performance; Actors and audiences; Writers, controllers and the place of theatre; Genre and tradition; Instruction and spectacle. It includes full chronologies, helpful text boxes and over twenty illustrations.

JANETTE DILLON is Professor of Drama at the School of English, University of Nottingham.

Cambridge Introductions to Literature

This series is designed to introduce students to key topics and authors. Accessible and lively, these introductions will also appeal to readers who want to broaden their understanding of the books and authors they enjoy.

- Ideal for students, teachers, and lecturers
- Concise, yet packed with essential information
- Key suggestions for further reading

Titles in this series:

Bulson *The Cambridge Introduction to James Joyce*
Cooper *The Cambridge Introduction to T. S. Eliot*
Dillon *The Cambridge Introduction to Early English Theatre*
Goldman *The Cambridge Introduction to Virginia Woolf*
Holdeman *The Cambridge Introduction to W. B. Yeats*
McDonald *The Cambridge Introduction to Samuel Beckett*
Peters *The Cambridge Introduction to Joseph Conrad*
Scofield *The Cambridge Introduction to the American Short Story*
Todd *The Cambridge Introduction to Jane Austen*

The Cambridge Introduction to
Early English Theatre

JANETTE DILLON

CAMBRIDGE
UNIVERSITY PRESS

CAMBRIDGE UNIVERSITY PRESS
Cambridge, New York, Melbourne, Madrid, Cape Town, Singapore, São Paulo

Cambridge University Press
The Edinburgh Building, Cambridge CB2 2RU, UK

Published in the United States of America by Cambridge University Press, New York

www.cambridge.org
Information on this title: www.cambridge.org/9780521542517

First published 2006

Printed in the United Kingdom at the University Press, Cambridge

A catalogue record for this publication is available from the British Library

ISBN-13 978-0-521-83474-2 hardback
ISBN-10 0-521-83474-0 hardback

ISBN-13 978-0-521-54251-7 paperback
ISBN-10 0-521-54251-0 paperback

For Brean

Contents

Illustrations

Tables

Preface

My aim in writing this book has been to offer an overview of early English drama from the earliest recorded vernacular texts in the late medieval period to the closing of the theatres in 1642. The year 1642 is an unusually precise date for the termination of a volume which is marked elsewhere, and especially in its earliest material, by vagueness and uncertainty over dating. The reader can see this vagueness clearly illustrated in Appendix 1, where select plays of the period are listed by date. Dating parameters range from 1376–1580 (for the York cycle: a stretch encompassing the known period of performance for a group of plays which were probably substantially altered and revised over that time) to a single year in which a play may be known to have been both written and performed (as in the case of the highly topical *A Game at Chess* in 1624). In other instances, such as the N-town cycle, the group of plays from which it was assembled is known to be a compilation including some quite disparate material dating from different years, so that the overall date assigned to the cycle in the chronology is based on what is known of the extant manuscript and its language rather than on any evidence of performance auspices, which is notably lacking. Hence some dates are 'harder' and more meaningful than others; and, though the book generally adopts the procedure of putting dates in brackets after plays named or discussed, it does not adopt that practice where to do so might be misleading, as is especially the case with the often revised and adapted medieval cycles.

Though I have described the book above as an 'overview', it is not a chronological survey, nor does it aim for quasi-neutrality or the smoothing over of controversy or disagreement. On the contrary, it aims to argue a case arising out of the unusual breadth of the period surveyed. Where most existing studies focus on one side or the other of an imaginary boundary between 'medieval' and 'early modern' (or 'Renaissance') drama, my aim is to look at the theatre of the nearly three centuries between about 1350–1400 and 1642 (with occasional comparison outside these limits) in an attempt to highlight its continuities as well as its divisions. All the descriptive terms for historical period division above are unsatisfactory in various ways: 'medieval' implies a period that comes in the 'middle', thus suggesting two more marked and definable periods on either side of it; 'early modern' implies a turn towards the modern and a perspective on the earlier period that views it teleologically as evolving towards the 'modern' that it is to become; 'Renaissance', on the other hand, implies sudden rebirth after relative dullness (C. S. Lewis' 'drab' age), thus looking backwards in a way that is as reductive as the forward perspective of 'early modern'. There is no escape from these terms, however, and this book uses them as part of the common currency of critical writing about the period. But I hope it does so with this difference: that instead of using them to seal a boundary between the medieval and the early modern, it allows them to describe different parts of the same picture, so that changes in the picture make sense within those parts of it that remain the same.

A further aim of the book is to let contemporary materials speak for themselves as much of the time, and often in as raw a state, as possible. This is the objective underpinning the shaded boxing of many quotations. By typographically isolating the quotation, boxes immediately allow the reader to see what someone else has said, and when, and to see that apart from, as well as within, the surrounding argument. The content of the boxes is always closely linked to the argument, sometimes very directly and immediately to the preceding sentence, and sometimes more generally, but the box allows the reader to absorb it in a slightly different way from the content of quotations integrated into the argument. Thus, where the argument over a paragraph or more is relying on quotations to illustrate the analysis of a particular play, for example, it is likely that those quotations will be typographically integrated into the surrounding prose; but where the quotations are doing separate work as well, and the reader is being invited to make his or her own assessment of their content, they will be shaded.

Quotations from plays have been taken, where possible, from plays in currently available anthologies, for ease of access, but spelling has been modernised throughout. Modernising spelling does occasionally distort meaning, especially in the case of medieval texts; but modernising the spelling of Shakespeare only, or of early modern plays only, two common editorial practices, perpetuates and highlights the imaginary boundary between medieval and early modern that the book as a whole rejects. For this reason, then, as well as for accessibility to student readers, it seemed appropriate to modernise spelling. The meanings of difficult words remaining are glossed in square brackets. Punctuation of early texts quoted follows editors where quotation is from a modern edition, but modernises slightly from unedited texts. Dates are rationalised to the current system, with the year beginning on 1 January. Money is counted under the old system, in pounds, shillings and pence, with twelve pence

(12d) making up one shilling (1s) and twenty shillings (20s) making up one pound (£1).

I have used a short citation system in order to keep endnotes to a minimum. All works from which quotations are taken are listed in the Bibliography. Authors and short titles only are supplied in the text or notes. Plays cited are listed in the bibliography by author, or by name in the case of anonymous plays, with an indication of the edition from which citation is taken. Notes clarify only ambiguous cases. Quotations from Shakespeare are taken from *The Riverside Shakespeare* unless otherwise indicated.

For simplicity and ease of reading, a decision was taken to provide author, title and date for shaded quotations, but not to note actual editions and sources of reference, which would have cluttered the boxes or extended the notes very considerably. Act, scene and line numbers are given for plays where possible, but some texts cited from early editions or from the Chadwyck-Healy database, compiled from such early editions, have no act divisions, sometimes no scene divisions and occasionally no line numbering. Where no author is cited, the text is anonymous.

I would like to acknowledge a particular debt to the collection of theatrical records assembled by Glynne Wickham, Herbert Berry and William Ingram in *English Professional Theatre 1530–1660* (Cambridge: Cambridge University Press, 2000). This is a wonderful resource, from which a significant number of my quotations from early documents are taken, and to which serious students of early drama should return if they wish to understand some of the documents quoted here within a fuller context. It may also be worth observing here that the reason for the bias towards fuller quotation from early modern than from medieval documents is due to the much greater fullness of extant records in the later period. My debt to the collected and ongoing volumes of the REED (Records of Early English Drama) project is as great as to Wickham, Berry and Ingram, but evidence of medieval theatrical practice is disparate and locally specific in such a way as to make its relevance often particular to the individual instance and less easily extractable from that context.

I wish to thank the University of Nottingham and the Arts and Humanities Research Board (now Council) for giving me the time to write this book. Above all, I am grateful to those friends and colleagues who have read drafts, offered advice, or discussed with me so many of the problems raised by a book of this kind, in particular Andy Gurr, Brean Hammond, Julie Sanders, Simon Shepherd, Sarah Stanton, Peter Thomson and Greg Walker. My apologies to them for any errors that remain.

Abbreviations

CHD	Chadwyck-Healy database of English drama, http://lion.chadwyck.co.uk/
DTRB	Ian Lancashire, *Dramatic Texts and Records of Britain: A Chronological Topography to 1558* (Cambridge: Cambridge University Press, 1984)
EEBO	Early English Books Online, http://eebo.chadwyck.com/
EETS	Early English Text Society
ELH	*English Literary History*
ELR	*English Literary Renaissance*
EPT	Glynne Wickham, Herbert Berry and William Ingram, eds., *English Professional Theatre 1530–1660*, Cambridge: Cambridge University Press, 2000
ES	E. K. Chambers, *The Elizabethan Stage*, 4 vols. (Oxford: Clarendon Press, 1923)
OED	*Oxford English Dictionary*, 2nd edition

Chapter 1

Places of performance

Performance spaces

Early theatrical performance in England was not linked either with professional companies or with purpose-built playhouses. Playing arose out of particular sets of circumstances in specific places at specific times: a group of travelling players arriving in town or calling at the great house of a local lord; a group of parishioners wishing to stage a play in order to raise money for a new roof for the church; a city wishing to honour a religious festival and attract visitors to the city; an enterprising individual staging versions of her neighbours' adulterous affairs in her back yard. This absence of any necessary tie to playhouses or professional companies means that it can be quite difficult to put a boundary around what should be classed as 'theatre'.

Performance in churches and churchyards, for example, widespread from medieval times into the early seventeenth century, constitutes a case in point. Scholars argue about whether we should properly seek to mark a boundary between church ritual and church drama and, if so, where it is to be drawn. The problem centres on our notion of performance. Few would argue that a church service is not 'performed' in some sense, but the terms 'theatre' and 'drama' seem to introduce a different dimension, and the former especially was historically used as a term of abuse by Reformers and Protestants attacking the ritual of the Catholic mass.[1] The fact is that the church was host to a whole spectrum of different kinds of performance, ranging from set speeches and responses, singing and the ritual acts of the mass, to slightly expanded and elaborated ritual enactments of liturgical material, sung Latin dramatisations of biblical material and secular, vernacular playing. This medley of practice, however, cannot be represented as an evolutionary development from 'church' drama to 'secular' drama. One reason why we now have such difficulty in making this distinction is that we are imposing it on a culture that did not operate within that kind of binary, but where the church was so inextricably entwined with both the state and everyday life that thinking through their separation would have been very difficult

1

1. Map of England, marking places of performance mentioned in the text.

for someone living in the period covered by this book, especially the early part.

A distinction between religious and secular performance is not one that the places of performance will support. Drama did not simply move, as scholars once argued, from inside to outside the church. Drama that we might consider secular was sometimes performed inside churches, at least from the sixteenth century, if not before, just as drama that we would consider religious might be performed outside churches. It is arguable, as John Wasson says, 'that far more than half of all vernacular plays of the English Middle Ages and Renaissance were in fact performed in churches'.[2] And vernacular plays might include plays defined, by later standards, as either religious or secular in content, or both simultaneously. Precisely one of the problems encountered by later scholars seeking to divide performance into these two categories is that in practice they constantly overlap: a 'religious' play like the Towneley *Second Shepherds' Play* deliberately sets a farce in which a stolen sheep is swaddled and laid in a cradle alongside a dramatisation of the birth of the Lamb of God, while 'secular' plays like John Bale's *King John* (*c.* 1538) or Shakespeare's history plays naturally set the discourse of politics within a framework of religious thinking (for example, about anointed kings and their duty to God as well as England, or the usurper's need to atone for his sin).

Some kinds of drama can be identified as fairly specifically tied to one performance location. Thus Latin liturgical drama can truly be described as 'church drama', since it was written only for performance within a church; the great cycle plays of biblical drama may be described as 'street theatre', since they were specifically written for performance in the streets of a given city; and court mask (or masque)[3] was designed for a single performance at court. But most plays were and had to be adaptable to a number of different performance locations, since most players travelled. From the King's Men to the smallest travelling company (4–6 was normal in the early sixteenth century, but some plays were written for even fewer),[4] companies expected to be able to put on their plays in whatever indoor or outdoor venue a town, village or great house offered them, from halls, inns, churches and chapels to open fields, innyards, churchyards and market-places.[5]

Enter Player

MORE   Welcome good friend, what is your will with me?
PLAYER My lord, my fellows and myself
        Are come to tender ye our willing service,
        So please you to command us.
MORE   What, for a play, you mean?
        Whom do you serve?
PLAYER   My lord Cardinal's grace.
MORE   My lord Cardinal's players? Now trust me, welcome.
        You happen hither in a lucky time,
        To pleasure me, and benefit yourselves.
        The mayor of London and some aldermen,

> His lady and their wives, are my kind guests
> This night at supper. Now, to have a play
> Before the banquet will be excellent.
> How think you, son Roper?
> ROPER   'Twill do well, my lord,
> And be right pleasing pastime to your guests.
> MORE   I prithee tell me, what plays have ye?
> PLAYER   Diverse, my lord: *The Cradle of Security*,
>   *Hit Nail o'th'Head*, *Impatient Poverty*,
>   *The Play of Four P's*, *Dives and Lazarus*,
>   *Lusty Juventus*, and *The Marriage of Wit and Wisdom*.
> MORE   'The Marriage of Wit and Wisdom'? That, my lads,
>   I'll none but that, the theme is very good,
>   And may maintain a liberal argument.
>   To marry wit to wisdom asks some cunning:
>   Many have wit, that may come short of wisdom.
>   Anthony Munday et al, *Sir Thomas More* (1592–3), III.2.45–68

Conceiving the performance space: *locus* and *platea*

The adaptability of performance to different kinds of places can be approached in terms of the overarching framework within which most styles of early performance are to be understood: namely *locus* and *platea* (terms made familiar through the groundbreaking work of Robert Weimann),[6] alternatively known as place and scaffold. This is basically a method of staging, a *use* of space rather than a demarcation or design of space; but it is necessary to understand a little bit about it in order to see how plays could be so adaptable to the various performance venues available before and after the building of designated playhouses. The two terms denote two interconnected ways of using space. While the place or *platea* is basically an open space, the *locus* can be literally a scaffold, but can also be any specifically demarcated space or architectural feature capable of being given representational meaning. Thus a door, an alcove, a scaffold, or a tent can represent a particular location, such as a house, a temple, a country, heaven or hell, or simply 'the place of (for example) Covetousness' (a conceptual rather than a properly physical place). The essential difference between a *locus* (of which there may be several) and the *platea* (which is by definition singular for any one performance) is precisely one of representational function: whereas a *locus* always represents, for a given stretch of time, a specific location, the *platea* is essentially fluid and frequently non-representational. It is not tied to the illusion, to the fictional places where the drama is set, but is often predominantly an actors' space, a space in which performance can be recognised as performance rather than as the fiction it intermittently seeks to represent.

If a comic doctor and his servant, for example, burst into a story about the conversion of a Jew who steals the sacrament, as happens in the Croxton *Play of the Sacrament* (1461–1520), it is no accident that we find them roaming round the *platea*, asking what ailments the audience have, making reference to people and places in the Croxton area, joking and interacting with the audience about familiar aspects of their contemporary world, whilst the characters who people the fictional conversion narrative remain still on their scaffolds. (Though they remain fixed on their scaffolds for the duration of this piece of action, however, they do occasionally cross the platea to get to other locations within the fiction at different points in the play.) Nor is it surprising that when the doctor and his man attempt to mount the scaffold which represents the Jews' house, the Jews beat them away and deny them access. For these two sets of characters embody two different worlds: one which is self-enclosed, illusionary, fictional, separate from the audience; and one which shares the audience's time and space, which is co-existent with them, sharing jokes with them in the knowledge that this is a performance and that two comics are here, now, to give the audience a good time. In the Digby play of *Mary Magdalene* (1480–1520), however, when Mary has to make a journey to Marseilles, she crosses the *platea* in a wheeled ship and arrives, probably, at a scaffold representing the palace of the King of Marseilles.[7] The *platea* is thus temporarily quite strictly representational. For the duration of the ship's crossing, combining seventeen lines of dialogue and some interjected song, it is the sea. But, unlike the scaffolds, which always and only represent single locations such as the King of Marseilles' palace or the castle of Magdalene in Bethany for the entire duration of the production, the *platea* will become many places, and sometimes no particular place, at different points in the action. Indeed, when an angel descends and appears to Mary just before the arrival of the ship, saying 'Abash thee not [be not abashed], Mary, in this place' (l.1376), the fluid meaning of the term 'place' is part of the overall meaning the play seeks to make. 'This place' is simultaneously the general location in which Mary is situated at that point of the narrative (Jerusalem) and the place of performance, where the audience sits in the here and now, seeing and hearing the enactment of past events as they have shaped the present. Moments later, when the ship arrives, the place must be understood to be a non-specific seashore.

The Play of the Sacrament and *Mary Magdalene* were probably performed in very different venues. In neither case do we know exactly where they were performed or how the venue was set up. The Croxton Play may have been staged partly outside and partly inside the parish church of Croxton, while

2. A conjectural reconstruction of the *Play of the Sacrament* in Croxton churchyard.

Mary Magdalene may have been staged in a number of different ways, perhaps in a round or a half round or perhaps drawing on the geographical features of a given secular site. What they have in common is the fundamental requirement of a combination of defined structures and open space, and this basic interplay between two kinds of space is deeply rooted in medieval and early modern drama across Europe. If we look at the interiors and exteriors of churches, one of the earliest known venues of performance, we see the potential for *locus* and *platea* staging in the combination of individual architectural features and the open spaces of the nave, the chancel and the 'crossing' (the space where the transept crossed the nave and chancel in cross-shaped churches). If we look at the standard design of great halls in manor houses, at court, in the universities and in the Inns of Court, we can see the potential specificity of features like the screens, the dais, the fireplace and the gallery operating in tension with the open space of the great rectangular frame. If we look at the very few staging diagrams extant in English manuscripts, we see a circular open space surrounded by representational structures.

3. A stage erected in the crossing in front of the roodscreen in the cathedral at Laon, 1566, for exorcism ceremonies. From Jean Boulaese, *Manuel de Victoire du Corps de Díeu sur l'Esprit Malin*, Paris 1575.

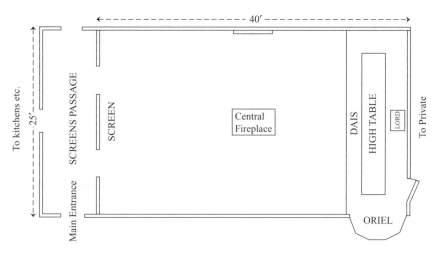

4. Floor plan of a great hall.

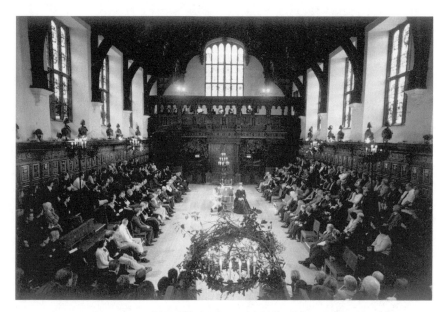

5. Performance of *Twelfth Night* in the hall of the Middle Temple, 2 February 2002.

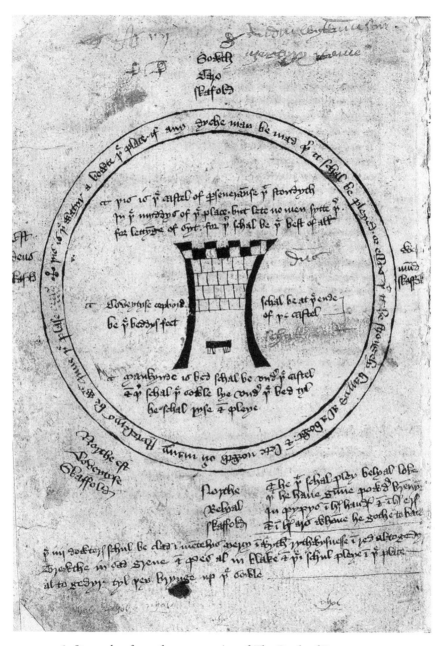

6. Stage plan from the manuscript of *The Castle of Perseverance*, late fifteenth century.

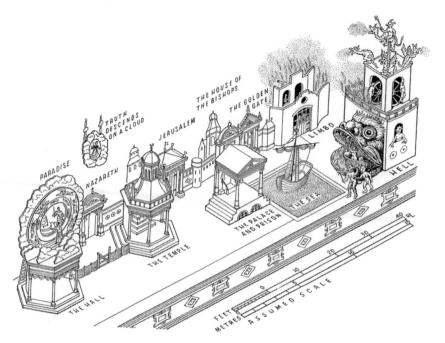

7. Reconstruction of the staging plan for the Valenciennes Passion Play, 1547.

European pictorial evidence suggests that the structures could be arranged in any number of ways: strung out in a line as at Valenciennes or arranged around a market square as at Lucerne. English urban ceremonies, such as coronation processions or royal entries, show the same combination of feature and space in the progression through open streets from one pageant location to another. (It was usual to adorn or build upon existing structures such as conduits, gates and other features: Glynne Wickham's photograph of the early fifteenth-century Market Cross at Shepton Mallet provides a good example of the kind of structure that naturally lent itself to performance in this way.)[8] Scholars are still divided about how much those cycle plays which used pageant wagons also used the street, but both urban ceremony, as described here, and court mask, which often brought elaborate pageant wagons into the open space of the hall and allowed the performers to descend from the wagon to perform in the open space, show clear precedents for a mode of performance that might use pageant wagons in conjunction with the surrounding space. On the other hand, performance on pageant wagons in narrow streets may have had very restricted opportunities to make use of the surrounding space.

A pageant, that is to say, a house of wainscot, painted, and builded on a cart with four wheels.
A square top to set over the said house.
A gryphon, gilt, with a fane [pennant] to set on the said top.
A bigger iron fane to set on the end of the pageant.
. . .
Six horse cloths, stained, with knobs and tassels.

Grocers' Company Records, Norwich, 1565

Then was there a device or a pageant upon wheels brought in, out of the which pageant issued out a gentleman richly appareled, that showed how in a garden of pleasure there was an arbour of gold, wherein were lords and ladies, much desirous to show pleasure and pastime to the Queen and ladies . . . then a great cloth of Arras that did hang before the same pageant was taken away, and the pageant brought more near. It was curiously made and pleasant to behold; it was solemn and rich, for every post or pillar thereof was covered with frise [ornamentally wrought] gold; therein were trees of hawthorn, eglantines, rosiers [rose-trees], vines and other pleasant flowers of divers colours, with gillofers [gillyflowers] and other herbs all made of satin, damask, silk, silver and gold, accordingly as the natural trees, herbs, or flowers ought to be. In which arbour were six ladies, all appareled in white satin and green.

Extract from description of the Golden Arbour pageant of February 1511, Hall's Chronicle (first published 1548)[9]

Simple precedents for this more restricted performance style include trestle and booth stages. A small stage erected on a trestle or barrels is relatively easily transportable in a horse-drawn cart and elevates the performers so that the performance becomes visible and accessible to a wider group of spectators. A curtain with dressing room space behind it at the back of such a stage turns it into a booth stage. It may be that performance on such stages made little use of the surrounding space; but the probability, given the likely range of venues and the strong performance tradition of *locus* and *platea*, is that, as with cycle performance, the possibility of using it was at least intermittently present. As Tydeman's reconstruction sketch of *Mankind* (1465–70) being performed in an innyard suggests, ascent and descent of the stage need not have been a very complicated matter.

What we see, then, is a wide range of individual variations on the basic arrangement of *locus* and *platea*, or spatial features in combination with open space. 'Standardization', as Peter Meredith puts it, 'is the last thing we should expect', even in the staging of similar kinds of events.[10] Whereas the York Corpus Christi cycle was staged over one day, for example, the Chester cycle eventually took place over three; where York and Chester were probably processionally

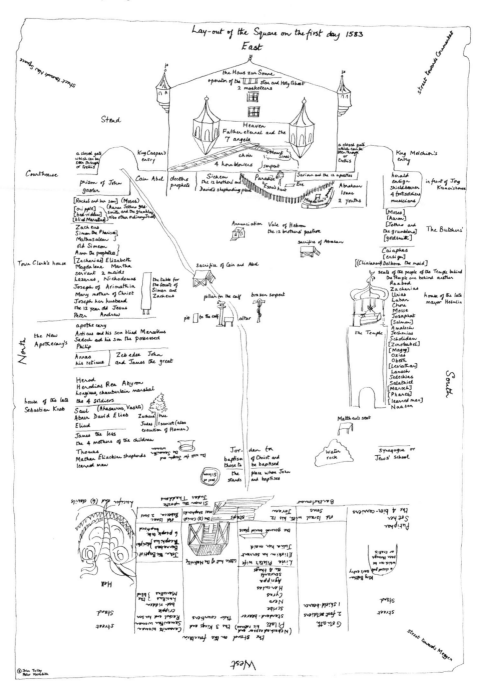

8a. Reconstruction of the staging plan for the first day of the Lucerne
Passion Play, 1583.

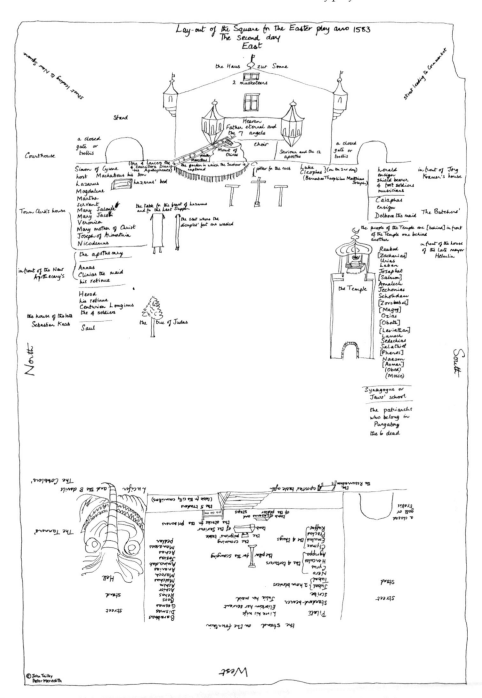

8b. Reconstruction of the staging plan for the second day of the Lucerne Passion Play.

9. Conjectural view of *Mankind* played on a booth stage in an innyard.

staged (that is, played at consecutive 'stations' around the town), N-town was probably staged in a fixed location; where York had twelve to sixteen stations, Chester had only four or five; and where York and Chester were probably performed only in those cities, the N-town plays may have toured.[11] (The name N-town derives from the banns, cited on p. 70 below. 'N' may stand for Latin *nomen*, meaning 'name'.) A wide range of effects, furthermore, could derive from *locus* and *platea* as separate features as well as from the different ways in which they could be scripted to interact with one another. Thus a *locus*, which might be any kind of marked structure, moveable or fixed, curtained or unenclosed, could operate to create a framing effect, offering the action within it as a picture for contemplation. The creation of formal symmetries and significant tableaux, perhaps drawing on existing visual tradition, as in books of hours, illustrated Bibles or other devotional literature, was thus a

10. The Annunciation. Illustration from a fourteenth-century manuscript of *Meditations on the Life of Christ*, at one time attributed to Saint Bonaventure.

possibility, as were other pictorial effects that anticipated the proscenium arch stage. The *platea*, on the other hand, might operate as unframed space, allowing both the boundary between performers and spectators and the space of each to become fluid. The combination of both these opposing modes of performance thus created an immensely flexible variety of staging effects.

Evidence and motives for performance

Most surviving early dramatic records, as a glance through the accumulating volumes of the Records of Early English Drama (REED) series or the Malone Society Collections will show, are accounts, which are by definition primarily concerned with listing and accounting for items of expenditure, not with detailing the place or content of performance. While such records often do tell us something about the geographical location of a performance, and sometimes specify more closely the actual site of performance, it can still be impossible to reconstruct the precise size and disposition of the playing space or, without knowing the content of what was performed, how it was used. Especially in the early period, before the building of permanent playhouses, the extant playtexts do not often coincide with the survival of other kinds of records (except in the case of the Corpus Christi plays) and it can thus also be difficult to tie the plays that survive to particular performance venues.

What we do learn from the extant accounts, however, is something of the range of motivations that could lead to the mounting of a play. The impetus for putting on a play might come from a number of different groups, and while Corpus Christi plays, sometimes mounted by urban trade guilds at the instigation of the city council, constitute the best surviving and best known form of medieval drama now, they were certainly not the most common form of drama in their time.[12] Civic drama, however, highlights an important difference between early and later motivations for staging plays. Where we tend to assume now that making money is the commonest reason for putting on a play and that amateur performances will be negligible in status and impact by comparison with professional theatre, early playing was not underpinned by the same assumptions. Only after the building of fixed theatres did the object of performing become primarily to make money for players, companies and theatre entrepreneurs; and when that began to happen, the level of outrage expressed provides some indication of how relatively new that state of affairs was (see chapter 3 below). Before that aims were more wide ranging, and such profit as was made funded a range of enterprises other than theatre itself.

These aims are of course closely tied to the patron and to the place of performance. The private players of a great lord or king, for example, might play before that lord's own household and his invited guests, and no payment would change hands; the object of the performance would be to entertain (and perhaps also teach) those present (see the exchange between Sir Thomas More and the player, pp. 3–4 above) and at the same time to signal the lord's social standing and largesse. Sometimes there might also be a subsidiary aim in performing a play with a particular message or piece of advice for some or all of the particular guests present. When the same lord's players toured, the function and message changed with different audiences: within the region of the lord's power and influence, his players functioned as a reminder of his position, his wealth and prestige and sometimes also perhaps of the kinds of views he held; outside the region they advertised the lord's status more widely and brought his name to the minds of those who might otherwise not think of him; and both the messages of the play's content and the social statement of the players' name and affiliation functioned differently in a town hall or a village square from the way they might function in the hall of another lord.

The interlude *Hick Scorner* (*c.* 1514), for example, was probably sponsored by Charles Brandon, favourite of Henry VIII, and performed at his London residence of Suffolk Place in Southwark. Its many local and topographical references to the London area, as Ian Lancashire has shown, would have made a particular kind of sense in the context of that performance. When Free Will enters with a rope and fetters saying:

> A, see! A, see, sirs, what I have brought!
> A medicine for a pair of sore shins.
> At the King's Bench, sirs, I have you sought,
>
> (lines 510–12)

his remark would have had especial relevance to both the location and the patron, since the King's Bench prison was located in Southwark and Charles Brandon himself was marshal of the prison in 1514.[13] If the play was performed outside Southwark, such closely topical lines would have had no special impact and may have been cut or altered for different performance venues.

We know of at least three specific places of performance for John Bale's *King John* (*c.* 1538), besides several more probable venues. Sponsored by Thomas Cromwell, the King's Secretary and Lord Privy Seal, the play was performed in St Stephen's Church in Canterbury in September 1538; before an invited audience in Archbishop Cranmer's household during the Christmas season of 1538–9; and in London, possibly at Cromwell House, in January 1539.[14] It may also have been taken on tour by Bale's company, almost certainly to be identified with Cromwell's own players, and was possibly performed at any of the range of places they toured, from York to Shrewsbury, Thetford, Cambridge and others.[15] The reason so much information survives about performances of this one play is partly due, as so often, to accounts (Cromwell's accounts list two payments to 'Bale and his fellows' for playing before him in September 1538 and January 1539), and partly to the fact that it caused trouble at a time when religious issues were highly sensitive. The production at Cranmer's residence aroused the audience to strong feelings for and against the Roman church, as the depositions taken from two witnesses, John Alford and Thomas Brown below, show.

> John Alford, of the age of 18 years, examined, saith that he had been in Christmas time at my Lord of Canterbury's, and there had heard an interlude concerning King John, about 8 or 9 of the clock at night; and Thursday, the second day of January last past, spake these words following in the house of the said Thomas Brown: That it is pity that the Bishop of Rome should reign any longer, for if he should, the said Bishop would do with our King as he did with King John. Whereunto (this deponent saith) that Henry Totehill answered and said, That it was pity and naughtily [wickedly] done, to put down the Pope and Saint Thomas; for the Pope was a good man, and Saint Thomas saved many such as this deponent was from hanging; which words were spoken in the presence of Thomas Browne and one William, servant unto the said Totehill.
>
> Deposition of John Alford, January 1539

> Thomas Brown, of the age of 50 years, examined, saith that about 8 of the clock on Friday the 3 day of January last past, as he remembreth, one Henry Totehill being in this deponent's house at Shawltcliff, this deponent told that he had been at my Lord of Canterbury's, and there had heard one of the best matters that ever he saw, touching King John; and then said that he had heard divers times priests and clerks say that King John did look like one that had run from burning of a house, but this deponent knew now that it was nothing true; for, as far as he perceived, King John was as noble a prince as ever was in England; and thereby we might perceive that he was the beginner of the putting down of the Bishop of Rome, and thereof we might be all glad. Then answered the said Totehill that the Bishop of Rome was made Pope by the clergy and by the consent of all the kings Christian. Then said this deponent, 'Hold your peace, for this communication is naught [wickedness]'. Then said Totehill, 'I am sorry if I have said amiss, for I thought no harm to no man'.
>
> Deposition of Thomas Browne, January 1539

Evidently, as will be discussed further in chapter 5 below, Cromwell's aim in sponsoring a play like *King John*, with its clear anti-Catholic thrust, was specifically propagandist. He wanted audiences to hear and respond to Bale's hostility to Rome and to turn positively towards the separatism that

Henry VIII sought to foster at that particular moment in time. Thomas Browne's deposition shows that he understood perfectly well that the climate of the time made Henry Totehill's views unspeakable. But all over England, wherever this play was performed, there must have been regional and individual differences in its reception, just as even here, in the Archbishop of Canterbury's own residence, the seat of the emergent Church of England, some individuals retained a strong loyalty to the Catholic past while others were either convinced that the Reformers were right or willing to subscribe to those views even if privately they retained some doubts. If the play toured in East Anglia, the region where John Bale himself had for twenty-four years before his conversion to the Reformist cause been a Carmelite friar, or in other locations with which he had a personal connection (York, Doncaster and Cambridge, for example), familiarity, personality and memory must have made some very specific contributions to the meanings of *King John* when performed in those areas.

Regionality is a very important aspect of dramatic performance throughout the period covered by this book. Regional cultures and economies differed very greatly from one another and, for reasons as yet insufficiently understood, the drama produced in different regions (or the apparent absence of drama in others) varied tremendously. The Corpus Christi cycles, for example, were primarily a northern and midland phenomenon. Extant cycle plays were performed at York, Chester and perhaps Wakefield (though evidence for the Towneley plays as a Wakefield cycle is coming increasingly under fire); lost cycles were probably performed at Beverley, Coventry, Newcastle, Norwich and perhaps also in some of the following: Doncaster, Durham, Exeter, Hereford, Kendal, Lancaster, Lincoln, Louth, Northampton, Preston and Stamford (though references to 'pageants' do not always mean plays, and references to Corpus Christi pageants or plays do not necessarily indicate the existence of extended play-cycles).[16] A Cornish-language cycle is also extant. The N-Town cycle, which, unlike the other extant cycles, is an amalgamation of material separately conceived and, as collected in the N-Town manuscript, probably intended for touring, is associated with East Anglia. Recent scholars have argued for Thetford or Bury St Edmunds as its primary location.[17] The evidence of dialect makes an East Anglian location at some point in the cycle's history a certainty, though it need not absolutely point us in the direction of East Anglia as its point of origin.

Outside the cycle plays, however, it is to East Anglia that extant evidence points again and again as the location of dramatic performance. East Anglia was, during the late medieval period, economically and culturally the most flourishing region of England outside London.[18] Its records are especially rich in demonstrating different sponsors, stimuli and communities for dramatic performance, and most of the medieval non-cycle plays in extant manuscripts are recorded in East Anglian dialect. The Carmelite houses at Maldon and Ipswich, where Bale was appointed prior in 1530 and 1533 respectively, were involved in plays and pageants; Mettingham College, a small community of secular canons in Suffolk, paid regularly for visiting entertainments; twenty-seven villages got together to fund a St George play in Bassingbourn, Cambridgeshire, in 1511; twenty-five places around Great Dunmow in Essex gave money every year for twenty-five years to fund collective performances for the broad community; and so on. Religious and secular communities alike sought to mount and/or view theatrical performance; and in many instances the two were not divided, but were working together as one parish or community, to organise a play for entertainment, education or some more specific and immediate end, like repairing a church steeple or rebuilding a bridge.

Once fixed playhouses began to be built in London, the difference between London and the other regions of England in theatrical terms became even more marked. While playing in inns and innyards, for example, represented a tradition widely shared across different regions, very few purpose-built theatres were constructed outside London during this early period of theatre-building. Three or four dedicated provincial playhouses outside London are known for the period, in York, Bristol (possibly two) and Prescot in Lancashire.[19] The city of London authorities, furthermore, were using the increasing prominence of playhouses as an excuse to shut down playing in inns within city limits. Though the players continued to defy the authorities with some success during the 1580s and early 1590s, no performances at London city inns are recorded after 1596.

it appeared unto me that it was your honour's pleasure I should give order for the stay of all plays within the city, in that Mr Tilney [Master of the Revels] did utterly mislike the same. According to which your lordship's good pleasure, I presently sent for such players as I could hear of: so as there appeared yesterday before me the Lord Admiral's and the Lord Strange's players, to whom I specially gave in charge and required them in her Majesty's name to forbear playing until further order might be given for their allowance in that respect. Whereupon, the Lord Admiral's players very dutifully obeyed; but the others, in very contemptuous manner, departing from me, went to the Cross Keys and played that afternoon, to the great offence of the better sort that knew they were prohibited by order from your lordship. Which, as I might not suffer, so I sent for the said contemptuous persons, who having no reason to allege for their contempt, I could do no less but this evening commit some of them to one of the compters [prisons], and do mean, according to your lordship's direction, to prohibit all playing until your lordship's pleasure therein be further known.
Letter from Mayor of London to Lord Burghley, 6 November 1589

Despite this growing difference between London, with its dedicated play-houses, and the regions, with their variety of ad hoc playing places, those play-ers who performed in the London theatres continued to tour very extensively. Indeed the most famous company of the 1580s, the Queen's Men, formed by royal command in 1583, was on tour more frequently than it played in London. It was not until the 1590s that the stranglehold of London-based fixed theatres really began to shift the emphasis away from touring; and in a sense the indica-tion that that point had been reached is the gradual demise of the Queen's Men (see further chapter 2 below). Prior to this, however, and to some extent long after, even those plays written for London companies performing in London playhouses had to be adaptable to a range of different venues at court and on tour. The company might be called to play at any number of different court venues, from the large halls at Whitehall and Hampton Court to the smaller halls and chambers of Richmond and St James' Palace or to locations the court might be visiting, such as Wilton House in Wiltshire or Christ Church Hall in Oxford. Such adaptability was made possible by two central and linked aspects of theatrical performance across the whole period: the basic similarity of design across many indoor spaces, from the great hall to the guildhall, and the staging tradition of *locus* and *platea*.

We may consider this need for flexibility through a brief look at what is perhaps the single best-known play of the whole period: Shakespeare's *Hamlet* (1600–1). The title page of the first quarto spells out in general terms three of the places where the play has been performed. We should note, first of all, that 'the city of London' is very specific and is unlikely to include reference to the performance venue that most automatically comes to mind for *Hamlet*: the Chamberlain's Men's own playhouse, the Globe. For the Globe was outside the limits of the city of London, in the liberty of the Clink, in Southwark (see further p. 46 below). It is difficult to know quite where the reference points to, since playing at city inns had been banned since before the first performance of *Hamlet*, and the Blackfriars Theatre, in a liberty geographically located inside the city walls, was not yet occupied by the Chamberlain's Men. The reference to the two universities is equally hard to interpret, since there is no external corroboration of the claim on record and the universities made a point of suppressing professional performance within a five-mile range of the city centre. Indeed both are on record as paying the players to go away rather than perform on occasion. Nevertheless a letter from the Privy Council to the chancellors of both universities in July 1593 implies by its very insistence on the need to suppress such performances that they were still successfully taking place in some instances: 'common players do ordinarily resort to the University of Cambridge there to recite interludes and plays'.[20]

THE
Tragicall Hiſtorie of
HAMLET

Prince of Denmarke

By William Shake-ſpeare.

As it hath beene diuerſe times acted by his Highneſſe ſeruants in the Cittie of London : as alſo in the two V-
niuerſities of Cambridge and Oxford, and elſe-where

At London printed for N.L. and Iohn Trundell.
1603.

11. Title page of the first quarto of *Hamlet*, 1603.

The point of considering the *Hamlet* title page here, however, is not so much to tie down the specific venues of performance as to indicate their range and variety. We may not be able to track down the precise venues involved but we can draw conclusions about the routine touring and adaptability of performance, even of plays strongly associated with permanent playhouses. This range of venues demands high adaptability of the company, who must move from the raised stage of a large outdoor amphitheatre like the Globe to performance in an indoor hall of varying size, with or without a raised stage. Yet one performance location influences another, and one effect of the flexibility of this period is that even the most seemingly disparate locations will have some features in common with one another (see further below, pp. 48–9). The universities had a long tradition of temporary stages that could be set up in college halls, thus allowing college performances to vary between conditions resembling household performance, on the floor of the great hall, and conditions closer to those that came to prevail in the permanent playhouses, with a raised stage for the players. (Court performance, it may be noted in passing, sometimes raised the spectators on scaffolds while positioning the players on the floor of the hall.)

We may close this brief discussion of *Hamlet* with one further recorded venue, this time of an amateur performance: a staging of the play on board ship.

> I invited Captain Hawkins to a fish dinner, and had *Hamlet* acted aboard me, which I permit to keep my people from idleness and unlawful games, or sleep.
>   Extract from journal of William Keeling, captain of an
>   East India Company ship, 31 March 1608[21]

This last example, though it has nothing to do with the range of venues that a professional company might play, should act as a reminder of the vast and unpredictable range of factors that may stimulate the performance of a play, and of how random the surviving record of such performance may be.

Festival time

Though the terms 'religious' and 'secular' are almost unavoidable and will continue to be used in this book, the present chapter opened with the contention that such binarism is falsely imposed on a culture in which religious and secular life were so closely intertwined as to be at times almost indistinguishable. In no area of everyday life was this truer than in the experience of time. People at all social levels, from courtiers to monks and to peasants, lived their lives within a structure organised by religious festivals. Sunday, a day of rest for those who laboured and a day of worship for most (worship ordered by statute for the latter part of the period as the duty of every parishioner),[22] punctuated the weekly cycle with predictable regularity, while the great festivals of Christmas, Easter and Whitsun, together with a host of other saints' days and high points of the Christian calendar, scripted the spaces for festivity into more everyday routine. Many festivals, such as Midsummer, were primarily pagan festivals, and these tended to be grouped together in the second half of the year, from summer to Christmas, with Christian festivals dominating the period from Christmas to summer. But it is doubtful whether the distinction between religious and secular festivals was widely recognised in practice. A festival such as Lammastide, for example, brought together a religious feast (St Peter Ad Vincula) with a secular occasion (harvest) in such a way as to make the two kinds of celebration seem codependent. Even the more literate and aware of the population, who understood the meaning of at least some specific festivals, may not have noticed a great deal of difference in the living through of one or another.

Certainly festival time was play time, even for those in religious orders (though this would be the group most likely to perceive a significant distinction between religious and secular festivals). Even monks and friars paid players to entertain them at Christmas, just as courts and households did. Though church festivals were times of reverence and religious celebration, they were also, and probably primarily, for the vast mass of the population, holidays. The performance of drama was always, in this early period, tied to festivals or other special occasions. Even after the establishment of fixed theatres began to move the culture away from this association with festival to a situation where plays were routine and 'everyday', at least in the capital city, private performances at court and elsewhere remained closely linked to festivals and special occasions. Sometimes the festive status of the day or time prohibited performance. Performances in the public theatres were forbidden on Sundays and during Lent, and very few plays were performed at court after Ash Wednesday during the period of Shakespeare's lifetime, though that changed in the later Stuart years, when plays became more routine throughout the year. Not all the occasions on which drama was performed would be religious, of course, but the general framing principle that performance was occasional as opposed to routine was only just coming into question in this period, and remained part of the cultural understanding of what performance was even as the playhouses challenged that understanding in practice.

Festivals were also naturally associated with the performance of ritual as well as with the performance of plays or drama, though this distinction between

Table 1.1 *A calendar of the principal festivals and feast days in Elizabethan England*

RITUALISTIC HALF		PROFANE OR SECULAR HALF	
25 December	Christmas – Nativity (Midwinter)		*Sheep-shearing*
26 December	Twelve Days of Christmas	24 June	Saint John the Baptist (Midsummer)
28 December	Holy Innocents	15 July	Saint Swithin
1 January	New Year		*Rush-bearing*
6 January	Epiphany	1 August	Lammas
7 January	Rock Monday	15 August	Assumption
7–14 January	*Plough Monday*		*Harvest-home*
21 January	Saint Agnes' Day	14 September	Holyrood Day
2 February	Candlemas	29 September	Michaelmas
3 February–9 March	*Shrove Tuesday*		*Parish wakes*
4 February–10 March	*Ash Wednesday*	28 October	Saint Simon & Saint Jude (Lord Mayor's Show)
14 February	Saint Valentine's Day	1 November	All Saints' Day
15 March–18 April	*Palm Sunday*	2 November	All Souls' Day
22 March–25 April	*Easter*	5 November	Guy Fawkes' Day
25 March	Lady Day (Annunciation)	11 November	Martinmas
30 March–3 May	*Hock Monday*	16 November	Saint Edmund's Day
31 March–4 May	*Hock Tuesday*	17 November	Accession Day of Queen Elizabeth
23 April	Saint George's Day	23 November	Saint Clement's Day
27/28/29 April–31 May–1/2 June	*Rogations*	25 November	Saint Catherine's Day
30 April–3 June	*Ascension*	30 November	Saint Andrew's Day (Advent)
1 May	May Day (Saint Philip & Saint James)	6 December	Saint Nicholas' Day
10 May–13 June	*Whitsun*	21 December	Saint Thomas' Day
17 May–20 June	*Trinity*		
21 May–24 June	*Corpus Christi*		

Note: The moveable feasts of the Church and the main non-calendary festivals (of peasants and parish) appear in italics. The dates correspond to the earlier and later limits for the moveable feasts given in the Book of Common Prayer.

ritual and drama constitutes another example of a binary that we apply to early theatre at our peril. Take, for example, the coronation of a king or queen. This was one of the most special of special occasions, a festival which combined religious with secular significance. Coronation itself was a religious ceremony akin to baptism: the king or queen would be anointed with holy oil in an elaborate ritual usually performed in Westminster Abbey. And the procession, even the spectators, were as much a part of the spectacle and performance as was the religious ceremony.

his grace, with the Queen, departed from the Tower through the city of London, against whose coming the streets where his Grace should pass were hanged with tapestry and cloth of Arras; and the great part of the south side of Cheap [Cheapside] with cloth of gold, and some part of Cornhill also; and the streets railed and barred, on the one side, from over against Grace Church unto Bread Street in Cheapside, where every occupation stood, in their liveries in order, beginning with base and mean occupations, and so ascending to the worshipful crafts. Highest and lastly stood the Mayor, with the aldermen. The goldsmiths' stalls, unto the end of the Old Change [Exchange], being replenished with virgins in white, with branches of white wax; the priests and clerks, in rich copes with crosses and censers of silver, with censing [perfuming with incense] his grace, and the Queen also as they passed . . .

Also before the King's Highness rode two gentlemen, richly appareled, and about their bodies traverse [across], they did bear two robes, the one of the Duchy of Guienne and the other for the Duchy of Normandy, with hats on their heads powdered [speckled] with ermines, for the estate of the same. Next followed two persons of good estate, the one bearing his cloak, the other his hat, appareled both in goldsmiths' work and broidery [embroidery], their horses trapped in burned [burnished] silver, drawn over with cords of green silk and gold, the edges and borders of their apparel being fretted [interlaced] with gold of damask. After them came Sir Thomas Brandon, Master of the King's Horse, clothed in tissue [rich cloth, often interwoven with gold or silver], broidered with roses of fine gold, and traverse his body a great baldric [strap worn diagonally over the shoulder and across the chest] of gold, great and massy, his horse trapped in gold, leading by a rein of silk the King's spare horse trapped bard wise [with a covering for breast and flanks], with harness broidered with bullion gold, curiously wrought by goldsmiths. Then next followed the nine children of honour, upon great coursers, appareled on their bodies in blue velvet, powdered with flower delices [fleurs de lys] of gold, and chains of goldsmiths' work, every one of their horses trapped with a trapper of the King's title, as of England and France, Gascony, Guienne, Normandy, Anjou, Cornwall, Wales, Ireland, etc. wrought upon velvets with embroidery and goldsmiths' work.

Then next following in order, came the Queen's retinue, as lords, knights, esquires, and gentlemen in their degrees, well mounted, and richly appareled in tissues, cloth of gold, of silver, tinsels [cloth interwoven with gold or silver] and velvets embroidered, fresh and goodly to behold. The Queen, then by name

Katherine, sitting in her litter, borne by two white palfreys, the litter covered and richly appareled and the palfreys trapped in white cloth of gold, her person appareled in white satin embroidered, her hair hanging down to her back, of a very great length, beautiful and goodly to behold, and on her head a coronal, set with many rich orient stones . . .

The morrow following being Sunday, and also Midsummer Day, this noble Prince with his Queen, at time convenient, under their canopies borne by the Barons of the Five Ports, went from the said Palace to Westminster Abbey upon cloth called vulgarly cloth of ray [striped cloth], the which cloth was cut and spoiled by the rude and common people immediately after their repair into the Abbey, where, according to the sacred observance and ancient custom, his Grace with the Queen were anointed and crowned by the Archbishop of Canterbury, with other prelates of the realm there present, and the nobility, with a great multitude of commons of the same. It was demanded of the people, whether they would receive, obey and take the same most noble Prince for their king, who with great reverence, love, and desire, said and cried, yea, yea.

Extract from description of Henry VIII's coronation, June 1509, Hall's Chronicle (first published 1548)

Were we to study coronations more fully, we would find that scripted pageants, usually constructed around allegorical, biblical or historical personages, were often staged along the procession route as a further embellishment of the performance; that the banquet, with its traditional challenger riding in to challenge any man to contest the king's right to rule, overlapped in its mode of performance with costly and extended jousts, often framed within a fictional allegorical setting; and that these in turn overlapped with elaborate indoor disguisings carrying on the allegorical fiction, and extending into the social side of the festivities with music and dancing. To divide the coronation performance up under either binary so far discussed, then (religious/secular or ritual/drama), would have made little sense to a contemporary audience. The magnificent 'secular' celebration at the Field of Cloth of Gold in 1520 included a spectacular mass alongside the feasting, jousting and masking. Both constituted one continuous performance over several days, highlighting different aspects at different times, surely, but never completely abandoning ritual for drama or drama for ritual. To understand this kind of performance is to understand its wholeness as well as its component parts.

Saturday, the 23rd [of June], a platform was built in the camp, and near it a chapel, a fathom and a half high, on pillars. It contained an altar and reliquaries, and at the side were two canopies of cloth of gold, with chairs for the legates of England and France, and the cardinals of France, and seats below for the French bishops. On another side were seats for the ambassadors of the Pope, the King of Spain, the Venetians and others . . . [T]he legates and cardinals started at

10 o'clock to go to the chapel, all in red camlet [soft silk or woollen cloth], and seated themselves under the canopies . . . The English chanters began by saying *tierce* [the third canonical hour of the day], which done, the English legate and the deacons, etc. changed their dress, and put on very rich vestments. The two Kings mounted the platform, and kneeled at the oratory, Francis on the right, and Henry on the left. The Queens did the like. . . . About noon the English legate commenced the high mass *De Trinitate*. The first introit was sung by the English chanters, the second by the French . . . The Cardinal de Bourbon, who brought the Gospel to the Kings to kiss, presented it first to Francis. He desired Henry to kiss it first, but he refused the honour. While the preface was being said, a great artificial salamander or dragon, four fathoms long, and full of fire, appeared in the air, from Ardre. Many were frightened, thinking it a comet, or some monster, as they could see nothing to which it was attached. It passed right over the chapel to Guisnes, as fast as a footman can go, and as high as a bolt shot from a crossbow . . . [T]he *Pax* [a tablet passed round for the kiss of peace] was presented to Cardinal Bourbon to take to the two Kings, who observed the same ceremony as before; then to the two Queens, who also declined to kiss it first, and, after many mutual respects, kissed each other instead. The benediction was given by the English legate, and one of the English secretaries made a Latin oration at the bottom of the chapel . . . The platforms and galleries, which contained great numbers of people, were so well arranged that everyone could see.

Extract translated from an anonymous
French description of the Field of Cloth of Gold (1520)

The closeness between ritual and drama is as true at the everyday level as at the level of special occasion, especially in the pre-Reformation period. Indeed the Reformers, as noted above, were hostile to both theatre and Catholicism partly because they saw each as an expression of the other. Protestantism, in embracing the inner life as primary and rejecting the necessity for intermediaries, was a movement against the ritual enactment of faith through intermediaries. It is notable, for example, that Hall's Chronicle, which lavishes twenty-eight folio pages on describing the Field of Cloth of Gold, has only a few sentences on the mass. The religious climate at the time of writing (after Henry VIII's divorce and separation of the English church from Rome) made such attention to Catholic ritual undesirable and possibly dangerous to publish. Thus the seven sacraments (baptism, confirmation, penance, marriage, ordination, the Eucharist and the last rites) shrank to two (baptism and marriage) in Protestant theology, and ritual occupied a much smaller part of everyday life. But throughout the fifteenth century people who went to mass regularly experienced its drama in a deeply embedded and embodied way in their lives. Since the laity made confession and received the sacrament very rarely, normally only once a year, the elevation of the host (the sacramental wafer consumed

12. Elevation of the host. From a Roman missal of the second half of the
fourteenth century.

in the mass) was the high point of the mass for them, and many rushed from
church to church in order to catch the moment of elevation more than once.
The ritual of elevation was already theatrical, with its focus on special vessels,
its accompanying bell-ringing, incense and candles and the dramatic gesture
of elevation itself; and the practice of witnessing the elevation through a tiny
aperture in the rood screen gave the event even more charisma, literally framing
the act of viewing in as prominent a way as any curtains or stage could have
done. Some priests made the ritual of elevation very theatrical indeed, and the
church issued specific instructions and warnings about precisely how it was to
be performed.

It is ordained to priests that, when they begin the canon of the mass, as *Qui pridie*, holding the host, they should not immediately raise it too high so that it can be seen by the people; rather, only keep it in front of their chests while they say *hoc est corpus meum* and then they should elevate it so that it can be seen by all.
Statute from Synod of Paris, 1198–1203

A few churches had machinery capable of making it truly spectacular, and Miri Rubin cites several bequests of money for enhancing the drama of church ritual.[23]

I bequeath . . . in honour of the sacrament, to make [a machine] which will rise and descend at the high altar, as angels go up and down, between the elevation of Christ's body and blood, and the end of the chant, *Ne nos inducas in temptacionem* [the Lord's Prayer].
Extract from the will of Thomas Goisman, alderman of Hull, 1502

The dragon made to hover miraculously above the mass at the Field of Cloth of Gold (box, pp. 27–8 above) is a particularly outstanding example of the kind of spectacle that might be staged when cost was no object. Its affinities with the mechanical descent of angels in street pageants or plays are obvious, though in both cases the aim is to inspire by amazement rather than primarily to trick spectators. Reformers, however, naturally delighted in exposing some of the machinery found in churches as cheap fakery.

the image of the rood that was at the Abbey of Boxley, in Kent, called the Rood of Grace, was brought to Paul's Cross, and there, at the sermon made by the Bishop of Rochester, the abuses of the vices[24] and engines, used in old time in the said image, was declared, which image was made of paper and clouts [patches, not necessarily of cloth] from the legs upward; each legs and arms [*sic*] were of timber; and so the people had been eluded [baffled] and caused to do great idolatry by the said image.
Wriothesley's Chronicle (mid-sixteenth century), entry for 1538
[The Boxley Rood incorporated springs and vices that could make it bow, shake its limbs, roll its eyes and move its lips in response to worshippers.]

The dramatic element in worship did not need to be quite so spectacular, of course. Preachers, for example, cultivated theatrical skills in order to touch the hearts of the listeners, and friars especially were known for their charismatic preaching. They typically added stories and songs to their teaching, sometimes singing religious lyrics to familiar secular tunes in order to make them attractive and memorable to the hearers. (On occasion the proximity of secular and religious culture could produce accidental confusion, as in the story, told by Gerald of Wales, of the priest who was kept awake by dancers singing secular songs in the churchyard and, instead of beginning mass with the familiar '*Dominus vobiscum*' [the Lord be with you], found himself repeating the words of the song: 'sweet leman [lover], thine are [mercy]').[25] Chaucer's Pardoner offers us a picture of how a travelling preacher might use rhetorical tricks and props (relics) to terrify his audience into repentance (and hence charitable offerings), and a fifteenth-century manuscript tells of a real preacher who 'to strike terror into his audience' suddenly pulled a human skull out from under his cloak as part of his performance.[26]

Processions too were a dramatic ritual routinely incorporated into everyday life. They might incorporate any or all of a range of props and costumes, including flowers, rushes, bells, crosses, flags, special liveries or other symmetrical dress. Floats and tableaux might further enhance the visual display, and, in the case of a Corpus Christi procession, the sacred host would be carried in a precious vessel, on or in a tabernacle structure placed on a bier and under a special canopy. As with the festivals themselves, processions were not necessarily perceived by the participants as either religious or secular. Processions accompanied urban midsummer celebrations and rural ceremonies such as beating the bounds (an annual ritual reaffirming parish boundaries by ritually walking them through) as well as religious feasts, and many secular rituals would display religious features.

Festivals were not merely dramatic in themselves, but often also the stimulus for other dramatic forms. The creation of a new festival could prompt the creation of a new dramatic form, and the demise of a religious ritual could equally precipitate the passing of an old dramatic form. Thus the establishment of the feast of Corpus Christi (meaning literally 'body of Christ' – a feast celebrating the Eucharist, the sacrament confirming the real presence of the body of Christ in the mass) in 1311 was soon celebrated with processions across Europe and, at some later date in the fourteenth century, gave rise in England to the great civic play-cycles. The earliest record of an extant cycle is that of York, in 1378, but the plays may well have been in existence for some time before that date either at York or elsewhere. The relationship between processions and play-cycles is not clear. Though processions may have included actors on floats representing tableaux of biblical events, there is no evidence that the plays evolved out of the processions, or even that plays and processions routinely existed side by side in the same place (though they did at York up to 1426, when Friar William Melton persuaded the city authorities to move the plays to the day before the procession, in order to avoid 'feastings, drunkenness, clamours, gossipings, and other wantonness' on the same day as the religious procession).[27] It so happened, moreover, that the new church feast, a moveable feast scheduled for celebration on the first Thursday after Trinity Sunday, could sometimes roughly coincide with the pagan festival of Midsummer, thus bringing religious and secular celebration into conjunction again.

The decline of the old religion brought with it a hostility to ritual and processional practices (see further chapters 3 and 5 below). Despite the hostility of the Reformed church to both ritual and theatre, however, both continued to flourish in changing forms. Even an evangelical like John Bale, whose own conversion to the Reformist cause from a devout and traditional branch of Catholicism, the Carmelite order, made him especially zealous in denigrating the old religion, and in condemning its idolatry and theatricality, sought out new forms of drama through which to express that zeal and convert others to the cause, rather than turn his back on the theatre completely. John Foxe, author of the best-known piece of Protestant polemic of the latter sixteenth century, commonly known as the *Book of Martyrs*, expressed the opinion that 'players, printers, preachers be set up of God as a triple bulwark against the triple crown of the Pope, to bring him down' and wrote Latin plays himself.[28] And Queen Elizabeth, keen to establish a church settlement that would curb the violence of polemic at either extreme, simultaneously maintained some of the old Catholic ritual in her own form of worship (keeping candles and a crucifix on the altar of her private chapel) and expressed her espousal of Reformed religion in long-established ritual forms (as in the coronation pageant in which she kissed a copy of the English Bible handed to her by the allegorical figure of Truth; see chapter 5 below). Indeed, one prominent area of social practice in which ritual continued to dominate and theatre in the narrower sense became ever more dominant, was the court, which set the example for the rest of the population to follow.

Court

The court had always been a centre of both ritual practice and theatrical patronage. It traditionally performed its own magnificence through a series of rituals, so that even the most potentially mundane of events became a ritual performance at court. The monarch, whether getting up, having dinner, resting or taking part in more obviously ceremonial activities, like public banquets, the reception of foreign ambassadors or the admission of knights to the Order of the Garter, was always on display, always performing. And this formal aspect of the royal household was to some degree replicated in noble or wealthy households throughout the land, where hierarchy and social order were enacted and reaffirmed in every movement.

> [Wolsey moved through his house] with two great crosses of silver borne before him; with also two great pillars of silver, and his sergeant-at-arms with a great mace of silver gilt. Then his gentlemen-ushers cried, and said: 'On, my lords and masters! Make way for my Lord's Grace!' Thus passed he down from his chamber through the hall. And when he came to the hall door, there was attendant [waiting] for him his mule, trapped altogether in crimson velvet and gilt stirrups. When he was mounted, with his cross bearers and pillar bearers also upon great horses trapped with red scarlet, then marched he forward, with his train and furniture [accoutrements] in manner as I have declared, having about him four footmen with gilt pole-axes in their hands.
>
> George Cavendish, *The Life and Death of Cardinal Wolsey* (1554)

The court itself was peripatetic at this period (though Whitehall Palace came increasingly to be regarded as the monarch's principal abode under the Stuarts), which was another factor taking courtly performance further afield than would now be the case. Queen Elizabeth in particular was noted for her progresses and her sometimes sudden visits to take up residence with courtiers and subjects, visits which put them under immense strain while they tried literally to keep court in their lesser houses and with their lesser resources. This was not merely a matter of feeding and accommodating the Queen and her retinue in the manner to which they were accustomed, but also of entertaining them with a degree of lavishness that would show proper love and respect. Many of the entertainments subjects offered to their monarch while on progress were published for the population at large to read; but perhaps the most famous is the entertainment laid on by the Earl of Leicester at his home of Kenilworth for Queen Elizabeth in 1575. The place of performance for such an entertainment, over several days, was the estate of Kenilworth itself, which was showcased through the flexible and varied use of its space for spectacular and astounding entrances. At one point the Lady of the Lake arrived 'from the midst of the pool, where upon a moveable island, bright blazing with torches, she floating to land, met her Majesty'. Mechanical descents were planned for Mercury in a cloud and Iris in a rainbow, but could not be performed due to 'lack of opportunity and seasonable weather'.[29]

When the court moved between the monarch's own palaces, however, and was host to the range of entertainments necessary both to keep the court amused and to impress foreign visitors, the places of performance varied from tiltyards and temporary buildings to indoor halls and chambers of varying sizes, depending on the nature and context of the performance. Temporary buildings were one type of space in which the building itself constituted part of the performance in a particularly marked way. Some of these buildings, such as the famous ones built under Henry VIII for the meeting with Francis I at the Field of Cloth of Gold in 1520 and the meeting with the Emperor Charles V immediately following, at Calais, were designed for that once-only meeting, and their function was primarily to dazzle the beholders with a sense of the power and prestige of a monarch capable of mounting such a one-off display. The buildings were hugely spectacular, and contemporary descriptions of them run to many pages. English temporary building tradition tended to combine a lower level of brick building, rising to about three feet of the building's total height, with a canvas superstructure, painted with a *trompe l'oeil* effect to look like brick, marble or some other permanent substance. Numerous glass windows sought to overwhelm the visitor with a sense of light in the interior, while silks and brocades were spread upon the floors and ceilings, further embellished with cut and embossed patterns and much gold and silver. The aim was to produce an effect of wonder: the building was to perform a level of spectacle that no building had performed before. The Calais banqueting house, for instance, known as the Roundhouse, was '800 foot round, after a goodly device, builded upon masts of ships in such manner as I think was never seen, for in it was the whole sphere portrayed'.[30] The Calais Roundhouse reveals not only the way such buildings functioned as more than mere spaces for entertainment, but the level of risk to which their fragility exposed them. A high wind blew the roof off before it could be put to use, and the whole company and entertainment had to move into the cramped space of the Exchequer. Such an outcome was always the risk of a temporary building; and the more expense and labour lavished on the building, the greater the statement it made against that background of risk. The building, even as it was destroyed, performed its owner's *sprezzatura* (the term is from Castiglione's *Book of the Courtier* and names the quality of carelessness, of seeming to perform gracefully entirely without effort, which he recommends his ideal courtier to cultivate).

Temporary banqueting houses became gradually less temporary as the period developed. Where a Henrician banqueting house, if it survived the weather, would typically be left standing for a short while so that beholders could continue to come and marvel at it after the event for which it was constructed, later banqueting houses tended to become semi-permanent. The wooden Elizabethan banqueting house built at Whitehall in 1581–2 for a visit by the Duke of Alençon remained standing until it was demolished in 1606 to make way for a new banqueting house for James I; and the 1607 building

13. Interior of Inigo Jones' banqueting house, looking south.

in turn remained standing until it was destroyed by fire in 1619 and replaced in 1622 by the Banqueting House designed by Inigo Jones which remains standing in Whitehall today. Banqueting, however, was only one of the elements of performance taking place inside such a building. A formal banquet to entertain honoured guests was part of a wider schedule of entertainment which interspersed feasting with masking or disguising, music and dancing. The double temporary building built at Greenwich for the visit of the French ambassadors in 1527 was unusual in allocating banqueting to one building and masking to the other. In most other temporary and many permanent buildings different forms of entertainment jostled side by side with each other in the same space. This conception of 'theatre' as part of an ongoing continuum of entertainment and performance is important both for understanding what theatre was and how plays sat alongside other forms of entertainment without very clear-cut distinction in the early period, and for understanding what a novel idea playhouses were at the end of the sixteenth century. Even as late as 1614 the Hope Theatre was designed to do double duty as a playhouse and a bearbaiting arena (although in practice it was mostly used for bear-baiting after 1617).

Coming at a building like the Hope from this distance in time, without paying attention to earlier tradition, can result in a patronising approach that overemphasises the 'popular' roots of Elizabethan theatre and condescends to some notional conception of lower-class pleasures, highlighting the presence of whores and cutpurses in the audience and the closeness of theatres to brothels and gambling dens. While it is certainly true that tradesmen and apprentices frequented the theatre and that theatres lay adjacent to other pleasures, the consumption of theatre as part of a cocktail mixed with other forms of entertainment is equally certainly not only a lower-class phenomenon. Just as public theatre allowed for an audience that might enjoy both bearbaiting and plays, and liked to see a bawdy jig or some dancing at the end of the play, so courtly entertainment might lead the court through a day of exciting physical exercise and spectacular viewing in the form of a joust or tournament into an evening of music, feasting, dancing and drama. But the point again, as with the false rigidity of modern distinctions between the religious and the secular or between ritual and drama, is that the boundaries between what we now seek to categorise as different forms of entertainment were less clear. The jousting, for example, might take place within a narrative framework which was then picked up by the indoor evening entertainments, perhaps costuming the dancers or setting the dramatic interlude within the same narrative frame. Nor, indeed, was the tiltyard without its theatrical set and costumes. Not only would the jousting knights and horses be costumed in rich and emblematic fabrics, colours and devices, but the Queen and her ladies might be watching the combat, themselves allegorically costumed, from a specially constructed spectators' box, devised to look like a castle.

Both tiltyards and indoor halls also hosted mobile stages in the form of pageant cars, which typically entered the space with a number of costumed performers on board, who then descended to enter the wider space, sometimes to speak and possibly to fight or to dance. Even fighting, however, was not, as one might imagine, restricted to the tiltyard, but might take place in an indoor space. Hall recounts one event in which combat, dance and dialogue were all part of the same extended drama, a barrier suddenly dropping down in the hall at the point of combat.

When the King and the Queen were set under their cloths of estate, which were rich and goodly, and the ambassadors set on the right side of the chamber, then entered a person clothed in cloth of gold, and over that a mantle of blue silk, full of eyes of gold, and over his head a cap of gold, with a garland of laurel set with berries of fine gold, this person made a solemn oration in the Latin tongue, declaring what joy was to the people of both the realms of England and France, to hear and know the great love, league and amity that was between the two kings of the same realms, giving great praise to the King of England for granting of peace, and also to the French King for suing for the same, and also to the Cardinal [Wolsey] for being a mediator in the same. And when he had done, then entered eight of the King's Chapel with a song and brought with them one richly appareled; and in like wise at the other side entered eight other of the said Chapel bringing with them another person, likewise appareled. These two persons played a dialogue, the effect whereof was whether riches were better than love, and when they could not agree upon a conclusion, each called in three knights, all armed. Three of them would have entered the gate of the arch in the middle of the chamber, and the other three resisted, and suddenly between the six knights, out of the arch fell down a bar all gilt, at the which bar the six knights fought a fair battle, and then they were departed, and so went out of the place. Then came in an old man with a silver beard and he concluded that love and riches both be necessary for princes, that is to say, by love to be obeyed and served, and with riches to reward his lovers and friends; and with this conclusion the dialogue ended.

Then at the nether end, by letting down of a curtain, appeared a goodly mount, walled with towers and vamures [outer walls of a fortress] all gilt, with all things necessary for a fortress, and all the mount was set full of crystal corals and rich rocks of ruby curiously counterfeited and full of roses and pomegranates as though they grew. On this rock sat eight lords appareled in cloth of tissue and silver cut in quatrefoils, the gold engrailed [ornamented with curved indentations] with silver, and the silver with gold, all loose on white satin, and on their heads caps of black velvet set with pearl and stone. They had also mantles of black satin; and then they suddenly descended from the mount and took ladies, and danced divers dances.

> Extract from description of the entertainment at Greenwich for the French ambassadors, May 1527, Hall's Chronicle (first published 1548)

There is even a record of a full-scale tournament being staged indoors at an entertainment for Henry VIII mounted at Lille in 1513, the horses on that occasion being shod in felt. Though many studies of Elizabethan and Jacobean theatre tend to concentrate first on Shakespeare and the public playhouses and second on a few Jacobean masques strongly focused on song and dance, the practice of incorporating combat and moving pageant stages into court performance did not come to an end with the early Tudors. The Four Foster Children of Desire, in the Elizabethan entertainment of that name staged in

1581, arrived at the Whitehall tiltyard the first day on a machine called 'a rolling trench' to besiege the so-called Fortress of Perfect Beauty and the second day in 'a brave chariot (very finely and curiously decked)';[31] and indoor masques at barriers continued to be performed through the Jacobean period.

> *a march being sounded with drums and fifes, there entered (led forth by the Earl of Nottingham, who was Lord High Constable for that night, and the Earl of Worcester, Earl Marshal) sixteen knights armed with pikes and swords, their plumes and colours carnation and white, all richly accoutred; and making their honours to the state as they marched by in pairs, were all ranked on one side of the hall. They placed, sixteen others like accoutred for riches and arms, only that their colours were varied to watchet [light blue] and white, were by the same earls led up, and passing in like manner by the state, placed on the opposite side . . . By this time, the bar being brought up, Truth proceeded.*
>
> Stage direction from *Barriers at a Marriage* lines 183–210, for the wedding of Frances Howard and Robert Devereux, January 1606

As the reference to the letting down of a curtain in the *Love and Riches* entertainment of 1527 shows, moveable pageant stages could be used in ways that anticipated later fixed stages. Though curtains were not installed in public playhouses before the closing of the theatres, court mask anticipated this later development, as it did so many other late developments of fixed staging, such as moveable scenic flats and the proscenium arch, developments brought into Jacobean court masque by Inigo Jones. Some of Jones' developments were truly innovative in an English context, but many of the features specific to masque staging, including most of the machinery for its spectacular effects, had been incorporated into masks and disguisings from the time of Henry VII, and were in widespread use in royal entries, Corpus Christi cycles and other forms of medieval theatre from at least the fourteenth century. Even the halpace (low platform) on which the King's throne was set for court masque was not new or specific to that form; halpaces had for many years been specially installed in churches for major events such as royal weddings so that the ceremony could be better viewed by the congregation. Jones certainly drew on Italian theatre and architecture for his designs and effects, but in so doing he was also drawing on a courtly tradition long established in England that sought to rival European precedent and impress European visitors through theatrical display.

Connections: court, civic, household and public theatre

Court theatre was not all a matter of masque, of course. Even under King James and his queen, Anna (who was mainly responsible for the major revival of masque in the early seventeenth century), much of the court's viewing was of invited performances, either by the monarch's own players, by his or her Chapel Gentlemen and Children, or by other companies.[32] At this level there truly was an exchange of theatrical commodities. Masque was exceptional in being performed once only and only at one, relatively elite venue, such as the court or a noble household.[33]

Various forms of court entertainment, however, were closely linked to civic entertainments from an early date. This connection is at its most obvious in royal entries, which aimed to entertain the monarch and the city together; but civic events such as the Midsummer Watch, the Lord Mayor's Show and even military parades, had strong affinities with the processions and pageantry of court revels. It is also the case that sometimes the same writers wrote for both court and city. John Lydgate's mummings in the 1420s and 1430s are an early case in point.[34] He wrote three for the court, three for the city of London, and one so far undetermined; and in addition he also wrote a description of Henry VI's entry into London in 1432 and an exposition of the pageants in a Corpus Christi procession. (The term 'mumming' is not clearly distinct from mask or disguising, and the manuscripts are in fact much looser than this in their terminology, describing these entertainments variously as 'ballades', 'mummings' and 'disguisings'. On terminology, see further chapter 4 below.)[35] Of the city mummings, one was written for a May Day dinner of the sheriffs of London; another was commissioned for performance before the Mayor by his own company, the Mercers; and a third was commissioned by the Goldsmiths' Company for performance before the same Mayor. But the format is not markedly different. All have a processional element, bringing in representative or allegorical figures in sequence; and all but one seem to have a single speaker pronouncing the text, which describes, or tells the story, or outlines the meaning of the figures presented. One, the *Mumming at Hertford* before the King, presenting some 'rude, uplandish people complaining on their wives', scripts a 'boistous [rough, coarse] answer' for the said wives, seeming to indicate dialogue; and two, the Mummings for the Mercers and the Goldsmiths, suggest that the presenter is costumed as a herald; but otherwise there is more similarity than difference between the court and civic shows.[36]

Most forms of theatre other than court and civic theatre toured, bringing adaptations of the same performances to very different audiences. It is impossible to know how far productions of the same play might be changed, in both content and staging, for different audiences and venues, but it is likely that different budgets and expectations changed the mode of performance significantly. Thus, while most town and village venues would have played in fairly bare spaces with few props, the court, accustomed to providing lavish costumes and large props (Revels accounts up to the 1580s often list payments for canvas 'houses' of various kinds), may well have supplied some of these to visiting performers, thereby encouraging them to develop a more dispersed style of performance and perhaps changing the dynamics between *locus* and *platea* from those that might obtain in simpler venues.

Just as a variety of troupes, both adult and children, visited and performed in the royal household, so the King's players, first recorded in the 1490s under Henry VII, and re-formed in many different incarnations under later monarchs, toured Britain, stopping first and foremost at noble households, but also in towns and villages along the way. At this level, however, theatre was still primarily working within a framework of patronage and occasional performance (occasional in terms of audiences, that is, even if the players were fairly fully occupied in regular performance). At what point theatre began to be regularly and widely available in one place is as yet an unanswered question. Theatre historians have traditionally identified the building of James Burbage's Theatre in 1576 as the point of origin. More recently, since the discovery of documents about the Red Lion, built in 1567, have shown it to be not an inn used for occasional playing, but something closer to a purpose-built playhouse than was previously thought, it has begun to be cited as the new point of origin. In fact the first recorded reference to a play in a known playhouse (though the reference concerns its prevention rather than its performance) refers to the Boar's Head, Whitechapel, in 1557, but the Boar's Head is not known to have been converted into a playhouse before 1598.

The revision of the idea of the Theatre as the first playhouse also functions to remind us how little we really know about what theatre was available beyond the court in London before 1576. A lawsuit brought by John Rastell, a playwright himself and the first English printer of plays, in 1530–1 provides evidence not only of an earlier Tudor stage, but also of the wider context for theatre in early Tudor London. Rastell's work has already cropped up several times in this chapter, though he has not yet had occasion to be named. He was the author of the *Love and Riches* dialogue performed at the Greenwich entertainments of 1527; he worked on the roofs of the Banqueting Hall at the Field of Cloth of Gold and the Calais Roundhouse in 1520; he designed the pageant at the Stocks, very close to his printing house at Paul's Gate, for the visit of the Emperor Charles V in 1522; he wrote and printed plays; and, as we learn from the lawsuit, he built a theatre in the grounds of his own house and ran a thriving costume hire business in London.[37]

Rastell brought the lawsuit against one Henry Walton, whom he accused of failure to return costumes left with him for safe-keeping while Rastell was in France. From the various testimonies it emerges that Walton, who had worked with Rastell on building the structures for the Greenwich revels, had also been employed to build a stage for Rastell at his own house in Finsbury at some date in the 1520s, perhaps around 1524. Tantalisingly, no evidence regarding the kind of plays staged at this venue emerges from the legal documents, but it is clear that here is a London citizen who also had connections with the court (not only did he work on court entertainments, but he was married to the sister of Sir Thomas More, and his daughter was married to the court playwright John Heywood) and who was thus producing plays for a potentially very mixed audience. Again, there is no evidence as to whether this was an invited or a paying audience, but the construction of a fixed stage would seem to point towards a business enterprise rather than the kind of ad hoc performance that would take place by clearing space in the hall of a noble household.

What is quite clear from the documents is that plays were being performed regularly enough in London to sustain a lucrative costume hire business, and it is the loss of this revenue that incites Rastell to sue Walton. The witnesses' statements specify the value of costumes as minutely as they are able to and often note in passing the practice of remaking and adapting old costumes. The tailor does not remember how long it took him to sew them, but states that Rastell's wife helped him with the sewing and that he was paid 4d per day in addition to being given food and drink. Two of the King's Players, George Mayler and George Birch, make statements on Rastell's behalf, and seem to have worn his costumes for their performances in the Greenwich revels (which would mean that some of the same costumes were being worn for courtly entertainments as for less elite and perhaps more public performances in the city).

George Mayler of London, merchant-tailor, of the age of 40 years, sworn and examined upon his oath, saith that he knew the said garments, but how many there be in number he remembereth not, for he hath occupied and played in them by the lending of Walton; and he saith they were worth 20s apiece and better; and he saith he knoweth well that he lent them out about a 20 times to stage plays in the summer and interludes in the winter, and used to take at a stage play for them and other, some time 40d, some time 2s, as they could agree, and at an interlude 8d for every time, but how many times he perfectly knoweth not, but by estimation 20 times a year in interludes. And he saith that he hath seen the curtains of sarcenet [very fine silk], but how many ells they contained he knoweth not, but it was worth 40d every ell; and he saith that he had buckram and tuke [lining materials], but how many yards he knoweth not, but it was better than 2d a yard. And further he saith that the summer when the King's banquet was at Greenwich he saw the same garments occupied in divers stage plays and occupied part of them himself by the lending of other players that Walton had lent them to to hire, which then were fresh and little worse for the wearing; and more he knoweth not.

George Mayler's deposition to the Court of Requests, 1531–2

It is impossible to know how public Rastell's enterprise was, or how many others in London may have been providing theatrical entertainment beyond the court, but several scraps of evidence suggest that the practice was not restricted to this single instance. One Felsted, a silk dyer, also ran a costume hire business in the capital, and was a known source for obtaining new and fashionable interlude-scripts for acting.

> according unto your ladyship's writing I will be in hand with Felsted, silk dyer, for the players' garments, and also to procure to get some good matter for them. But these new ecclesiastical matters will be hard to come by.
>
> Letter from John Husee to Lady Lisle, 3 October 1538

> I have been with Felsted and given him earnest for a suite of players' garments, which he will keep for you, and an interlude which is called *Rex Diabole*. (Spark knoweth the matter.) I will do my best to get some of these new scripture matters, but they be very dear; they asketh above 20s for an interlude.
>
> Letter from John Husee to Lady Lisle, 5 October 1538

Felsted, as Meg Twycross suggests, may have offered a 'total package', providing scripts and costumes together.[38] A courier called John Wilkinson was also named in an injunction of 1549 forbidding him to host interludes in his house; and acts passed by the London authorities legislating against the performance of plays routinely included private houses amongst the list of prohibited playing places.

> These [authorities] are, in the Queen's Majesty's name, straightly [rigorously] to charge and command that no manner of person or persons whatsoever, dwelling or inhabiting within this city of London, liberties and suburbs of the same, being innkeepers, tablekeepers, taverners, hall-keepers or brewers, do or shall, from and after the last day of this month of May now next ensuing, until the last day of September then next following, take upon him or them to set forth, either openly or privately, any stage play or interludes, or to permit or suffer to be set forth or played within his or their mansion house, yard, court, garden, orchard, or other place or places whatsoever, within this city of London, the liberties or suburbs of the same, any manner of stage play, interlude, or other disguising whatsoever.
>
> Proclamation from London Guildhall, 12 May 1569

Known records offer a limited guide to what kinds of plays were being performed at these city and non-aristocratic household venues in early Tudor London. John Husee's letters to Lady Lisle show a keen interest in plays on the burning religious issues of the day at precisely the same time as Cromwell was sponsoring Bale to produce Reformist propaganda plays, but both Bale and Lady Lisle are performing or arranging performance in places outside London (Lady Lisle is looking for an interlude for performance at her Calais household over Christmas). Rastell's interests are the best guide we have to the range of material that may have been shown in a London gentry household. He is known as the writer of *The Four Elements* (1517–20), though that was written before his stage was built. A note at the head of the printed edition of this play, however, clarifies that Rastell conceived of it as a play adaptable to different audiences: 'if ye list [like] ye may leave out much of the sad [serious] matter', and the play's lengthy prologue also spends considerable time justifying the need to mix serious matter with 'merry conceits' in order to educate a less learned audience.

> But because some folk be little disposed
> To sadness [seriousness], but more to mirth and sport,
> This philosophical work is mixed
> With merry conceits, to give men comfort
> And occasion to cause them to resort
> To hear this matter, whereto if they take heed
> Some learning to them thereof may proceed.
>
> John Rastell, Prologue to *The Nature of the Four Elements*
> (1517–20), lines 134–40

Rastell is also known as the possible translator of a Spanish play, *Calisto and Melibea* (*c.* 1523–5?), as the printer of Medwall's *Fulgens and Lucres* (*c.* 1496–7, printed 1512–16), the first printed English play, and as one of two proposed authors for the play *Gentleness and Nobility* (*c.* 1519–28). Since the other candidate for authorship is Rastell's son-in-law, John Heywood, the play remains a likely candidate for Rastell's stage whichever of them wrote it. Like *The Four Elements*, it mixes 'toys and jests' with serious content in order to 'make merry pastime and disport' (as the extended title matter indicates) and it encourages its audience to think about serious philosophical questions. Such aims would fit with the range of Rastell's known activity, from court revels to household performance and printing, and would fit too with the expressed interests of Sir Thomas More's circle, with which Rastell was connected by marriage. More, an advocate of the capacity of drama to educate the less literate members of the population, was not only known, as the extant play about him emphasises, as a willing and generous sponsor of players visiting his own household, but as a talented improviser himself in his earlier life.

> though he was young of years, yet would he at Christmas tide suddenly sometimes step in among the players and, never studying for the matter, make a part of his own there presently among them, which made the lookers on more sport than all the players beside.
>
> William Roper, *Life of Sir Thomas More* (c. 1566)

The establishment of fixed playhouses

The household, then, at a range of social levels, was an active venue for performance inside as well as outside London before the building of permanent playhouses. So too were guildhalls, churches and inns as well as a range of more ad hoc spaces, as repeated London edicts against playing confirm (see e.g. box on p. 42 above). The earliest specific known London location for the performance of plays (excluding the court and taking 'plays' in a relatively narrow sense) is Clerkenwell, where the prioress petitioned the King to protect priory property against damage by Londoners attending '*miracles* [miracles; see chapter 3] *et lutes* [wrestling matches]' there c.1300. The London clerks are regularly recorded towards the end of the fourteenth century and into the fifteenth century as performing at Skinners Well, in the Clerkenwell area, over a period of a few days, sometimes before the King, Queen and nobles.[39] Other specified auspices for London performance outside the court include the Inns of Court and several trade guilds. Both normally used their own halls for performance. An early record of such performance is John Foxe's record of an interlude performed at the Carpenters' Hall in Shoreditch in 1541. The parish of of St Andrew's, Holborn, also paid for annual plays from 1503 to 1507; while Trinity Hall was rented out to players by the church of St Botolph's without Aldersgate from 1557 to 1568, a period including over one hundred performances.[40]

Inns are a well documented venue for the later sixteenth century. The Saracen's Head in Islington was in use in 1557, the same year as the lost play, *A Sackful of News*, was stopped at the Boar's Head, but it is not recorded again after this date. Four inns in particular are known as performance venues in London from the 1570s: the Bel Savage on Ludgate Hill (in use for plays by 1575), the Bull at Bishopsgate (from 1577), the Bell in Gracious (now Gracechurch) St (from 1576–7) and the Cross Keys adjacent to it (from 1577 or 1578). Almost nothing is known about how much conversion work was done on any of these, though the Bel Savage stage was high enough to put a person 'in danger to break his neck' if he fell off.[41] The city, however, was hostile to performance within city limits and lobbied and legislated continuously to try to ban it. The problem with maintaining such a ban, however, was that the interests of the city conflicted with those of the court. This was partly a matter of private interests, since some members of the Privy Council were also patrons of the players (Henry Carey, Lord Chamberlain 1585–96 and Charles Howard, Lord Admiral 1585–1619, for example) and partly a matter of protecting the Queen's access to a useful resource, since inviting professional companies to perform at court was much cheaper than devising

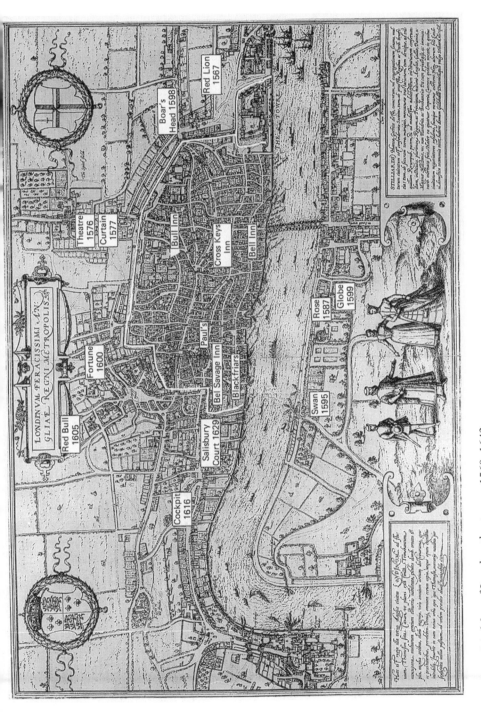

14. Map of London theatres, c. 1560–1642.

Boar's
Head 1598

Red Lion
1567

Theatre
1576

Curtain
1577

Bull Inn

Cross Keys
Inn

Bell Inn

Rose
1587

Globe
1599

LONDINVM FERACISSIMI AN
GLIÆ REGNI METROPOLIS.

Red Bull
1605

Fortune
1600

Paul's

Bel Savage Inn

Blackfriars

Salisbury
Court 1629

Swan
1595

Cockpit
1616

in-house entertainment from scratch. There was therefore tension between the London authorities and the Privy Council, and actors were confident enough on account of their powerful backing to defy the city on occasion (see box, p. 20 above).

When playhouses began to be built they were thus strategically placed outside the city limits. The edict banning playing during time of plague cited in the box on p. 42 is precise in specifying the area in which the ban applies as 'this city of London, liberties and suburbs'. For most purposes, however, the city had no power to legislate for the liberties and suburbs. The boundary of its authority, once coincidental with the city walls, by this date extended a little way beyond the walls in places, to what were known as the 'bars' (sometimes marked by chains across the street). 'Suburbs' designated adjacent areas outside the boundary, while 'liberties' were areas free of city jurisdiction due to ancient privilege (often the site of former religious houses, as in the case of the Blackfriars) and could be located physically within the boundaries while remaining legally beyond them. The Theatre and the Curtain, the first two major theatrical enterprises, were built close to one another outside the city's northern boundary, while the next group of playhouses to be built clustered within the liberties of the Clink and Paris Garden in Southwark. Southwark itself had come inside city jurisdiction in 1550, but the Clink and Paris Garden, as liberties, remained outside it.

The swift expansion of outdoor fixed playhouses is testimony both to the enormous popularity of playgoing and to London's fast-growing population. It was an expansion that was to continue into the seventeenth century, as the population grew even further (from *c.* 15,000 in 1576 to *c.* 200,000 in 1642) and theatregoing became a more regular part of everyday life in the capital. If there is one thing scholars have learned from recent discoveries and excavation, as at the site of the Rose Theatre, it is that there is no 'standard' model that can be applied to all playhouses, but that individual playhouses differed significantly from one another. Nevertheless, the playhouses of the period can be broadly divided under two headings: indoor and outdoor. Outdoor theatres were all unroofed (apart from a roof over the stage in most later ones) and mostly circular (the Fortune and the Red Bull being the exceptions to this).

Outdoor playhouses	
Red Lion	1567–?
Newington Butts	?1576–?1599
Theatre	1576–98
Curtain	1577–c.1625
Rose	1587–?1606
Swan	1595–c.1637

Boar's Head	1598–c.1616 (in use until c.1604)[42]
Globe	1599–1644 (fire in 1613; rebuilt in 1614)
Fortune	1600–61 (fire in 1621; rebuilt in 1622–3)
Red Bull	?1605–c.1663
Hope	1614–56

The circular shape may have owed something to classical tradition, but it also recalled certain kinds of *locus* and *platea* arrangements, as in the Cornish rounds (on which the circular staging diagrams for the Cornish cycle plays are based) and the staging shown for *The Castle of Perseverance* (1397–1440) in the Macro manuscript (see illustration above, p. 9), where the scaffolds surround the *platea* in a circular design. There was thus continuity as well as innovation in the earliest purpose-built theatres. What was new above all was the scale and magnificence of the enterprise, as Johannes de Witt, a Dutch visitor to London in 1596, noted. The four amphitheatres he writes about at this date are the Theatre, the Curtain, the Rose and the Swan.

In London are four amphitheatres of obvious beauty, which from their diverse signs receive their diverse names. In them a different play is daily presented to the people . . . Of all the theatres, however, the largest and most distinguished is the one whose sign is a swan (commonly, the Swan theatre), which, to be sure, accommodates three thousand people in seats. [It is] built of an accumulation of flint stones (of which in Britain there is a vast abundance), supported by wooden columns which, on account of the colour of marble painted on them, can deceive even the most acute, whose form, at least, since it [the playhouse] seems to represent the general notion of Roman work, I have drawn above.

> Notes by Johannes de Witt copied by Arend van Buchell, c. 1596 (translated from the Latin)

The practice of painting or disguising one surface to look like another (here, wood to look like marble), while innovative in popular theatre, was, as we have seen, a long-established tradition in temporary court theatres.

The dimensions of both stages and playhouses could vary tremendously (see Appendix 3, Known dimensions of playing spaces), but certain features of the basic design were shared. Thus the Globe had a capacity of up to 3,000 and a rectangular stage measuring up to 49′6″ wide, while the capacity of the Rose has been estimated at 2,200 and its stage was hexagonal and tapering, measuring 37′6″ (tapering to 27′6″) × 15′6″ (later extended to 17′); but both had thrust, open stages, surrounded by standing spectators; galleries accommodating further spectators; and a tiring house backing the stage from which the actors entered through two or three doors. (The de Witt sketch of the Swan

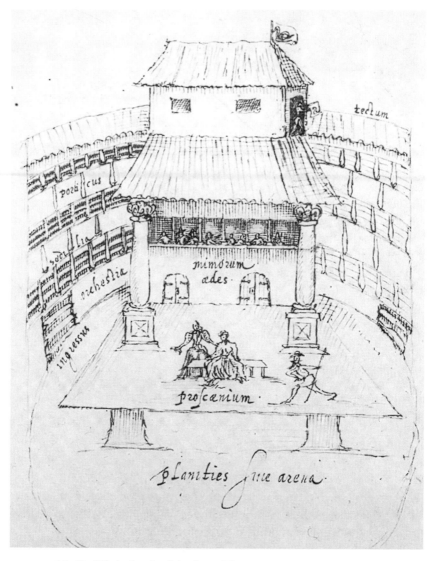

15. De Witt's sketch of the Swan Theatre.

shows only two doors, but other evidence suggests that many playhouses had a third door, also used as a discovery space, in between.) The tiring-house wall, furthermore, had a gallery space that could be used by actors or musicians. And these features too had some continuity with earlier tradition despite their variability. The practice of performing in front of a wall with two doors for entrances and exits and sometimes a gallery above was strongly reminiscent of indoor performance in great halls, where one possible arrangement was against the hall screen, with its gallery and two doors.[43] Square or rectangular theatres like the Fortune and the Hope recalled this indoor tradition more strongly, though the surrounding of an open yard by galleries and standing space was perhaps even more reminiscent of innyard playing. But whatever the shape of the playhouse in this period, the audience surrounded the actors on three or four sides of the stage in both indoor and outdoor playhouses (the de Witt sketch and the pictures printed in William Alabaster's *Roxana* (1632) and Henry Marsh's *The Wits, Part I* (1662) show the likely use of the stage balcony by audience as well as players),[44] and the degree of distance or intimacy in that arrangement depended on the relative sizes of the stage, the theatre and the audience.

The indoor theatres were even more evidently dependent on earlier tradition, especially since most of them were conversions of halls originally designed for other purposes. The two Blackfriars theatres, for example, converted different parts of the original Blackfriars monastery, the buttery and the dining hall.

Indoor playhouses	
St Paul's	1575–1606 (not in use 1590–9)
First Blackfriars	1576–84
Second Blackfriars	1600–66 (not in use after 1642)
Whitefriars	1609–14
Cockpit/Phoenix	1616–?1665 (not in use after 1661)
Porter's Hall	1615–17
Salisbury Court	1629–66

Like the amphitheatres, they were galleried spaces surrounded on three sides by audience, their stages were entered from the tiring house wall, and that wall sometimes had a gallery that could be used as a performance space; but unlike most of the amphitheatres, the indoor theatres were rectangular, they seated all spectators and they were reliant on artificial lighting in the form of candles. There were other differences too. The indoor theatres were smaller and more exclusively located than the amphitheatres, hosted performances only once a week, rather than daily, and charged more for admission. The capacity of the Blackfriars has been estimated at about 700, while Paul's, within the cathedral precinct, held only 50–100.

Performance on the stages in these fixed playhouses remained based on a principle of *locus* and *platea*. Despite the fixed dimensions of the stage in a given playhouse (variable, of course, across different playhouses), the stage itself, thrust into and surrounded by the audience, could be used as yet another form of open space, or *platea*, while the tiring house doors or large free-standing props might function as *loci*. This continuing principle meant that the localisation of scenes in plays performed in these playhouses was only ever intermittent. Some scenes had a specifically designated location (those in the arbour in *The Spanish Tragedy* (1585–9) or the graveyard in *Hamlet*, for example), but many more are unlocated in any very specific sense, which makes for an open-ended and receptive relation with the audience's time and space. When Antonio, Salerio and Solanio in *The Merchant of Venice* (1596–7), for example, enter and begin speaking to each other in the first scene, no obvious props or dialogue indicate where they are as they talk, and the scene does not particularly encourage us to ask this question. When Lancelot, the clown, enters in a later scene (II.2) speaking directly to the audience and telling them comic anecdotes about his service in Shylock's household, there is even less interest in the question of location: it is irrelevant to the kind of drama being played at that moment on the stage. Even a scene which has a clear and specified location, like the graveyard scene in *Hamlet*, can momentarily allow the audience's sense of their own location in the here and now to overwhelm the fictional location of Denmark, as when the gravedigger, ignorant of Hamlet's identity, tells him that the Prince Hamlet has been sent to England:

> HAMLET Ay, marry, why was he sent into England?
> 1 CLOWN Why, because 'a was mad. 'A shall recover his wits there, or if 'a do not, 'tis no great matter there.
> HAMLET Why?
> 1 CLOWN 'Twill not be seen in him there, there the men are as mad as he. (V.1.150–5)

Location, when specified, is often specified through language alone, which is the reason why the scene on Dover cliff in *King Lear* (1605–6) could act so powerfully on a contemporary audience (see chapter 5 below). It is also the reason why the stage could not only change the represented location so easily and instantly, but also accommodate 'simultaneous staging', or two locations at once, as when Kent remains on stage in the stocks, in a location understood to be in front of Gloucester's castle, while Edgar enters to deliver a soliloquy, presumably located elsewhere, and exits (*King Lear*, II.3). The phemonenon, including this example, is discussed more fully by Bernard Beckerman, who also observes that most of the plays performed at the Globe during its first decade, 1599–1609, need nothing but a bare stage, not even a stool.[45]

As playhouse building developed, its 'innovations' continued to be influenced by tradition.

Item paid for carpenter's work and making the throne in the heavens the 4 of June 1595 £7 2s

Extract from Philip Henslowe's *Diary*, June 1595[46]

The building of a roof over the stage and the incorporation of descent machinery into the 'heavens', as it was known, drew on staging traditions familiar across a range of different forms of theatre that had used mechanical ascents and descents since at least the fourteenth century, from street pageants for royal entries to both cycle and non-cycle drama. The insertion of a trapdoor into the stage followed on from the vertical conception of a three-tiered universe embedded in, for example, the pageant wagons for cycle drama, with their sometimes very elaborate heavens and their hell-mouths under the stage. Such a conception of the universe may, of course, also be problematised and parodied through staging, as it is, for example, in *Hamlet* (1600–1), when Hamlet jokes with the ghost in the 'cellarage' below (I.5.151) or leaps into the grave to fight Laertes (V.1).

Props too were mainly conservative. Some of the large props listed in Philip Henslowe's inventories for the Rose recall earlier traditions at different levels from popular to elite (another binary often too rigidly imposed on a culture where so much performance was either to mixed audiences or adapted for different audiences).

Item: 1 rock, 1 cage, 1 tomb, 1 hell-mouth
Item: 1 tomb of Guido, 1 tomb of Dido, 1 bedstead
Item: 8 lances, 1 pair of stairs for Phaeton
. . .
Item: 1 lion skin; 1 bear's skin; and Phaeton's limbs, and Phaeton chariot; and Argus' head
Item: Neptune fork and garland
Item: 8 vizards [masks]; Tamburlaine bridle; 1 wooden mattock [agricultural tool]
. . .
Item: 1 lion; 2 lion heads; 1 great horse with his legs; 1 sackbut [wind instrument]
Item: 1 black dog
Item: 1 cauldron for the Jew
  Extracts from an inventory of the Admirals' Men's properties, Henslowe's *Diary*, 10 March 1598[47]

First, a pageant with four wheels;
Hell mouth;
3 devil costumes, 3 two-faced masks;
2 evil soul costumes (shirts, hose, masks, wigs);
2 good soul costumes (shirts, hose, masks, wigs);
2 pairs of angels' wings 'with iron in the end';
. . .
1 cloud and 2 pieces of wooden rainbow;

God's costume (shirt, halo with gilt mask);

. . .

1 heaven of iron with a hub/wheel of wood;

2 pieces of red cloud and gold stars for heaven;

2 pieces of blue cloud painted both sides;

3 pieces of red cloud with sunbeams of gold and stars for the 'highest of heaven'; a long narrow border of the same work;

7 large angels 'holding the Passion of God', one of them has a 'fane of laton' [possibly a metal shield] and a cross of iron in its head;

4 smaller gilt angels 'holding the Passion';

9 smaller angels painted red to 'run about in heaven';

a long thin cord to make the angels run about;

Extracts from an inventory of props for the Last Judgement pageant at York, 1433[48]

The first item on Henslowe's list of props and costumes, the rock, is a prop found again and again in different kinds of performance. The Queen of Marseilles and her baby are cast on to a rock in the Digby *Mary Magdalene*; court pageants from the time of Henry VIII regularly incorporate rocks, both on and off pageant wagons (see e.g. box, p. 37 above); Revels accounts demonstrate that a rock was specially constructed for *The Knight of the Burning Rock*, a lost play performed by Warwick's Men's at court in 1579; a rock was again central to the mask of *Proteus and the Adamantine Rock*, performed at court by the gentlemen of Gray's Inn in 1595, close in date to Henslowe's inventory; and rocks continue to appear in different kinds of performances.

In staging shows that included such large props, the playhouses had two possibly conflicting traditions to draw on: the symmetrical arrangements of some indoor and outdoor spaces, where the features of a wall, incorporating say, two doors and a gallery, or three buttresses, or different sized niches symmetrically arranged in a line, or the frame of a pageant wagon, predisposed the space towards symmetrical staging; and the dispersed staging of a random outdoor topography (a field with a stream and a mound, for example) or the Tudor court, where a number of 'houses' or props may have been distributed either randomly or symmetrically across the hall. While it is difficult to know what kind of balance between symmetrical and more randomly dispersed effects may have been dominant at any given time, we can certainly see evidence from playhouse texts as well as earlier plays that symmetrical effects were scripted in places, and that large props could often be strongly emblematic. Thus in Kyd's *Spanish Tragedy* (1585–9), for instance, we not only see symmetry scripted in the scene where Lorenzo and Balthazar enter on either side of their prisoner, Horatio (I.2), or in the language (which in turn scripts movement) in which Horatio and Belimperia advance their courtship (II.2); we also see the arbour (illustrated on the play's 1615 title page) in which they express their love reappear as the arbour in which Horatio is hanged, and probably again (perhaps differently dressed but possibly also in the same location) as the scaffold on which Pedringano is hanged (III.6) (see p. 54). The single surviving contemporary illustration perhaps depicting a scene staged in this early period, the drawing attributed to Henry Peacham c.1595 of a scene possibly from Shakespeare's *Titus Andronicus* (1592), shows a prominent horizontal symmetry, with opposing groups of characters arranged on either side of the central point of Titus' spear (see p. 55).[49]

Staging throughout the period, then, could be either centred or decentred. Occasionally a particular genre or performance space will favour one style or the other (seventeenth-century masque behind a proscenium arch, or cycle plays on pageant wagons), but most performance modes are able to draw on both, moving between the particular pleasures of symmetrical, centred effects and the very different pleasures of a freer and more decentred use of space. The two case studies below look briefly at some of these effects in two plays at different moments in time.

Case study: *Mankind* (1465–70)

Mankind is a morality play, that is, broadly speaking, a play dramatising the moral choices in a human life that lead to their salvation or damnation. (The question of genre is more fully discussed in chapter 4 below). Several medieval morality plays follow a structure like that of *Mankind*: a central human figure is led astray by vices personified (here Mischief, New Guise, Nowadays and Nought) before being converted to a better life by personified virtue or virtues (here Mercy). Like most medieval plays, *Mankind* survives in only one manuscript, and there are no records of performance to tell us where or how it was first staged. All the information we have is so-called 'internal' evidence, that is, the evidence of the text itself. We may look at external evidence of the kinds of communities that might receive visiting players, but we have nothing that ties any recorded performance to this play (since plays are not usually named in such records). The East Midlands dialect of the play helps to locate the text geographically; and East Anglian place names in the text suggest that the play probably toured within the area indicated by the concentration of those names (parts of Norfolk, Suffolk and Cambridgeshire, but mainly the northern part of East Anglia). Surviving records of payments to players suggest that players might tour over an area this size playing in a range of locations, from village halls and religious houses to innyards, marketplaces and open fields.

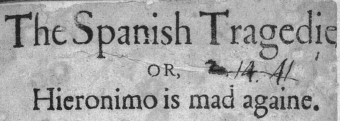

The Spanish Tragedie

OR,

Hieronimo is mad againe.

Containing the lamentable end of *Don Horatio*, and
Belimperia; with the pittifull death of *Hieronimo*.

Newly corrected, amended, and enlarged with new
Additions of the *Painters* part, and others, as
it hath of late been diuers times acted.

LONDON,
Printed by W. White, and are to be sold by I. White
and *T. Langley* at their Shop ouer against the
Sarazens head without New-gate. 1615.

16. Title page of *The Spanish Tragedy*, 1615.

17. Drawing attributed to Henry Peacham, possibly of Shakespeare's *Titus Andronicus*.

The play seems to address a socially mixed audience; though presumably if the audience on a particular occasion was relatively unmixed, parts of the play could be highlighted or omitted accordingly. As it has come down to us, the text includes some rather sophisticated Latin jokes, which only the educated (who would in this period comprise mainly the clergy) could understand; some very 'aureate' English, polysyllabic, Latin-derived and always verging on the incomprehensible; and some highly colloquial and often obscene comic dialogue which mocks the Latin and puts Latin endings on to recognisably English words. It would be unwise to make any hard and fast equation between these different registers and the different social groupings in the audience, however. The notion that clerics would only accept serious matter, or that farm labourers would only appreciate low comedy is both misconceived and patronising; and the play in any case functions via the interaction of the two modes, not by presenting them as episodically or conceptually separate. Yet the presence of this range of address can nevertheless be viewed as part of the play's necessary flexibility in touring to different audiences.

In addressing itself to 'ye sovereigns that sit and ye brothern that stand right up' (line 29), the play suggests a performance area that combined both sitting and standing space (though this need not have been the case for every performance: travelling players were experienced in adapting the script to suit the venue). There are also two references to a 'house', first when one character greets another with the phrase 'Ye be welcome to this house' (line 209), and later when a player makes reference to 'the goodman [host] of this house' (line 467), as someone outside the fiction of the play. The second reference occurs about half-way through the play, when the players invite the audience to make a cash contribution if they wish to see Titivillus, the devil. Clearly the figure of the devil must have been one of the most attractive and familiar figures in the repertoire, since the play relies here on the fact that the audience will want to pay in order to see this attraction rather than disperse without paying. The player suggests that 'the goodman of this house' make the first contribution.

The request for money makes it unlikely that the place of *Mankind's* performance was a private house. Collecting from an audience who were guests might have offended both guests and householder; and troupes who visited private households looked to the lord of the house for payment (see *Sir Thomas More*, pp. 3–4 above). A public house seems more likely. Collection in an inn or innyard, where people were voluntarily gathered and free to come and go would have been quite acceptable, and probably expected. And this in turn makes it possible that the troupe performing it could have been a freelance group without a patron, making a living on the road. The play requires only six performers if the same actor doubles as Mercy and Titivillus. Further references within the play seem to endorse the possibility of inn or innyard performance. Characters call for an ostler (who saw to the horses) and a tapster (who drew the ale). In favour of performance inside the building is the character Mankind's reference to his intention to go into the yard to relieve himself, which suggests that the player is indoors at that point; against it, however, is his later announcement of an intention to 'haste me to the ale-house' (line 609).

Perhaps both kinds of performance took place, and the players adapted the lines in question as necessary. Scripts for travelling players had to be adaptable by definition, and even if the evidence of this one surviving manuscript suggests performance in an inn or innyard, this cannot be taken to imply that the play was only performed in these kinds of locations. One very flexible and transportable mode of performance favoured by travelling players, and usable in innyards as well as other places, was the booth stage, which could be set up in any open space, indoors or out (though its use outdoors is better documented). In this way a group of players, even a small group with only a horse-drawn cart to transport their materials, could travel independently across the country performing wherever they had a booking or could find an audience. Whatever the precise form of staging used, we can look at it, as an earlier section of this chapter has already argued, in terms of *locus* and *platea*, the oscillation between defined and undefined space and between the fictional world of the play and the here and now of the audience.

Mankind does not script movement as clearly as the place-and-scaffold plays discussed in the section above on *locus* and *platea*, but indications of the same approach to play-space are present. The vices, for example, evidently move between the audience and the fiction, clearing space as they go amongst the audience to encourage them to join in an obscene song ('Make room, sirs, for we have be long! / We will come give you a Christmas song' (lines 332–3)) and subsequently to collect for the appearance of Titivillus: 'We intend to gather money, if it please your negligence, / For a man with a head that is of great omnipotence' (lines 461–2). It is clear too, from Nowadays' classic call to 'make space and beware!' (line 475), that Titivillus enters through the audience. The references to the ale-house and the yard noted above also encourage the audience to recognise the place in which they actually sit as co-present with the setting the play seeks to represent.

Further features of the dialogue seem to indicate that performance could be made very specific to place and that awareness of place as co-present with the fiction is an essential aspect of the way the play engages its audience. References to 'Pychard of Trumpington' (line 508), 'William Baker of Walton' (line 510), 'Master Allington of Bottisham' (line 515) and others have been investigated, and the fact that most of these references can be tied to individuals or families documented as living in late fifteenth-century East Anglia suggests that the players were consciously targeting specific communities. Clearly the naming onstage of known individuals in the audience creates a knowing and intimate relationship between performers and spectators, one that happily allows the world of the spectators to coexist with the fictional world of the play.

At one point the play plays comically with this double awareness by drawing the audience's attention to the fact that the stage is a bare board. The character Mankind has been getting on with his work, digging with his spade, and the audience has been encouraged to imagine how productively he is labouring by the comment of another character, who says

> Ey, how ye turn the earth up and down!
> I have be, in my days, in many good town,
> Yet saw I never such another tilling!
>
> (lines 362–4)

Shortly afterwards, however, the devil conceives the idea of hiding a board under the earth so that Mankind's digging becomes impossible and he gives up in frustration. On a stage which is no more than a board and trestle this whole episode becomes a joke about the stage. A piece of board obviously cannot be 'hidden' on a board stage; it lies on top of it, self-evidently of the same texture and hardness as the stage itself. When Mankind pretends to dig a board surface with his spade his action is, in stage terms, no different from when he was pretending to dig earlier and the audience was willingly complicit with the fiction that he was turning over earth. Now, however, the audience is no longer encouraged to maintain that imaginative distance from the materiality of the stage; it is deliberately invited to inspect the seam between the stage and its fiction and to enter into a different and more intimate moment of shared knowing with the actors.

Case study: *The Masque of Blackness* (1605)

Nothing could be further from the ad hoc casualness of touring performance, moulding itself to each new place of performance, than the Jacobean masque, performed once only in a very specific place, often the Banqueting Hall at Whitehall. Masque borrows from the earlier 'mumming' or 'disguising', which often took the form of a surprise visit that cultivated the appearance of spontaneity. Such an occasion, for example, was the Christmas visit of a group of mummers to the young prince, the future Richard II, in 1377: the disguised mummers played a game of dice with the prince, set up to allow him to win costly prizes (a ball, a cup and a ring, all of gold), and then danced with him. Henry VIII's masks and disguisings in the early sixteenth century show a repeated interest in these same features of disguise and affected spontaneity; but Jacobean court masques were another matter. Even the first spectators were unsure how to categorise them. Sir Dudley Carleton, recounting the performance of *The Masque of Blackness*, Jonson's first masque, hesitated about what to call it: 'At night we had the Queen's masque in the Banqueting House, or rather her pageant.'[50] Planned for months in advance and prepared at huge expense, Jacobean masques were performed to a specially commissioned text and on an elaborate, purpose-built, perspective stage. The two names most famously associated with it are those of Ben Jonson, who wrote the texts, and Inigo Jones, who designed the intricate sets and spectacular effects.

The Masque of Blackness, devised for the Jacobean court by Jonson and Jones, was performed on Twelfth Night (6 January) 1605. It cost at least £2,000 (though contemporary rumour whispered that costs were up to or in excess of £3,000), a huge sum in a period when the building costs of the Fortune Theatre in 1600 were £600 and the standard payment to an author for a new play was £6 (see table 1.2). The text of the masque demonstrates clearly that music, spectacle and dancing were at least as important as any words spoken: it incorporates 99 lines of stage directions, 47 lines of song and several dances as against 163 lines of spoken verse, and other records show that the dancing usually took up most of the evening. As Jonson's prefatory note indicates, the aim of the written text was to record 'the honour and splendour of these spectacles . . . in the performance' (lines 1–2), which would otherwise pass into oblivion; and the stage directions show that a major concern of performance was to astonish.

Table 1.2 *Comparison of selected theatre-related costs with artisans' wages*

Item	Pounds Ster.	No. Years' Wgs.
Construction Costs: Burbage's "Theatre"	£666	44.4 Years
Construction Costs: Henslowe's "Rose"	£816	54.4 Years
Construction Costs: "The Globe"	£600	40 Years
Construction Costs: Henslowe's "Fortune"	£600	40 Years
Average Constructions Costs (4 Theatres)	£673	45 Years
Land Rent, Annual: Burbage's "Theatre"	£14	11 Months
Average Play Production Costs: Annually	£900	60 Years
Average Building Maintenance Costs: Annual	£100	6.7 Years
Average Daily Receipts: "Globe" or "Rose"	£8.5	7 Months
Annual Receipts: "Globe" or "Rose"	£1955	130.33 Years
Average Daily Receipts: "Blackfriars"	£15.75	1 Year
Average Daily Receipts: Globe/Blackfriars	£23.25	1.6 Years
Annual Receipts: Globe/Blackfriars	£6545	436.3 Years
Costumes/Properties: "The Swan"	£300	20 Years
Buy-in, Buy-Out Share: Acting Companies	£70–£90	4.6 Years
Sharer's Annual Salary	£180	12 Years
Playwright's Fee + "Benefit" Performance	£14.5	1 Year
Heminges' Minimum Income (1623)	£1000	66.7 Years
Henslowe's Theatre Expenses (1593–1603)	£2399	160 Years
Shakespeare's Cash Bequests (in Will)	£387	25.8 Years
Cooke's Cash Bequests (in Will)	£150	10 Years
Alleyn's Upkeep Costs: Dulwich Manor	£1700	113.3 Years
Purchase Price of Dulwich Manor	£10,000	666.7 Years

A curtain displaying a landscape scene fell to reveal an artificial sea *'shoot forth, as if it flowed to the land, raised with waves which seemed to move, and in some places the billow to break'*; six tritons moved in front of this sea, and behind them two *'sea-maids'* flanked the figures of Oceanus and Niger mounted upon *'two great sea-horses, as big as the life, . . . the one mounting aloft, and writhing his head from the other'*. A *locus*, then, was very clearly established, using framing devices unfamiliar and as yet unavailable to popular theatre, a curtain and a backdrop. The locus is further reinforced by a large prop: the masquers, playing twelve nymphs, *'were placed in a great concave shell, like mother of pearl, curiously made to move on those waters, and rise with the billow; the top thereof was stuck with a chevron of lights which, indented to the proportion of the shell, struck a glorious beam upon them as they were seated one above another'*. Six huge sea-monsters swam on either side of the shell, bearing twelve torch-bearers, and the whole scene behind *'seemed a vast sea'* (lines 20–66).

Naming names is an important feature of the stage directions, and this opening direction ends by attributing '*the bodily part*', or the set, to '*Master Inigo Jones*' (line 73). The Queen and her ladies, who play the daughters of Niger, are all individually named alongside the parts they play and the symbols they bear. All of this adds to the sense that what a masque text does is record an occasion, not offer a script for performance. The very uniqueness of that occasion is part of its glamour and appeal; and the text that records it seeks to celebrate the specificity of each of its elite participants. Significantly, however, while Jonson and Jones incorporate their own names as well as those of the courtly masquers into the record, they are not concerned to record the names of those professional actors (from the King's Men) who took the speaking parts.

Though the Queen and her ladies performed as masquers, King James himself did not perform in this or any other masque. He was, however, the central participant in the occasion. The whole design of the place of performance revolved around him: his chair of state, raised on a dais and covered with a canopy, was centrally placed, and the perspective of the stage was designed for the eye of this single, central spectator, who was always in some sense the subject of court masque and whose presence gave the masque its meaning. The opening stage direction is explicit about the gearing of the whole performance towards this single, central point: the horizon, it tells us, was at the level of '*the state*' (the chair of state), and the lines of perspective were designed to draw the eye towards the conspicuous '*decorum*' of its '*wandering beauty*' (lines 67–71). But that beauty was fully perceptible only from the single perfect viewpoint of the monarch. Most of the audience was seated around the walls on three sides of the hall in order to leave the central space clear for dancing. As Orgel and Strong note, '[i]t is no accident that perspective stages flourished at court and only at court, and that their appearance there coincided with the reappearance in England of the Divine Right of Kings as a serious political philosophy'.[51]

The position of the King's seat, therefore, was not just a matter of his seeing, but, even more importantly, of his being seen; and the audience, by the same token, rated their view of the King more highly than their view of the perspective stage. Thus the dais becomes almost another *locus*, reifying the King into a representation of kingship. When the King's representatives came to inspect the planned layout at Christ Church Hall, Oxford for a sequence of performances planned for the King's visit in 1605, they 'utterly disliked the stage at Christ Church, and above all, the places appointed for the chair of state, because it was no higher, and the King so placed that the auditory could see but his cheek only'. The University's defence of the design, 'that by the art perspective the King should behold all better than if he sat higher', was clearly seen as a less important consideration than that the King should be well seen, and the halpace was moved further back from the stage. The result was that the King

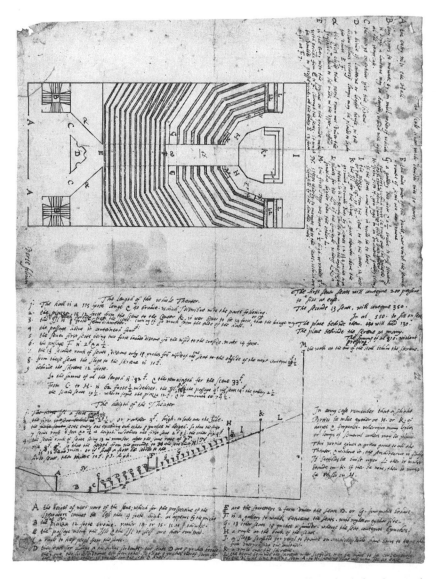

18. Plan for the conversion of Christ Church Hall, Oxford, for the royal visit in August 1605.

could not hear the speeches properly, and fell asleep during the third night's performance.[52]

As the king's role underlines, there was no clear divide between performers and audience. The central spectator was as much on view as the events on stage. Masque, by its nature, breaks down the distinction between actors and spectators, and this is evident in other ways too. Besides the fact that a group of those on stage are themselves members of the court rather than professionals, masques normally lead up to the point where the masquers literally descend from the stage and invite the courtly spectators to dance, thus effacing even further the boundaries between both performers and audience and between performance-space and audience-space. The inhabitants of the carefully framed *locus* of the masque stage descend into the *platea* (which contains within it the further quasi-*locus* of the King's throne) and fill it with the formally scripted movements of dance. The movement from *locus* to *platea* is both like and unlike that of *Mankind*. It is like it insofar as the actors move away from the safety and enclosure of the fiction and the script to become physically closer to and more immersed in the world of the spectators; but it is unlike it both in that these actors are already known members of the spectators' world and in that the moment of their entry (or re-entry) into that world is formal, constrained and submissive, not rough and imperative. This is to change, as we shall see later.

The fact that the whole event, not just what happens on stage, is theatre is evident in the competitiveness surrounding attendance and seating arrangements. Which ambassadors to invite, and how close to the king each might sit offered the potential for rivalry, flattery and ceremony, and provided part of the spectacle on view to lesser spectators. The spectacle extended both before and after the staged show; the entry of the King was as choreographed as anything on stage; and the place of performance was as much a source of pleasure as the masque itself.

> While waiting for the King we took pleasure in admiring the decorations, in observing the beauty of the hall, with two orders of columns one on top of the other, their distance from the wall the full width of the passage . . .
>
> every box was full, especially with most noble and richly dressed ladies, six hundred and more in number. . . .
>
> As he entered the hall fifteen or twenty cornets and trumpets began to play, antiphonally and very well. After his majesty had been seated under the canopy alone, . . . he had the ambassadors sit on two stools, and the great officers and magistrates sat on benches.
>
> Orazio Busino, Chaplain to the Venetian Embassy, describing
> *Pleasure Reconciled to Virtue*, 24 January 1618

Though the ambassador quoted above is describing a later masque, performed in the second Banqueting Hall, built in 1607–8, after *The Masque of Blackness*, we may assume that the entry of the royal party was always a spectacle worth attending to in itself. As this account suggests, the masque functioned as importantly to display and affirm to court society its own internal hierarchy and to offer up monarch, court and country for the admiration of foreign ambassadors, as to entertain.

The subject of *The Masque of Blackness* is a politically contentious issue in gracious disguise. The unifying 'conceit' (or extended imaginative framework) is that the daughters of Niger, instructed to seek out a land with a name ending in '*tania*', discover that the country signified is in fact 'Britannia', where their blackness is to be metamorphosed into whiteness (the cultural assumption being that this could only be a desirable outcome). 'Britain' was not a name in current use before James (though it had an ancient pedigree), but one that James, as King of Scotland and England from 1603, was keen to reintroduce. Parliament, however, was less keen, and James encountered some dogged opposition to his attempts to get both the name and the notion of a united Britain accepted. The masque therefore performs ideological work by endorsing and celebrating the name of Britain in a quasi-mythological way.

Yet, at the same time, masque did aim to entertain, not only via its spectacle, but also by its creation of the opportunity for some aristocratic partying. Following *The Masque of Blackness*, the revels continued with a banquet, which, Carleton reported, 'was so furiously assaulted, that down went table and tresses [trestles] before one bit was touched'; 'and one woman amongst the rest lost her honesty, for which she was carried to the porter's lodge being surprised at her business on the top of the terrace'.[53] A masque for the King of Denmark's visit the following year was notable above all for the drunkenness of its participants: the lady playing the Queen of Sheba tripped up the steps to the chair of state and upset her gifts of wine, cream, jelly and other assorted food and drink into the Danish king's lap; he then got up to dance with her, but fell down in front of her and had to be carried off to a bed of state; the figures of Hope and Faith vomited in the lower hall; and Peace, in her determination to get close to the King, used her olive branch to beat those who stood in her way. As Sir John Harington ironically summed up the proceedings: 'The entertainment and show went forward, and most of the presenters went backward, or fell down; wine did so occupy their upper chambers.'[54] The formal constraint with which the masquers re-entered the world of the spectators breaks down completely at this point, and the actors merge much more closely with the spectators than even the comic antics and communal singing of the actors in *Mankind* ever allow them to do.

Masques, then, could be seen as evanescent moments of glory, allegorical spectacles that sought to present what Jonson rather pretentiously called 'more removed mysteries' (Preface to *Barriers at a Marriage* (1606), line 16), or they could be dismissed, in the scornful tones of Francis Bacon, as 'but toys'.[55] Underpinning the 'removed mysteries' were certainly some hard facts at odds with such an idealised conception of masque: the king's extravagance, Parliament's anger at the outlay, and emerging tensions between Jonson and Jones.

Chapter 2

Actors and audiences

Pre-playhouse companies

Before the establishment of dedicated playhouses, playing companies were of differing and sometimes nebulous status. Generally speaking, companies at the elite end of society were more clearly named and defined and perhaps also narrower in the range of venues they played than groups of common players. Thus the King's Players, the Earl of Leicester's Players, the Gentlemen and Children of the Duke of Northumberland's Chapel, and so on, were all named after their particular patron, while a host of unnamed and often unrecorded groups of players toured different venues, both invited and uninvited. It is very difficult to assess numbers of companies before and during the fifteenth century, when extant records of companies begin, but identifiable companies become numerous from the start of the sixteenth century; and by 1525, according to John Wasson, 'there were more companies active than there would be at any time during Queen Elizabeth's reign, the period when dramatic activity is supposed to have been at its height'.[1]

There was all the difference in the world between the social status of these two broad groupings. Whilst those in the service of noble households were attached to a great lord, wore his livery, received a financial retainer from him, together with food and clothing while in residence, and were entitled to his protection, those whose primary occupation was commercial and more random performance were seen as equivalent to vagrants. Yet there was common ground between the two in terms of performance practice, since both groups toured and hence had to be adaptable to different playing spaces (see the extract from *Sir Thomas More*, pp. 3–4 above). Even the King's Players did not play only at court, but at venues ranging from other noble households to London guildhalls and smaller town halls.[2]

In the city of Gloucester the manner is (as I think it is in other like corporations) that when players of interludes come to town, they first attend the mayor, to inform him what nobleman's servants they are, and so to get licence for their

65

public playing; and if the mayor like the actors, or would show respect to their lord and master, he appoints them to play their first play before himself, and the aldermen and common council of the city; and that is called the mayor's play, where everyone that will comes in without money, the mayor giving the players a reward as he thinks fit, to show respect unto them. At such a play my father took me with him and made me stand between his legs, as he sat upon one of the benches, where we saw and heard very well.

Robert Willis, *Mount Tabor* (1639)

The only group that did not regularly tour was the household chapel (see chapter 1, note 32 above), since its primary duty, to sing at mass and prayers, was a daily requirement in noble households. Chapel Gentlemen, however, might occasionally be invited to perform outside the patron's household. Chapel Children and Gentlemen might be called upon to perform separately or together in secular household entertainments as well as religious ritual and drama, and probably collaborated with other members of the household, such as minstrels, on these occasions.[3] The capacity to diversify and collaborate is an index of how flexible and adaptable all kinds of performers might be in this period: chapels might be called upon to act just as interluders might expect to incorporate singing, dancing, instrumental playing, clowning, mime, acrobatics and swordplay into their performance.

The size of playing companies and chapel groups varied considerably according to circumstances, though chapels were generally much larger than playing companies. Before the accession of Elizabeth companies varied from two to six players.[4] Even the King's Players had only four or five men under Henry VII. The presence of a boy (as in the 'four men and a boy' depicted arriving at the household of Sir Thomas More in the play of that name (III.2.72)) did not become standard until the later sixteenth century. The group there is represented as being Cardinal Wolsey's players; but a more lowly group of players, without a noble patron, might have been very similarly constituted, though perhaps more likely to play in innyards and market squares than in the halls of great houses. Some troupes gradually expanded to seven or eight in the 1560s and 1570s, but larger numbers on a wide scale came only with the establishment of permanent playhouses. All kinds of performers, of course, including bearwards, jesters, jugglers, acrobats, musicians and dancers, toured either solo or in smaller or larger groups. Companies playing at the new playhouses typically formed around a core group of eight to twelve sharers (actors literally having a share in the company, and thus participating in both the investment and the profit). Hired men and boys, together with stage hands and musicians, made up the rest of the company.[5] Those performing plays at all levels were male,

19. Leicester Town Hall.

with men or boys taking the women's parts, and doubling of parts being standard practice. Very few female performers are on record; and none in England, so far as we know, were members of established companies. An occasional female dancer, tumbler or singer turns up in court records, and females were established professionals in some parts of Europe (as in the Italian *commedia dell'arte* tradition, for example), but they remained outside the sphere of English professional or semi-professional playing companies throughout the period covered by this book.

Those companies with noble patrons were more secure and more durable than those who set out to perform for profit without such backing. Sir Thomas More's first question to the company arriving at his house is 'Whom do ye serve?' and the answer to that question is the players' passport to being allowed to perform before More's guests. One noble lord paid his respects to another by welcoming the other's household servants. As the play shows, no price is negotiated; the play is performed in expectation of an unspecified reward, and a noble lord demonstrated his liberality through the size of his gift. Indeed much is made of this in the play, where More is outraged to find that the servant who delivers his gift to the players takes some of the money for himself. Within the patron's household too, the relationship between players and patron is one of gift exchange: the players perform for the household in return for the lord's maintenance and protection, and part of what that maintenance comprises is the gift of his name as well as the essentials of food, clothing and shelter. It is the authority and social standing of that name that stands between the players and vagrancy, as the Act Against Vagabonds clarifies in 1572.[6]

All and every person and persons . . . being whole and mighty in body and able to labour, having not land or master, nor using any lawful merchandise, craft or mystery whereby he or she might get his or her living and can give no reckoning how he or she doth lawfully get his or her living; and all fencers, bearwards, common players in interludes and minstrels, not belonging to any baron of this realm or towards any other honourable personage of greater degree; all jugglers, pedlars, tinkers and petty chapmen; which said fencers, bearwards, common players in interludes, minstrels, jugglers, pedlars, tinkers and petty chapmen, shall wander abroad and have not licence of two justices of the peace at the least. . . . shall be taken, adjudged and deemed rogues, vagabonds and sturdy beggars.

Act for the Punishment of Vagabonds, 1572

May it please your honour to understand that forasmuch as there is a certain proclamation out for the reviving of a statute as touching retainers, . . . we, . . for avoiding all inconvenience that may grow by reason of the said statute, are bold to trouble your lordship with this our suit, humbly desiring your honour that (as you have been always our good lord and master) you will now vouchsafe to retain us at this present as your household servants and daily waiters [attendants], not that we mean to crave any further stipend or benefit at your lordship's hands but our liveries as we have had, and also your honour's licence to certify that we are your household servants when we shall have occasion to travel amongst our friends as we do usually once a year, and as other noblemen's players do and have done in time past.

Letter from Leicester's players to the Earl of Leicester, c. 1572

Exactly how the relationship between a patron and his players functioned is a much larger question than can be explored here, but it is clear not only that different patronised groups (players, minstrels, chapel gentlemen and chapel children, for example) had different status and relationships to the patron, but also that the nature of those relationships changed over time. When the Earl of Leicester's players in 1572 asked him to retain them as his household servants without payment and thereby to license them to travel without risk of being arrested as vagabonds, they were evidently entering into a different relationship with him from that of players in the earlier sixteenth century who had truly formed part of a great lord's household; and when King James took over the Lord Chamberlain's Men as the King's Men on his accession as King of England in 1603, his relation to them was clearly different from that of Henry VIII to the company of players who went under his name, and may have spent much of their working lives as tradesmen, or of Elizabeth I to the company assembled under her name by Sir Francis Walsingham in 1583 out of the major professional companies.[7]

One further group of players not so far considered is amateur players, though the term 'amateur' is really out of place during a period before any playing companies could be described as fully professional. The most famous, though not the most widespread, form of medieval drama (continuing in fact down to the 1570s), was the Corpus Christi play (also now known as mystery plays), sponsored and mainly performed by urban trade guilds. Despite the subsequent fame of these plays, however, only a few towns, mostly in the North and Midlands (see p. 19 above), hosted these annual performances. One reason why they have become so well known is that, by comparison with popular touring theatre, their scripts survive much more fully, which is partly because they belong within a more literate and clerical tradition than secular interludes. Though the plays were a civic initiative, their subject matter was biblical history; clerics may have had some involvement in the writing of the texts; and both the church and the city had an interest in maintaining and overseeing the texts, especially as the Reformation advanced and scripts became a focus of potential controversy and even heresy (see further chapter 3).

Theatre historians have traditionally assumed that each guild relied on its own members to act its play, but the surviving evidence points to a situation in which at least some of the actors were chosen from outside the guild for their acting ability. In York an ordinance of 1476 decreed that no actor should perform more than twice (meaning more than two parts?) on the day of the play and that auditions should seek to maintain minimum levels of skill and suitability in those who performed.

> yearly in the time of Lenten there shall be called afore the Mayor for the time being four of the most cunning [skilful], discreet [civil] and able players within this city to search, hear and examine all the players and plays and pageants throughout all the artificers belonging to Corpus Christi Play. And all such as they shall find sufficient in person and cunning to the honour of the city and worship of the said crafts for to admit and able, and all other insufficient persons either in cunning, voice or person to discharge, ammove [remove] and avoid.
>   York ordinance, April 1476

Scholars have argued both for and against the presence of the clergy as performers, but the looseness of contemporary terminology (see further chapter 4) makes it impossible to know whether many apparent records of clerical participation actually refer to plays and/or acting or to other forms of performance and participation. The terms 'clerk' and 'cleric' too were not distinct, as they are in present-day usage, and could refer to educated men in either civil or religious employment or working outside such anachronistic distinctions. John Lydgate, for example, was a monk, a writer of civic entertainments and a court poet writing for performance before Henry VI (see p. 39 above). Outside England there are occasions when it is clear that clerics were performing, as in the application for a dispensation to grow beards in order to perform at Amboise in 1507.[8] As with the touring companies, women almost certainly did not perform, and men took the women's parts. The well-known, but isolated, reference to the 'wives [women] of Chester', interpreted by some as evidence of women performing in the Chester plays, is more likely to be a reference to women financing or supporting the production in some other way.

> The worshipful wives of this town
> Find of our Lady th'Assumption
> It to bring forth they be bound
> And maintain with all their might.
> Chester Early Banns, 1539–40

Casts for these plays could be much larger, precisely because they were predominantly amateur and occasional productions not designed for touring. Parallels between the cyclic form of these plays, however, should not blind us to differences in the way they were mounted in different towns, and it has been suggested that the N-town cycle, named for the banns that allow any specific name to be substituted for the anonymous 'N-town', was in fact a touring production. (The banns were pronounced during the so-called 'riding of the banns', a festive procession with music which took place a few days before the performance and announced the content of the coming play.)

> A Sunday next, if that we may,
> At six of the bell, we gin [begin] our play
> In N-town.
> N-Town Proclamation, lines 525–7

It is more probable, however, that the script rather than the production 'toured', just as several of the York plays found their way into the Wakefield Cycle.

The growth of professionalisation

The process of professionalisation, ongoing through the second half of the sixteenth century, reached an important high-water mark with the establishment of fixed theatres (though there was no immediate change in companies' touring practices).[9] The building of permanent playhouses represented the arrival of a commercially organised theatre industry, in which actors who made acting their primary occupation and often had a financial share in the company (and sometimes the building) to which they belonged, took control and reversed the situation in which they had up to now stood. Instead of responding to invitations to perform or approaching a town council or noble lord to ask permission to perform, they now began to invite spectators to pay a fixed charge to enter the players' own dedicated theatre-space and thus stimulated the gradual formation of a regular theatre-going public paying for an advertised and freely available commodity. The invitation still worked in the old way, from patron to players, for court performances, but the change in popular practice nevertheless impacted on the court, if in a different way. During the first two decades of the reign, in the absence of a commercial theatre industry or a company of Queen's Men, children's groups, including the Queen's own Children of the Chapel Royal, performed twice as often as adult companies at court. The balance shifted significantly following the building of permanent theatres in London, so that the commercial adult companies came to dominate the court schedule as well as popular theatre. It also became gradually less common for the court to mount its own performances, supplied and paid for by the Revels Office, as the opportunity to pay for professional players, funding their own props and costumes for the most part, provided high-quality entertainment much more cheaply. Increasingly the Privy Council's stated reason for defending the players against the London authorities, who would have been happy to see them fold altogether, was the need to rehearse their plays in public before bringing them before the Queen.

> licence hath been granted unto two companies of stage players retained unto us, the Lord Admiral and Lord Chamberlain, to use and practise stage plays, whereby they might be the better enabled and prepared to show such plays before her Majesty as they shall be required at times meet and accustomed, to which end they have been chiefly licensed and tolerated as aforesaid.
> Letter from Privy Council to Master of the Revels and magistrates of Middlesex and Surrey, 19 February 1598

The building of the Theatre, though it was not quite the first public playhouse, was a significant and symbolic economic event. James Burbage built it at a cost of about £700, and had to take on his brother-in-law, John Brayne, builder of the Red Lion, to help him finance it. As a building, the Theatre displayed a level of richness and ostentation which enraged its detractors. John Stockwood, in a sermon preached at St Paul's Cross, called it a 'gorgeous playing place', and William Harrison, writing in 1576, the year in which the Theatre was built, expressed the belief that 'it is an evident token of a wicked time when players wax so rich that they can build such houses'.[10] It was no accident that it was James Burbage who built it, or that he did so in 1576. Burbage was the leader of Leicester's Men, who were granted a new and special privilege in May, 1574: a royal patent allowing them to perform throughout the city and liberties of London and all over England.[11] The London authorities responded, however, by attempting to regulate playing within the city in a much more draconian way, effectively ending performance at city inns and insisting on the need to eradicate any potentially offensive or seditious content in plays.

Whereas heretofore sundry great disorders and inconveniences have been found to ensue to this city by the inordinate haunting of great multitudes of people, specially youth, to plays, interludes and shows, namely occasion of frays and quarrels, evil practices of incontinency in great inns, having chambers and secret places adjoining to their open stages and galleries, inveighing and alluring of maids, specially orphans and good citizens' children under age, to privy and unmeet contracts, the publishing of unchaste, uncomely and unshamefast speeches and doings, withdrawing of the Queen's Majesty's subjects from divine service on Sundays and Holydays – at which times such plays were chiefly used, – unthrifty waste of the money of the poor and fond [simple-minded] persons; sundry robberies by picking and cutting of purses; uttering of popular, busy and seditious matters; and many other corruptions of youth, and other enormities besides that also sundry slaughters and mayhemmings of the Queen's subjects have happened by ruins of scaffolds, frames and stages, and by engines, weapons and powder used in plays . . . Now, therefore, to the intent that such perils may be avoided and the lawful, honest and comely use of plays, pastimes and recreations in good sort only permitted . . . be it enacted by the authority of this Common Council, that from henceforth no play, comedy, tragedy, interlude nor public show shall be openly played or showed within the liberties of the city, wherein shall be uttered any words, examples or doings of any unchastity, sedition, nor suchlike unfit and uncomely matter . . . And that no innkeeper, tavern keeper nor other person whatsoever within the liberties of this city shall openly show or play, nor cause or suffer to be openly showed or played, within the house, yard, or any other place within the liberties of this city any play, interlude, comedy, tragedy, matter, or show, which shall not be first perused and allowed in such order and form, and by such persons as by the lord mayor and court of aldermen for the time being shall be appointed.

Act of Common Council, 6 December 1574

Burbage's decision to build an outdoor amphitheatre in Shoreditch, outside the jurisdiction of the city of London, set the precedent for the theatre building that followed, which concentrated primarily in the northern suburbs and the Southwark liberties on the south bank of the Thames. But a different line of development, focusing on indoor hall playhouses, was becoming established simultaneously. At the same time as Leicester's Men were taking this crucial step towards professionalisation, so too were the children's companies, performing indoors in liberties within the city walls (see p. 46 above). Paul's Boys, the choristers of St Paul's cathedral, began performing regularly in a playhouse within the cathedral precinct in 1575, and the Chapel Children began performing in the Blackfriars a year later, the same year as Burbage built the Theatre.

There were important differences between the two groups of companies arising out of their playhouses and their London locations. For one thing, amphitheatres had much larger capacities than indoor halls. Whereas Johannes de Witt, a Dutch visitor to London probably in 1596, estimated the capacity of the Swan, built the previous year, at 3000, the capacity of the second Blackfriars Theatre (in use by the Chapel Children from 1599) may have been only 600–700. And the more exclusive nature of the children's performances was further emphasised by the fact that they performed weekly rather than daily, and charged a minimum of six times the minimum of one penny at the Globe.

And thus every day at two o' clock in the afternoon in . . . London two and sometimes three comedies are performed at separate places wherewith folk make merry together, and whichever does best gets the greatest audience. The places are so built, that they play on a raised platform, and everyone can well see it all. There are, however, separate galleries and there one stands more comfortably and, moreover, can sit, but one pays more for it. Thus anyone who remains on the level standing pays only one English penny, but if he wants to sit, he is let in at a further door, and there he gives another penny. If he desires to sit on a cushion in the most comfortable place of all, where he not only sees everything well but can also be seen, then he gives yet another English penny at another door. And in the pauses of the comedy, food and drink are carried round amongst the people, and one can thus refresh himself at his own cost.

Thomas Platter's account of his visit to London in 1599
(translated from the German)

But this is to leap forward to the end of the century, by which time, as Platter's description above shows, theatre culture in London was thriving and well established. There were several stages on the journey to that point, the first of which was in 1583. On Sunday 13 January 1583, a seating scaffold collapsed at the bearbaiting arena in Paris Garden, in Southwark, killing eight spectators.

As the Act of Common Council quoted above demonstrates, it was not the first time seating had collapsed in an entertainment venue, but the fact that the occasion was a Sunday in 1583 lent fuel to the fire of the city authorities and of the anti-theatrical lobby generally.

> God hath in his judgement showed a late terrible example at Paris Garden, in which place in great contempt of God the scaffolds are new builded, and the multitudes on the Sabbath day called together in most excessive number.
> Letter from Mayor of London to Privy Council, 3 July 1583

> For surely it is to be feared, besides the destruction both of body and soul that many are brought unto by frequenting the Theatre, the Curtain and such like, that one day those places will likewise be cast down by God himself.
> John Field, *A Goodly Exhortation, by occasion of the late judgement of God, showed at Paris Garden* . . . (1583)

Two months later Sir Francis Walsingham, the Queen's secretary, instructed Edmund Tilney, Master of the Revels, to hand-pick a new company of players to bear the Queen's name. The narrative is related rather more idealistically after the fact by Edmund Howes, in his continuation of Stow's *Annals* some years later.

> Comedians and stage-players of former times were very poor and ignorant in respect of these of this time: but being now grown very skilful and exquisite actors for all matters, they were entertained into the service of divers great lords, out of which companies there were twelve of the best chosen, and, at the request of Sir Francis Walsingham, they were sworn the Queen's servant's and were allowed wages and liveries as grooms of the chamber. And until the year 1583, the Queen had no players.
> Edmund Howes' continuation of John Stow's *Annals* (1615)

The Queen's Men, comprising all the best players of the day, three of them from Leicester's Men, gained prestige and security even beyond that of a royal patent from having the personal protection of the monarch. Not surprisingly, they became the dominant company for the next five years, in London, nationally and at court. They appeared three times at court in the Christmas season of 1583–4, and no other adult troupe was invited to perform at court at all until the Admiral's Men in 1588–9. Numbering twelve sharers, they were considerably larger than playing companies had been before 1583, and they were licensed by the Privy Council to play at two city inns: the Bull in Bishopsgate Street and the Bell in Gracious Street. If they also played at the new purpose-built playhouses, as seems likely, they would not have needed Privy Council authority to do so. Their licence to play inside the city, however, was much coveted and much 'borrowed' by other companies looking for a way round the law.

> It may please you to know that the last year when such toleration was of the Queen's players only, all the places of playing were filled with men calling themselves the Queen's players.
>
> Letter from Common Council of London to
> Privy Council, c. November 1584

Yet, despite their popularity and privilege in London, they were primarily a touring company, still for most of the time following in the old tradition of long journeys across England (and occasionally further, to Scotland and Ireland) and performing in an open, physical and improvisatory style inherited from medieval interludes. (It is perhaps no more than an interesting coincidence that their first recorded appearance is in East Anglia, where so many records of earlier performance are concentrated.) Their most famous player, Richard Tarlton, was a clown, known for his physical comic routines and his improvisatory wit, and when the company divided into two after Tarlton's death, one group was especially known for the skill of its tumblers.[12] The Queen's Men were last recorded performing in London in 1594, but they remained the most successful touring company of their day until their dispersal in 1602–3.

The removal of the Queen's Men from the London scene in 1594 coincided with, and perhaps partly prompted, the rise of the two companies that were to dominate and stabilise the London scene for many years to come: the Admiral's Men (whose star actor was Edward Alleyn and whose most famous dramatist was Marlowe) and the Chamberlain's Men (whose star was Richard Burbage and whose major dramatist was Shakespeare). Each company was associated with a major entrepreneur, the Admiral's Men with Philip Henslowe, who owned the Rose, and whose so-called *Diary* (covering the years 1592–1603) remains our best guide to company practice in the 1590s, and the Chamberlain's Men with James Burbage, Richard's father, whose company later came to establish the innovative practice of shared ownership of their theatre.[13] A brief run-in between Pembroke's Men and the Privy Council over a now lost play called *The Isle of Dogs* performed at the Swan in 1597, may have had the paradoxical long-term effect of securing the stability of the Admiral's and Chamberlain's Men. The Privy Council's immediate reaction was draconian: they imprisoned one of the writers and two of the actors on grounds of sedition and passed a decree prohibiting all plays for three months and ordering the demolition of all the London amphitheatres (the last part never put into effect).

But the following year they reinforced the position of the two companies who had not crossed them by issuing a decree limiting the London companies to these two. In 1600 a further order attached each company to a particular playhouse, the Chamberlain's to the Globe and the Admiral's to the Fortune; and in 1602 a third company, Worcester's Men, was licensed to play at the Boar's Head. These same three companies became attached to the royal households following King James' accession in 1603. They became the King's, Prince's and Queen's Men respectively, and remained, with some name-changes, the major three companies throughout the rest of the period.[14]

From 1592, when Henslowe's *Diary* begins, it is possible to see how one company operated from day to day. The London repertory theatres operated a punishing schedule, performing a different play every afternoon, increasingly excepting Sunday, possibly rehearsing in the mornings (though almost nothing is known about rehearsal practices) and putting on a new play every three weeks or so.[15] Preparations had to move at high speed, with new plays going into production within about three weeks of the script being purchased and actors learning new parts while continuing to perform their existing repertory of roles. Over a period of three years a leading actor with the Admiral's Men like Alleyn had to play about seventy-one different parts, including fifty-two or so new to him in that time.[16] From this schedule we can see how quickly theatre-going became embedded at a popular level into the lives of Londoners. It has been estimated that in 1595 up to 15,000 people a week were attending performances by two companies, and that in 1620, when six playhouses were operating, that number could have risen to 25,000.[17]

The companies played in their London outdoor amphitheatres most weeks of the year, breaking only for the thirty-seven days of Lent and a summer tour of about eight weeks, unless plague interrupted these conditions (see table 2.2). The London authorities closed the theatres when plague deaths rose above normal, and there were occasional periods of prolonged infection when the closures lasted for well over a year.[18] Companies struggled to survive under these conditions, though once the King's Men were retained members of the royal household under James I, they occasionally received payment without performance to enable them to survive in times of plague, beginning with a payment of £30 during the long closure of 1603.

Players gradually became an integral part of parishes where playhouses were constructed, and were expected to operate with some consideration for the surrounding area, restricting their times of performance with regard to evening prayers, for example, and contributing to the cost of poor relief in the parishes where they played. When the Privy Council first opposed plans for the building of the Fortune playhouse in the parish of St Giles without Cripplegate, residents

Table 2.1 *Playing seasons at Rose to November 1597*

Company	Season	Possible performances	Actual performances	Plays	New plays	Weeks in which new plays opened
1. Strange's Men	19 Feb. 1592–22 Jun. 1592	123	105	23	5	2, 8, 10 14, 16
2. Strange's Men	29 Dec. 1592–1 Feb. 1593	35	29	12	2	2, 5
3. Sussex's Men	27 Dec. 1593–6 Feb. 1594	42	30	12	1	5
4. Sussex's & Queen's Men	1 Apr. 1594–8 Apr. 1594	8	8	5	0	
5. Admiral's Men	14 May 1594–16 May 1594	3	3	3	0	
6. Admiral's Men	17 Jun. 1594–26 Jun. 1595	328	273	36	20	2, 4, 5, 7, 9, 11, 14, 15, 19, 21, 22, 25, 26, 35, 36, 38, 42, 44, 46, 48
7. Admiral's Men	25 Aug. 1595–27 Feb. 1596	187	151	30	10	1, 2, 4, 6, 8, 10, 14, 20, 23, 26
8. Admiral's Men	12 Apr. 1596–28 Jul. 1596	107	84	25	7	3, 4, 6, 9, 11, 12, 15
9. Admiral's Men	27 Oct. 1596–12 Feb. 1597	109	75	18	8	6, 7, 8, 10, 11, 12, 14, 16
10. Admiral's Men	3 Mar. 1597–16 Jul. 1597	136	109	21	6	4, 9, 11, 13, 14, 18
11. Admiral's Men	11 Oct. 1597–5 Nov. 1597	26	9	6	1	1

of the area petitioned them to allow the project to go ahead, mainly on the grounds that they could not afford to do without the contribution to poor relief that the players were promising.[19] Players might also offer or be asked to contribute to poor relief on tour. Churchwardens in West Ham, Essex, justified permitting players to perform in the church by the fact that they made such a contribution.[20] Given that many players resided at least some of the time in the same area as they played, it was in their interests to show respect towards the communities they lived and worked in.

> [The players] have undertaken to me that, where heretofore they began not their plays till towards four o'clock, they will now begin at two and have done between four and five and will not use any drums or trumpets at all for the calling of people together and shall be contributories to the poor of the parish where they play, according to their abilities.
>
> Letter from Lord Chamberlain to Mayor of London, 8 October 1594

Table 2.2 *Dates of playhouse closures due to plague, 1563–1642*

Year or year extent	Month or season	Kind of closure
1563–4	30 Sept.–Jan.	
1569	31 May–30 Sept.	
1572	?[a]	
1574–5	15 Nov.–Easter	
1577	1 Aug.–31 Oct.	
1578	10 Nov.–23 Dec.	
1580	17 Apr.–31 Oct.	
1581	10 July–18 Nov.	
1582	summer–autumn	
1583	summer–26 Nov.	
1584	?summer	
1586	11 May	precautionary restraint
1587	7 May	precautionary restraint
1592	23 June–29 Dec.	
1593	1 Feb.–26 Dec.[b]	
1594	3 Feb.–1 Apr.	
1596	22 July–27 Oct.	
1603	19 Mar.–29 Apr., 1–12 May	[Mar.–Apr.; June–][c]
1604	12 May–9. Apr[d]	[–Apr., June–Sept.]
1605	5 Oct.–15 Dec.[e]	[Mar.; Oct.–Dec.]
1606	? July–? Nov.	[Mar.–Apr.; July–Dec.]

Table 2.2 (cont.)

Year or year extent	Month or season	Kind of closure
1607	? July[f]–? Nov.	[Jan.–Mar.; May–Dec.][g]
1608	? July–	[Jan.–Mar.; Aug.–]
1609	– Dec.[h]	
1610		[–Jan.; Mar.; July–Nov.]
1611		[Feb.–Mar.]
1612		[Mar.–Apr.; Nov.–Dec.]
1613		[Feb.–Mar.; July–Dec.]
1625	12 May–24 Nov.[i]	
1630	8 July–28 Nov.	
1636	12 May–	
1637	–2 Oct.	
1640	23 July–29 Oct.	
1641	15 July–9 Dec.	

Notes:

[a] Indicates indirect or imprecise evidence, e.g. based on Harrison's *Description of England*, or Stowe.

[b] A heavy year for plague: over 15,000 identified plague deaths, more than half the total mortality for the year, continuing through 1594.

[c] Lists in square brackets from Barroll, *Politics, Plague, and Shakespeare's Theater*, Appendix 2, 217–26.

[d] This closure began on 19 Mar. 1603 when Elizabeth entered her final illness; in Apr. it continued as a closure for plague. *Henslowe's Diary* (209, 225) indicates some playing in May, but then none until after Lent 1604. Stowe indicates 30,000 plague deaths during the year; none the less, that winter the court had its plays. Possibly playing resumed before Lent; but restraint was withdrawn in Apr. 1604.

[e] Order of the Privy Council, BL Add. MS 11402, f. 107, 109; printed in *MSC* i. 4–5: 371–2.

[f] The Lord Mayor asked the Council to stop plays in a letter, 12 Apr. 1607 (*MSC*, i. 1: 87–8). The plague bill by the end of Apr. was 43; it then fell until July.

[g] Barroll considers (I think wrongly) that the cold weather which froze the Thames Dec.–Feb. would have stopped playing.

[h] Plague deaths were heavy: 2,262 in 1608; 4,240 in 1609; the epidemic persisted into 1610. See Dekker, *Work for Armourers* (1609, *Non-Dramatic Works*, iv. 96).

[i] The year of James's death and of greatest plague mortality on record, with 35,417 deaths.

Sources:

E. K. Chambers, *The Elizabethan Stage*, App. E (*ES* iv 345–51).

R. A. Foakes and R. T. Rickert (ed.), *Henslowe's Diary* (Cambridge, 1961).

G. E. Bentley, *The Jacobean and Caroline Stage* (7 vols.; Oxford, 1941–68), ii. 667–72.

J. Leeds Barroll, *Politics, Plague and Shakespeare's Theater*.

Though much has been made of the idea that early theatres, especially those south of the Thames, were positioned in low-life neighbourhoods, populated by brewhouses, whorehouses and bull and bearbaiting rings, William Ingram has shown that the parish of St Saviour's, where the Rose, the Swan, the Globe and the Hope were located, did not, as one might expect if there was real opposition to the players, suddenly become an undesirable place of residence following the building of the Swan and the Globe.[21]

Some communities, of course, resisted players' attempts to move into the district, and it was for this reason that James Burbage, having purchased the Blackfriars monastic buildings (previously accommodating the first Blackfriars playhouse, p. 49 above) in 1596, could not use it for performance until several years later, after the Blackfriars Children had given up their lease in 1608. Several prominent residents of the district, including George Carey, Lord Hunsdon, the Chamberlain's Men's own patron, opposed the opening up of the playhouse under an adult company in 1596 on the grounds that it would be a social nuisance.

one Burbage hath lately bought certain rooms in the same precinct near adjoining unto the dwelling houses of the right honourable the Lord Chamberlain and the Lord of Hunsdon, which rooms the said Burbage is now altering and meaneth very shortly to convert and turn the same into a common playhouse, which will grow to be a very great annoyance and trouble, not only to all the noblemen and gentlemen thereabout inhabiting, but also a general inconvenience to all the inhabitants of the same precinct, both by reason of the great resort and gathering together of all manner of vagrant and lewd persons that, under colour of resorting to the plays, will come thither and work all manner of mischief, and also to the great pestering and filling up of the same precinct if it should please God to send any visitation of sickness as heretofore hath been.

Blackfriars residents' petition to the Privy Council, November 1596

But that opposition had apparently decreased by the time the King's Men returned to the idea of performing there in 1608.

The Blackfriars became available again to the King's Men as a result of the fall from favour of the Blackfriars Children. This was the point at which the trajectory of the children's companies' development separated most radically from that of the adult companies. We have seen that Paul's Boys and the Chapel (later Blackfriars) Children had begun regular performances in fixed venues during the mid 1570s, around the same time as the adult companies were beginning to become established in permanent theatrical venues. The two boys' companies joined forces in 1583, the year when the Queen's Men were formed, and it is conceivable that the conjunction was not coincidental, but that the boys' companies were responding to and imitating the adult initiative that sought to strengthen the prestige and status of the profession through selection and amalgamation of its best resources. The collaboration did not last, however, and both companies had closed down by 1590. The most radical difference between these two companies and the companies that reopened under the same names in 1599 (Paul's) and 1600 (Blackfriars) was, as Andrew Gurr emphasises, that the early pretext that the children were acting as part of their education was now abandoned for open commercialisation, and the boys remained in their companies into maturity.[22]

> but there is, sir, an aery [nest] of children, little eyases [fledgling hawks], that cry out on the top of the question, and are most tyrannically [outrageously] clapp'd for't. These are now the fashion, and so berattle [assail] the common stages – so they call them – that many wearing rapiers are afraid of goose-quills [pens] and dare scarce come thither.
> William Shakespeare, *Hamlet* (1600–1), II.2.339–44

The question of how different the children's repertoire was from the adult is one that has provoked ongoing disagreement since company rivalry, even amounting to 'war', between the 'private' and the 'public' theatres was first proposed. Interpreting the famous lines in the Folio text of *Hamlet* which seem to openly acknowledge rivalry between adult and child companies is more problematic than is first apparent. Later scholars have qualified and nuanced the larger arguments in a number of ways. Roslyn Knutson has recently proposed cooperation as a more useful paradigm than rivalry for understanding relations between companies, and many others have noted not only the finer distinctions between invidual repertoires, whether boy or adult, but also some degree of crossover between public and private theatres, most notably after the King's Men began to play routinely at both.[23] While some of the most interesting work remaining to be done is undoubtedly in identifying the specificities of individual company repertoires, some broad-brush distinctions can nevertheless be made between the adults and the boys. Perhaps the clearest of these is that, while the adult companies for the most part contained their satirical gibes within acceptable limits, the boy companies finally went too far and lost their professional lives as a result.

[The King] had vowed [the Blackfriars Children] should never play more, but should first beg their bread, and he would have his vow performed. And therefore my Lord Chamberlain . . . should take order to dissolve them, and to punish the maker [the playwright] besides.

Letter from Sir Thomas Lake to the Earl of Salisbury, 11 March 1608

Despite all the changes in company status and practice brought about by increasing professionalisation and commercialism, some traditional practices remained strikingly strong. Throughout most of the period, for example, despite the growth of both 'public' and 'private' playhouses in London, companies continued to play at court and to tour the provinces, playing a wide range of venues.[24] Thus the old-fashioned virtues of flexibility and adaptability continued to inflect performance even as some new and fashionable plays were being written specifically for one place rather than another, or succeeding or failing with particular audiences. Jonson's *Poetaster* (1601), written for the Blackfriars Children, mocked the Globe for performing 'humours, revels and satires that gird [gibe] and fart at the time' ((III.4.190–1); *The White Devil* (1612–13) failed at the Red Bull before then coming to play regularly at the indoor Phoenix; the printer of *The Knight of the Burning Pestle* (1607) lamented the failure of the Blackfriars audience to appreciate its satire against citizens. But at the same time a huge range of plays might be taken anywhere from amphitheatres to hall theatres and from court to country, and even star London actors expected to trail the country for two months of the year.

My good sweet mouse, I commend me heartily to you and to my father, my mother and my sister Bess, hoping in God though the sickness be round about you, yet by his mercy it may escape your house . . .

   Mouse, you send me no news of any things. You should send of your domestical matters, such things as happen at home, as how your distilled water proves, or this or that or any thing, what you will. And, Jug, I pray you, let my orange tawny stockings of woollen be dyed a very good black against I come home, to wear in the winter. You sent me not word of my garden, but next time you will; but remember this in any case, that all that bed which was parsley, in the month of September you sow it with spinach, for then is the time. I would do it myself but we shall not come home till All Hallowtide. And so sweet mouse, farewell, and brook our long journey with patience.

Letter from Edward Alleyn, on tour, to his wife in London, 1 August 1593.
[The mother, father and sister Alleyn refers to in the letter are his in-laws.]

Born two years after Shakespeare, in 1566, Alleyn married Joan Woodward, Henslowe's stepdaughter, in October 1592, a move that brought business and personal life together in a way that was characteristic of the time, not only in the theatre industry. By May 1593 he was on tour with Lord Strange's Men, while plague ravaged London, and was to remain on the road for most of rest of the year.[25]

Despite the new and fashionable plays being produced all the time in the capital, many more traditional kinds of plays continued to be performed at particular venues and on tour. Thus Corpus Christi plays were performed at Prescot and Lancaster until 1603; morality play structure was remodeled to create Protestant propaganda (*Enough is as Good as a Feast, c.* 1568) or controversial and spectacular theatre (*Dr Faustus,* 1588?) or fashionable court or popular drama full of topical allusion (*King Lear,* 1605–6); and the Red Bull continued to play 'drum and trumpet' plays (militaristic, action-packed plays appealing to civic or patriotic values) long after the more fashionable companies and theatres had ceased to perform them.

Audiences

Audiences sometimes paid and sometimes did not, depending on the nature and place of performance. Invited guests, whether at court or in any household, would not be expected to pay, though at certain types of court performance, such as tournaments, it was possible for a non-invited, paying audience to attend alongside the household and its guests. The performance of a morality play, *St Christopher,* at Gowthwaite Hall, home of the recusant Sir John Yorke, in 1609–10, drew an audience of local people so large (more than 'fourscore or a hundred persons') that it was necessary to turn some away.[26] One of the problems, of course, before the building of permanent playhouses, was the difficulty of finding a way of making the spectators pay, a difficulty street performers still face today. One way, as in *Mankind* (p. 56 above), was to make a collection at a point when spectators would be inclined to stay rather than leave. Another was to finance the play in advance through loans or subscriptions, methods well documented in rural communities.

It is salutary to remember that drama in London was not always the grandest in scale or investment. John Coldewey has described a sequence of 'semi-professional' productions in Essex and Kent indicating a level of dramatic activity well beyond the casual. At Chelmsford in 1562, indeed, the expenditures reveal a summer dramatic festival, involving large sums of money and run by a hired and very well paid London 'property player', whose duties combined those of the modern stage manager, designer and director.[27] Yet another way of making money was to set up and charge for seating in prime viewing locations, whilst allowing others to stand free of charge. Thus at the York Corpus Christi performance, for example, the city rented out concessions on the different stations (the places where the pageant wagons stopped) to the highest bidder, who in turn sold the seats to those willing to pay.

The Corpus Christi plays were primarily funded by the guilds, whose own interests were served not only by the opportunity to showcase their trade and status and the influx of spectators with money to spend in the city, but by the city's protection and regulation of their interests. (In some cases plays were tied quite closely to the trade of those performing, as in Shipwrights staging the Noah play, with the building of the ark, at York. The allocation of the Doomsday play to the Mercers, traders in expensive cloths, such as silk and velvet, was an opportunity for them to display their wealth and prestige through the elaboration of the special effects as well as the rich cloths themselves.) The whole city benefited from the prestige and money that came via the plays, which even attracted royal visitors with some frequency, especially in Coventry, located close to Kenilworth Castle.

Guilds retained their association with performance, though recorded performances at guildhalls outside London mostly indicate simple use of the town's major indoor space rather than the sponsorship of a particular guild. Inside London, however, the sponsorship of plays by individual guilds is more clearly demonstrable. The entry fee of one penny recorded by the Merchant Taylors in 1574, for example, is parallel with the penny still charged at the Globe in 1599. (Outside the theatre a penny bought, for example, a one-pound loaf of bread.)

> Whereas at our common plays and such like exercises which be commonly exposed to be seen for money, every lewd [ignorant] person thinketh himself (for his penny) worthy of the chief and most commodious place without respect of any other either for age or estimation in the common weal, which bringeth the youth to such an impudent familiarity with their betters that oftentimes great contempt of masters, parents, and magistrates followeth thereof . . .
>
> Accounts of Merchant Taylors' Company, 16 March 1574

The sneering tone audible here finds a parallel in the attitudes expressed towards audiences at public playhouses. Thomas Dekker shows contempt for the lowest social levels of the audience; and a Florentine recounting the eccentricities of the Venetian ambassador in the second decade of the seventeenth century reports the way one social group might turn on another, whether as a result of xenophobia or class hostility or both.

your stinkard has the selfsame liberty to be there in his tobacco fumes which your sweet courtier hath, and . . . your carman and tinker claim as strong a voice in their suffrage, and sit to give judgement on the play's life and death as well as the proudest Momus among the Tribe of Critic.

Thomas Dekker, *Gull's Hornbook* (1609)

[The Venetian ambassador] went the other day to a playhouse that is called the Curtain . . . , a place as dubious as they come, and where you would never see the face of a gentleman, let alone a nobleman. And what made it worse, so as not to have to pay sixpence [he chose not] to go to one of the boxes and not even to be seated in one of the degrees [galleries] they have there but preferred to stand below the middle, among the rabble of porters and carters, pretending that he needed to stay close by because he was hard of hearing, as if he really understood what was being recited.

But that is not all, for in the end, when one of the actors took leave of the audience and invited it to come back the next day and to pick a play, he actually named one. But the crowd wanted another and began to shout *'Friars, Friars'* because they wanted one that usually took its name from the friars, meaning [in Italian] *'frati'*. Whereupon our blockhead turned to his interpreter [who] explained that this was the name of a comedy about friars. So, loosening his cloak, he began to clap his hands just as the mob did and to shout 'frati, frati'. As he was shouting this, the people turned to him and, assuming he was a Spaniard, began to whistle in such a way that I cannot imagine that he would ever want to return to that place. But he has not given up visiting the other theatres and almost always with a single servant.

Undated letter from Antimo Galli to the Florentine Secretary of State, 1611–15

As the player's invitation to the audience to choose a play for the next day in Antimo Galli's letter illustrates, plays were, probably from about the time of the opening of fixed playhouses, performed daily except for Sundays, the period of Lent and plague closures. There were at first no intervals or act divisions in public theatres (though act divisions are often inserted into early plays by later printers), but practice at indoor playhouses, where intervals were necessary in order to trim the candles, gradually became more widespread in the seventeenth century. Food and drink were sold before and possibly during performances at outdoor amphitheatres, where some of the audience stood around the stage. 'Jigs', usually bawdy song and dance routines, were performed at the end of plays, even after tragedies, up to about 1612 and were an opportunity for the clown to shine.[28] Act breaks at the indoor theatres were occupied by music and dancing, and the Blackfriars consort was famous for its musical skill. Indoor playhouses, where audiences were all seated, also began the practice of allowing audience members to sit on stools on the stage, thereby purchasing an opportunity to make themselves the object of the audience's gaze, even to the point of disrupting the play. Dekker famously satirises the typical gallant, who interrupts the quaking prologue by swaggering on with his stool and his sixpence in his hand, and plays also mock this fashion.[29]

> Today I go to the Blackfriars Playhouse,
> Sit i' the view, salute all my acquaintance,
> Rise up between the acts, let fall my cloak,
> Publish a handsome man and a rich suit,
> As that's a special end, why we go thither.
>   Ben Jonson, *The Devil is an Ass* (1616), I.6.31–5

Many of these elements, together with several accounts of audiences throwing things, mounting the stage and rioting at playhouses, suggest an audience that was neither silent nor passive[30]; yet it must be borne in mind that most remaining descriptions of audiences come from relatively hostile or contemptuous sources, and it is unlikely that the companies would ever have performed anything other than comedies and rabble-rousing heroics if audiences had not been capable of listening and responding to the full variety of plays that were in fact on offer.

> In the last few days the King's players have been here. They acted with enormous applause to full houses . . . They had tragedies too which they acted with skill and decorum and in which some things, both speech and action, brought forth tears.
>   Moreover, that famous Desdemona killed before us by her husband, although she always acted her whole part supremely well, yet when she was killed she was even more moving, for when she fell back upon the bed she implored the pity of the spectators by her very face.
>   Letter from Henry Jackson to G.P., September 1610 (translated from the Latin)

The spectator reporting on *Othello* above was a fellow of Corpus Christi College, Oxford. He does not specify the place of performance, which could have been an innyard or perhaps a college. Either way, an Oxford audience cannot be contrasted in any simple way with a potentially more popular audience. Students, then as now, were not noted for their quiet behaviour; members of the public often attended college performances; and crowds sometimes led to problems amongst university as well as public playhouse spectators.[31] In any case a deep emotional engagement with plays, even to the point of tears, is also recorded at public playhouses, where spectators wept for the death of Shakespeare's heroic Talbot.

> How would it have joyed brave Talbot (the terror of the French) to think that after he had lain two hundred years in his tomb, he should triumph again on the stage, and have his bones new embalmed with the tears of ten thousand spectators at least (at several times) who, in the tragedian that represents his person, imagine they behold him fresh bleeding.
>
> Thomas Nashe, *Pierce Penniless his Supplication to the Devil* (1592)

Audiences also wept at religious plays, as the author of a hostile fifteenth-century tract noted.

> Oft sythes [times] by such miracles playing men and women, seeing the passion of Christ and his saints, been moved to compassion and devotion, weeping bitter tears.
>
> *Treatise of Miracles Playing* (1380–1414)

And Thomas Heywood, an actor and dramatist himself as well as the author of an important defence of the stage, took it for granted that total immersion in the fiction was one crucially available mode of engagement.

> To turn to our domestic histories, what English blood, seeing the person of any bold Englishman presented, and doth not hug his fame and honey at his valour, pursuing him in his enterprise with his best wishes, and, as being rapt in contemplation, offers to him in his heart all prosperous performance, as if the personator were the man personated? So bewitching a thing is lively and well-spirited action, that it hath power to new-mould the hearts of the spectators and fashion them to the shape of any noble and notable attempt.
>
> Thomas Heywood, *An Apology for Actors* (1612)

In trying to arrive at a broad view of how audiences behaved we must remember that many of the most memorable records that survive are recorded precisely because they were out of the normal run in some way. Lord Thurles' deliberate blocking of Captain Essex's view at the Blackfriars in 1632, resulting in Thurles drawing his sword to run Essex through, was out of the ordinary, as were the several accidents on record, where scaffolds fell killing audience members or muskets or cannons went off in the wrong direction, killing spectators or setting fire to the playhouse.[32]

It is partly the case that different playhouses played different repertories for different audiences, though too much can also be made of this. A late seventeenth-century historian of the theatre reports that the Fortune and the

Red Bull 'were mostly frequented by citizens, and the meaner sort of people' and identifies the Blackfriars as having the highest reputation amongst the others. Its players, he says, 'were men of grave and sober behaviour', implying a distinction between their calibre and that of other players.[33] On the other hand, while the King's Men, playing at the Blackfriars from 1609, may have been noted for their respectability by that point, the children's company occupying the Blackfriars before them were closed down for their insolence, and the King's Men themselves performed much of their repertory at the Globe as well as the Blackfriars; so the idea of fixed repertories and reputations at any single playhouse must be treated with some caution. Plays and printers' notes show clearly, however, that contemporaries were aware of fashions and divisions that set them apart. Yet men and women of all social classes shared a common impulse to take up this newly widespread form of entertainment, which kept them up to date with both fashion and news.

> With these and many more amusements, the English pass their time, learning at the play what is happening abroad; indeed men and womenfolk visit such places without scruple.
>
> > Thomas Platter's account of his visit to London in 1599 (translated from the German)

The reactions of several playgoers to what they saw are on record, and responses range from accounts of the plot, the spectacle and the acting to determination to derive a moral lesson from the play. Simon Forman, for example, who kept notes on the plays he went to see, enjoyed the spectacle of the witch scenes in *Macbeth* (1606) and saw the *The Winter's Tale* (1609) as warning spectators to 'Beware of trusting feigned beggars or fawning fellows'.[34] Heywood, as noted above, also believed in theatre's capacity to educate and inspire to good behaviour. Tastes could be both personal and wide-ranging, of course. Roslyn Knutson concludes from her study of the commonplace book of a gentleman named Edward Pudsey that 'when Pudsey went to the playhouse or bought a play in quarto, he appears to have been looking for *sententiae*, witty similes, and cultural opinion on clothing, jewelry, baldness, music, women, and boorish behavior, not for the latest fashion in genre or the greatest dramatic poetry'.[35]

Audience–actor relations

'The actors', as Bernard Beckerman writes, 'did not regard the stage as a place but as a platform from which to project a story.'[36] The survey of different places of performance in chapter 1 shows how regularly the spatial conditions for viewing were shared, open and interactive, the audience sharing space and light with the actors, the actors' space only sometimes defined by a stage and even then by a stage thrust into the spectators' space. These conditions, together with the need for flexibility in different venues, chapter 1 argued, fostered a fluidity of performance that can be spatially conceptualised through the terms *locus* and *platea*. Performance, in other words, is 'simultaneously representation and being';[37] the actors participate in two worlds, the real world in which the representation takes place (which we may call 'this world') and the fictional world represented in the drama (which we may call 'the other world'); and the play moves between these two worlds from moment to moment. The movement is both physical and conceptual. The audience's perception moves between this world and the other world as the actors move in physical space. The other world is marked by its difference and distance from the audience, again materially as well as imaginatively. Costumes, props and marked features of the space are all signs of the fictional world, and the more distant from the audience or the closer to large props or marked spatial features the actor's body is, the more easily he is perceived as inhabiting that fictional world. The closer to the edge of the performance space the actor moves, and the less conspicuous his markers of difference seem (or, to put it another way, the more conspicuous his own presence as actor rather than as character seems to be), the more easily he is perceived as inhabiting the same world and time as the audience.

The figure most markedly moving between the two worlds of the audience and the fiction in medieval drama was the figure known as the 'Vice', who was often the leader of the troupe and usually its star performer. His name often appears first or in special type in the cast lists of early printed plays. The Vice represented vice or sinfulness either explicitly or implicitly, and his name varied between labeling him allegorically as a vice (Mischief in *Mankind*, Pride in *Nature* (c. 1490–1500), Iniquity in *King Darius* (c. 1564–5)) and suggesting his difference from the more narrowly conceived allegorical figures by allowing the negativity of the name to shade into a more frivolous register through rhyme or alliteration (Hardydardy in *Godly Queen Hester* (1529–30), Nichol Newfangle in *Like Will to Like* (c. 1567–8)). His part was often very physical and highly comic, written for an actor with skills in song, dance, acrobatics and clowning; and this range of performance styles, together with the ways he had to occupy space in order to pursue this range, gave him a labile existence between fictional role and extraneous clown or acrobat. We can see in *Mankind*, for example, how Mischief's mockery of Mercy within the fiction of the play (lines 45–63) functions within the audience's reality both as a temptation to laugh with vice and as a reminder of how easily one may slide into vice and sneer at virtue. Aspects of the Vice are visible in both the clowns and the villains of later drama, who slip in and out of the fiction in similar ways, ducking out of their relationships with other characters in the play in order to make a direct relationship with the audience through direct address and physical proximity. Though the organisation of companies became more complex with the building of permanent playhouses, clowns were often still star performers, known for their singing, dancing and improvisation, and dominating the jig that usually followed the play in the public theatres. Richard Tarlton, the earliest and most famous of those we know by name, was a favourite of the Queen, sometimes called to perform solo before her. The great years of the Queen's Men, of whom he was a founder member in 1583, were from then until his death in 1588. Will Kemp, the Chamberlain's Men's clown until 1599, may have prompted Shakespeare's writing of Hamlet's well-known invective against clowns who threaten to overwhelm the plays they perform in.

And let those that play your clowns speak no more than is set down for them, for there be of them that will themselves laugh to set on some quantity of barren spectators to laugh too, though in the mean time some necessary question of the play be then to be consider'd. That's villainous, and shows a most pitiful ambition in the fool that uses it.

William Shakespeare, *Hamlet* (1600–1), III.2.38–45

In another sense, of course, all the performers in early drama have a certain freedom to move in and out of the playworld, not only because of the spatial features explored in chapter 1, which plunged them physically into the midst of the spectators, often without very clearly marked boundaries, but also because the performers' bodies were often conspicuously at odds with the parts they were adopting. This is especially true of children's companies, where there was a continuously visible gap between the child actor and the role, and of women's parts, which were always taken by men (though reactions such as Henry Jackson's to *Othello* indicate the degree to which such conventions could become so normalised as sometimes to blind spectators to their presence). Hamlet's observations on acting conventions, however, indicate that it is not only particular classes of performer who can move across the boundary between the worlds of the audience and of the fiction. Even a tragic protagonist can be scripted to stimulate awareness of the gap between the two; and this dramatic flow between immersion in the fictional world and awareness of the world of the here-and-now creates an audience capable of scepticism, criticism and laughter, as well as empathy, emotion and tears. Bertolt Brecht, later describing an effect he called '*Verfremdung*' [perhaps best translated as 'distancing'], did not invent the effect but rather refined techniques for producing it based on his study of early theatre. His interest in white light, emblematic costumes and props and visible scene changes, for example, as ways of producing a critical mode of viewing were aspects of an intention more reconstructive than original. An audience's capacity for one kind of reaction need not, however, as some critics have supposed, inhibit its capacity for the other. The mixed dramaturgy characteristic of both medieval and early modern theatre can, as this and subsequent chapters seek to demonstrate, move an audience between very different kinds of engagement with the drama from moment to moment.

The mixture of acting styles and modes of engagement is visible in the text of plays from the beginning to the end of the period. A comically realistic response of bewilderment, for example, is scripted for the N-Town shepherds when they hear the sacred and unfamiliar Latin words of the angels' '*Gloria in Excelsis Deo*':

> FIRST SHEPHERD Ey! Ey! This was a wonder note
> That was now sungen above the sky.
> I have that voice full well I wot [know],
> They sang, 'Gle, glo, glory'.
> SECOND SHEPHERD Nay, so mote I the [as I hope to thrive], so was it not.
> I have that song full well inum [understood].
> In my wit well it is wrought,
> It was 'Gle, glo, glas, glum'. (N-town, *The Shepherds*, lines 62–9)

But the third shepherd is scripted to move beyond the realm of realism, to a mysterious understanding of the divine song as an announcement of the birth of Christ, and the play moves from realism into ritual as all three shepherds leave the stage singing a Latin anthem. Mixed perspectives can be so closely sequenced or entwined as to be almost inseparable. Shakespeare's Cleopatra, preparing for death, is intermittently, and sometimes simultaneously, a tragic queen preparing for the most intense moment of the fictional narrative; a boy-actor explicitly making reference to that gap between actor and character as s/he gives voice to the fear that Caesar will have 'some squeaking Cleopatra boy my greatness / I'th' posture of a whore' (*Antony and Cleopatra* (1606), V.2.220–1); and a comic actor/courageous queen joking with the clown who brings the serpent. When s/he calls for her crown and her 'best attires' and gives Charmian leave thereafter 'To play till doomsday' (V.2.228–32), she is simultaneously a character immersing the audience in the part of a proud woman taking control of her own destiny and a player dressing up for a tragic role and alluding to a long-familiar dramatic form. Both queen and actor are dressing up; both the world and the Corpus Christi play end with Doomsday. Notions of dramatic unity or consistency of character are irrelevant to this kind of theatre, which seeks to move an audience through a number of registers of engagement rather than to seal them hermetically into one.

What we know of acting styles confirms a range from the formal, pictorial and emblematic, to the emotive, the rhetorical and the realistic. But what the examples above seek to show is that the extreme ends of the register are neither separate nor incompatible, and that the effects produced are not uniquely or necessarily tied to the acting styles with which we might automatically link them today, in an age when the dominance of television realism might persuade us that the most realistic acting is necessarily the most emotive. Looking back to the accounts of audience reaction documented above, we see potentially disparate ways of moving audiences to tears: the concentration on Desdemona's face suggests a naturalistic style of performance; brave Talbot's death was probably performed in a highly rhetorical and heroic acting style; and the plays showing the suffering of Christ and the saints may have moved audiences to tears by allowing them a prolonged, still moment in which to view and meditate on iconic and often very familiar tableaux of ritual punishment, humiliation and death, including crucifixion. Some of the stage pictures of religious theatre may have resembled images in stained glass windows and devotional books so strongly as to provoke tears in the very moment of their recognition (see illustrations, p. 15 above). But iconographic stagecraft was not a feature only of medieval or religious drama. The discovery space is regularly used on the later stage to create meaningful tableaux (Faustus in his study (*Dr Faustus*, 1588?), Miranda and Ferdinand playing chess (*The Tempest*, 1610), the Duchess of Malfi's children seemingly dead, for example (*The Duchess of Malfi*, 1612–14)), and iconographic moments totally outside framed space can be so powerful as to stand out in the memories of modern as well as earlier audiences. Even today, people who have never seen a performance of *Hamlet* may recognise the familiar image of Hamlet holding Yorick's skull.[38]

While we can see elements of realistic characterisation in early drama (and we will notice them all the more if these are what we set out to look for), there are certain formal, non-realist characteristics that define medieval and early modern dramaturgy (and by implication acting) as different from post-Naturalist theatre.[39] (Case studies below will take up these points in relation to individual plays.) Early acting is demonstrative, gestural, explicit and focused on stage picture to a degree that is unfamiliar now. The opening stage direction of *The Play of Adam*, a twelfth-century Anglo-Norman play, specifies how the actors are to be coached to behave in a way that underlines word with gesture.

all the actors must be trained to speak with deliberation, and to make gestures that are in keeping with what they are saying; they must not add or take away a syllable in their lines, but rather pronounce them all distinctly, and deliver everything they have to say in the proper order. Every time someone mentions paradise he is to look at it and point it out with his hand.

Play of Adam (c. 1146–74), opening stage direction (translated from the Anglo-Norman)

When Adam and Eve are sent out of paradise, the stage direction indicates that they beat their breasts; and when they see thorns and thistles growing where they have planted their seeds, they '*fall prostrate to the ground struck with violent grief; and then, as they sit up they will strike their breasts and their thighs, showing the grief they have suffered*.'[40] Several characters in medieval drama, furthermore, would routinely have been played in masks, thus inhibiting a mode of engagement like empathy; and the widespread practice of doubling, which demanded that an audience accept a performer in two or more different roles, would also have served to inhibit any total immersion in the character's role.[41] In any case, it is self-evident that empathy would be a totally misplaced audience response to a non-human figure like God the Father or the devil; and indeed the gold mask of the first and the false head or false nose of the second would make such a response highly unlikely. When we bear in mind, however, that Edward Alleyn played the Jew of Malta in a false nose and Faustus in a surplice emblazoned with a cross (to protect himself, as an actor, from the blasphemies of his role), we see that later performance retains the traces of its medieval origins. Masque (or mask) as a genre, of course, carried that more emblematic and pictorial performance style right through to the closing of the theatres and beyond.

Plays of this period are frequently presentational as well as representational, that is, explicit about what they seek to show or mean as well as, or sometimes rather than, implicit in their showing. They often begin with a prologue and end with an epilogue, sometimes drawing a moral or inviting the audience to pray or (later) to applaud. Characters frequently announce themselves by name when they enter or tell the audience what their role is, and this is a feature that remains especially characteristic of the villain, a figure descended from the medieval Vice.[42] Characters, sometimes allegorical, who stand outside the fictional frame may enter between episodes of the action to instruct the audience on how to understand it (like Contemplacio in the N-Town cycle: 'This matter here made is of the Mother of Mercy; / How by Joachim and Anne was her conception . . .' (*Joachim and Anna*, lines 9–10 etc) or sit on stage throughout as an implicit pointer for the audience as to the play's meaning (like Revenge in *The Spanish Tragedy*).

Asides are another way in which early theatre prioritises clarity and a direct appeal to the audience over realism. As Bernard Beckerman suggests, 'the Globe players, in the staging of asides, did not think in terms of creating an illusion of actuality but of relating the crucial elements of the narrative to each other'. And Beckerman illustrates at length how the tendency to make emotion explicit in speech, more strongly associated with the early part of the period, continues even into plays that we now think of as having a rather inward turn, like *Hamlet*.[43]

> GERTRUDE Thou turn'st my eyes into my very soul,
> And there I see such black and grained spots,
> As will not leave their tinct. (III.4.89–91)
>
> . . .
>
> Oh Hamlet, thou hast cleft my heart in twain. (III.4.156)
>
> HAMLET But break my heart, for I must hold my tongue. (I.2.159)
>
> William Shakespeare, *Hamlet* (1600–1)

Many of the most explicit revelations of feeling are made through the medium we now call soliloquy, which is often best understood as a direct address, in confidence as it were, to the audience. Our most familiar encounter with early drama now, through the medium of filmed and televised versions of Shakespeare's plays, invites us to engage with those plays in a way that is more anachronistic than we may realise, and one of the ways in which this is most evident is in performers' and directors' uncertainty over what to do with soliloquy, which needs a live audience to make sense. Voice-over; the utterance of words into an imagined middle distance; direct address to camera; all of these strike a false note which does not help us to enter into the dramaturgy at its root, which is based on the simultaneous recognition of 'this world' and 'the other world'. Soliloquy is the dominant mode of many of the most fully rounded characters of early theatre, and at the same time one of its least realistic modes of operation.

The problem of seeking to translate early theatre to later, recorded media brings together issues of acting style and space. Where film and television alternate between the long shot and the close-up, inviting us to take pleasure in scenic sweep and in the workings of the 'naturally' mobile face, early drama, like any live theatre, gives the audience choice about where to look even as it scripts them to engage with either the whole stage or a small part of it, so that as they vary their gaze, they are constantly aware of the alternative possibilities with which that chosen gaze is in tension. They know that their view of the stage is never complete, and that their look at the whole stage, full or empty, differs from their close focus on an individual performer or prop. Early theatre alternates between engaging an audience through the formal creation of stage pictures (from the framed emblems of the pageant wagon and the perspective pictures of the proscenium arch stage of masque to the formal procession through the great doors of the public playhouses) and more restricted and restrained movements that interrupt or disrupt those symmetrical and rhythmical pleasures. *King Lear*, for example, opens mid-conversation between two lords and the bastard son of one of them, postponing for thirty lines or so the ceremonial entry of Lear and his family and retinue to the sound of a sennet, a sequence of notes on the trumpet or cornet. The disruption of Lear's plan for the smooth allocation of the divided kingdom according to set rhetorical speeches is then manifested first through Cordelia's asides, which interrupt the audience's engagement with the broad sweep and high rhetoric of public interaction on a full stage, demanding that they focus momentarily off-centre on her still, individual body and private thoughts, and then through her radically disjunctive refusal to be drawn into a rhetoric parallel with that of her father and sisters: 'Nothing, my lord' (I.1.86).[44] The change in focus is visual, spatial and aural; and the aural register includes not only voices, differently pitched, speaking publicly or aside, but also the presence or absence of music, background noise or silence. And audiences feel the texture of each moment not only against other moments in that same play, but against their experience of other plays. Thus the first two of Shakespeare's *Henry VI* plays (1591–2) open with an ordered ceremonial entry to musical accompaniment, led by the King and filling the stage with his lords and retinue, but the third strikes an audience with its difference, opening in the midst of battle, with alarums sounding, and the random and disorderly entrance of embattled lords wondering how the King has escaped them.

Playscripts show certain kinds of performance and certain modes of acting and occupying space persisting over the whole period. The presence of song and dance, for example, is much more prominent in drama throughout the early period than it has been in most twentieth-century drama. Though performance is moving back again now towards the inclusion of such varied textures, musical performance through most of the three hundred years from the eighteenth to the twentieth century was conceived of as separate from 'drama', which in turn was understood to be mainly a matter of the spoken word. There were also, however, changes in acting style which were recognised and singled out by contemporaries. In particular there seems to have been a visible distinction between the playing styles of the two star actors, Edward Alleyn and Richard Burbage.[45] Ben Jonson described two of Alleyn's most famous roles, Tamburlaine and Tamercham, as having 'nothing in them but . . . scenical strutting, and furious vociferation'; and 'strutting' is a term used elsewhere too to describe a particular kind of acting going out of fashion by about 1600. Hamlet, that unstoppable critic of theatrical styles, had something to say about this too, as by now we should expect.

> O, there be players that I have seen play – and heard others praise, and that
> highly – not to speak it profanely, that, neither having th'accent of Christians, nor
> the gait of Christian, pagan, nor man, have so strutted and bellow'd, that I have
> thought some of Nature's journeymen had made men, and not made them well,
> they imitated humanity so abominably.
>
> William Shakespeare, *Hamlet* (1600–1), III.2.28–35

Nor did Shakespeare stop with Hamlet. In *Troilus and Cressida*, written around the same time as *Hamlet*, he has another jibe at the 'strutting player' when he lets Ulysses draw a parallel between Achilles, mocking Agamemnon, and such a figure.

> And like a strutting player, whose conceit
> Lies in his hamstring, and doth think it rich
> To hear the wooden dialogue and sound
> 'Twixt his stretch'd footing and the scaffolage [scaffoldage, i.e.
>   stage-boards],
> Such to-be-pitied and o'er-wrested seeming
> He acts thy greatness in.
>
> William Shakespeare, *Troilus and Cressida* (1602), I.3.153–8

'Strutting', both Hamlet and Ulysses make clear, was linked to noise, to a resounding step and a 'bellowing' voice. Heightened physical movement and heightened speech went together; and we can see 'strutting' scripted across a range of parts.[46] Tyrants in the mystery cycles, for example, speak a common rhetoric of violence, and it is no accident that Herod's raging, as a famous Coventry stage direction indicates, took him out into the street beyond the pageant wagon. Verbal excess naturally performs itself through physical and spatial emphasis and expansion.

> KING HEROD   I ride on my rowel [spur] rich [powerful] in my reign [kingdom]
>   Ribs full red with rape [violence] shall I rend [tear]
>   Poppets [puppets] and pap-hawks [?sucklings] I shall putten in
>   pain,
>   With my spear preven [prove], pichen [stab] and to pend [pinch].
>   The gomes [men] with gold crowns ne get never again,
>   To seek those sots [fools] sondes [messengers] shall I send.
>   Do howlot howten, hoberd and hein [make owl (i.e. woman),
>   clown and villain hoot]
>   When her [their] barns [children] bleed under cradle bend,
>   Sharply I shall hem shend [destroy],
>   The knave [male] children that be

In all Israel country;
They shall have bloodly ble [faces]
For one I called unkind [unnatural].
The Death of Herod (c. 1450–75), lines 9–21

MULY MAHOMET   Now have I set these Portugals awork,
To hew a way for me unto the crown,
Or with your weapons here to dig your graves,
You dastards of the night and Erebus,
Fiends, fairies, hags that fight in beds of steel,
Range through this army with your iron whips,
Drive forward to this deed this Christian crew,
And let me triumph in the tragedy,
Though it be seal'd and honour'd with my blood,
Both of the Portugal and barbarous Moor.
George Peele, *The Battle of Alcazar* (c. 1589), lines 1227–36

Richard Burbage, by contrast, was praised for making audiences feel that they were seeing, not theatre, but real life (or, in this case, death).

Oft have I seen him leap into the grave,
Suiting the person, which he seem'd to have
Of a sad lover, with so true an eye
That there I would have sworn he meant to die.
Oft have I seen him play this part in jest,
So lively, that spectators, and the rest
Of his sad crew, whilst he but seem'd to bleed,
Amazed, thought even then he died in deed.
Anonymous funeral elegy for Richard Burbage (1619)

The term 'personation', first recorded in the Induction to Marston's *Antonio and Mellida* (written probably 1599–1600), came to stand for this more naturalistic style. And around the same time Hamlet, in his lengthy instructions about good and bad acting, was warning the players visiting Elsinore not to shout out their lines like the town-crier, not 'to saw the air too much with your hand', not to 'out-Herod Herod' (III.2.1–14). 'True', or acceptable, acting, by 1629, was 'naturall unstrayn'd Action'.[47]

[The actor requires] a comely and elegant gesture, a gracious and bewitching kind of action, a natural and familiar motion of the head, the hand, the body, and a moderate and fit countenance suitable to all the rest . . . [He should not] use any impudent or forced motion in any part of the body, nor rough or other violent

> gesture; nor on the contrary . . . stand like a stiff starched man, but . . . qualify everything according to the nature of the person personated.
>   Thomas Heywood, *Apology for Actors* (1612)

'In overacting tricks', according to Thomas Heywood, actors 'may break into the most violent absurdities'.[48] But what is designated overacting is a matter of theatrical fashion. When medieval tyrants and Elizabethan warriors ranted to excess, such excess was presumably, for the many years during which this style lasted, felt to be necessary and appropriate to the acting of certain kinds of roles.

It should not be thought that the emergence of a fashion for greater restraint simply replaced the older, more rhetorical style. Increased realism and interiority developed alongside a continuation of various kinds of formal, patterned and excessive performance. Tragicomedy and masque, for example, both genres that flourished especially towards the latter end of the period under study here, are very far from being realistic in their structures, and actors' performances in masque, as the scripts demonstrate, could never have been remotely naturalistic or understated. Nor was performance style, even in the outdoor amphitheatres, ever dominated by one style to the exclusion of others. Actors and spaces are both more flexible and more subtle than that. Even now, actors responding to the dimensions and spaces of the excavated Rose and the reconstructed Globe have mixed reactions. They notice, sometimes overwhelmingly, the great size of the Globe stage and the boldness it requires of the actor; yet this sense of immensity may be linked to a sense of surprise arising out of the discovery that there is also a potential for intimacy in interacting with an audience in such a space. Ian McKellen, visiting the Rose site in 1989, said, 'Well, I don't need to over-act here.'[49] This is partly, but not wholly, a matter of the Rose's smaller dimensions. Willy Russell has spoken of his experience of acting in the reconstructed Globe as producing 'this strange paradox that you feel almost a sense of shock with all those people around you, but when you go out there you have an intimacy with them which you don't have in other theatres'; and Gaynor MacFarlane, having directed there, notes the difference between the feeling of the theatre from the stage and from the auditorium: 'From the stage it is warmer and more intimate, smaller, even.'[50]

Costumes and props

> *First entereth Wisdom in a rich purple cloth of gold with a mantle of the same ermined within, having about his neck a royal hood furred with ermine, upon his head a cheveler [wig] with brows [artifical eyebrows], a beard of gold of Cyprus*

> *(cloth of gold) curled, a rich imperial crown thereupon set with precious stones and pearls, in his left hand a ball of gold with a cross thereupon and in his right hand a regal sceptre.*
> *Wisdom* (c. 1460–70), opening stage direction

Few early English plays offer full descriptions of costume, but where they do it is evident that costume could be central to both meaning and spectacular effect. The stage direction that opens the play of *Wisdom*, a morality play, shows the importance of costume at the levels of both functionality and display. Wisdom's costume strikes the viewer simultaneously with its richness, its visual appeal and its symbolic meaning, purple, ermine and cloth of gold combining with crown, orb and sceptre to communicate that this figure is a great king. (Statutes and proclamations regulated the apparel that could be worn outside the theatre in early modern England: cloth of gold and purple were routinely forbidden to those below the order of Earl.)[51]

Clothes, in society as well as in theatre, were much more expensive in relation to other costs than they are now. Costumes for plays performed in Cambridge colleges were so valuable that they were stored in chests in the Master's living quarters or kept locked in the college tower with the silver; and John Rastell's suit against Henry Walton for costumes lent to him for safekeeping and not returned shows the value of costumes very clearly. Not only do the depositions list the value of each costume item by item, some costing over 20 shillings (£1) each, but they also reveal how many times the same material might be reworked into different costumes before finally disintegrating.[52] As Suzanne Westfall points out, Rastell's estimate of the total value of his costumes at 20 marks (£13 6s 8d) is equivalent to one year's salary for all four of the King's Players at the time.[53]

Besides representing the company's major expense for display purposes, however, costumes signified within the fiction. Given the prevalence of doubling throughout the period, moreover, continuity of costume was one way in which an audience recognised which character a given actor was playing. Seeing the same actor double in contrasting parts, of course, was another aspect of performance in this period that encouraged audiences to maintain a simultaneous awareness of actor and role and could thus bring an ironic awareness into the viewing. The casting list for Bale's *Three Laws* (c. 1538), for example, printed with the first edition of the play, tells us that Bale played the three parts of Baleus Prolocutor, Infidelity and Christian Faith; the authority-figure, the Vice and a Virtue named as the opposite of this Vice.

Wigs, masks and conspicuously rich or grotesque costumes identify figures like gods, angels and devils (Wisdom above is also God the Father), but costumes otherwise generally resemble the spectators' clothes. A change of costume may signal a temporary condition, such as readiness for bed (a nightcap) or a journey (boots), or a change of state (such as madness or sickness), or disguise. Clothing often needs to be read as a kind of shorthand for statements about the character. Occupation, social class, moral status all could be signalled through clothes. When Everyman enters for the first time in the play of that name, the likelihood that he is wearing conspicuously fashionable clothing is indicated by Death's deduction that 'His mind is on fleshly lusts and his treasure' and by the way Death addresses him: 'Whither art thou going / Thus gaily' (*Everyman* (*c.* 1510–19?), lines 82–6). Osric's hat and the way he uses it in *Hamlet* give us the same impression of shallow gallantry.

If a character's moral status changes, costume can show that too. Thus Mankind's jacket gets shorter as he falls in with the vices in *Mankind*; Mary Magdalene vows to 'inhabit me with humility' (*Mary Magdalene*, line 683) when she repents her life of sin; and Lucre (Money) literally spots the face of Conscience as he succumbs to temptation in *Three Ladies of London* (*c.* 1581). Colours are especially symbolic in religious drama, and may be carefully prescribed, as they are for the four daughters of God under the staging diagram for *The Castle of Perseverance* (1397–1440): 'The four daughters shall be clad in mantles: Mercy in white, Righteousness in red altogether, Truth in sad [sober] green, and Peace all in black.'[54] And costumes for allegorical characters may be even more explicit than that in signalling what the character is, as with Money in *All For Money* (*c.* 1572–7), whose gown is half yellow and half white, the white half '*having the coin of silver and gold painted upon it*'.

Hand-held props served many of the same functions as costume, signalling occupation, status, temporary conditions and so on. A glance back at the props lists cited in chapter 1 (pp. 51–2) shows something of the range that two very different playing groups in different contexts might have (though the reason these lists were cited in chapter 1, with reference to the discussion of performance space, is that so many of those listed are large props, or part of what we would now call the set). Travelling players, especially in the early part of the period, however, would have very few material resources of this kind and would often expect to borrow props at the venue. The players who visit Sir Thomas More in the play of that name have a bridle and a dagger, but have to send one of their number off to Ogle's (a well-known London supplier of theatrical props in the late sixteenth century) for a last-minute beard after More has made his choice from the plays on offer (p. 4 above). *Mankind* illustrates not only the range of standard small props that any travelling company might carry for use in a variety of interludes (purse, whip, spade, rosary, net, plate, fetters, a hangman's noose), but also the symbolic way in which props might operate. Mankind's spade, for example, is a strongly emblematic and didactic object shaping the audience's understanding of the play. He is carrying it when he enters. The implied connection with Adam, the first man, and hence with all mankind, would have been obvious to many fifteenth-century spectators, but Mankind's first line underlines the point, announcing that 'we' (both character and audience) are derived 'Of the earth and of the clay' (line 186). He makes the sign of the cross before taking up his spade to follow worthy labour and (again the point is made very explicit) 'to eschew idleness' (line 330). When the vices seek to disrupt his work he drives them away with his spade, then constructs a pause in the narrative in order to allow the audience to focus on the stage picture and its meaning, which he glosses for the audience with a Latin quotation from the Bible:

> Yet this instrument, sovereigns, is not made to defend.
> David saith: '*Nec in hasta, nec in gladio, salvat Dominus*' [Not by the spear or sword does the lord save).
>
> (lines 397–8)

As if this were not clear enough, Mercy underlines the point further for the audience:

> For with his spade, that was his weapon,
> Newguise, Nowadays, Nought hath all to-beaten.
>
> (lines 422–3)

The emblematic functioning of props continues in a wider variety of contexts, secular as well as religious, in the Tudor and Stuart theatre. The Bible, for example, becomes a crucial emblem of godly Protestantism, while rosaries and Catholic clerical costume signal wickedness in Protestant plays. When Faustus finds Mephistopheles too hideous to look upon as a devil, for example, he asks him to return as 'an old Franciscan friar' because 'That holy shape becomes a devil best' (*Dr Faustus*, sc.3, lines 28–9). *The Spanish Tragedy* shows how props can play an equally forceful and emblematic role in a secular play, and some of them would have been already familiar from earlier, travelling interludes. Andrea's scarf, for example, is handed from person to person in a significant way. We first see it when Horatio comes to Belimperia, Andrea's love, having taken it from the arm of his dead friend on the battlefield. At that point we discover that the scarf was a gift from Belimperia to Andrea on his departure for battle, and she entreats Horatio to 'now wear . . . it both for him and me' (I.4.48). It thus changes in significance from being a token of Belimperia's love for Andrea, to a token of Horatio's love for Andrea, to a foreshadowing of Belimperia's love for Horatio; and that foreshadowing is swiftly confirmed later in the same scene, when Belimperia drops her glove for Horatio to take up.

When Horatio is murdered, the 'handkercher besmeared with blood' (II.6.51) that Hieronimo, his father, takes up as a token of his determination to revenge Horatio's murder is most probably perceived by the audience as the same scarf that Belimperia gave Horatio, since that is the signficant item he would keep on his person. Hieronimo keeps that same scarf on his own person until the last scene, but produces it in between when he encounters another father of a murdered son, offering it to him to 'wipe thine eyes, / Whiles wretched I in thy mishaps may see / The lively portrait of my dying self' (III.xiii.83–5). At the bloody climax of the play, he again holds it up as a material symbol of all he has lost and all he has endured in working out his vow of vengeance (IV.4.122–9). Other props in the play share some of the same heavily invested, recurrent quality. The rope and dagger that Hieronimo carries when he enters in Act III, scene 13, are traditional stage signs of despair and thoughts of suicide; and though Hieronimo casts them aside as he steels himself for revenge, his wife, Isabella, who enters with a dagger a few scenes later, plunges it into herself. When Horatio asks for a knife in the last scene, the fulfilment of this pattern is played out to excess as he stabs himself and the Duke. And the scaffold on which Pedringano is hanged may be the same prop that functioned as the arbour in which Horatio was hanged (see title page, p. 54 above).

Case study: *The Death of Herod*

The Death of Herod is from the N-Town cycle, of which little is known for certain regarding staging and auspices, despite its very full stage directions. Scholars used to think that plays other than the Passion Play within the N-Town cycle were processionally staged, but consensus has now swung towards stationary place-and-scaffold staging. Placed as it is within a cycle of biblical plays, *The Death of Herod* brings together elements of both mystery and morality form. It begins by dramatising a biblical event, the slaughter of the innocents, and ends by showing the allegorical coming of Death to Herod.[55] Characters announce themselves ('I am Death, God's messenger' (line 177) or otherwise perform themselves as essences (see Herod's opening rant, quoted on pp. 96–7 above). Their words and gestures mutually underline each other in ways that invite the audience to pause and focus on iconic stage pictures: 'Upon my spear / A girl I bear' (lines 109–10); 'In seat now am I set as king of mights most' (line 129); 'Now am I set at meat' (line 155); 'see how proudly yon caitiff sit at meat' (line 194). Herod's boasting as he sits at dinner following the massacre of the innocents changes him from the biblical Herod of the Corpus Christi plays to the figure of Pride familiar from morality plays; and it is this transition that triggers the coming of Death: 'I heard a page make praising of pride!' (line 168).

Costumes contrast the two central protagonists, but props suggest an ironic parallel between them. Herod is costumed as a powerful king, while Death's costume is implied by his closing stanza: 'I be naked and poor of array / And worms gnaw me all about' (lines 272–3). But both may have been masked; and the spear with which Death threatens Herod ('With my spear slay him I shall / And so cast down his pride' (lines 205–6)) grimly echoes Herod's own spear, with which he threatens 'poppets [puppets] and pap-hawks [sucklings]' (line 11) with violence, and the spears of Herod's soldiers, whose violence is openly staged as they slaughter children before their crying mothers.[56] Herod kills, commands killing and laughs at death; but Death has the last laugh by killing Herod in swift and sudden silence, in the midst of his own noise and carousing. The stage direction, translated from the Latin, simply reads: '*Here, while the trumpets blow, Death shall kill Herod and the two Soldiers suddenly, and the Devil shall receive them*' (line 232). The devil rejoices loudly, as Herod rejoiced in his slaughter of the innocents, and Death turns to address the audience directly with the explicit moral of the play:

> Of King Herod all men beware,
> That hath rejoiced in pomp and pride;
> For all his boast of bliss full bare,
> He lieth now dead here on his side.
> . . .
> Now is he as poor as I;
> Worms' meat is his body;
> His soul in hell full painfully
> Of devils is all to-torn [torn to pieces].
> (lines 246–57)

The message is clear: 'look ye dread me night and day; / For when Death cometh ye stand in doubt [you never know when death will come]' (lines 274–5). The play is open and unembarrassed about its manipulation of biblical history to teach a moral lesson, recognising its duty to the audience as taking clear priority over any literal-minded faithfulness to history or the Bible.

Case study: *Tamburlaine* Parts One and Two (1587–8)

The Prologue to the first part of Marlowe's *Tamburlaine* self-consciously puts a distance between itself and some of the traditional fare of the popular English stage, the 'jigging veins of rhyming mother-wits, / And such conceits as clownage keeps in pay' (lines 1–2), suggesting a newness and excitement about the 'high astounding terms' of Tamburlaine's rhetoric (lines 1–5). Though the verse-form – blank verse – is different from most of what has gone before, however (blank verse first having been used in English drama in *Gorboduc*, performed at the Inner Temple in 1562), there are notable continuities with medieval drama, and Tamburlaine's proud, defiant, threatening voice has clear echoes of medieval tyrants' set-pieces. The major difference is that, whereas medieval audiences were positioned to despise tyrants, later audiences were expected to admire Tamburlaine, 'the scourge of God' (the phrase, highly ambiguous in the relation it declares between Tamburlaine and God, is used several times over in both plays).

Edward Alleyn made the part famous, but the plays script the use of props, costumes and stage pictures to construct a star role for Tamburlaine, so stellar, in fact, that the popularity of the first play demanded the writing of a sequel, as the prologue to the second part indicates. The extant Rose inventories list three items specifically designed for Tamburlaine, his bridle, his coat with copper lace and his breeches of crimson velvet[57]; and the first scene in which Tamburlaine appears shows him changing his costume in order to look like the great conqueror he aspires to be:

> Lie here, ye weeds that I disdain to wear!
> This complete armour and this curtle-axe
> Are adjuncts more beseeming Tamburlaine.
> (Part One, I.2.41–3)

As in medieval drama, speech underlines and reaffirms stage picture; and in *Tamburlaine* this feature is intensified by Marlowe's habit of having a second character ratchet up the effect with an even more rhetorical word-picture of the same thing:

> TECHELLES As princely lions when they rouse themselves,
> Stretching their paws and threat'ning herds of beasts,
> So in his armour looketh Tamburlaine.
> Methinks I see kings kneeling at his feet,
> And he with frowning brows and fiery looks
> Spurning their crowns from off their captive heads.
> (Part One, I.2.52–7)

The plays are constructed, as medieval allegorical drama is, through a sequence of memorable emblems. The bridle, listed in Henslowe's inventory of 1598, is a reminder of one of the most notorious emblematic moments, when

20. Antony Sher as Tamburlaine, RSC Swan, 1992.

Tamburlaine enters '*drawn in his chariot by Trebizond and Soria* [two con-
quered kings] *with bits in their mouths, reins in his left hand, in his right hand
a whip, with which he scourgeth them*' (Part Two, IV.3.1). The length and detail
of the stage direction show how much attention is paid to constructing the
right effect; and the use of the whip may be interestingly compared with its use

in earlier drama. Noted above (p. 100) as a common prop in medieval plays, its use there is most often for self-scourging, in order to show penitence. In *Tamburlaine*, however, it is an image of triumphant, precisely inhuman refusal to submit to any higher law. At the point of death Tamburlaine passes on his whip and crown to his son and makes him mount the royal chariot by way of constructing an image of immortality in seeing his kingdom at least pass to his son before he dies.

The self-consciousness with which the *Tamburlaine* plays script stage pictures is evident in the way they consciously point to such pictures as shows within shows, making the audience aware of theatricality and preventing them from full immersion in the fiction. Having imprisoned Bajazeth, the defeated Turkish Emperor, in a cage, for example, Tamburlaine dresses himself '*all in scarlet*' (Part One, IV.4.1), taunts Bajazeth to a fury, and then turns to Zenocrate to ask the rhetorical question: 'How now, Zenocrate, doth not the Turk and his wife make a goodly show at a banquet' (IV.4.60–1). The effect is like watching the play stage a courtly masque in which a pageant wagon carrying further performers is brought on for the entertainment of the on-stage spectators. Victory and defeat for Tamburlaine are a matter of who reduces whom to the status of mere spectacle:

> THERIDAMAS It seems they meant to conquer us, my lord,
>   And make us jesting pageants for their trulls.
> TAMBURLAINE And now themselves shall make our pageant,
>   And common soldiers jest with all their trulls.
>
> (Part Two, IV.3.88–91)

It is in the confrontation of death that both the continuity with, and the difference from, medieval morality structure is most evident. Death is personified in language, but not literally staged as a character from early in Part One and recurrently thereafter (see e.g. Part One, II.7.8–11; V.1.111–18; Part Two, II.4.81–4, III.4.11–14). At times the language is such as to suggest that Death really is present as a character on stage, as in *The Death of Herod*. Tamburlaine, threatening the virgins of Damascus, warns them thus, for example:

> For there sits Death, there sits imperious Death,
> Keeping his circuit by the slicing edge.
> But I am pleased you shall not see him there;
> He now is seated on my horsemen's spears,
> And on their points his fleshless body feeds.
>
> (Part One, V.1.111–15)

But in the scene where Tamburlaine himself truly has to confront death, the question of whether Death appears as a performer is an open one. Just as Death entered to Herod at the point where his boast was most offensive to God, so Tamburlaine seems to make the triumph of death inevitable by his very refusal to acknowledge his vulnerability to it:

> Sickness or death can never conquer me.
>
> (Part Two, V.1.221)

> What daring god torments my body thus
> And seeks to conquer mighty Tamburlaine?
> Shall sickness prove me now to be a man,
> That have been termed the terror of the world?
>
> (Part Two, V.3.42–5)

In contrast to the suddennness of Herod's death, Marlowe allows Tamburlaine to fight death through several scenes and long speeches and shows him ordering drums to strike up as though preparing for physical battle against the possibility of death (Part Two, V.3.57–63). As Death either appears or seems to appear on stage in person before Tamburlaine, Marlowe challenges the framework of the earlier drama by depicting Death recoiling and advancing by turns in response to Tamburlaine, as opposed to continuing inexorably towards his goal:

> See where my slave, the ugly monster Death,
> Shaking and quiv'ring, pale and wan for fear,
> Stands aiming at me with his murd'ring dart,
> Who flies away at every glance I give,
> And when I look away comes stealing on. –
> Villain, away, and hie thee to the field!
> I and mine army come to load thy bark
> With souls of thousand mangled carcasses. –
> Look where he goes! But see, he comes again
> Because I stay.
>
> (Part Two, V.3.67–76)

The audience's admiration for Tamburlaine is actively solicited by his long speech of determination to resume battle, a lyrical speech full of longing for the farthest reaches of the world and summed up by the memorable line: 'And shall I die, and this unconquered?' (V.3.151). There is no fixed viewpoint from which to judge him. His discourse is now of God and now of the gods; he rants against Mahomet and claims to adore 'The God that sits in heaven' as 'God alone' (V.1.200–1); yet he repeatedly makes the satanic claim to be invincible and the equal of any god. His final farewell is an unrepentant acceptance of death that reaffirms his ongoing claim to be the scourge of God: 'For Tamburlaine, the scourge of God, must die' (V.3.249). The comparison with the moral message that brings closure to *The Death of Herod* is stark. Where the audience is given clear instructions on how to think and behave in the medieval play, here they are left in a moral maze, understanding Tamburlaine's defiance, unlike Herod's, to be a possible index of heroism. Where the medieval play leaves an audience in no doubt of its didactic intention, the later play operates in an expanding, secular world, in which the responses demanded of the audience seem to position them intermittently inside and outside a moral framework. The certainties which informed the relationship between medieval religious drama and its audiences have given way to a more fluid and uncertain exploration of the individual's place in the world.

Chapter 3

Writers, controllers and the place of theatre

Authors and plays

There is widespread uncertainty about who wrote the earliest plays in this period. Not only do we know the names of very few dramatists, but we know very little about what kind of men they were. We can be sure that almost all of them would have been men, since most women were illiterate or barely literate. (A few women wrote plays in the later part of the period, but these were mainly for closet performance. No plays by women were publicly performed, which is why there is no discussion of female dramatists in this book.) For the same reason, many of the men who wrote plays must have been clerics, since the clergy constituted the social grouping most likely to be literate; and the religious subject matter of most of the extant plays confirms the probability of clerical authorship in many cases (though this is not to say that all religious drama was written by clerics). The anonymity of authors, especially before the coming of printing in the late fifteenth century, however, is not confined to plays and is not merely a function of the absence of print. Authorship was simply not invested with the same degree of importance as it is now, and the craft of the author in the Middle Ages was understood as more derivative than original.[1] 'Authority' came from the Greek and Latin classics; and medieval vernacular authors typically represented themselves as standing on the shoulders of giants, the giants being those ancient predecessors from whom they had borrowed material. Chaucer did a great deal to enhance the status of the vernacular writer, but the idea of authorship was slower to become attached to plays than to other literary works.

Even as printing gradually began to change the visibility and status of plays, they remained a very small section of the book trade, a subliterary genre published in the form of sixpenny pamphlets. Printers' names continued for some time to take precedence over authors' names on title pages, and more care was taken to name the performance venue than the author, indicating that printed plays were thought of at this stage as tied to performance more than to literary notions of authorship.[2] The earliest printed versions of Shakespeare's plays did not carry his name, which is why in later years, once his name had become a selling point, it was possible to claim him as author of all manner of anonymous plays. Eight of his plays were in print before a quarto of *Love's Labour's Lost* bearing his name on the title page was published in 1598.[3]

Yet, as Lukas Erne has recently argued, the 1590s were a key time of transition, during which more plays were gradually coming into the medium of print as well as performance, if only in relatively small numbers. A few plays achieved high popularity both on stage and in print, running to several editions over a few years; and the inclusion of occasional extracts from plays in anthologies of verse 'flowers' (high points of poetry) shows the beginning of a more literary response to dramatic texts.[4] English plays, as David Kastan writes, were in transition from being 'the ephemera of an emerging entertainment industry' to becoming 'the artifacts of high culture'; and those who wrote them were, as Julie Stone Peters has shown, very gradually coming to be perceived as 'authors', a word that 'dignif[ied] the craft of play-making'.[5] Single authorship, however, was not the norm for plays at this time. Payments in Henslowe's *Diary* show not only a majority of plays written by two, three and four authors rather than one, but also payments for revisions by later authors to popular plays, which suggests a very fluid and provisional conception of the dramatic text.[6]

Stephen Orgel, discussing three promptbooks for performances of Shakespeare's *Macbeth*, *Measure for Measure* and *1* and *2 Henry IV* between 1625 and 1635, shows how radically they were cut and revised for performance and notes particularly the 'systematic deletion' of lines that were to become, in subsequent centuries, precisely those known as most famously 'Shakespearean'. For the reviser of the first two, Orgel comments, 'the essential Shakespeare play is action, not poetry'.[7] On the other hand, while the evidence clearly supports Orgel's argument that 'the text of a play was thought of as distinctly, essentially, by nature, unfixed', that is not the whole story. It is also the case that a few authors (and some printers) seem to have conceived of dramatic compositions in two forms, one for the stage and one for the page.

To the gentlemen readers and others that take pleasure in reading histories. Gentlemen, and courteous readers whosoever: I have here published in print for your sakes the two tragical discourses of the Scythian shepherd, Tamburlaine, that became so great a conqueror and so mighty a monarch. My hope is that they will be now no less acceptable unto you to read after your serious affairs and studies than they have been (lately) delightful for many of you to see, when the same were showed in London upon stages. I have (purposely) omitted and left out some fond [foolish] and frivolous gestures [movements, attitudes, expressions], digressing (and in my poor opinion) far unmeet for the matter, which I thought might seem more tedious unto the wise than any way else to be regarded, though (haply) they have been of some vain conceited fondlings [fools] greatly gaped at, what times they were showed upon the stage in their graced deformities. Nevertheless now, to be mixtured in print with such matter of worth, it would prove a great disgrace to so honourable and stately a history.

> Printer's Epistle to the Readers, *Tamburlaine* (printed 1590)

The comical satire of Every Man Out of His Humour. As it was first composed by the author B.J. Containing more than hath been publicly spoken or acted. With the several character of every person.

> Ben Jonson, from title page of *Every Man Out of His Humour*, as printed in 1600

The tragedy of the Duchess of Malfi. As it was presented privately, at the Blackfriars; and publicly at the Globe, by the Kings Majesty's Servants. The perfect and exact copy, with divers things printed, that the length of the play would not bear in the presentment.

> John Webster, from title page of *The Duchess of Malfi*, as printed in 1623

The promptbook cuts discussed above are one response to a fact that we also have to take into account: that many of Shakespeare's plays survive in versions too long for acting. Perhaps he too had a sense of there being both 'readerly' and 'actorly' versions of his texts.[8]

Plays were often produced at high speed, sometimes to capitalise on a piece of current news or to follow up a popular play with a sequel or a competitor. Shakespeare was unusually slow in producing only two plays per year on average (and he was unusual too in writing for only one company for so long and from such an early date). Thomas Heywood, by contrast, claimed to have had 'an entire hand, or at least a main finger' in 220 plays.[9] Dramatists, furthermore, were nakedly writing for the market in a way that aristocrats and gentlemen circulating poetry in manuscript (like Sir Philip Sidney below) were not. Though some were university-educated, most were of middling social status. Shakespeare was the son of a glover, Kyd of a scrivener (a professional scribe) and Marlowe, though educated at Cambridge, of a cobbler. Jonson's stepfather was a bricklayer, and Jonson himself was the butt of jokes because he too was put to that trade for a time.

After selling his play to a company for performance, a dramatist had no ownership or 'copyright' (the term did not exist) in his work. The play became the property of the company, and only they could then decide to sell it on to a publisher. But the author could make good money from selling his work to the companies or theatre entrepreneurs like Henslowe if he was prolific. The standard payment for a new play during the period of Henslowe's *Diary* was £5 or £6, rising to around £10 over the next decade (cf. table p. 59), and the practice of authors' benefit productions (where a day's takings from performance went to the author) was established before the closing of the theatres in 1642. So too, though not until relatively late, was the practice of contracting an author to write an agreed number of plays for a given company in return for a weekly wage. A lawsuit between the dramatist Richard Brome and the owners and players of Salisbury Court gives evidence of both these practices: Brome was contracted to write three plays a year for three years from 1635 in return for 15s a week and a benefit performance for each play.[10]

Contempt for the native tradition can be seen in Sir Philip Sidney's *Apology for Poetry* (printed in 1595, but possibly written as early as 1579 and certainly circulating in manuscript before Sidney's death in 1586). Though he thought the academic *Gorboduc*, performed privately before the Queen by gentlemen training for the law, a worthy, if faulty, attempt to imitate classical precedent, he despised the implausible conventions of the popular theatre.

> But if it be so [i.e. faulty] in *Gorboduc*, how much more in all the rest? where you shall have Asia of the one side, and Afric of the other, and so many other under-kingdoms, that the player, when he cometh in, must ever begin with telling where he is, or else the tale will not be conceived. Now ye shall have three ladies walk to gather flowers and then we must believe the stage to be a garden. By and by we hear news of shipwreck in the same place, and then we are to blame if we accept it not for a rock. Upon the back of that comes out a hideous monster with fire and smoke, and then the miserable beholders are bound to take it for a cave. While in the meantime two armies fly in, represented with four swords and bucklers, and then what hard heart will not receive it for a pitched field?
> Philip Sidney, *Apology for Poetry* (printed 1595)

The status of plays was changing during this period, but as late as 1612 Sir Thomas Bodley, in setting up his new library in Oxford, excluded them from the collection as 'riff-raffs'.[11]

> I can see no good reason to alter my opinion for excluding such books as almanacs, plays, and an infinite number that are daily printed of very unworthy matters and handling . . . Haply some plays may be worthy the keeping, but hardly one in forty . . . the more I think upon it, the more it doth distaste me, that such kind of books should be vouchsafed a room, in so noble a library.
> Letter from Sir Thomas Bodley to Thomas James, 1612

A mere four years later, Jonson was opposing the contempt of men like Sidney and Bodley in his decision to include his plays in a folio edition of his *Works* in 1616. Until this point, plays had only ever been published in quarto, a relatively small and cheap format. A folio volume, on the other hand, was a large-format, prestige form of publication, considerably more expensive than either a quarto book or entrance to a public theatre. In publishing his plays in folio, Jonson was staking a claim for their status as literature and incurred some mockery for it.

> Pray tell me Ben, where doth the mystery lurk,
> What others call a play you call a work.
>> Anon, 'To Mr Ben Jonson demanding the reason why he called his plays works' (printed 1640)

No further plays by any author, however, were published in folio again until 1623, when the first folio edition of Shakespeare's plays was printed, seven years after his death. In the folio collection, as David Kastan notes, 'the theatrical authorizations that mark the quartos are gone; there is no mention that any text is here "as it was played"; indeed the acting companies are never mentioned by name ... The texts themselves are offered ... original and still uncontaminated, the title page promising that the plays are "Truly set forth according to their first ORIGINAL".'[12] The Bodleian Library, so sneering about plays in 1612, had a copy of the First Folio expensively bound in 1624.

As late as 1633, however, Thomas Heywood, an older dramatist who had been writing plays since the 1590s, explained the absence of an edition of his collected works partly on the grounds that he never had much interest in having his plays read.

> True it is, that my plays are not exposed unto the world in volumes, to bear the title of Works, as others. One reason is, that many of them by shifting and change of companies, have been negligently lost; others of them are still retained in the hands of some actors, who think it against their peculiar profit to have them come in print; and a third, that it never was any great ambition in me, to be in this kind voluminously read.
>> Thomas Heywood, 'To the Reader', *The English Traveller* (1633)

To some degree, dramatists had low status because plays and players did. Though some praised the theatre, many more detractors are on record, and the detractors typically write at much greater length than the approvers. William Prynne's *Histriomastix* (third box below), was over a thousand pages long; and even motivated members of the general public could on occasion be provoked to lengthy diatribes against the theatre.

> The daily abuse of stage plays is such an offence to the godly, and so great a hindrance to the gospel, as the papists do exceedingly rejoice at the blemish thereof, and not without cause. For every day in the week the players' bills are set

up in sundry places of the city, some in the name of Her Majesty's men, some the Earl of Leicester's, some the Earl of Oxford's, the Lord Admiral's and divers others: so that when the bells toll to the Lectorer [i.e. for the public reading of the Scriptures] the trumpets sound to the stages whereat the wicked faction of Rome laugheth for joy, while the godly weep for sorrow. Woe is me! The playhouses are pestered when churches are naked: at the one it is not possible to get a place; at the other void seats are plenty.

The profaning of the Sabbath is redressed[13]; but as bad a custom entertained, and yet still our long-suffering God forbeareth to punish. It is a woeful sight to see two hundred proud players get in their silks, where five hundred poor people starve in the streets. But if needs this mischief must be tolerated, whereat (no doubt) the highest frowneth, yet for God's sake (sir), let every stage in London pay a weekly pension to the poor.

> Letter from an anonymous army officer to Sir Francis Walsingham, the Queen's Secretary, 25 January 1587

playing is an ornament to the city, which strangers of all nations repairing hither report of in their countries, beholding them here with some admiration; for what variety of entertainment can there be in any city of Chistendom more than in London?

> Thomas Heywood, *An Apology for Actors* (1612)

most common actors, who are usually the very filth and off-scouring, the very lewdest, basest, worst and most perniciously vicious of the sons of men.

> William Prynne, *Histriomastix* (1632)

Both sides have vested interests, of course. Heywood, as a dramatist and actor himself, has an evident stake in arguing for the virtues of the theatre, while Prynne and the army officer, as hard-line Protestants, or 'Puritans', stand within a long tradition of religious hostility to the theatre. (The term 'Puritan' was first used as a term of abuse in the 1560s; Puritans themselves used the terms 'godly' and 'ungodly', as the army officer does in the first of the three quotations above, to refer to themselves and their opponents.)[14]

The Christian church, however, had shaped negative attitudes towards the theatre from the time of the late Roman empire onwards. Indeed, as Alexandra Johnston has pointed out, 'almost all indications of the existence of plays in England before the last quarter of the fourteenth century are couched in terms of prohibitions'.[15] Some scholars have emphasised that church hostility was primarily towards certain abuses, such as the use of churches and churchyards for secular performance, or the blasphemy or obscenity of particular kinds of performance, or the participation of clerics (who were forbidden by canon law to act in vernacular plays, though their participation in liturgical drama was permitted).

> Steracles [spectacles], plays and dances that are done principally for devotion and honest mirth to teach men to love God the more and for no ribaldry nor meddled [mixed] with no ribaldry nor lesings [lies] are lawful, so that the people be not letted [hindered] thereby from God's service nor from God's word hearing and that there be no error meddled in such steracles and plays against the faith of holy church nor against the statutes of holy church nor against good living. All others are defended [forbidden] both in holiday and work day.
>   *Dives and Pauper* (c. 1405–10), ch. xvii

> Item that the minister and churchwardens shall not suffer any lords of misrule or summer lords or ladies or any disguised persons or others in Christmas or at May games or any minstrels, morris dancers or others at rushbearings or at any other times to come unreverently into any church or chapel or churchyard and there dance or play any unseemly parts with scoffs, jests, wanton gestures or ribald talk, namely [especially] in the time of divine service or of any sermon.
>   Archbishop Grindal's Register, York 1576

But the line between targeted and general hostility is a thin one, and even if 'the church' as a whole was not hostile to theatre per se, it is evident that many within it were hostile to the very roots of theatre. In particular, the fact that theatre is by definition pretence presented a problem to Christian ethics.

> players in the play which is commonly called *miracula* use masks, beneath which the persons of the actors are concealed. Thus do the demons, whose game is to destroy souls and lure them by sin: in which play, masks are used, that is, curious adornments, and dancing is used, in which the feet run to evil.
>   John Bromyard, *Summa Praedicantium* (c. 1325–50) (translated from the Latin)

Thus, even religious drama could not escape the charge of fraudulence. In some ways, as the anonymous *Treatise of Miracles Playing* (1380–1414) argues, imitating sacred things was even worse than imitating the secular world, because it dressed up a lie to look like truth. Religious drama, according to this treatise, is mere signs, play without deeds. The writer is part of an early Reformist movement known as Lollardy, which attacked many of the same aspects of the Catholic church as later Protestantism did, such as relics, pilgrimages and other potentially 'idolatrous' aspects of worship. Playing with God's works, he believes, is disrespectful and blasphemous, functioning as a trap set by the devil to catch men for Antichrist. If Passion plays move audiences to tears, as they did (p. 87 above), those tears are not virtuous tears, shed in recognition of sin, but a merely superficial response to outward shows.

This anxiety about the dangers of illusion continues into the later Puritan discourse of the sixteenth century, when a real avalanche of writing against the theatre gathered particular force from the 1570s onwards, with the establishment of permanent playhouses.[16] The hostility to illusion as a form of deceit issues in three more particular aversions, two especially linked to the growth of the theatre as an industry. The first of these two is the dislike of men dressing up as women, an aspect of theatre made much more prominent by its visibly increasing presence and permanence in London.

> In stage plays for a boy to put on the attire, the gesture, the passions of a woman; for a mean person to take upon him the title of a prince, with counterfeit port and train; is by outward signs to show themselves otherwise than they are, and so within the compass of a lie.
>
> Stephen Gosson, *Plays Confuted in Five Actions* (1582)

This was seen by some as an open transgression of biblical injunctions against cross-dressing.

> The law of God very straitly [strictly] forbids men to put on women's garments. Garments are set down for signs distinctive between sex and sex; to take unto us those garments that are manifest signs of another sex is to falsify, forge and adulterate, contrary to the express rule of the word of God, which forbiddeth it by threatening a curse unto the same.
>
> Stephen Gosson, *Plays Confuted in Five Actions* (1582)

Yet the same critics who attacked the sin of cross-dressing would have been at least equally outraged by the idea of putting women on the stage. Though there are occasional records of women performing in an amateur or individual capacity, the idea of their belonging to professional companies was virtually unthinkable in England.

> Our players are not as the players beyond sea, a sort of squirting bawdy comedians, that have whores and common courtesans to play women's parts, and forbear no immodest speech or unchaste action that may procure laughter; but our scene is more stately furnished than ever it was in the time of Roscius, our representations honourable and full of gallant resolution, not consisting like theirs of pantaloon, a whore, and a zany [figures in *commedia dell'arte*], but of emperors, kings, and princes.
>
> Thomas Nashe, *Pierce Penniless* (1592)

A French company including female actors was hissed off the stage at the Blackfriars in 1629 (though audiences flocked to see them), and William Prynne lost his ears for referring to actresses as 'notorious whores' at a time when Queen Henrietta Maria and her ladies were taking part in court performances (see further below).[17]

The second aversion is to players and theatres as encouraging sin. Actors, according to this line of attack, are idle and dissolute; theatres are places of crime and immorality; and the subject matter of plays excites the passions of spectators, teaching them such evils as wantonness, rebellion, murder, swearing and deceit. In this view, plays should be banished altogether from a Christian commonwealth.

> [Plays] are public enemies to virtue and religion, allurements unto sin, corrupters of good manners, the cause of security [(false) confidence] and carelessness, mere brothel houses of bawdry; and bring both the gospel into slander, the sabbath into contempt, men's souls into danger, and finally the whole commonweal into disorder.
>
> Anthony Munday, *A Second and Third Blast of Retreat from Plays and Theatres* (1580)

The third aversion, finally, and one with which Puritans were to be associated ever after, not always fairly, is to pleasure itself as transgressive.

> Comedies so tickle our senses with a pleasanter vein, that they make us lovers of laughter and pleasure without any mean, both foes to temperance.
>
> Stephen Gosson, *Plays Confuted in Five Actions* (1582)

The sentiment is akin to the distaste more carefully and subtly expressed by Sidney (also strongly Protestant) for the vulgar laughter excited by the popular theatre (see p. 155 below).

The growth of control: church and state

Before the 1530s, though the church routinely attempted to restrict the involvement of the clergy in performance outside the church and to prevent the use of churches and churchyards for inappropriate kinds of performance, there was no state control or censorship of the content of dramatic performance. This changed, however, with the coming of the Reformation and the resultant awareness of the propagandist potential of plays in an age when few could read. The first sign of intervention is evident in the censorship of the Chester cycle in 1532 to erase previous references to the authority of the Pope, and, though some cycle plays continued in performance until 1579 (the date of the last performance at Coventry), this was the beginning of a widespread and lengthy attempt, more actively pursued by some authorities than others, to suppress elements of the Catholic dramatic tradition.

> This day, upon intelligence given to the said commission that it is meant and purposed that in the town of Wakefield shall be played in Whitsun week next or thereabouts a play, commonly called Corpus Christi play, which hath been heretofore used there, wherein they are done [given] to understand that there be many things used which tend to the derogation of the majesty and glory of God, the profanation of the sacraments and the maintenance of superstition and idolatry, the said commissioners decreed a letter to be written and sent to the bailiff, burgesses and other inhabitants of the said town of Wakefield that in the said play no pageant be used or set forth wherein the majesty of God the Father, God the Son, or God the Holy Ghost, or the administration of the sacraments of baptism or of the Lord's supper be counterfeited or represented, or anything played which tend to the maintenance of superstition and idolatry, or which be contrary to the laws of God and of the realm.
>
> Order from Diocesan Court of High Commission in the North to the Wakefield authorities, 27 May 1576

Elizabethan government policy towards the religious cycle drama became increasingly interventionist through the 1570s until virtually all the cycle plays were suppressed by the end of the decade.[18] On the other hand, however, as Paul Whitfield White has recently emphasised, the suppression of religious drama could hardly be said to be a matter of central policy before the Northern Rebellion of 1569 and the excommunication of Elizabeth in 1570, which hardened the state's dealings with the old religion.[19] Prior to that point there was room for attitudes that with hindsight, now that Protestantism and Catholicism have so long been clearly separated, look conflicted and contradictory. White focuses on the example of John Careless, a Protestant weaver and stage-player imprisoned for 'lewd and seditious behaviour' in 1553, but released for one day to play in the Coventry Corpus Christi play. Neither Careless, it seems, nor John Foxe, who told his story, saw any incongruity in combining performance in the old religious drama with a fervent commitment to the new Reformed faith.

From an early date, nevertheless, some Reformers used drama to attack the old religion, and certain kinds of old-style drama were seen as potentially inflammatory. Thomas Cromwell, secretary to Henry VIII, instituted a deliberate oppositional programme of anti-Catholic drama to be toured around England, and the strength of feeling aroused by Bale's *King John* when it was performed at Archbishop Cranmer's residence in 1538–9 (pp. 17–18 above) gives some indication of the kinds of impact this campaign had. Pro-Catholic drama had the same capacity to incite feeling, and the King was predictably eager to quell any sign of sedition before it got out of hand.

> Trusty and well-beloved, we greet you well. And whereas we understand by certain report the late evil and seditious rising in our ancient city of York, at the acting of a religious interlude of St Thomas the Apostle, made in the said city on the 23rd of August now past; and whereas we have been credibly informed that the said rising was owing to the seditious conduct of certain papists who took part in preparing for the said interlude, we will and require you that from henceforward ye do your utmost to prevent and hinder any such commotion in future, and for this ye have my warrant for apprehending and putting in prison any papists who shall, in performing interludes which are founded on any portions of the Old or New Testament, say or make use of any language which may tend to excite those who are beholding to the same to any breach of the peace.
>
> Letter from Henry VIII to the justices of York, c. 1536–7

It is hardly surprising, then, that the first government statute censoring the content of plays in 1543 was a statute dealing primarily with religion.

> **Licence and Censorship: a select chronology**
>
> 1543 Act for the Advancement of True Religion allowed the performance of moral plays rebuking vice and promoting virtue provided that they 'meddle not with interpretations of scripture, contrary to the doctrine set forth, or to be set forth, by the King's Majesty'.
>
> 1545 Proclamation including 'common players' as liable for punishment alongside vagabonds and masterless men.
>
> 1549 Act of Uniformity forbidding interludes, plays etc containing anything 'depraving and despising' the Book of Common Prayer.
>
> 1549 Proclamation warning people not to 'play in the English tongue any kind of interlude, play, dialogue or other matter set forth in form of play in any place public or private within this realm' for a period of three months.
>
> 1551 Proclamation seeking to enforce statutes against players and 'divers other disordered persons' involved in any kind of sedition or lawbreaking and explicitly forbidding any performance of plays and interludes in English without special licence from the King or Privy Council.
>
> 1553 Proclamation ordering 'evil disposed persons' who play interludes or print books 'concerning doctrine in matters now in question and controversy, touching the high points and mysteries of Christian religion' to cease such activities.

1556	General Order against strolling players spreading sedition and heresy throughout the kingdom.
1559	Act of Uniformity reenacted the provision against 'depraving and despising' the Book of Common Prayer.
1559	Proclamation outlining the fundamentals of Elizabethan censorship: prohibiting all plays and interludes not licensed for performance by a town council or two Justices of the Peace and instructing these officers not to permit any play 'wherein either matters of religion or of the governance of the estate of the Commonwealth shall be handled, or treated: being no meet matters to be written or treated upon, but by men of authority, learning and wisdom, nor to be handled before any audience but of grave and discreet persons'.
1572	Act Against Vagabonds (see p. 68)
1574	Royal patent issued to Leicester's Men, permitting them to perform throughout the realm so long as their plays were first seen and allowed by the Master of the Revels.
1581	Full powers of censorship over performance (but not printing) of plays invested in the Master of the Revels, who could now license and suppress plays at his discretion and imprison players or playwrights who disregarded his authority.
1597	Privy Council Order that playhouses be demolished and playing within three miles of London prohibited for three months.
1603	Proclamation forbidding all forms of entertainment on Sundays.
1603	Royal patents making the Lord Chamberlain's Men the King's Men and Worcester's and the Admiral's Men the Queen's and Prince's Men respectively.
1606	Power to license plays for print transferred to Master of the Revels. Act to restrain Abuses of Players, forbidding use of the names of God, Jesus, the Holy Ghost or the Trinity
1642	Parliamentary Ordinance suppressing all public performance (renewed in 1647 and 1649)[20]

The table above covers only the major landmarks in the progress of censorship, but it is clear from those that throughout the period of this study two aspects of the content of plays especially worried the state, the handling of religion and of politics, and two aspects of performance gave most cause for concern, the size and social class of the audience. But large audiences were naturally drawn to hot topics, and both dramatists and spectators became adept at handling controversy in a way that protected the perpetrators from the harshest penalties of censorship legislation. Dramatists and players protected themselves against the charge of meddling in current affairs by blaming audiences for falsely reading in such allusion where none was intended; but audiences knew very well that 'application' was necessary to their understanding of a great deal of the material staged before them and would have nodded knowingly at Jonson's disavowal of such sharp practice.

> Application is now grown a trade with many, and there are those that profess to have a key for the deciphering of every thing, but let wise and noble persons take heed how they be too credulous, or give leave to these invading interpeters, to be over-familiar with their fames [reputations], who cunningly, and often, utter their own virulent malice, under other men's simplest meanings.
> Ben Jonson, Epistle to *Volpone* (1607)[21]

> ARETINUS You are they
> That search into the secrets of the time,
> And, under feign'd names, on the stage, present
> Actions not to be touch'd at; and traduce
> Persons of rank and quality of both sexes,
> And, with satirical and bitter jests,
> Make even senators ridiculous
> To the plebeians.
> PARIS [an actor]. . . .
> . . . they make that a libel, which the poet
> Writ for a comedy.
> Philip Massinger, *The Roman Actor* (1626), I. 3.36–47

Underpinning the growth of censorship legislation was a sense on the part of both those in authority and those subject to it that plays could make a difference. Censorship legislation was often produced in reaction to an offending play. Thus the proclamation of 1549 forbidding all plays for three months was prompted by the Kett rebellion, which began with the assembly of a large crowd at Wymondham, Norfolk, to see a play; and the order for the demolition of London playhouses in 1597 was a response to another lost play also seen as seditious, *The Isle of Dogs*. It landed Jonson, one of its co-authors, in prison, along with two members of Pembroke's Men, the company who performed it. The variation in the responses to such incidents by the monarch or the state, however, can be difficult to explain at this distance in time. When the Earl of Essex, for example, had a play of *Richard II*, probably Shakespeare's, staged on the eve of his rebellion against the Queen in 1601, the players escaped with mere questioning and were performing again at court within the month, on the eve of Essex's execution; and King James, though he occasionally made an example of companies and playwrights who took too many liberties (*Sejanus* (1603), *Eastward Ho* (1605), *The Isle of Gulls* (1606), Chapman's *Biron* plays (1607–8)), was a source of amazement to some of those around him for his level of tolerance towards topical theatre.

> Consider for pity's sake what must be the state and condition of a prince, whom the preachers publicly from the pulpit assail, whom the comedians of the metropolis bring upon the stage, whose wife attends these representations in order to enjoy the laugh against her husband.
>
> Letter from the French Ambassador, 14 June 1604

> the play[er]s do not forbear to represent upon their stage the whole course of this present time, not sparing either King, state, or religion, in so great absurdity, and with such liberty, that any would be afraid to hear them.
>
> Letter from Samuel Calvert to Ralph Winwood, 28 March 1605

While James may have been unusually lax unless someone else was complaining (as the French Ambassador did about the *Biron* plays, for example), he was also part of a long tradition in which theatre offered counsel to monarchs and lords relatively freely and those in power were expected to receive it magnanimously.[22]

> We see sometimes kings are content in plays and masks to be admonished of divers things.
>
> Thomas Scott, *Vox Regis* (1624)

Thus *Hick Scorner* (*c.* 1514) could criticise the Duke of Suffolk's self-interested policy of marrying for money, *Gorboduc* could warn Queen Elizabeth of the dangers of not ensuring the succession and Jacobean and Caroline masques could offer criticism of royal policy, and only very rarely were the repercussions negative.[23] This was partly a matter of not going too far. Charles I, reading through Massinger's *The King and the Subject* (1638), which was dangerously outspoken about taxation without the approval of parliament, responded not by punishing the writer or even vetoing the play, but simply by demanding that it be changed.

> This is too insolent, and to be changed.
>
> Charles I, note on Massinger's *The King and the Subject*, as recorded in Henry Herbert's Office Book, 5 June 1638

His judgement of the play as 'too insolent' implies both an expectation and a tolerance of some level of insolence. But above all repercussion or the absence of it was a matter of time and place. As Elizabeth's 1559 proclamation explicitly acknowledged, drama that might be acceptable before a select audience of 'grave and discreet persons' (as at the Inns of Court, where *Gorboduc* was performed) was not acceptable in the public playhouses, where a different perspective on a controversial topic might lead to riot.

City and state in tension

Where the monarch and the Privy Council were broadly supportive of public theatre, not least because they increasingly wished to invite the companies to perform at court, the city was much more hostile. Fixed playhouses, as we saw in chapter 1, were prudently located outside the city boundary by the entrepreneurs who built them, whilst the city increasingly sought to outlaw any form of public playing inside its boundary. London was governed by three authorities, the Court of Aldermen (headed by the lord mayor), the Court of Common Council and Common Hall. Their hostility to theatre was rooted in a mixture of religious and civic concerns.[24] They were anxious about the potential effects of theatre on orderly city life, about playhouses competing for attention with divine service and sermons, about workers and apprentices leaving their work in the afternoons to attend plays, about the spread of infection where large groups of people were gathered together and, even more than that, about the potential for riot and rebellion in such gatherings. Church and city were often at one in their feeling that London would be a better place if the playhouses were closed down for good.

there is no one thing of late is more like to have renewed this contagion [i.e. plague], than the practice of an idle sort of people, which have been infamous in all good commonweals: I mean these *histriones*, common players, who now daily, but specially on holy days, set up bills, whereunto the youth resorteth excessively and there taketh infection: besides that God's word by their impure mouths is profaned, and turned into scoffs: for remedy whereof in my judgement ye should do very well to be a mean, that a proclamation were set forth to inhibit all plays for one whole year (and if it were forever, it were not amiss) within the city, or three miles compass, upon pains as well to the players, as to the owners of the houses where they play their lewd interludes.

Letter from Edmund Grindal, Bishop of London, to Lord Burghley, 23 February 1564

We have signified to your Honours many times heretofore the great inconvenience which we find to grow by the common exercise of stage plays . . . [N]either in polity nor in religion they are to be suffered in a Christian commonwealth, specially being of that frame and matter as usually they are, containing nothing but profane fables, lascivious matters, cozening [defrauding] devices and scurrilous behaviours, which are so set forth as that they move wholly to imitation and not to the avoiding of those faults and vices which they represent. Among other inconveniences it is not the least that they give opportunity to the refuse [worthless] sort of evil disposed and ungodly people that are within and about this city to assemble themselves and to make their matches for all their lewd and ungodly practices; being as heretofore we have found by the examination of divers apprentices and other servants who have confessed unto us that the said stage plays were the very places of their rendezvous appointed by them to meet with such other as were to join with them in their designs and mutinous attempts, being also the ordinary places for masterless men to come together and to recreate themselves.

Letter from Lord Mayor and Court of Aldermen to Privy Council, 28 July 1597

In 1597, as the censorship table above shows, the Privy Council took action. The order is dated 28 July, the same date as the Mayor's letter, but the Privy Council was motivated, as we have seen, primarily by the disruptive performance of *The Isle of Dogs* at the Swan earlier that month. In practice, moreover, the playhouses were not destroyed and the restraint on playing was relaxed a month early.[25]

The other factor that might motivate the Privy Council to take action against playhouses was their capacity to personalise an attack and thereby give offence in high places. Even when such lampooning was disguised, neither the Privy Council nor the Master of the Revels, as well versed in the art of 'application' as the playhouse audiences, was as alert to nuances of performance as to nuances of text.

We do understand that certain players that use to recite their plays at the Curtain in Moorfields do represent upon the stage in their interludes the persons of some gentlemen of good desert and quality, that are yet alive, under obscure manner, but yet in such sort as all the hearers may take notice both of the matter and the persons that are meant thereby. This being a thing very unfit, offensive and contrary to such direction as have been heretofore taken that no plays should be openly showed but such as were first perused and allowed, and that might minister no occasion of offence or scandal, we do hereby require you that you do forthwith forbid those players, to whomsoever they appertain, that do play at the Curtain in Moorfields, to represent any such play.

Privy Council Order to Middlesex magistrates, 10 May 1601

In the play of *the Ball*, written by Shirley, and acted by the Queen's players, there were divers personated so naturally, both of lords and others of the court, that I took it ill.

Henry Herbert, Office Book, 18 November 1632

Similarly, plays offending other countries at times when the government was seeking to maintain good relations, such as Chapman's *Biron* plays, which gave offence to the French ambassador in 1608, or *A Game at Chess*, which went out of its way to insult the Spanish in 1624, were closed down. Indeed Elizabeth's proclamation of 1559 was itself a response to a complaint from the Spanish Ambassador about plays insulting his country.[26]

Outside stress-points of this kind, the Privy Council more commonly ignored the pleas of the city and insisted on the need to tolerate the players by way of providing recreation for the people (drawing them 'from sundry worser exercises') and, later, rehearsing plays for performance before the monarch.[27] When complaints about plays and playhouses were mounted in response to the proposed building of the Fortune Theatre in 1600, the Privy Council responded by restricting playing to two companies at two playhouses only, while insisting on the need to maintain public performance despite its abuses.

> it is manifestly known and granted that the multitude of the said houses and the misgovernment of them hath been made and is daily occasion of the idle, riotous and dissolute living of great numbers of people that, leaving all such honest and painful course of life as they should follow, do meet and assemble there and of many particular abuses and disorders that do thereupon ensue. And yet nevertheless it is considered that the use and exercise of such plays (not being evil in itself) may with a good order and moderation be suffered in a well governed state and that, her Majesty being pleased at some times to take delight and recreation in the sight and hearing of them, some order is fit to be taken for the allowance and maintenance of such persons as are thought meetest in that kind to yield her Majesty recreation and delight and consequently of the houses that must serve for public playing to keep them in exercise. [The Chamberlain's Men are thus approved to perform at the Globe and the Admiral's Men at the Fortune.]
>
> Privy Council Order, 22 June 1600

The players, confident of the backing of lords more powerful than the city authorities, could afford to be insolent on occasion. William Fleetwood, the Recorder of London (a legal position with criminal and civil jurisdiction over London) wrote to Lord Burghley, the most powerful member of Elizabeth's Privy Council, in 1584 to complain that when he had sent for James Burbage, owner of the Theatre, Burbage had refused to come, saying 'that he was my Lord Hunsdon's man and that he would not come at me'.[28] (A 'supporter of plays and playing throughout his life', the first Lord Hunsdon was Henry Carey, the Queen's cousin and Lord Chamberlain from 1585 until his death in 1596. He was patron to three companies at different times.[29]) Even when the mayor was only a spokesman for the government, the players sometimes disobeyed him. When Lord Burghley ordered the mayor of London in 1589 to put a temporary stop to all plays inside the city, Lord Strange's Men, the mayor reports, 'in very contemptuous manner departing from me, went to the Cross Keys [a city inn] and played that afternoon'.[30] Players evidently expected state authority to overrule city authority for the most part, and to work in their favour; and mostly it did.

The Revels Office

The Revels Office was a court institution which changed status considerably over the period of this study.[31] Before it became a separate office it was part of the Office of the Tents, which was a department of the Chamber, the division of the royal household responsible for organising and servicing the private life of the monarch. Responsibility for servicing the royal household was divided between three areas of activity, presided over by three ceremonial figures, the Lord Steward, the Lord Chamberlain and the Master of the Horse. The Steward and the Chamberlain shared responsibility for the management of ceremony and entertainment at court, which might take place in any of the royal palaces, or in special temporary banqueting halls built for particular occasions (see pp. 34–5 above). Westminster Palace was the principal residence of the monarch up to the fire of 1512. Henry VIII favoured Greenwich Palace for some years between then and the rebuilding of York Place as the Palace of Whitehall in the 1530s. By the time of James I the court had become considerably less peripatetic and more fixed at Whitehall; but throughout the period the Revels Office might be asked to mount performances at any of a range of palaces, mainly in the south east of the country, and the court would also expect to be entertained on progress at the private households of wealthy courtiers.

Masters of the Revels were at first simply minor court officials, or occasionally courtiers, asked to organise the festivities for particular occasions, as, for example, the Earl of Essex organised the entertainment of ambassadors at the court of Henry VIII in February 1510. In this same year, however, the term 'Master of the Revels' is first found in use. Richard Gibson, who kept the accounts of court revels from 1510 to his death in 1534, in this year referred to Henry Wentworth, a gentleman usher of the Privy Chamber, by this title; and Wentworth's ongoing involvement with the organisation of revels between 1508 and 1510 suggests the beginnings of a more formalised, semi-permanent role. Sir Henry Guildford, a personal friend of Henry VIII's, acted regularly in this capacity from 1510 to at least 1527, and Richard Gibson, Yeoman of the Revels under Guildford, served as his assistant over a long period of stability, which was also a very active one in terms of revels. The first permanent appointment to the position of Master of the Revels was Sir Thomas Cawarden in 1545.

At this point, however, the role had little or nothing to do with censorship or control. It was a supervisory role, which in itself calls attention to the highly collaborative nature of revels in the early period. Dramatists in the later professional playhouses working together on new material and working over other dramatists' older materials were drawing on a long-standing tradition of collaborative preparation of entertainment at both a popular and elite level. Indeed one of the reasons why 'authorship' was so much less important then than it is now is that revels were 'devised' (the more common fifteenth- and sixteenth-century term) by a group of people working together to create a spectacle in which spoken text might be just one element or absent altogether. Different skills and ideas came together to produce court revels, but not necessarily in a way that conceived of individuals as singly responsible for writing, design and so on. Richard Gibson, like other early Tudor Yeomen of the Revels, was a master tailor, though his skills and interests clearly went far beyond the preparation of costumes. John Rastell, around the same time, wrote and printed plays, designed a pageant with moving parts for the entry of Charles V, worked on the roofs of the banqueting houses at Calais and Guisnes, ran a costume hire business and had a stage constructed in his garden. The strict division of labour between writer and designer was not sharpened until the quarrel in the 1620s between Ben Jonson and Inigo Jones. As late as 1573 a memo outlined the ideal Master of the Revels as bringing together a wide range of skills.

> the cunning of the office resteth in skill of device [devising], in understanding of histories, in judgment of comedies, tragedies and shows, in sight of perspective and architecture, some smack of geometry and other things.
> Note by Edward Buggins, Yeoman of the Revels, 1573

By this time, as the above quotation shows, the post had changed to become one in which judging other plays was at least as important as devising them from scratch. More and more plays for court performance were being chosen by the Revels Office on a competitive basis, a much cheaper option than planning and producing revels entirely in-house.

> Six plays being chosen out of many and found to be the best that then were to be had, the same also being often perused and necessarily corrected and amended (by the aforesaid officers), then they being so orderly addressed (prepared) were likewise thoroughly apparelled and furnished with sundry kinds and suits of apparel and furniture [equipment], fitted and garnished necessarily and answerable to the matter, person and part to be played; having also apt houses

made of canvas, framed, fashioned and painted accordingly, as best might serve their several purposes. Together with sundry properties incident, fashioned, garnished and bestowed as the parties themselves needed and required.
    Revels Office accounts, 1572

Expensive court masks thus declined in favour of plays as the major form of court entertainment under Elizabeth, not to be revived in a major way until 1604, under the new King James.

The changing remit of the Master of the Revels, and his increasing responsibility for the conduct and licensing of public theatre is evident from the new patent issued to him in 1581. The patent was issued to Edmund Tilney, who became the longest-serving Master of the Revels, holding the post from 1579 to 1610. His powers were extended to control all plays, players and playing places.[32] At first, according to the terms of the patent, players were to perform their plays before him or his deputy (which they did in the Revels Office premises in the former St John's Priory in Clerkenwell), but by 1590 the volume of plays was too great for this practice to continue, and companies were required to submit the scripts for inspection instead.

It is at this point that we begin to have access through written record to the kinds of thing the Master censored. The earliest record of his intervention is in the play of *Sir Thomas More* (1592–3). The play was submitted to Tilney at a time when racial tensions were running high in London. There had been serious riots in the summer of 1592, and the following year the London authorities had to count the total number of foreigners living in London in response to shopkeepers' complaints that foreigners were not content with English goods, but were insisting on setting up their own shops in competition. The next day a warning was found in the Dutch churchyard:

Ye strangers that do inhabit in this land
Note this same writing, do it understand . . .
Since words nor threats nor any other thing
Can make you to avoid this certain ill
We'll cut your throats, in your temples praying.
    Written on the wall of the Dutch churchyard in London, 1593

The point which particularly provokes Tilney's intervention is the play's attempted dramatisation of Evil May Day, a riot against foreigners in London in 1517. He wanted all references to foreigners changed specifically to 'Lombards', presumably in order to maintain the distance between the historical riot and the present-day situation, and ordered that the riot be reported, with the emphasis on More's own good conduct in restraining it, rather than staged, which might prove incendiary in performance.

> Leave out . . . the insurrection wholly with the cause thereof and begin with Sir Th. More at the mayor's sessions with a report afterwards of his good service done being Sheriff of London upon a mutiny against the Lombards only by a short report and not otherwise at your own perils.
>
> Edmund Tilney, marginal note on *Sir Thomas More* (1592–3)

Sir Thomas More is the only censored play manuscript surviving from Tilney's long period of office as Master of the Revels. Extant play manuscripts for the whole period are few (there are only eighteen), but extant play manuscripts showing the censor's hand are even fewer. *The Second Maiden's Tragedy* (1611) and *Sir John Van Olden Barnavelt* (1619) show the intervention of Sir George Buc, and *The Launching of the Mary, or the Seaman's Honest Wife* (1633) of Sir Henry Herbert. Between them they show an overriding concern to deflect any dangerously topical application, as does Herbert's Office Book, the only surviving documentary record of a Master of the Revels' practice. Most revealing of all with regard to such practice, perhaps, is Herbert's treatment of Massinger's *Believe as You List* (1631).

> I did refuse to allow a play of Massinger's because it did contain dangerous matter, as the deposing of Sebastian King of Portugal by Philip the Second and there being a peace sworn 'twixt the Kings of England and Spain.
>
> Henry Herbert, Office Book, 11 January 1631

Having first refused it a licence in order to avoid offence to Spain at a time of peace, he was prepared, five months later, to license an obvious reworking of it which merely translated the location from contemporary Spain to ancient Syria, leaving the application to recent history perfectly evident. 'The only difference', Richard Dutton argues, 'was that a discreet veil of historical distance has been drawn over it, requiring an interested party (such as the Spanish Ambassador) actively to draw parallels with the present rather than letting them speak for themselves. Incontrovertibly, Herbert knew that such parallels *would* be drawn, but he did not see it as part of his duty to police the intentions of authors or the inferences to be drawn by audiences, beyond points of specific provocation.'[33] In time of war or otherwise open enmity, potential offence to the countries in question was much more likely to pass the censor, and Tilney condoned offence to Spain in plays written around and after 1588, the time of the Armada crisis.

Intervention and obstruction: the York Creed Play

Since the relationship between theatre and authority changed so much over the period 1350–1642, I have here selected four moments in that history in order to show the range of practice and response and some of the points of change and continuity over time. In starting with the York Creed Play, I am consciously choosing to discuss a play that no longer survives, because its very non-survival tells us so much about the processes of circulation and control and about the cultural shift from the fifteenth to the sixteenth century.

The Creed Play was bequeathed to the York Guild of Corpus Christi by William Revetour, deputy civic clerk of the city, in a codicil to his will in 1446.[34] This suggests that it was already in performance before this date and that, in entrusting it to the Guild of Corpus Christi, Revetour intended to ensure its continued performance in the city. Religious guilds (as opposed to trade guilds) were fraternities bringing together clergy and laity, dedicated to prayer and good works and founded for a specific aim, as, in the case of the Corpus Christi Guild, to honour the Eucharist. The content implied by the play's title is confirmed by documents of 1449–51 and 1465 describing it as a play 'containing the Articles of the Catholic faith' designed 'for the instruction of the people . . . in very truth so that the Creed may be carried to the ignorant' and listing props and costumes for St Peter, Christ and the apostles.[35] The guild account roll of 1449–51 stipulates performance 'every twelve years or more often if possible by the City of York openly and publicly . . . and to the glory of God and especially for the instruction of the people', and later documents talk about performance every ten years. In September 1483 a special performance was given before King Richard III. Though records are incomplete, the ten-year pattern seems to have been followed from 1495 to 1535, when the last recorded performance was given.

During the next decade the Reformation began to make its mark very strongly in England. The Ten Articles of 1536 expounded the new basis of religious doctrine, and royal injunctions of 1536 and 1538 aimed to put these changes in doctrinal emphasis into practice. The 1536 injunctions sought to eradicate superstitious beliefs regarding pilgrimages, relics and images and required the clergy to expound the Ten Articles and to teach their flocks the Lord's prayer, the creed and the commandments in English. The 1538 injunctions ordered the removal of images from churches and the placing in churches instead of an English Bible. From 1536 onwards the monasteries were dissolved, images in churches were desecrated and the days of religious guilds were clearly numbered. After a brief return to a more conservative policy in the later years of Henry VIII's reign, anti-Catholic legislation became more vehement again under Edward VI. The Act of Dissolution in 1547 disbanded all guilds and confiscated their property. The Creed Play passed to the Hospital of St Thomas, but it is highly unlikely that it was performed during those years. Attempts were made to revive it in 1562 and 1568, but the records show the city taking care to check with the authorities about whether it could be approved for performance. The Dean of York's response on checking the text of the play in 1568 is highly self-aware about the way the climate has changed for religious drama.

> surely mine advice should be that it should not be played; for, though it was plausible 40 years ago, and would now also of the ignorant sort be well liked, yet now, in the happy time of the gospel [i.e. the Reformation], I know the learned will mislike it, and how the state will bear with it I know not.
>
> Letter from Matthew Hutton, Dean of York, to the Mayor of York, 1568

The Dean's distinction between what was possible or 'plausible' forty years ago and what is possible now marks a clear awareness of how thinking has shifted and control has tightened, and his sense of the gap between what 'the ignorant sort' and 'the learned' will like gives us a very strong sense of why the government might wish to censor this kind of play.[36]

Negotiating boundaries: *The Lady of May* (1578–9)

> Her most excellent Majesty walking in Wanstead Garden, as she passed down into the grove, there came suddenly among the train one apparelled like an honest man's wife of the country; where, crying out for justice, and desiring all the lords and gentlemen to speak a good word for her, she was brought to the presence of her Majesty, to whom upon her knees she offered a supplication, and used this speech.
>
> Philip Sidney, opening of *The Lady of May* (1578–9)

When Elizabeth, on progress, visited one of her noble subjects, the entertainment characteristically performed the appearance of spontaneity. Though readers now are accustomed to think of *The Lady of May* as Sir Philip Sidney's first known literary work, for Sidney it was in the first instance an exercise in flattery and courtly politics, devised for his uncle, the Earl of Leicester, on the occasion of Elizabeth's visit to his manor of Wanstead in Essex, probably in 1578. It was first printed untitled in 1599, at the end of Sidney's *Arcadia*; its title is a late and literary imposition on an essentially performative event. As such, it could not be called in for inspection before it took place, as the York Creed play was by the ecclesiastical authorities or as later public-theatre plays were by the Master of the Revels. Like the agate beads that are presented to Elizabeth at the end of this entertainment, the whole performance is in the nature of a gift to the Queen, not a commodity offered for public consumption.

Such gifts were nevertheless part of a courtly and political exchange between the main participants, who are all performing, whether or not they take part in the scripted mask. (Sidney himself may have taken the part of Rombus, the schoolmaster and the Queen is invited to choose between the Lady of May's two suitors at the end.) The Queen's progress, and her walk through the garden and grove at Wanstead are a part of an ongoing performance: no-one understood better than Elizabeth how every public appearance might be nuanced to impress the spectators in particular ways. Her gesture of kissing the Bible at her coronation procession is a classic example of this; but her progresses show this same understanding of how to improvise in order to inflect the performance of monarchy in deliberate ways. Visiting Edward Rookwood, a Catholic who had taken the oath acknowledging the Queen's supremacy over the Pope, at his Suffolk manor in August 1578, she turned the occasion into a piece of religious showmanship when Rookwood refused to kiss her hand.

And to decipher the gentleman to the full, a piece of plate being missed in the Court, and searched for in his hay house, in the hay rick such an image of Our Lady was there found, as for greatness, for gayness and workmanship, I did never see the match; and after a sort of country dances ended, in her Majesty's sight, the idol was set behind the people . . . Her Majesty commanded it to the fire, which in her sight by the country folks was quickly done, to her content, and unspeakable joy of everyone but some one or two who had sucked of the idol's poisoned milk.

Letter from Richard Topcliff to the Earl of Shrewsbury, 30 August 1578

A shrewd performer herself, Elizabeth understood equally well that performances given for her by others were often part of a political agenda, and there is no record of her taking action against any of those involved in private performances of this kind before her.

we went to the Queen's rooms and descended to where all was prepared for the representation of a comedy in English, of which I understood just as much as the Queen told me. The plot was founded on the question of marriage, discussed between Juno and Diana, Juno advocating marriage and Diana chastity. Jupiter gave the verdict in favor of matrimony after many things had passed on both sides in defense of the respective arguments. The Queen turned to me and said, 'This is all against me'.

Spanish Ambassador, describing attending a Gray's Inn entertainment at court, 1565

On the occasions quoted above the explicitness of the records makes it a simple matter to see how performance might enact a political agenda. But in the case of *The Lady of May* there is no such conveniently explicit commentary extant to clarify its meaning, though most scholars have assumed that there is a coded meaning, as indeed the text itself suggests, when the Lady tells the Queen: 'this I will say, that in judging me, you judge more than me in it' (line 281). Interpretations range from seeing it as a plea for Elizabeth to send troops to intervene on behalf of beleaguered Protestants in the Netherlands (Leicester and Sidney were both active in the Protestant cause); as a critique of the French Catholic Duke of Alençon's marriage suit to the Queen; as a proposed 'cure' for recusancy; as a plea for favour towards the Earl of Leicester personally; or as an autobiographical plea on Sidney's part for a more active military role. In deciding what the undeclared political meaning of a given performance might be, however, critics must have recourse to comparison with external events; and if, as has been the case with *The Lady of May*, the date of the entertainment is not completely clear, tying its topical meaning to particular events becomes a very provisional activity. Elizabeth made two progresses to Wanstead, one in May 1578 and one in May 1579, and the arguments that can be made for specific topical agendas necessarily differ depending on which issues seem to critics at this distance to have been uppermost in the minds of all concerned at those different dates.[37] And a further difficulty emerges when the early printed texts are compared with the Helmingham Hall manuscript, which adds a different ending.[38]

In scripting the Queen's choice into its text, the *Lady of May* also takes the risk that the Queen will not choose as Leicester and Sidney hope; and Stephen Orgel has argued that this was indeed the case.[39] The text itself, which is, as its opening makes clear, a report of the performance after the event, coyly withholds any account of the Queen's reasons for her choice:

> *This being said, it pleased her Majesty to judge that Espilus did the better deserve her; but what words, what reasons she used for it, this paper, which carrieth so base names, is not worthy to contain.* (lines 282–4)

At least some of the participants and spectators present at the time will have understood the implications of both the *Lady of May*'s agenda and Elizabeth's response. If its agenda, whatever that was, gave any offence to the Queen, it may have been an occasion for private reprimand; but it is equally likely that the fictional framing of the intervention, slight and blurred though it was, allowed all parties to dismiss it after their debate had been played out in this ludic form.

Intervention and action: *A Game at Chess* (1624)

The most famous case of non-censorship over the whole period is Thomas Middleton's play, *A Game at Chess*, performed at the Globe in the summer of 1624. First licensed by the Master of the Revels, then staged for an unprecedented run of nine consecutive days, excluding Sunday, while the King was out of London, it satirised Spain and especially the former Spanish Ambassador, Count Gondomar. A contemporary letter reporting the content of the play and clearly recognising the chess game as an allegory of present Anglo-Spanish relations, shows how bold the play was in its meddling with matters of state.

> when I returned from your Lordship hither upon Monday, I was saluted with a report of a facetious comedy, already thrice acted with extraordinary applause: a representation of all our Spanish traffic [business], where Gondomar his litter, his open chair for the ease of that fistulated part,[40] Spalato etc. appeared upon the stage. I was invited by the reporter Sir Edward Gorge (whose balance gives all things weight to the advantage) to be also an auditor thereof, and accordingly yesterday to the Globe I rowed, which house I found so thronged, that by scores they came away for want of space, though as yet little past one; nevertheless loath to check the appetite, which came so seldom to me (not having been in a playhouse these ten years) and such a dainty not every day to be found, I marched on, and heard the pasquin [satire], for no other it was which had been the more complete, had the poet been a better statesman. The descant was built upon the popular opinion, that the Jesuits' mark [aim] is to bring all the Christian world under Rome for the spirituality and under Spain for the temporality . . . The whole play is a chess board, England the white house, Spain the black. One of the white pawns, with an under black doublet, signifying a Spanish heart, betrays his party to their advantage, advanceth Gondomar's propositions, works underhand the Prince's coming into Spain . . . Surely these gamesters [i.e. the players] must have a good retreat, else dared they not to charge thus Princes' actions, and ministers', nay their intents. A foul injury to Spain, no great honour to England . . . every particular will bear a large paraphrase, which I submit to your better judgment.
>
> Letter from John Holles to the Earl of Somerset, 11 August 1624[41]

As Jerzy Limon has shown in his book, *Dangerous Matter*, the entire theatre season of 1623–4 offered an unprecedented concentration of plays dealing with political matters, primarily foreign policy. Some scholars since have argued that the play must have had the backing of powerful sponsors for it to be licensed, as it was, by Henry Herbert, the Master of the Revels; but others have pointed to the timing as crucial.[42] Negotiations between England and Spain regarding a marriage between Prince Charles and the Spanish Infanta had continued over several years up to their failure in the autumn of 1623. There was immense public hostility to a Catholic marriage for the Prince, so that when the Prince and the Duke of Buckingham returned to England in October 1623, having failed in their enterprise, there were bonfires in the streets of London. By the time the play was staged, then, it was within the context of a general anti-Spanish mood shared by Charles and Buckingham, and the play was unlikely to present a problem to the English authorities. As one contemporary commented, however, 'had so much been done the last year, they had every man been hanged for it'.[43]

Richard Dutton argues that the only person likely to take offence by the time the play was staged was the one who did: Don Carlos de Coloma, resident Spanish Ambassador in London at the time of the play's performance.[44]

> this comedy has forced me to put my pen to paper and to beg . . . for one of two things. Either let Your Majesty give the order for the aforementioned authors and actors to be punished in a public and exemplary fashion . . . or let Your Majesty order that I be given a ship to sail to Flanders with the appropriate safe passage which you give to the ambassadors of other Kings.
>
> Letter from Don Carlos de Coloma to James I, 7 August 1624

> There were more than 3000 persons there on the day that the audience was smallest. There was such merriment, hubbub and applause that even if I had been many leagues away it would not have been possible for me not to have taken notice of it.
>
> Letter from Don Carlos de Coloma to the Conde-Duque Olivares, 10 August 1624

He duly complained and the King took action against the offenders when he returned to London, but the punishments were light. Performance was immediately stopped and Middleton was arrested, but the closure of the company was brief, and Middleton remained in his post as City Chronologer.

Intervention and reprisal: women performing

Attitudes towards female performance, as we have seen, were markedly more negative in England than elsewhere. The queens of James and Charles, however, coming from different countries and cultures (Anna was Danish and Henrietta Maria French), brought changes to court practice long before such changes worked through to the public theatres. It was Anna, James' Queen, who was more directly responsible for the revival of masque than the King himself, and her appearance with her ladies in blackface in *The Masque of Blackness* clearly crossed the boundary of what the court considered acceptable. One courtier,

Dudley Carleton, writing to a friend after the event, expressed his disgust with such a spectacle, condemned the costumes as 'too light and courtesan-like for such great ones' and was astounded by the willingness of the Spanish Ambassador to kiss the Queen's hand, even though 'there was danger it would have left a mark on his lips'.[45] But queens were above any authority to censor, and the French Ambassador, as we have seen, marvelled at the King's tolerance of a wife who attended performances in order to enjoy seeing her husband mocked (p. 122 above). It is therefore not surprising to find significant shifts in theatre practice often originating at an elite social level.

If Queen Anna used masques to express occasional opposition towards James and his policies, however, Henrietta Maria fostered interest-groups opposi-tional to Charles in a much more consistent way. According to one contem-porary, writing in 1630, the court 'was never so full of factions and enmities and emulations as it is now'.[46] Though Henrietta Maria was herself a Catholic, practising a moderate form of Catholicism known as Devout Humanism, her ties in England were nevertheless, as were those of her native France, coinciden-tally Protestant by virtue of being hostile to Spain. 'To be on the side of France against Spain', Erica Veevers summarises, 'meant to be vaguely on the side of Protestant Parliamentarians.'[47] Henrietta Maria was a great lover of theatre and had been brought up taking part in court theatre in France. From her arrival in England, she was actively involved in the performance as well as the sponsor-ship of court drama. At the same time, however, in the public theatre, women were excluded from English companies and French actresses were hissed off the stage. As always throughout the period, there was one rule for those under the law and another for those above it. Henrietta Maria and her ladies not only took speaking parts on stage within the first year of Charles's reign, a thing unprecedented in England, but played male roles. Even the fact that the perfor-mance was given before a carefully selected audience did not insulate it from shocked reactions, and several contemporaries commented disapprovingly on seeing women wearing beards and male apparel and hearing the Queen herself speak on stage.[48]

William Prynne, as noted above (p. 117), made reference to actresses as 'notorious whores' at precisely the moment of the Queen's performance in Walter Montagu's pastoral, *The Shepherds' Paradise*, in January 1633. Time, place and social class came together coincidentally in such a way as to result in the draconian punishment of Prynne.[49] Yet while Prynne lay imprisoned in the Tower awaiting trial, a play probably also written some years earlier now acquired new pointedness. James Shirley's *The Bird in a Cage* may have been written in 1629–30, but it was printed early in 1633, and the title page states that it was performed at the Phoenix in Drury Lane (also known as the

Cockpit), where Henrietta Maria's Men played. The play presents a Princess and her ladies agreeing to perform a play and specifically highlights the issue of their sex. Donella, the most forceful of the group, encourages the others to have confidence in their own abilities: 'Do not distrust your own performance, I ha' known men ha' been insufficient, but women can play their parts' (III.iii; p. 42, lines 1–3), and there are jokes about women wearing beards and playing the parts of kings and gods. The printed edition carries a sarcastic dedication to William Prynne, in his 'happy retirement' (i.e. imprisonment), in which Shirley delights in warning him how far the printed text must fall short of the pleasures of performance: 'for it comprehending also another play or interlude, personated by ladies, I must refer to your imagination, the music, the songs, the dancing, and other varieties, which I know would have pleased you infinitely in the presentment' (lines 9, 18–22). Prynne was sentenced in February 1634, condemned to lose his ears, pay a fine of £5000 and remain in perpetual imprisonment. Four years later, re-examined by the court, his ears were found to be have been incompletely cropped and were cut again.

Ironically, *The Bird in a Cage*, though it mocked Prynne, deprived of his liberty, was itself centrally concerned with questions of individual freedom at a time when the increasing absolutism of a monarch determined to rule without parliament was making itself felt. The play's main plot opens with a duke depriving his daughter of her liberty so that she cannot marry without his consent. The scene plays up the Princess's sense of outrage at being 'cag'd up' (I.i; p. 7, line 6), and the plot turns to the Duke challenging Rolliardo (who is in fact the Princess's beloved Philenzo in disguise) to gain access to the imprisoned Princess. Again, much is made of Rolliardo's unrestricted movement ('it seems he makes himself free of all places'; I.i; p. 11, line 32), and images of freedom and imprisonment dominate both the language and the action. Bonamico regains the Duke's favour by making him a gift of a huge cage filled with various birds (used to introduce allusions to various contemporary political figures and events); the Princess and her ladies take the story of Jupiter and Danae (a princess confined in a seemingly inaccessible tower) as the subject of their interlude; and Rolliardo finally manages to penetrate the Princess's captivity by having himself conveyed in Bonamico's birdcage. Rolliardo steps into the Princess's view at the moment she opens the cage and declares himself 'the truest prisoner' (IV.ii; p. 57, line 34). The comic ending resolves itself into freedom for both Philenzo/Rolliardo and the Princess. If Prynne, in prison, ever saw a text of the play so pointedly dedicated to him, he might have reflected with some bitterness on the relative freedom of princesses, whose loss of liberty in stories is always a prelude to a happy ending, and who, in real life, are so much more free to break the rules than their social inferiors.

Powerful theatre?

All the examples above, taken from different times and places, should function as a reminder that government control and censorship of both the stage
and printed books was above all a matter of time and place. Dean Matthew
Hutton explicitly voices the importance of historical moment and social class in
determining what he can allow; *The Lady of May*, seeking to spring its delicately
veiled politics on the Queen as she passes, runs the risk of being simply brushed
aside rather than taken seriously enough to produce a strong reaction of any
kind; *A Game at Chess* passes the censor because it appears at just the right
moment; and the unfortunate timing of Prynne's publication to coincide with
the Queen's own performance determines the extremity of his punishment. It
must be remembered, too, that Prynne's text was not a play but a prose treatise,
a form taken more seriously by the authorities than drama.

   Alongside the handful of plays that got into trouble with the authorities, is the
much larger group that successfully encoded their political content within limits
acceptable to the authorities, while at the same time consciously directing their
audiences to consider political questions. Some critics, notably Paul Yachnin,
have argued that the reason theatre was allowed to get away with so much
was that it was seen by those in authority as powerless. The companies, he
argues, 'won from the government precisely what the government was most
willing to give – a privileged, profitable, and powerless marginality'.[50] But
while this would explain the leniency of some situations (the light response
to *Richard II*, for example), it scarcely explains either those situations where
the punitive response was harsh (the closing down of the Blackfriars Children,
for example) or the continuing growth of legislation aimed at controlling the
theatre. It is certainly the case that successive governments sought to forbid
the theatre to handle matters of politics or religion while at the same time
allowing it in practice to do so with some frequency; and it is also true that this
contradictory behaviour creates the space for later critics to read early theatre
as either powerful or powerless.[51]

   What the contradiction surely represents, however, as suggested above, is
the differences of time and place. Theatre was capable of moving audiences
powerfully, to riot or rebellion; but this does not mean that it routinely or
frequently did so. Governments took action to repress or control theatre in the
wake of popular insurrections or complaints from foreign powers. Yet despite
increasingly rigorous legislation and licensing systems, theatre remained an
arena in which the protective armour of fiction and analogy could create a
space for the voicing of contentious issues; and, because theatre, at least in
London, was so widely accessible even to the illiterate, it was perhaps the form

that spoke to the largest constituency of the king's subjects. 'Application', as Jonson's Epistle to *Volpone* shows, functioned as a key for audiences and a cover for dramatists, who could hope to escape punishment by arguing that their intentions had been misconstrued. In Prynne's case, that defence was rejected. His prosecutors, reporting the view expressed by some that 'he had no ill intention, no ill heart, but he may be ill interpreted', went on to argue that '[t]hat must not bee allowed him in excuse, for he should not have written anything that would bear construction' ('construction' meaning the same as 'application', discussed above).[52] For writers of plays, such harshness of judgement was a less likely outcome, since what they had written was not, and could not be, identical with what was performed, not only because the text might vary from the licensed script, but because performance makes its own meanings in excess of text. In the case of the 1601 performance of *Richard II*, for example, the actors were questioned, but Shakespeare did not come under suspicion, the play having been written several years before and only now becoming topical through 'application' on the part of the conspirators, some spectators and the authorities.[53] Eastern European countries under communist regimes in the twentieth century were equally well versed in using performances of Shakespeare to point up political allusions of relevance to audiences separated from the writing of the plays by several centuries and geopolitical frontiers.

In representing controversial matters as readable from different perspectives, the theatre gave audiences ways of thinking about things that might conflict with the conformity that kings and queens attempted to enforce by burning books, instructing preachers what to preach, forbidding discussion of particular topics and punishing those who infringed these edicts. It is worth remembering that, although the theatres did not in fact close until 1642, there were moves from various quarters throughout the period to close them down. Such moves suggest an ongoing fear of theatre as powerful at least some of the time and in some places. The huge gap between between court performance and popular performance in terms of what could be allowed to develop must underline the sense that city and state authorities feared the power of theatre over popular, mass audiences. Yachnin, focusing on the explicitness of scripts, argues that 'the polemical theater of the early and middle Tudor period gave way to the recreational theater of Elizabeth's reign', suggesting that theatre lost rather than gained in power over time.[54] But the moves outlined in chapters 1 and 2, from ad hoc playing places to permanent playhouses and from small touring companies to large, established groups with shares in theatre as a business enterprise, represented a move from small-scale to large-scale, from relative amateurism to professionalism, from scattered audiences in random places across the country to daily performance across a range of venues in the capital to an estimated audience of 25,000 a week around 1620.[55] Even if its content were indeed less bold, as Yachnin believes, it was arguably becoming more rather than less powerful by virtue of the sheer numbers it now reached and its potential for arousing a more mass response. The huge growth in the presence and popularity of theatre between 1350 and 1642 meant that such ripples as it did produce had the potential to become real waves too dangerous to be ignored.

Chapter 4

Genre and tradition

Terminology and boundaries

Chapter 1 began with some discussion of the terms 'theatre', 'performance', 'ritual' and 'drama', arguing that some of the divisions now so familiar in our thinking are inapplicable to early performance. This chapter takes up that argument more fully, beginning with those same general terms and moving into discussion of narrower, more specific terms, such as 'comedy' and 'tragedy', 'morality play' and 'history play'. But the discussion must be framed by an understanding particular to, and evolving over, this early period of theatre, that even seemingly specific terms were much broader and looser then than we might like them to be. Paradoxically, given that this chapter takes genre as its focus, in order to understand the distinctiveness of early performance we must often be willing to suspend or qualify the impulse to pigeonhole types of performance according to theoretical conceptions of genre. Though we may look for clarity and fixity, what we find, often, is overlap and blurring of boundaries.

This is not just a matter of terminology, but of performance itself. But, if we begin with the terminology, it will soon be evident how the problem develops. The word 'performance' was not in use in this theatrical or quasi-theatrical sense until the eighteenth century, though occasional earlier usage, where the word really means 'completed action', may seem to point the way towards later use, especially when used thus in the theatre: 'eche out [eke out] our performance with your mind', asks the Chorus in *Henry V* (1598–9; Act III, Chorus 35). 'Theatre' was a term consciously borrowed from the classical lexicon, and not in use to refer to the art of performance until the seventeenth century. When James Burbage named his playhouse the Theatre he was deliberately recalling the classical past, though his polygonal, almost circular playhouse in fact recalled the shape of an amphitheatre (literally, 'double theatre') rather than that of a theatre, which was semicircular.[1] This is why the term 'amphitheatre' has come into widespread currency among modern critics as a term for the outdoor playhouses of the early modern period. The term 'theatre', moreover, when first taken into wider use, referred only to the building, not to what took place inside it, though 'playhouse' remained the word in common use for the building throughout the later period of this study. Before the building of Burbage's Theatre, and of playhouses generally, the word was so unfamiliar that the Wyclifite translation of the Bible, in the late fourteenth century, had to explain it as 'common beholding place'.

Even the term 'play' was far less clear-cut than it is now, and this was partly a matter of terminology and partly a matter of practice. The English word 'play' (and Latin '*ludus*', which it translated) could mean any kind of game, festivity or performance, so that it is often impossible in reading records of this period to distinguish between dramatic and non-dramatic events. An ongoing argument between scholars now about the degree to which the saint play, for example, was rare or widespread in medieval England hinges on the double question of how many of the records linking saints' names to some kind of playful or festive event are instances of plays, and what the definition of a 'play' is.[2] 'Drama' and 'dramatic' were terms very rarely used before the seventeenth century.

A further difficulty, given that theatre was so closely tied to special occasions before the building of permanent playhouses, is that 'revels' (a word in very common use) tended to run together different kinds of performance into one long continuous entertainment. If we look back to Hall's account of the entertainment for the French Ambassadors at Greenwich Palace in May, 1527 (quoted on p. 37 above), we can see an example of this in practice. Prior to the extract quoted, the court and the Ambassadors have attended a spectacular banquet, full of rich and strange dishes, devised in the shapes of birds and animals. The first spectacle that nowadays we might call a 'performance', but would be less likely to call 'theatre', and even less likely to call 'drama', is the processional entry of the King and Queen and their guests, not described by Hall, but undoubtedly a visually striking event, especially given the construction of a stunning new double banqueting house for this very occasion. The next part of the event is described by Hall as 'a solemn oration', and, though the speaker is costumed, again we might not now be likely to choose terms like 'theatre', 'drama' or 'play' for this kind of performance. In fact Gasparo Spinelli, the Venetian Secretary in London, identifies him as Mercury; and this element of fictional representation brings the performance closer to our modern sense of what might constitute a play. (Indeed one of the criteria regularly used by critics seeking to differentiate 'liturgical drama' from the liturgy itself (the words of the church service) is an emphasis on the 'as if', the element of impersonation or representation in the action.)[3] The entrance of the chapel singing after Mercury's speech might be thought of as primarily a musical recital, except that the chapel enters in two symmetrical groups, each led by a richly dressed speaker, thus calling attention to visual and spatial display.

The debate between the two speakers as to 'whether riches were better than love' is the closest thing to what we might begin to call a 'play' (and indeed is sometimes referred to as the 'play' of *Love and Riches*, probably by John Rastell). It is not fictional, and neither of the speakers is apparently representing any thing or person other than themselves (though, as we have seen, reports of an earlier speaker differ on this question), but it is scripted and costumed, and not very different from the dialogues John Heywood writes for the Tudor court, usually now categorised as plays or 'interludes' (another word to return to, but essentially a subcategory of 'play'). The two speakers being unable to agree, the dialogue gives way to a mock-tournament, which is essentially inside the framework of the 'play', since an old man comes in after the combatants have departed to pronounce a conclusion 'that love and riches both be necessary for princes'.

The conclusion of the play, however, does not conclude the revel as a whole, which moves almost seamlessly into the next phase as a curtain is lowered at the screen end of the hall to reveal a pageant stage representing a fortress on a rock, with lords seated upon it who descend to dance with ladies in the hall. The entertainment continues beyond the length of the extract quoted, and, following this stretch of dancing, the Princess Mary and her ladies issue forth from a cave and dance with the lords of the mount. The appearance of the Princess is a reminder of the political functionality of revels and the particular occasion to which these revels are tied: the French embassy's visit to negotiate a peace treaty between England and France and a marriage between Henry's daughter, Mary, and either Francis I or his second son, the Duke of Orleans. Showcasing the Princess, aged eleven at this time, as a suitable bride is part of the aim of this mask. Spinelli, characteristically alert to this function, says she was considered beautiful by the Viscount of Turenne, but too small and thin to be married within the next three years.[4]

Six maskers enter suddenly after the eight lords and ladies have danced and again dance with ladies; and following this the King and the Viscount of Turenne are whisked out of the hall to change costume, then re-enter with six others in Venetian-style masking apparel, their faces masked with beards of gold. They then dance for a long time with ladies in the hall, until the Queen and her ladies pluck off all the masks, revealing the maskers' identities. At last all return to the banqueting chamber for another 'banquet' (in the sense of 'dessert'); and only after that do they retire to bed, 'for the night was spent, and the day even at the breaking'.[5] The final spectacle is that of the double banqueting hall itself, which is left standing for three or four days, so that all may come and see its richness and ingenuity.

Picking out the dramatic from the non-dramatic events in this day of revels, then, or the play from what is not the play, is no straightforward matter, and very much an anachronistic concern of our own time. Hall nowhere uses the word 'play', but does distinguish an 'oration' and a 'dialogue' from the surrounding spectacle, and might well, in other descriptions, have called upon the words 'mask' (or 'meskelyn' or 'meskeler'), 'mumming' (or 'mummery'), 'disguising', 'pageant' or 'revel' to outline events. All of these words are used loosely and often interchangeably. Even where they seem to represent something specific, as 'mask' does when Hall first introduces it in describing the Twelfth Night revel of 1512 as something new 'after the manner of Italy, called a mask, a thing not seen afore in England', that specificity is elsewhere undermined by descriptions that conflate or parallel different terms, or by others using different terms for the same thing.[6] Fifty years later, by which time the definition of a 'play' from the surrounding events was clearer, it was still the case nevertheless that court entertainments, such as progresses, mingled one kind of spectacle with another very freely, weaving plays into a much wider and richer tapestry of events.[7]

Kinds of medieval theatre

Many kinds of medieval theatre go by more specific names, but it is important to be aware, first, that many of these were applied later than the practices themselves and, second, that the seeming specificity of the terms usually masks a degree of overlap between them. One of the most widespread distinctions now in use to categorise medieval drama, for example, is the distinction between 'cycle' and 'non-cycle' drama. But neither of these terms was in use during the medieval period, not is the distinction as fixed as it might seem to be. The N-town cycle, for example, was compiled in cycle form by a scribe bringing together three separate groups of plays, and, more recently, the Towneley cycle has been argued to be not a cycle at all, but a mid-sixteenth-century compilation; while elsewhere, plays that look like fragments from cycle plays survive separately and individually, as in the Brome play of *Abraham and Isaac*.[8] Someone writing on the first page of the N-town manuscript in the sixteenth century, called it 'the play called Corpus Christi', a designation relating to its association with the church festival of Corpus Christi (p. 31 above); but the cycle plays were not always and everywhere performed at this time (in Chester, for example, they were moved to Whitsun), so the label 'Corpus Christi play' is also imperfect. We should note too the medieval tendency to refer to the whole cycle as a 'play' in the singular, with the term 'pageant' most often used to designate the individual playlets.

Even less satisfactory than 'Corpus Christi play', however, are the terms 'mystery' and 'miracle' play. 'Mystery (play)', a term not used until the eighteenth century, has sometimes (erroneously, according to the *OED*) been supposed to derive from Latin '*mi[ni]sterium*' (trade, occupation; cf French *métier*), thus seeming to highlight the plays' links with the craft guilds. Not all the cycles had such links, however; indeed, N-town and the Cornish cycle almost certainly did not. 'Miracle', a term in common use in both Latin (*miraculum*) and the vernacular from early on, is even more confusing because its terms of reference are both so wide and so ambiguous. Sometimes it seems most likely to mean a play containing a miracle or miracles, as when a twelfth-century writer describes a play on the life of St Katherine performed at Dunstable *c.* 1100–19 as one of the kind 'which in common speech we call *miracula*'. William Fitzstephen, writing in the later twelfth century, without quite using the term as a name for a dramatic genre, describes the plays performed at London's Skinners Well as showing 'the miracles wrought by Holy Confessors or the sufferings which glorified the constancy of Martyrs'.[9] John Bromyard and the *Treatise of Miracles Playing*, as quoted in Chapter 3 above, do use the term to refer to a kind of drama, but it is not clear how narrowly specific that is.[10]

Critics often group much of the non-cycle drama under the heading of 'morality play', another term first coined in the eighteenth century. Early writers occasionally referred to 'morals' or 'moral plays' but not in a way consistent enough to give these terms very clear currency.[11] Indeed, the printer of *Everyman* (*c.* 1510–19?), a play now usually considered a classic 'morality play', defines the piece in a puzzling way, choosing the word 'treatise' as primary and merely likening the text to a 'moral play'.

> Here beginneth a treatise how the high Father of Heaven sendeth Death to summon every creature to come and give account of their lives in this world, and is in manner of a moral play.
> *Everyman* (c. 1510–19?)

Much more widely and broadly used are the terms 'interlude' (in use from at least *c.* 1300) and 'stage play' (from the early sixteenth century), both frequently combined in official documents and other general contexts seeking to be fairly inclusive about forms of theatre (see the table of Licence and Censorship in chapter 3 above).[12] The King's Players are described in 1494 as the 'players of the King's interludes', and Sir Thomas Elyot uses the terms inclusively in his dictionary of 1538 in glossing '*ludii* and *ludiones*' as 'players in interludes or stage plays'. Uses like this, however, which seem to render 'interlude' and 'stage play' synonymous, are undercut by instances that imply a clear distinction between them, as when one of the King's Players, called as a witness in a lawsuit regarding some costumes owned by John Rastell, talks about the costumes being hired out for 'stage plays in the summer and interludes in the winter', adding that the charge for costume hire was 8d for an interlude and up to 40d for a stage-play (p. 41 above). Different interpretations of this distinction have been suggested, including the possibility that interludes were indoor and stage-plays outdoor performances or that admission was charged for stage-plays and not for interludes. There is nothing to rule out either reading, nor are the two suggestions mutually incompatible.[13]

Early terminology, then, is too loose or ambiguous to allow clear-cut generic categories to emerge, and later terminology imposes an anachronistic generic rigidity. Plays such as *The Death of Herod*, discussed in chapter 2 above, collapse the boundary between cycle and non-cycle drama and between biblical history and moral allegory, while the numerous plays described on their earliest printed title pages as 'interludes' vary from the religious-moral-allegorical (*Nature* (*c.* 1490–1500), *Mundus et Infans* (*c.* 1507–8) and *Youth* (*c.* 1513), for example), to the more secular and political (*Fulgens and Lucres* (*c.* 1496–7), *Gentleness and Nobility* (*c.* 1519–28), *The Play of the Weather* (*c.* 1519–28)), while still others combine religious with topical or political messages (*Hick Scorner* (*c.* 1514), *Magnificence* (*c.* 1519–20), *Godly Queen Hester* (1529–30)).

Early Tudor theatre

Given that generic terminology is so slippery, it might seem that a clearer way to categorise performance is via the place or auspices of performance, where known, but this is not straightforward either. First, it is often the case that where a text survives, records of its place and auspices do not, or vice versa; and secondly, even where there are clear records of both, as in the case of *Fulgens and Lucres*, we do not know that the play was only ever performed in this one location. Indeed, touring, as discussed in chapter 2 above, was the norm for most kinds of performance up to the end of the sixteenth century. A few particular kinds of court performance, such as expensive masks and disguisings, could only ever have been funded by and for an elite, but interludes written by men like John Heywood and John Rastell may have been performed both at court and much more widely. Some of the prefatory matter in early printed plays registers a clear expectation that different auspices will dictate a different way of performing the same play.

A New Interlude and a Merry, of the Nature of the Four Elements, declaring many proper points of philosophy natural, and of divers strange lands, and of divers strange effects and causes; which interlude, if the whole matter be played, will contain the space of an hour and a half; but if ye list ye may leave out much of the sad [serious] matter, as the messenger's part and some of Nature's part and some of Experience's part, and yet the matter will depend [hang together] conveniently, and then it will not be past three quarters of an hour of length.

John Rastell, *The Nature of the Four Elements* (1517–20), prefatory matter

Thus the familiar distinction between popular and elite performance is not really tenable either, since we know so little in most instances about how widely performances circulated either geographically or socially. There is some truth in Greg Walker's argument that 'by the very fact of their written form, all the dramatic texts which we now possess are "elite" creations', in so far as writing and to some extent printing were the activities of an educated few; but the written creations of an elite could easily have become accessible to a wider and less literate audience through performance.[14] Even audiences in elite venues included servants and other working people. Hall's Chronicle gives us several insights into the way 'the rude people' behaved at such events, tearing and spoiling the pageant wagons, even stripping the costumes of the King and courtiers, in pursuit of expensive souvenirs that could then be sold on.[15]

Despite this flexibility across elite and popular theatre, however, the distinction can still be useful to a degree in contributing to the analysis of different threads in the fabric of theatrical tradition. It is clear, for example, that performances of Greek and Latin plays and of vernacular plays modelled upon them, addressed themselves in the first instance to a social elite, even though other spectators might also be present; and the humanist classical revival is one of the developments marking a distinction between medieval and early Tudor theatre. 'Humanism' is the term used to describe the rediscovery and close study of ancient Greek and Roman texts in fifteenth- and sixteenth-century Europe. More broadly it also designates the intellectual and cultural focus on those areas of thought still sometimes referred to as the 'humanities' (grammar, rhetoric, poetry, philosophy and history), arising out of a close engagement with ancient texts.[16] Italian classical scholars were encouraged to come to England under Henry VII, following the lead of earlier English humanists such as Duke Humphrey of Gloucester and John Tiptoft, Earl of Worcester, who employed Italians as their Latin secretaries (Latin being the language of international scholarship and diplomacy throughout Europe at this time). Henry VIII's court maintained equally active European links, cultivating Italian and French fashions in revels, entertainment and the arts. The fashion for performing classical plays began at the court of Ferrara with a performance of Plautus' *Menaechmi* in 1486, and the first known performance of a classical play at the English court was the performance of a 'goodly comedy of Plautus', the name of which is unrecorded, in the Great Chamber at Greenwich in March 1519.[17] Performances of classical plays at the universities predated this, beginning at King's Hall, Cambridge in 1510–11, but their performance at court signalled their arrival into more mainstream culture.[18] As with the revelling of May 1527, outlined above, this 1519 performance was part of a continuous stream of entertainment, with masks and dancing followed the classical play. (In this respect, too, the English court was following Italian practice, which mixed performances of classical plays into a surrounding medley of *intermezzi*, dialogues and dances.)[19] Cardinal Wolsey, who was especially interested in Italian and classical fashion, may have been involved in this production, about which very little is known, and was certainly responsible for performances of *Menaechmi* by his own Chapel Gentlemen in January 1527 and Terence's *Phormio* by the Children of St Paul's in January 1528.[20] The performance of *Menaechmi* was followed by an Italianate chariot entry that impressed even Gasparo Spinelli.

a stage was displayed, on which sat Venus, at whose feet were six damsels, forming so graceful a group for her footstool, that it looked as if she and they had really come down from heaven. And whilst everybody was intently gazing on so agreeable a sight, the trumpets flourished and a car appeared, drawn by three boys stark naked, on which was Cupid, dragging after him, bound by a silver rope, six old men, clad in the pastoral fashion, but the material was cloth of silver and white satin. Cupid presented them to his mother, delivering a most elegant Latin oration in their praise.

Letter from Gasparo Spinelli to his brother, Lodovico, 4 January 1527[21]

It may be noticed that all these early productions of classical plays are of comedies, and it is also the case that the earliest English plays imitating classical form are comedies: *Thersites* (1537), *Ralph Roister Doister* (c. 1547–8), *Gammer Gurton's Needle* (c. 1551–4) and *Jack Juggler* (1553–8). The most notable difference between these plays and drama deriving from native tradition is the stronger sense of unity binding them, so that it begins to be appropriate for the first time to use the generic term 'comedy' in approaching them. Before this date, we may think of comedy as an ingredient in theatrical practice, rather than as a descriptor of theoretical genre; but now, in this narrowly specific strand of humanist theatre, comedy emerges as a unified structural form, sometimes arranged according to a classical five-act model (first used in English drama in *Ralph Roister Doister*), importing character types like the boasting soldier or the clever slave (servant), and concluding with the resolution of errors and misunderstandings. Within that more unified framework, however, even comedy conceived in imitation of classical models typically injects a strong element of native tradition or local interest into its form. *Gammer Gurton's Needle*, for example, adapts recognisably classical character-types and plot-shapes to the vernacular setting of an English village, thus exploiting the possibilities for rustic humour, and *Jack Juggler* (whose name, as Peter Happé notes, suggests a link with the very English stage-figure of the Vice) encodes witty play on the topical question of Reformed church doctrine ('juggling' was a routine term used to condemn Catholic forms of worship).[22]

Tragedy was slower to spread into vernacular theatre. As with comedy, where Terence was the most familiar model, Roman tragedy (especially the work of Seneca) was better known than Greek tragedy. The earliest known performance of a classical tragedy in England was Alexander Nowell's production of Seneca's *Hippolytus* at Westminster School in the mid 1540s, and very few further early productions of classical tragedy are known.[23] There are no records of early English court performance of classical tragedy. *Gorboduc*, performed in 1562, first at the Inns of Court in London, effectively England's 'third university' (besides Oxford and Cambridge), and then at Whitehall before the Queen, was the first English tragedy modelled on classical form. Like some of its comic predecessors, it used a five-act structure and a unified approach to plot and character; but aspects of its dramaturgy, again like that of its comic predecessors, may be thought of as overlapping with native tradition. Its pioneering use of dumbshows preceding each act, for example (though they are closely united with the overall theme of the play by function, since they enact the theme of the forthcoming act) is closely in tune with the visual and spectacular mode of earlier native masks and disguisings, where meanings are characteristically represented primarily through visible emblems and stage pictures, sometimes with no speech at all. Its content, furthermore, constituted a clear intervention in contemporary politics, with regard to the fraught question of the succession in the context of the Queen's unmarried state, as an eyewitness account makes clear that some, and perhaps all, of the audience understood.

> There was also declared how a strange duke, seeing the realm at division, would have taken upon him the crown, but the people would none of it. And many things were said for the succession to put things in certainty.
>
> Anonymous report of the first performance of *Gorboduc*, at the Inner Temple, January 1562

As Bruce Smith and Kent Cartwright have shown, '"influence" is perhaps a less apt term . . . than "confluence"' for the dynamic relationship between

classical and native modes of dramaturgy in England.[24] Many learned dramatists imitated vernacular tradition in the same way as more popular dramatists
imitated some elements of classicism. We may see some of the similarities and
differences by comparing two plays written very close in time in the 1560s:
Thomas Preston's *King Cambyses* (*c.* 1558–69) probably written for touring,
with its instructions to potential actors on how to allocate thirty-eight parts
among eight players, and *Damon and Pythias* (1564–5), written by Richard
Edwards, Master of the Chapel Children, for performance by the Chapel Children at Merton College, Oxford and at court, before the Queen. The apparent
distinction between a popular, touring play and one for private performance
before a select audience is undermined, however, by the fact that the prologue
of *Damon and Pythias* is altered, as the title page indicates, 'for the proper use
of them that hereafter shall have occasion to play it, either in private, or open
audience'. It is possible, too, that *Cambyses* was performed at court, and the
play concludes by asking the audience to pray for the Queen.[25] Both plays thus
anticipate different groups of players performing the plays in different kinds
of venues before different kinds of audiences.

More importantly for this chapter, both plays show a similar uncertainty over
genre and/or terminology. *Cambyses*, incorporating several deaths, culminating
in the death of King Cambyses himself, is described on the title page as 'A
Lamentable Tragedy, mixed full of pleasant mirth', but the running heads (the
title as it appears across the top of the pages inside the book) call it 'A Comedy
of King Cambyses'. (The word 'comedy', however, when it first came into use,
could mean simply 'play', as did its cognate forms in some other European
languages. See further below.) Edwards advises his audience that because his
Damon and Pythias contains 'matter mixed with mirth and care', he has decided
to call it a 'tragical comedy' (Prologue, lines 37–8). The running heads confirm
this; but the 1571 title page calls it merely an 'excellent comedy'. Edwards also
stakes a claim to seriousness which seems to be setting itself against conventional
expectations of the stage, warning any members of the audience expecting to
see 'toys' [trifles] (Prologue, line 3) that they will be disappointed. His aim is
a classical one, to follow Horace in observing 'decorum' (Prologue, line 26):

> rightly to touch
> All things to the quick and eke [also] to frame each person so
> That by his common talk you may his nature rightly know.
> . . .
> The old man is sober, the young man rash, the lover triumphing in joys,
> The matron grave, the harlot wild and full of wanton toys.
>
> (Prologue, lines 14–20)

A lamentable tragedy

mixed ful of pleasant mirth, conteyning *the life of*
CAMBISES king of PERCIA, from the beginning
of his kingdome vnto his death, his one good deed of ex-
ecution, after that many wicked deeds
and tirannous murders, committed by and
through him, and last of all, his odious
death by Gods Iustice appoin-
ted. Don in such order as
foloweth. By
Thomas Preston.

The diuision of the partes.

Councel, Huf, Praxaspes, Murder, Lob, the 3. Lord.	*For one man.*	Prologue, Sifamnes, Diligence, Crueltie, Hob, Preparatiõ the 1. Lord.	*For one man.*
Lord, Ruf, Commons cry, Cõmõs cõplaint Lord smirdis, Venus.	*For one man.*	Ambidexter Triall.	*For one man.*
Knight, Snuf, Small habilitie, Proof, Execution, Attendance, second Lord,	*For one man.*	Meretrix, Shame, Otian, Mother, Lady, Queene.	*For one man.*
Cambises, Epilogus.	*For one man*	Yung childe Cupid.	*For one man*

21. Title page of *Cambyses*, 1570.

Neither play is divided into acts or scenes; but both plays have didactic prologues, with *Damon and Pythias* focusing more explicitly on the question of the play's genre, while *Cambyses* indicates that its story is to be understood as showing the requirements of a good prince and briefly summarises the fall of its protagonist, making the classical comparison with Icarus, rather as *Dr Faustus* does some thirty years later. Both dramatise stories centring upon a tyrannical king, though neither Cambyses nor Dionysus rants like an unregenerate medieval Herod. Indeed, Cambyses, as Preston's source shows, is noted for his one good deed in flaying Sisamnes, his corrupt deputy, and Dionysus is converted to virtue through the actions of Damon and Pythias. Both plays show their closeness to medieval tradition in other ways, however. Both mix allegorical with human characters, and both have a figure of good counsel to clarify the King's failings for the audience (Counsel in *Cambyses* and Eubulus (meaning 'Good Counsel' in Greek) in *Damon and Pythias*). Both also show their transitionality between medieval and later tradition in having clowns thrust in alongside classical figures (Venus and Cupid in *Cambyses*, the Muses in *Damon and Pythias*). Of the central clownish figures, Ambidexter in *Cambyses* is more truly in the tradition of the Vice than is Grim the Collier in *Damon and Pythias*, and *Cambyses* also has three ruffians with rhyming names, Huff, Ruff and Snuff, who are strongly reminiscent of the alliterative trio of New Guise, Nowadays and Nought in *Mankind*.

The way characters speak and present themselves in *Cambyses* is also more medieval than in *Damon and Pythias*, in so far as they present and state their positions and qualities openly to the audience

> SISAMNES Even now the king hath me extoll'd and set me up aloft;
> Now may I wear the border'd guard [ornamental border] and lie in
> down-bed soft; (lines 113–14)

> AMBIDEXTER My name is Ambidexter; I signify one
> That with both hands finely can play. (lines 150–1)

Characters in *Damon and Pythias* tend more to reveal than to declare their qualities, and use a much fuller range of metrical patterns than *Cambyses*, whose clumping fourteeners Shakespeare had such fun parodying in *A Midsummer Night's Dream* (1595):

> Now am I dead,
> Now am I fled;
> My soul is in the sky.
> Tongue, lose thy light,
> Moon, take thy flight,
> Now die, die, die, die, die.[26]
>
> (V.1.301–6)

In line with its more presentational mode of representing characters, *Cambyses* is also shorter, less fully developed than *Damon and Pythias* and more strongly focused on visually signposting the stages of the narrative and their significance. Thus Shame enters with a black trumpet, underlining his emblematic costume and prop with words that drive the point home:

> From among the grisly ghosts I come from tyrants' testy train;
> Unseemly Shame, of sooth, I am, procured to make plain
> The odious facts and shameless deeds Cambyses King doth use.
> (lines 341–3)

The detail of the stage directions speaks both of bold spectacle, of how to effect it and of the gap between stage action and the action it represents.

Smite him in the neck with a sword to signify his death. (line 460)
Flay him with a false skin. (line 464)
A little bladder of vinegar pricked
[SMIRDIS] . . . Behold, now his blood springs out on the ground. (lines 726, 729)
Stage directions and text from Thomas Preston, *Cambyses* (c. 1558–69)

The combination of explicitness with literal-mindedness, seen too in the stage direction instructing Cambyses himself to '*quake and stir*' as he dies (line 1171), is presumably what prompts Shakespeare to turn this kind of dramaturgy to comic purposes in *A Midsummer Night's Dream*, but we have seen its more seriously powerful legacy in *Tamburlaine*, also constructed around a series of very explicit stage pictures reinforced by verbal text. And Shakespeare, though he mocked *Cambyses* again in making Falstaff utter his intention to perform Henry IV in the Boar's Head tavern 'in passion . . . in King Cambyses' vein' (*1 Henry IV*, II.4.386–7), was also seeking thereby to accommodate and defuse a play whose deeper influence on him he may have recognised. Falstaff, braggart, clown and cowardly soldier, owes something to the image of Ambidexter, 'with an old capcase on his head, an old pail about his hips for harness [armour], a scummer [skimming ladle] and a potlid by his side and a rake on his shoulder' (line 125); and Falstaff's parody of both Henry IV and Prince Hal in the tavern scene where he acknowledges 'King Cambyses' vein' may also draw on Ambidexter's parodic positioning in relation to King Cambyses' high-sounding military project.

    Damon and Pythias, as Ros King has shown, was also very influential, even offstage, in university life. 'Nearly eighty years after the play was written', she notes, 'Ralph Kettle, the idiosyncratic President of Trinity College, Oxford, seizing a bread-knife and singing the refrain from the play's shaving song, cut off the hair of one of his wealthy, upper-class students as he sat at table.'

As this incident suggests, it was Grim the Collier rather than Damon and Pythias who retained the greatest hold over later imaginations, and Malvolio in Shakespeare's *Twelfth Night* (1600–1) may owe something to Grim.[27]

Theory and practice

It is clear from both Edwards' prologue and from the plays themselves that the generic terms 'tragedy' and 'comedy' can be applied only with some difficulty and distortion to vernacular English drama in this period. Edwards' attempt to validate the term 'tragical comedy' (a forerunner of 'tragicomedy', a term which would not come into regular use until the seventeenth century) represents a pioneering early theoretical engagement with genre. European writers had begun to become more theory-conscious about drama with the rediscovery of Aristotle's *Poetics*, printed in Latin translation in 1498, but not widely known until after the publication of Francesco Robertello's commentary in 1548.[28] Roger Ascham, like Richard Edwards, conveys the exciting sense of doing something new that he and his Cambridge friends felt as they began to compare the theory with the practice of classical tragedy.

> When Mr Watson in St John's College at Cambridge wrote his excellent tragedy of *Absalom*, Mr Cheke, he and I, for that part of true imitation, had many pleasant talks together, in comparing the precepts of Aristotle and Horace *De Arte Poetica*, with the examples of Euripides, Sophocles and Seneca. Few men, in writing of tragedies in our days, have shot at this mark.
> Roger Ascham, *The Schoolmaster* (1570)

Aristotle's best-known admirer in England, however, was Sir Philip Sidney, though Sidney, like Ascham and his friends, may not have known Aristotle's work directly, but rather through European commentators like Robortello.[29] As we saw in chapter 3, Sidney's admiration for classical theory and English attempts to follow its prescriptions were linked to a marked distaste for the popular stage, which openly defied the supposedly Aristotelian unities, as Sidney understood them (though Aristotle, it should be noted, did not in fact prescribe unity of time or place, only unity of action). Even *Gorboduc*, Sidney lamented, could not 'remain as an exact model of all tragedies' because it represented many days and many places.[30] As for his contemporaries, they simply did not understand, according to Sidney's analysis, that drama was 'tied to the laws of poesy, and not of history', so that dramatists were free to 'feign' their subject matter in order to make it accord with the unities. Their plays, then, were 'neither right tragedies, nor right comedies', and Sidney reserves especial venom for the mixing of tragic and comic elements that Edwards sought to present in such a positive light. His contempt for this generic instability is evident in the term he coins to name it: 'mongrel tragi-comedy'.

> But besides these gross absurdities, how all their plays be neither right tragedies, nor right comedies, mingling kings and clowns, not because the matter so carrieth it, but thrust in clowns by head and shoulders, to play a part in majestical matters with neither decency nor discretion, so as neither the admiration and commiseration, nor the right sportfulness, is by their mongrel tragi-comedy obtained . . . So falleth it out that, having indeed no right comedy, in that comical part of our tragedy, we have nothing but scurrility, unworthy of any chaste ears, or some extreme show of doltishness, indeed fit to lift up a loud laughter, and nothing else: where the whole tract of a comedy should be full of delight, as the tragedy should be still maintained in a well-raised admiration.
>
> But our comedians think there is no delight without laughter; which is very wrong, for though laughter may come with delight, yet cometh it not of delight, as though delight should be the cause of laughter; but well may one thing breed both together. Nay, rather in themselves they have, as it were, a kind of contrariety . . . Delight hath a joy in it, either permanent or present. Laughter hath only a scornful tickling.
>
> Philip Sidney, *Apology for Poetry* (printed 1595)

What Sidney clearly hates, and audiences equally clearly loved, is mixed dramaturgy, the invasion of serious matters by clowns, with their physical humour, their improvisatory wit and their defiance of the rules.[31] The earliest star of the Elizabethan theatre known to us by name was a clown, Richard Tarlton; and the longevity of the Vice in English dramatic tradition owes much to his clowning skills. Even Shakespeare, however, despite his willingness to mingle clowns with kings, seems to have had reservations about clowns who exceeded their brief (p. 90 above). Yet the mingling of kings and clowns on the popular stage resembles another classical precept sufficiently to give it a degree of theoretical respectability. The notion, of which Sidney also approves, that it is good to bring together *utile et dulce*, the useful and the pleasing, can function as a justification for retaining elements of a popular tradition that dramatists know will please an audience. John Lyly, writing for elite audiences at court and at the Blackfriars Theatre in the 1580s, is apparently influenced by both Sidney and classical drama, and echoes Sidney's wording in his prologues, yet his statements of intent could stand as unwitting defences of less learned drama.[32] 'We have mixed mirth with counsel and discipline with delight, thinking it not amiss in the same garden to sow pot-herbs that we set flowers', he writes in the Blackfriars prologue to *Campaspe*, while insisting in his Blackfriars prologue to *Sappho and Phao* (probably first performed, with *Campaspe*, in 1583–4) that his intention is 'to move inward delight, not outward lightness, and to breed (if it might be) soft smiling, not loud laughing'. The direct response to Sidney and the attempt to differentiate this stagecraft from that of popular tradition are evident; but the conceptual framework of mixing mirth with matter remains the same.

Shakespeare, who knew Sidney's *Apology*, worked within that same native framework but approached the learned tradition with much less respect, joking about Sidney with the more knowing amongst his audience as he openly flouts his precepts. Not only does he thrust several different clowns into *As You Like It* to disrupt the unity of the Duke Senior plot, but he scripts for them a dialogue that deliberately recalls Sidney's own theoretical terms in order to make nonsense of them.

> TOUCHSTONE Truly, I would the gods had made thee poetical.
> AUDREY I do not know what 'poetical' is. Is it honest in deed and word? Is it a true thing?
> TOUCHSTONE No, truly; for the truest poetry is the most feigning, and lovers are given to poetry; and what they swear in poetry may be said as lovers they do feign.
> AUDREY Do you wish then that the gods had made me poetical?
> TOUCHSTONE I do, truly; for thou swear'st to me thou art honest. Now if thou wert a poet, I might have some hope thou didst feign.
>
> William Shakespeare, *As You Like It* (1599–1600), III.3.15–27

> For that a feigned example hath as much force to teach as a true example (for as for to move, it is clear, since the feigned may be tuned to the highest key of passion) . . . So then the best of the historian is subject to the poet; for whatsoever action . . . the historian is bound to recite, that may the poet (if he list) with his imitation make his own, beautifying it both for further teaching, and more delighting, as it pleaseth him.
>
> Philip Sidney, *Apology for Poetry* (printed 1595)

Thus one strand of popular theatre plays with its own learnedness, challenging an elite model of theatre with knowing wit.

The persistence of 'mingle-mangle'

> If we present a mingle-mangle, our fault is to be excused, because the whole world is become an hodgepodge.
>
> John Lyly, Prologue to *Midas* (1589)

Shakespeare and his contemporaries, even as they became more aware of rule-bound notions of genre, continued to play with such concepts more often than follow them. Shakespeare himself wrote two tightly structured comedies observing the classical unities of time and place at the beginning and end of his career (*The Comedy of Errors* (1594) and *The Tempest* (1610)), and Jonson, his younger contemporary, regularly restricted his plays in this way; but the shift from an open, episodic structure towards a more tightly unified generic structure was sporadic and slow. Generally, until well into the seventeenth century, the notion that different kinds of engagement belonged in different kinds of plays was alien. Dramatists sought variety instead, as so many title pages suggest (see fig. 22 below). They looked for opportunities to insert music, singing, dancing, clowning, dogs, bears and spectacular effects of all kinds; they looked to make audiences laugh and weep from moment to moment. Tragedy and comedy were ingredients, not definitions, and the experience of a play was one of plenitude rather than unity.[33] As earlier chapters have shown, it was a virtue in plays to be flexible, open to improvisation and adaptation, cutting and extending, and it was not uncommon for the prefatory material to advise on how the play might be adjusted for different companies and audiences.

This liking for diversity was not a popular as against an elite preference, nor was there a clear distinction between the kinds of variety presented before elite and popular audiences, except in so far as wealth and learning imposed certain restrictions. Not only did many of the same plays travel between court, private and public venues, as we have seen, but Queen Elizabeth famously liked Tarlton's comic routines with a dog as much as did playhouse audiences. Catholicity of taste in entertainment was widespread at all levels, and individual components were not necessarily or regularly separated.

> Her Majesty . . . is very well. This day she appoints to see a Frenchman do feats on the rope in the Conduit Court. Tomorrow she hath commanded the bears, the bull and the ape to be baited in the tiltyard. Upon Wednesday she will have solemn dancing.
> Letter from Rowland White to Sir Robert Sidney, 12 May 1600

Though the Queen might see dancing and bears on consecutive days, just as the Hope Theatre, built in 1614, showed plays and bearbaiting on different days, other occasions might equally well bring such kinds of things together in sequence, as in the court revels Hall describes, or into even closer proximity, as when bears are brought right into the play in *The Winter's Tale* (1609) or the immensely popular *Mucedorus* (1588–98).

One reason why it is important to consider genre from a theatrical as well as a theoretical and literary perspective is that the two are in conflict in this period.

M. William Shak-ſpeare:

HIS
True Chronicle Hiſtorie of the life and
death of King L E A R and his three
Daughters.

With the vnfortunate life of Edgar, *ſonne*
and heire to the Earle of Gloſter, and his
ſullen and aſſumed humor of
T O M of Bedlam:

As it was played before the Kings Maieſtie at Whitehall vpon
S. Stephans *night in Chriſtmas Hollidayes.*

By his Maieſties ſeruants playing vſually at the Gloabe
on the Bancke-ſide.

LONDON,
Printed for *Nathaniel Butter,* and are to be ſold at his ſhop in *Pauls*
Church-yard at the ſigne of the Pide Bull neere
Sᵗ. *Auſtins* Gate. 1.6 0 8.

22. Title page of *King Lear*, 1608.

Literature, with some exceptions, tends to privilege a unitary conception of the fictional world, as does later, realist drama; but early theatre routinely moves in a more fluid way between the two worlds of the fiction and the audience. At one level this is an accidental effect of its cultivation of variety; but at a more sophisticated level it is also a matter of self-conscious intention. Metatheatricality, the deliberate calling attention to the gap between the fiction and its performance, is endemic to medieval and early modern theatre, and its effects may be earnest or playful or both together. When Christ at the end of the York Crucifixion play instructs the audience to look at his wounds 'And fully feel now, or ye fine [before you go], / If any mourning may be meet [appropriate]' (lines 256–7), the exposure of the gap between fiction and real life is urgent and instructive; when two servants begin to address a company who do not yet know themselves to be an audience in rhyming verse, asking them whether there is to be a play performed, at the start of *Fulgens and Lucres* (*c.* 1496–7), the effect is witty and pleasurable; and when Hamlet/Richard Burbage, performing in the Globe Theatre, vows to remember the ghost 'whiles memory holds a seat / In this distracted globe' (*Hamlet*, I.5.96–7), the effect is to mix a temporary and pleasurable recognition of play with ongoing engagement in Hamlet's pain.

Early theatre is not, of course, without realism or the capacity to immerse the audience temporarily in an imaginative, unified, fictional world, and the tendency towards realism increases as the period advances. The opening of *Hamlet* plunges the audiences into a fully imagined world of darkness and fear already in process in a way as unlike the servants' direct address to the audience in *Fulgens and Lucres* as could be conceived. But the realism of that opening is not maintained consistently throughout *Hamlet* or indeed any other early modern play. The disunity or 'mingle-mangle' of *Hamlet*, for example, may be made clear by asking the question: where is Gertrude when Ophelia dies?

> GERTRUDE There is a willow grows askaunt [sideways over] the brook,
> That shows his hoary leaves in the glassy stream,
> Therewith fantastic garlands did she make
> Of crow-flowers, nettles, daisies, and long purples
> That liberal shepherds give a grosser name,
> But our cull-cold [chaste] maids do dead men's fingers call them.
> There on the pendant boughs her crownet weeds
> Clamb'ring to hang, an envious sliver broke,
> When down her weedy trophies and herself
> Fell in the weeping brook. Her clothes spread wide,

And mermaid-like awhile they bore her up,
Which time she chaunted snatches of old lauds [hymns],
As one incapable of her own distress,
Or like a creature native and indued [habituated]
Unto that element. But long it could not be
Till that her garments, heavy with their drink,
Pull'd the poor wretch from her melodious lay
To muddy death.

William Shakespeare, *Hamlet* (1600–01), IV.7.166–83

Even this framing of the question, however, highlights the assumptions with which we come. When we use the personal names of the characters in this way we betray our own preferred sense of them as rounded and distinctive individuals. But stage-directions and speech-headings in early printed versions of the play refer inconsistently to Gertrude as 'Queen', 'Lady', or 'Mother', as well as 'Gertrude', revealing their own greater concern with the function and status of characters than with consistent individuality or personality.

Gertrude reports Ophelia's death to us, so if the play's fictional world were supposed to be fully and consistently in place with the same degree of realism as it is at the start, it would make sense for us to ask where she was and what she was doing while she watched Ophelia drown. Yet the experience of watching or reading the play is not one that usually prompts most spectators or readers to ask this question. They know that this is an inappropriate response. They know, as they read or hear Gertrude speak these lines, that this is not a piece of realism, but a lyrical moment inserted to produce a different kind of engagement and a different kind of pleasure. The speech is there to create a pause, to make space in a hectic narrative for the still contemplation of Ophelia's death. Gertrude is an appropriate speaker for several reasons: she is a woman, sympathetic to Ophelia, not involved in any tension or conflict with her and not bearing any responsibility for her madness or death. The symbolic rightness of Gertrude as speaker and the lyrical beauty of the speech itself should combine to erase realist considerations at this point, and should also serve to display some of the advantages of mixed over unified dramaturgy. 'Mingle-mangle' should not be understood as inadequate, inferior or a step on the evolutionary ladder towards unity. What mingle-mangle allows is an engagement that changes from moment to moment, an experience that sets the satisfactions of intermittent realism alongside the complications of other responses in tension with those satisfactions. Early modern theatre is less interested in maintaining a consistently plausible world of illusion, than in making and breaking illusion as necessary for the scene in question, in shaping dramatic material according to the criterion of particular effects for particular moments.

The range and flexibility of such a mixed drama is surely one reason why dramatists did not seek to impose a more rigid generic unity on their material. Yet it is also the case that patterns in dramatic writing are not so free and conscious as the previous sentence might suggest. Dramatists' choices about how to write are not made in a cultural vacuum, but determined by a number of factors, one of which is the inheritance of a dramatic tradition. New plays, as they emerge, are in dialogue with the theatrical past, and the experience of watching a play draws always and necessarily on such previous experience of watching other plays as the spectator may bring. Spectators bring expectations with them based on their previous experience of plays; dramatists may consciously fulfil or thwart such expectations; and genre itself is a matter of expectation. Genre and expectation are mutually shaping: repeated fulfilment of the same dramatic pattern produces the expectation of its further repetition; further repetition reinforces that pattern to the point where it can be named as a genre; and establishment of the genre reinforces the expectation of its fulfilment. Plays can then give pleasure or excitement or satisfaction by fulfilling or disrupting expectations. Thus, for example, the shape of the morality genre gives pleasure by regularly showing the Mankind-figure saved from eternal damnation; but Marlowe's *Dr Faustus* excites, and offers a different kind of pleasure, by disrupting that expectation and showing Faustus damned.[34] Shakespeare's *Love's Labour's Lost* (1594–5) adds the additional pleasure of highlighting the audience's awareness of genre expectations as it breaks them.

BEROWNE	Our wooing doth not end like an old play: Jack hath not Gill. These ladies' courtesy Might well have made our sport a comedy.
KING	Come, sir, it wants a twelvemonth an' a day, And then 'twill end.
BEROWNE	That's too long for a play.

William Shakespeare, *Love's Labour's Lost* (1594–5), V.2.874–8

It is not merely in the structure of plays that genre is recognised, however, and early modern plays retain the traces of medieval genres in many more ways. Particular characters, costumes and visual images may deliberately recall earlier counterparts, for example. When audiences saw Alleyn wear a false nose to play Barabas in *The Jew of Malta* (*c.* 1589–90), they were seeing a continuity with medieval devils; when Barabas fell into a cauldron of his own devising they were seeing a continuity with the medieval hell-mouth; when the Porter in *Macbeth* (1606) came to open the stage-doors in response to the knocking on them, making a stream of jokes about being a 'devil-porter' opening the gates of

Hell to sinners, they knew they were being asked to recall the Harrowing of Hell plays from the mystery cycles; and when *Volpone* (1606) opened with an image of Volpone surrounded by heaps of gold they recognised not only Marlowe's Barabas at the start of *The Jew of Malta*, but also the numerous allegorical images of Goods, Money or Covetousness in earlier moral plays like *Everyman* (*c.* 1510–19?) or in later ones such as *All For Money* (*c.* 1572–7). Even as late as *A Game at Chess* (1624), the wicked characters were still being kicked into a bag, as into a medieval hell-mouth, at the end of the play. Meanings were made through the dialogue between one play and others, and the framework within which audiences processed such meanings depended partly on their ability to recognise the different implications such traces acquired within the changed framework of a different genre.

In addition to issues of theatre history and dramatic tradition, of course, there are also more material causes for generic fluidity. One is the conditions of writing outlined in chapter 3: the prominence of collaboration; the allocation of different scenes or plots to different writers; the requirement to revise and rewrite earlier plays to bring them up to date; and the commercial impetus to pull the punters in. Another is the conditions of performance: the openness of the space and the dynamic between *locus* and *platea*, which created different ways of interacting with an audience (see chapter 1); the shape of the space and the fact that the spectators were distributed in such a way as to be able to view one another as much as the play; daylight performance, at least in outdoor amphitheatres; and, in many cases, the relative permeability of the boundary between actors' and audiences' spaces and the willingness to cross such boundaries as there were from time to time.

Unity

Two starting points are especially common in modern discussions of early modern dramatic genre. Both, predictably, are Shakespearean: Polonius' remarks about the visiting actors in *Hamlet* and the categorisation of Shakespeare's plays by Heminges and Condell, for the First Folio collected edition of his works in 1623.

POLONIUS The best actors in the world, either for tragedy, comedy, history, pastoral, pastoral-comical, historical-pastoral, tragical-historical, tragical-comical-historical-pastoral, scene individable, or poem unlimited; Seneca cannot be too heavy, nor Plautus too light.

William Shakespeare, *Hamlet* (1600–1) II.2.396–401

Mr William Shakespeare's Comedies, Histories, and Tragedies Published according
to the True Original Copies
Title page of the First Folio edition (1623)

At one level, Polonius' absurdly overcomplicated list at least shows that thinking
within generic categories was becoming more usual; and there is other evidence
to support this. Legal documents, for example, which spoke in terms of 'stage
plays' and 'interludes' in the sixteenth century (see chapter 3 above), were
beginning to use more specific generic terms, in addition to the two earlier
terms, in order to ensure completeness of coverage.

Know ye that we of our special grace . . . do license and authorise these our
servants, Lawrence Fletcher, William Shakespeare, Richard Burbage, Augustine
Philips, John Heminges, Henry Condell, William Sly, Robert Armin, Richard Cowley
and the rest of their associates freely to use and exercise the art and faculty of
playing comedies, tragedies, histories, interludes, morals, pastorals, stage-plays
and such others . . . as well for the recreation of our loving subjects as for our
solace and pleasure when we shall think good to see them during our pleasure.
Royal Patent for the King's Men, 17 May 1603[35]

The difference between the royal patent and Polonius' overcategorisation, however, is that, where the patent has the wholly serious intention of making its
terms as complete as possible, Shakespeare's intention in *Hamlet* is to mock
Polonius and, through him, the pseudo-specificity of emergent genre-theory.
And at the same time, of course, the particular mode of his satire, whereby he
joins an increasingly comical number of terms together, also points to the gen-
uine overlap between categories in early modern dramatic practice. We have
already seen how early dramatists and printers struggled to name what they
were producing (a 'tragical comedy', a 'lamentable tragedy, mixed full of pleasant mirth', and so on); and, despite the development of a greater degree of clarity
about genre in the seventeenth century, loose terminology and overlap between
categories remained endemic. As late as 1620, the author of *The Two Noble
Ladies* was still struggling with categorisation and collapsing potentially three
major categories into one in describing the play as 'a tragi-comical history'.

While performance is happy to play with notions of genre and to subject them
to irony, print tends to push harder towards generic fixity, and, if its formula-
tions of genre occasionally sound comical, that effect is usually unintentional.
The First Folio's 'catalogue of the several comedies, histories, and tragedies contained in this volume' undoubtedly encourages the reader to approach the plays
with a set of generic expectations. As many critics have pointed out, however,

the Folio groupings are problematic in several ways: many of the plays are differently categorised from the way they are labelled in quarto editions; several are listed in categories that now seem to conflict with their content; and one, *Richard III, is* listed as a history in the 'catalogue' but entitled a tragedy inside the volume.[36] As Samuel Johnson commented in his *Preface to Shakespeare* (1765), neither Shakespeare nor '[t]he players, who in their edition divided our author's works into comedies, histories, and tragedies, seem . . . to have distinguished the three kinds by any very exact or definite ideas'.[37] Later critics have tended to agree with him. To take a random recent example, we may note that the 2003 issue of *Shakespeare Survey*, taking 'Shakespeare and Comedy' for its theme, included three essays on tragedies. Despite this dialogue across the boundaries of genre, however, it is worth looking briefly at the standard terms coming into common use in English during the early modern period.

'Is not a comonty a Christmas gambold [leaping], or a tumbling-trick?', asks Christopher Sly in *The Taming of the Shrew* (1590–91; I.2.137–8), thereby demonstrating his unfamiliarity with the term 'comedy'. Both tragedy and comedy, as we have seen, were terms deriving from Latin, and came into use to describe particular dramatic structures as the result of the humanist revival of interest in the classics. Prior to this usage, they were in common medieval use to refer to non-dramatic narratives, a comedy being a narrative with a happy ending (like Dante's *Divine Comedy*) and a tragedy being the story of 'prosperity for a time that endeth in wretchedness' (like Chaucer's *Troilus and Criseyde*).[38] When 'comedy' and its cognate terms in other European vernacular languages were first adopted with primary reference to plays, however, in the mid sixteenth century, they could be used very vaguely, to mean merely 'play', as well as in a more specific sense, and the term 'comedian' simply meant 'actor'.[39] The specific senses of 'comedy' and 'tragedy' never became as clear in vernacular use as they had been in classical use, and they broadly carried over the medieval sense of happy and unhappy endings from narrative into dramatic form, with usually a marked emphasis, in tragedy, on death over any other kind of unhappy ending.

The history play lacks the clear generic marker of ending, and is characteristically much more provisional and open than tragedy or comedy. It is usually associated with the decade of the 1590s and with public theatres, and David Bevington's pioneering work in *Tudor Drama and Politics* showed it to be clearly associated with England's wartime aspirations during that period, and to recede with the failing years of Elizabeth and the peace policy of James I from 1603. Despite broad critical agreement about its central axis in the 1590s, however, the history play has never been easy to define, and there is a general lack of agreement about how it should be identified. The term 'history play' was not in use during the sixteenth century, and the term 'history' was used in so loose a way (often closer in sense to modern 'story') that its presence or absence in play titles is unhelpful in reaching a definition of dramatic genre.[40] Its overlap with tragedy, furthermore, is notable time and again, as play after play ends with the death of a king. In Thomas Heywood's *Apology for Actors*, where the text uses the term 'tragedy', the marginal note uses the term 'historical play'. Above all we should take note that historical writing, whether in dramatic or non-dramatic form, was supremely susceptible to 'application'.

> men might safely write of others in manner of a tale; but in manner of a history, safely they could not: because, albeit they should write of men long since dead, and whose posterity is clean worn out; yet some alive, finding themselves foul in those vices which they see observed, reproved, and condemned in others, their guiltiness maketh them apt to conceive, that, whatsoever the words are, the finger pointeth only at them.
>
> John Hayward, dedication to *Lives of the Three Normans* (1613)

Richard II (1595) and *Sejanus* (1603) are two cases in point (see chapter 3 above). And to cite *Sejanus* as a history play, furthermore, is to make the point about the difficulty of defining the genre. Modern critics, perhaps following the First Folio, rarely include plays about ancient history within the category, but Thomas Heywood did (p. 175 below).

More than any other genre, tragicomedy flags up the paradoxes of generic classification in itself. On the one hand it seems to signal a new precision about genre in that it seeks to give a new name to an existing grey area between tragedy and comedy.

> A tragicomedy is not so called in respect of mirth and killing, but in respect it wants deaths, which is enough to make it no tragedy, yet brings some near it, which is enough to make it no comedy; which must be a representation of familiar people, with such kind of trouble as no life be questioned, so that a god is as lawful in this as in a tragedy, and mean people as in a comedy.
>
> John Fletcher, Preface to *The Faithful Shepherdess* (1608–9)

Fletcher was consciously imitating the Italian playwright Giambattista Guarini, whose play, *Il Pastor Fido* [*The Faithful Shepherd*] was published in Italian in 1590, first performed in 1598, and translated into English in 1602, and it would seem that both Fletcher and Guarini thought of themselves as innovators in dramatic practice. On the other hand, however, 'tragical comedy' and even 'tragi-comedy' had already been coined, as we saw earlier in this chapter, by Richard Edwards and Philip Sidney, for very different purposes, and numerous plays written and performed earlier than *The Faithful Shepherdess* seem to hover between tragedy and comedy: Shakespeare's *Much Ado About Nothing* (1598), for example, or the group of plays later known as his 'problem plays'; or, even earlier, George Whetstone's *Promos and Cassandra* (1578), Shakespeare's main source for *Measure for Measure* (1603).

In the end, despite the intensifying interest in defining genre in the seventeenth century, it remains, as Susan Snyder argues in her discussion of genre in Shakespeare, a matter of 'shape rather than limitation, in musical terms a kind of ground on which - and sometimes against which - [Shakespeare] played the individual descant of each play'.[41] Though this is certainly widely true of the period, not just of Shakespeare's plays, a Shakespearean play that now has immense cultural prestige as one of the great tragedies, *King Lear* (1605–6), provides a particularly good example of the degree to which genre in the early modern period must be understood as in dialogue with earlier and contemporary dramatic theory and practice, rather than as subject to any set of precepts, including those of Aristotle, so often falsely offered as the right and only framework from which to analyse early modern dramatic form.[42]

In excess of unity: *King Lear* (1605–1606)

King Lear begins, as *Hamlet* does, by plunging us into a seemingly real world, mid-conversation, as Kent and Gloucester discuss the King's division of the kingdom and Gloucester's bastard son, but almost as soon as that world has been established it begins to give way to a strange, fairy-tale world in which a King asks which of his three daughters loves their father most and invites them to declare their love in turn. As in all the best fairy-tales, the youngest, Cordelia, loves him most, but her reply does not satisfy her father's expectation, and the two wicked daughters worm their way into their father's affections whilst the youngest is banished. Kent, the traditional type of the good counsellor, tries to dissuade Lear from 'this hideous rashness' (I.1.149), but succeeds only in rousing his fury. The scene positively invites a staging which lines up good characters and evil characters on either side of the King in the middle, and invites the audience to view, at this early point, from a relatively simple and clear-cut moral perspective. It is, in fact, not quite so simple as this even at this early point, since Cordelia's deviation from the ideal of the dutiful daughter would certainly have raised more problems for a seventeenth-century audience with stronger views on the subordination of daughters to their fathers than it does for a modern audience; but the broad moral outline is nevertheless clear, as Kent's intervention confirms.

This clear moral shape, emphasised as it probably was by the horizontal lines of staging outlined below, is reminiscent not only of folk-tale and romance, but also of a specifically dramatic shape, that of the medieval moral play. It typically centred on the moral choices to be made by an everyman-figure in the course of his life, especially within the framework of the summons of death, which brought the course of that life into direct and urgent relation to God's judgement. Clear imitation of the characters' moral alignment in terms of staging, along horizontal and/or vertical lines, was almost certainly a regular feature of such plays. Angels and devils, or allegorical virtues and vices, may have appeared from above or below, or from stage-right or stage-left, according to their status, and the soul of the mankind-figure was eventually going to move either up or down, to heaven or hell, or to the right or left hand of God. The same staging pattern is visible in the Doomsday cycle plays, where angels and devils appear from above or below and the saved must finally be separated from the damned. Even if the visual pattern were not there in the staging, however, the clear categorisation of the characters at this point with Lear as having a choice to make, and other characters as good or bad, offering truth or dissimulating rhetoric, would have led an early modern audience to recognise the frameworks of an earlier dramatic tradition and to have begun viewing the play from within those horizons of expectations, though those horizons would be in constant tension with the expectations aroused by the strongly realist and conversational opening, pointing towards a more open-ended kind of dramaturgy.[43] Thus, from the start, the play signals a contradictoriness in excess of any single formulation of genre. It both summons and disavows the earlier generic traditions of morality and cycle plays.

This alternation between different ways of viewing continues as the play develops. When Edmund, the bastard son so informally discussed at the opening of the play as one at whose 'making' there was 'good sport' (I.1.22), enters alone in the next scene, speaking directly to the audience and dedicating himself to 'nature' (in the sense of his own baseness, as determined by his birth), the audience is positioned to make a relationship with this character reminiscent of the classic relationship with the Vice, who typically took control over the stage and the audience in this same bold way, speaking with similar directness about his own vicious nature. Yet the style of the conversation that follows when Edmund's father, Gloucester, enters is different. Though Edmund successfully deceives and misleads Gloucester as the Vice would mislead the gullible mankind-figure, the plot-lines and the conversation are naturalistic rather than allegorical. Edmund becomes absorbed into the same character-register as Gloucester, speaking in the same way as he does rather than continuing to signal his difference from the other characters, his distance from the fiction or his control over the stage, as the Vice might do. He is not scripted here to collude with the audience through asides, as the Vice might. The play immerses him in the temporary deception and expects the audience to remember that deception is the game. But when he does step away from the fiction and towards the audience, as he does when Gloucester goes out, he makes an explicit allusion to dramatic genre which forces the audience to take a giant leap outside their immersion within the fiction to consider the degree to which this play is and is not like its predecessors. As he mentions his brother, Edgar, that very brother enters, prompting Edmund to make this comment: 'Pat: he comes like the catastrophe of the old comedy; my cue is villainous melancholy, with a sigh like Tom o'Bedlam' (I.2.124–6). The play, which will end tragically, jokes at this early point about a piece of scripting that resembles the predictable shape of old-style comedy by producing the right character 'coincidentally' on cue; and the joke, furthermore, is carried on into a self-conscious reference to the predominantly comic convention of disguise, citing the very disguise (of a bedlam beggar) that Edgar himself will later take on with such tragic consequences. The level of knowing playfulness about genre within broadly tragic form is daring and on the edge of breaking out of generic confinement.

Other elements in the play carry strong echoes of medieval dramaturgy: the stripping away of Lear's one hundred knights (I.3, I.4, II.4) recalls the gradual falling away of Everyman's friends in the play of that name; the tableau of Kent in the stocks (II.2) recalls the figures of virtue put in the stocks in *Hick Scorner* (*c.* 1514) and *A Satire of the Three Estates* (1552–4); the tableau of Lear kneeling to Cordelia for forgiveness recalls scenes such as Mankind's kneeling to Mercy for forgiveness in the play of *Mankind* (1465–70); and the recalling of earlier plays enriches the meaning of the moment in this play by putting a traditional moral and didactic perspective into dialogue with the elements of the new context.[44] Lear's kneeling to Cordelia towards the end of the play (IV.6.53), for example, though it resembles Mankind's kneeling to Mercy, does not simply reduce Lear to the position of all humanity nor Cordelia to one quality. Each of them is also a rounded individual with a history and a relationship. The ways in which an audience responds to Lear's kneeling are as much determined by Cordelia's earlier refusal to submit to Lear's demand that she quantify her love for him; by his elder daughters' humiliation of him; by his own mock-kneeling to Regan ('On my knees I beg / That you'll vouchsafe me raiment, bed, and food' (II.4.144–5)); and by his loss of reason in between those early moments and this point of recovery as they are by the moral dimension supplied by the fleeting recognition of Lear and Cordelia as humbled Mankind and forgiving Mercy. And all of those moments in turn help to determine the response to the final tableau in which Lear holds the dead Cordelia in his arms, a tableau that takes the audience a very long way from the kinds of experience available in medieval morality plays.

Above all, perhaps, the echoes of morality play recall with sadness the certainties about death specific to that genre. Framed as they were by Christian theology, morality plays offered the certainty that there was a God who judged mankind and who had the power to save penitent sinners. Salvation itself could not be a certainty, but the reassuring faith in divine justice and mercy gave a providential shape to life as presented through the genre of morality play. When *King Lear*, however, glances back at that dramatic tradition, it does so from within a fictional world no longer framed by certainties about life and death. *King Lear* offers no reassurance that there is meaning in either life or death. Edgar tries to play God with Gloucester, his father, and Gloucester, saved from one death by Edgar, dies before Edgar can reveal himself as Gloucester's loving son. Lear, reconciled with Cordelia, has time only to glimpse the happiness they might have together before Cordelia is slain; and within moments of her death Edmund revokes the order to have her killed. The closing moments offer no closure, no meaning, but despairing bewilderment:

> KENT Is this the promised end?
> EDGAR Or image of that horror?
> ALBANY Fall, and cease. (V.3.237–8)

For Albany, life on earth is merely 'this great decay' (V.3.271); for Lear, Cordelia's death makes no sense in the scheme of things ('Why should a dog, a horse, a rat, have life, / And thou no breath at all' (V.3.280–1)); Lear's own death as he struggles to revive her merely ratchets up the suffering for those left behind ('Break, heart, I prithee break!' says Kent at line 287) and leaves them crushed, Kent choosing death and Edgar accepting the burden of rule with a heavy heart. There is no sense that death fits into any divine pattern.

It is worth recalling at this point that Shakespeare's source, *The True Chronicle History of King Leir* (c. 1588–94) did not end tragically, but with the survival and reconciliation of Lear and Cordelia. Nahum Tate rewrote Shakespeare's play with a happy ending to please late seventeenth-century audiences, and Dr Johnson, whose critical remarks on First Folio notions of genre are quoted above (p. 164), preferred Tate's ending to Shakespeare's, which he found unbearable.[45] Shakespeare's manipulation of the source play was contradictory in generic terms. On the one hand he added features strongly associated with comedy: a double plot; the fool; disguise; and the retreat into a 'green world'.[46] On the other hand he scripted madness and death into both plots; dropped the fool without explanation towards the end of Act III; made the central disguise that of a mad beggar and left it in place too long for happy resolution; and turned the traditional comic green world into a bare heath. Reconciliation is either withheld or granted too late, and death itself is the only certainty. The play is a tragedy in the sense that it has an unhappy ending, but not by any classical definition of the genre. Like so many early modern plays, it knowingly chooses a rich and complex dialogue with other genres over generic unity.

Chapter 5

Instruction and spectacle

Theatre as instruction

The dominant assumption about theatre in Western culture for well over a century has been that it will imitate life. We not only expect to see much of what we consume in film and television as well as theatre fulfilling this assumption, but also like to quote historical comments that seem to show that this has always been the case.

> Epic poetry and the composition of tragedy, as well as comedy and the arts of dithyrambic poetry and (for the most part) of music for pipe or lyre, are all (taken together) *imitations*.
> Aristotle, *Poetics* (4th century BCE) (translated from the Greek)

> the purpose of playing, whose end, both at the first and now, was and is, to hold as 'twere the mirror up to nature: to show virtue her own feature, scorn her own image, and the very age and body of the time his form and pressure.
> William Shakespeare, *Hamlet* (1600–1), III.2.20–4

Yet it is self-evidently not the case that drama has always been predominantly realist in nature, nor do these familiar statements really endorse the idea that drama essentially sets out to copy life. Whole books have been written on what Aristotle meant by the term *'mimesis'*, translated above as 'imitation'.[1] It is enough to note here that translation often distorts or reduces a word in another language, and that 'representation', an alternative term favoured by many translators of Aristotle's *'mimesis'*, does not carry the same implications of 'copying' that 'imitation' does. The very examples of mimetic arts that Aristotle cites alongside drama – poetry and instrumental music – make clear that he cannot be thinking in terms of art as straightforwardly copying life.

We should note that Renaissance commentators typically do not take *mimesis* to mean imitation in that sense.

171

Nature never set forth the earth in so rich tapestry as divers poets have done; neither with pleasant rivers, fruitful trees, sweet-smelling flowers, nor whatsoever else may make the too much loved earth more lovely. Her world is brazen, the poets only deliver a golden . . . Poesy therefore is an art of imitation, for so Aristotle termeth it in his word *mimesis*, that is to say, a representing, counterfeiting, or figuring forth – to speak metaphorically, a speaking picture – with this end, to teach and delight.

   Sidney, *Apology for Poetry* (printed 1595)

For Sidney art is not a simple copy of life, but an idealised representation of it which is capable, by virtue of the fact that it is superior to life, of teaching and delighting its audience. It is a reflection less *of* life than *on* life, aiming to demonstrate how life could be if it reached its fullest potential. The mirror of art should not merely or neutrally reflect a surface but should show the essences within, and teach by example. This is what Hamlet implies when he says that playing should 'show virtue her own feature, scorn her own image'. And when, later in the play, Hamlet forces his mother to look in a glass, it is so that she will see, not a simple reflection, but 'the inmost part' of herself; and what she sees indeed by the end of Hamlet's speech is 'black and grained spots' imprinted on her soul (III.4.20, 90). What the quotations from Sidney and Shakespeare reveal is that the dominant assumption underpinning approaches to art, including theatre, in the early modern period and before, was that it should teach, and should do so through delight.

   Chapter 3 showed the extent to which theatre was under attack throughout the period of this book. The most common ground of its defence was that it was a form of teaching. In the medieval period the emphasis of this defence was towards its capacity to strengthen faith and inspire to devotion, though that emphasis shifted over time towards a more secular conception of moral improvement. Quotations below seek to show how widespread and self-evident over a long period, both in drama and in other records, was the view that theatre enhanced the faith and improved the virtue of the beholders.[2]

[The purpose of the liturgical ceremony of burying the cross is] for the strengthening of the faith of the unlearned multitude and of neophytes [novices].
   Regularis Concordia (965–75) (translated from the Latin)

[a cleric] may in the church, through this reason,
Play the resurrection, –
That is to say, how God rose,

God and man in might and los [renown], –
To make men be in belief good
That he rose with flesh and blood;
And he may play, withouten plight [danger]
How God was born in yule night,
To make men to believe steadfastly
That he light [alighted] in the virgin Mary.

    Robert Manning, *Handling Sin* (early 14th C), lines 4641–50

Lady [Abbess] Katherine of Sutton . . . desir[ed] to eradicate the . . . torpor [of the nuns] and stimulate the faithful to greater devotion.

    MS description of an Easter play at Barking Abbey (1363–76) (translated from the Latin)

First, as to the cause of the founding of [the Pater Noster Guild], it should be known that after a certain play on the usefulness of the Lord's Prayer was composed, in which play, indeed, many vices and sins are reproved and virtues commended, and was played in the city of York, it had such and so great an appeal that very many said: 'Would that this play were established in this city for the salvation of souls and the solace of the citizens and neighbours.' Wherefore, the whole and complete cause of the foundation and association of the brothers of the same fraternity was that that play be managed at future times for the health and reformation of the souls, both of those in charge of that play and of those hearing it. And thus, the principal work of the said fraternity is that the play should be managed to the greater glory of God, the deviser of the said prayer, and for the reproving of sins and vices.

    York Pater Noster Guild Returns, 1388–9 (translated from the Latin)

a certain very religious man, Brother William Melton of the order of Friars Minor, a professor [teacher] of scripture and a most famous preacher of the word of God, coming to this city [York], has commended the said [Corpus Christi] play to the people in several of his sermons, by affirming that it was good in itself and most laudable.

    York A/Y Memorandum Book, 1426 (translated from the Latin)

[The Chester plays were produced] for the augmentation and increase of the holy and catholic faith of our saviour Christ Jesu and to exhort the minds of the common people to good devotion and wholesome doctrine thereof.

    Chester Early Banns, 1539–40

Now have we told you all bedeen [together]
The whole matter that we think to play.
When that ye come, there shall ye seen
This game well played in good array.
Of Holy Writ this game shall been,
And of no fables by no way.

  N-town Proclamation, lines 516–21

Thou toldest me that other day
That all the substance of this play
Was done specially therefore;
Not only to make folk mirth and game,
But that such as be gentlemen of name
May be somewhat moved
By this example for to eschew
The way of vice and favour virtue;
For sin is to be reproved.

  Speaker B to speaker A, *Fulgens and Lucres* (c. 1496–7), lines 2317–25

Come near virtuous matrons and womenkind,
Here may ye learn of Hester's duty;
In all comeliness of virtue you shall find
How to behave yourselves in humility.

  Prefatory verse, *Godly Queen Hester* (1529–30)

Oh children, learn, learn by your mother's fall
To follow virtue, and beware of sin,
Whose baits are sweet and pleasing to the eye,
But being tainted, more infect than poison,
And are far bitterer than gall itself,
And liv'd in days where you have wealth at will,
As once I had, and are well match'd beside:
Content yourselves, and surfeit not on pride.

  An adulterous wife speaks to her children in *A Warning for Fair Women*
  (1596–1600), lines 2474–11

Oh women, women, you that have yet kept
Your holy matrimonial vow unstained,
Make me your instance. When you tread awry,

> Your sins like mine will on your conscience lie.
>> An adulterous wife speaks to the audience in Thomas
>> Heywood, *A Woman Killed with Kindness* (1603), xiii.141–4

> If we present a tragedy, we include the fatal and abortive ends of such as commit notorious murders, which is aggravated and acted with all the art that may be to terrify men from the like abhorred practices. If we present a foreign history, the subject is so intended, that, in the lives of Roman, Grecians, or others, either the virtues of our countrymen are extolled, or their vices reproved . . . If a moral, it is to persuade men to humanity and good life, to instruct them in civility and good manners, showing them the fruits of honesty, and the end of villainy.
>> Thomas Heywood, *Apology for Actors* (1612)

Occasionally, the emphasis was on teaching factual knowledge rather than morality:

> And though some men think this matter too high
> And not meet for an audience unlearned,
> Methink for man nothing more necessary
> Than this to know, though it be not used
> Nor a matter more low cannot be argued.
> For though the elements God's creatures be
> Yet they be most gross and lowest in degree.
>> John Rastell, Prologue to *The Nature of the Four Elements* (1517–20), lines 106–12

> plays have made the ignorant more apprehensive [discerning], taught the unlearned the knowledge of many famous histories, instructed such as cannot read in the discovery of all our English chronicles.
>> Thomas Heywood, *Apology for Actors* (1612)

Even more occasionally acting itself was seen as a moral pursuit by comparison with other leisure activities, as when William Keeling had his company act Shakespeare's plays on board ship in order to keep them from 'idleness and unlawful games, or sleep' (p. 23 above). Thomas Heywood, the great apologist for actors and acting, also cited instances of plays shaming murderers into confessing their sins and frightening enemy armies, overhearing the sounds of a stage-battle, into running away.[3] More often, theatre's detractors argued that it did indeed teach, but that it taught the very sins it portrayed as opposed to the avoidance of them (see the letter from the London Mayor and Aldermen quoted on p. 123 above); and players were then held up as living examples of the theatre's failure to teach virtuous behaviour.

> If any goodness were to be learned at plays it is likely that the players themselves, which commit every syllable to memory, should profit most, because that, as every man learneth so he liveth; and as his study is, such are his manners. But the daily experience of their behaviour showeth that they reap no profit by the discipline themselves. How, then, can they put us in any good hope to be instructed thereby, when we have the sight of such lessons but an hour or two as they study and practise every day, yet are never the better?
>
> Stephen Gosson, *Plays Confuted in Five Actions* (1582)

Evidently some spectators, however, as we saw in the case of Simon Forman (chapter 2 above), who understood *The Winter's Tale* to be teaching the audience about the dangers of 'trusting feigned beggars or fawning fellows', did look for moral and practical lessons as well as pleasure from theatre.

'Quick books': the medieval drama of devotion

> sithen [since] it is leveful [lawful] to han [have] the miracles of God painted, why is [it] not as well leveful to han the miracles of God played, sithen men mowen [may] better readen the will of God and his marvellous works in the playing of them than in the painting, and better they been holden in men's mind and ofter rehearsed by the playing of them than by the painting, for this is a dead book, the tother a quick [living].
>
> *Treatise of Miracles Playing* (1380–1414)[4]

Despite the long-standing hostility to theatre explored in chapter 3, especially on the part of the church, it is nevertheless the case that vernacular drama arose within the context of a movement within the church to educate the laity as a way of reinforcing their faith. Prior to the fourteenth century, the vast bulk of all written material in Europe was in Latin, and thus readable only by a tiny minority of educated elite, especially clerics. During the fourteenth century new materials in English, aimed both at a less literate clergy (hugely reduced in numbers and education after the ravages of the Black Death in 1349) and a wider audience, began to be disseminated by the church. 'Primers', books of prayers and devotions used to teach reading (literally 'first books'), began to be produced in English for the first time, and numerous other kinds of material, including stories of the life of Christ and the lives of the saints, Christianised histories, explanations of the basic prayers and tenets of Christianity and religious lyric poetry, became available to those who could read English (still a small minority, but notably larger than the group who could read Latin).

The friars, who came to England towards the end of the thirteenth century, were very influential in making the word of God more accessible to ordinary people, and many devotional books in English were the result of their efforts. In the first instance, however, the friars reached the illiterate laity through their sermons, since they did not preach primarily in churches, but wandered the country preaching to audiences in the open where they found them. Their sermons were often skilled pieces of performance, incorporating popular tales by way of example, sometimes embellished with snatches of poetry or song, and people flocked to hear them. Several scholars have suggested that sermons and drama may have been linked, and certainly numerous medieval plays contain sermons or doctrinal exposition (see, for example, Mercy's sermon at the opening of *Mankind*; St Paul's sermon on the seven deadly sins in *The Conversion of St Paul* (1480–1520); or the commentary on the Magnificat in the play of *The Visit to Elizabeth* in the N-Town cycle). As G. R. Owst has pointed out, the Croxton *Play of the Sacrament* dramatises a popular sermon *exemplum* (a story told to illustrate a point), and the speech of the resurrected Lazarus in the Towneley cycle follows John Bromyard's sermon on the dead almost word for word.[5] It is possible that friars in England linked their sermons to performances of plays, as occasional fragments of evidence seem to suggest and as we know they did elsewhere in Europe. David Jeffrey notes that several Italian manuscripts include sermons and plays together and cites an English verse sermon which makes explicit reference to a play that is to follow.[6]

> if ye wellet [will] stille been
> in this play ye mowen iseen [may see]
> this man havede [had] land and lede [people]
>   Verse sermon on St Nicholas (13th century)

On 29 March, which was Good Friday . . . Friar Ruberto started again his daily preaching in the square . . . [A]t the end of the said sermon on the Passion he performed this play: that is, he preached at the top of the square outside the door of San Lorenzo where a platform was prepared . . . And there, when it was time to show the Crucifix, out of San Lorenzo came Eliseo de Cristofano, barber at the Gate of Sant'Agnolo, representing the naked Christ with a cross on his shoulder and the crown of thorns on his head; and his flesh seemed beaten and scourged, as when Christ was scourged. And there several armed men took him to be crucified. And they went down towards the fountain, around the crowd, as far as the entrance to the Scudellare, and they turned at the Exchange and returned to the door of San Lorenzo and went onto the said platform; and there, in the middle of the platform, someone went towards him in the garb of the Virgin Mary dressed all in black, weeping and speaking sorrowfully, as was done in the similar play of the Passion of Jesus Christ; and when they arrived at the scaffold of Friar Ruberto, he stood there for a long time with the cross on his shoulder, and all the while the people wept and cried for mercy. Then they put down the said cross and took up a crucifix which was already there, and they erected the said cross; and then the wailing of the people grew louder. At the foot of the said cross, Our Lady started her lament together with St John and Mary Magdalene and Mary Salome, and they said some stanzas from the lament of the Passion. Then came Nicodemus and Joseph of Arimathea, and they freed the body of Jesus Christ from the nails, put it in the lap of Our Lady, and then laid it in the sepulcher; and throughout the people continued to weep loudly. And many said that there had never been performed in Perugia a more beautiful and pious play than this one. And on that morning six friars were professed: one was the said Eliseo, who was a foolish youth . . . And after three or four months the said Friar Eliseo . . . left the friary and returned to the barber's trade, and they call him Lord God; and then he married and was a greater scoundrel than before.

Chronicles of the city of Perugia for the year 1448 (translated from the Italian)

The weeping of the Perugia audience throughout Friar Ruberto's spectacle in Perugia shows how this clerical initiative to strengthen the faith of the laity sought to reach out to them through the emotions. This kind of response, based on a highly emotional reaction to church teachings, mainly on the life of Christ, was known as 'affective piety'. Drama and sermons were part of a performance-based teaching which could touch even the most illiterate levels of society, but books in English, especially illustrated books, were also an influential part of the movement to educate, and may have influenced both the narrative detail and the visual composition of performance.

We must now treat of the Passion of our Lord Jesus. He who wishes to glory in the Cross and the Passion must dwell with continued meditation on the mysteries and events that occurred. If they were considered with complete regard of mind, they would, I think, lead the meditator to a (new) state. To him who searches for it from the bottom of the heart and with the marrow of his being, many unhoped-for steps would take place by which he would receive new compassion, new love, new solace, and then a new condition of sweetness that would seem to him a promise of glory. . . .

When the Lord Jesus, led by impious men, reached that foul place, Calvary, you may look everywhere at wicked people wretchedly at work. With your whole mind you must imagine yourself present and consider diligently everything done against your Lord and all that is said and done by Him and regarding Him. With your mind's eye, see some thrusting the cross into the earth, others equipped

23. The crucifixion. *Speculum Humanae Salvationis,* Speyer: Peter Drach der Ältere, *c.* 1480.

with nails and hammers, others with the ladder and other instruments, others giving orders about what should be done, and others stripping Him. Again He is stripped, and is now nude before all the multitude for the third time, His wounds reopened by the adhesion of His garments to His flesh. Now for the first time the Mother beholds her Son thus taken and prepared for the anguish of death . . . Oh, what bitterness her soul is in now! I do not believe that she could say a word to Him: if she could have done more, she would have, but she could not help Him further. The Son was torn furiously from her hands to the foot of the cross.

Meditations on the Life of Christ (late 13th century) (translated from the Latin)[7]

Looking across the broad spread of extant medieval drama texts, it is immediately evident that almost all of them are religious (see p. 69 above), and this in turn means that they are routinely shaped towards a didactic end. Morality plays usually end with repentance, mercy and salvation. Mystery cycles end with doomsday and the lesson that some souls are damned while others are saved. Other kinds of plays survive in very small numbers, but the wish to draw out a moral or religious lesson is evident across the board: St Paul escapes from prison with the help of God in *The Conversion of St Paul*; Mary Magdalene ascends into heaven in the Digby *Mary Magdalene*; the Jews are converted in the Croxton *Play of the Sacrament*. The regular framing of a plot, which is already didactically shaped, within the explicitly moral discourse of prologues and epilogues takes this a stage further, so that the audience can be left in no doubt as to how to understand the message of the play. A prayer is also often part of the epilogue, thus binding the audience into a community that understands itself as a congregation.

PRIEST Sovereigns [sirs], of this process thus endeth the sentence
[narration]
That we have played in your sight.
Almighty God, most of magnificence,
Mote [may] bring you to his bliss so bright,
In presence of that king!
Now, friends, thus endeth this matter.
To blisse bring tho[se] that been here!
Now, clerks [clerics] with voices clear,
Te Deum laudamus let us sing.
Digby *Mary Magdalene* (1480–1520), lines 2132–40

BISHOP Christ's commandments ten there be.
Keep well them; do as I you tell.
Almighty God shall you please in every degree,
And so shall ye save your souls from hell.
For there is pain and sorrow cruel,
And in heaven there is both joy and bliss,
More than any tongue can tell.
There angels sing with great sweetness.

To the which bliss he bring us
Whose name is called Jesus,
And in worship of this name glorious
To sing to his honour *Te Deum Laudamus*.
Croxton *Play of the Sacrament* (1461–1520), lines 916–27

> GOD THE FATHER SITTING IN JUDGEMENT And they that well do in this
>   world, her wealth [their good] shall awake;
> In heaven they shall heined [exalted] be in bounty and in bliss.
> And they that evil do, they shall to hell-lake
> In bitter bales [torments] to be brent [burnt]: my judgement it is.
> My virtues [powers] in heaven then shall they quake;
> There is no wight in this world that may scape this.
> All men example hereat may take
> To maintain the good and menden her miss [amend their sins].
>
> Thus endeth our games.
> To save you from sinning,
> Ever at the beginning
> Think on your last ending!
> *Te Deum laudamus* [We praise you, O God]
>   *The Castle of Perseverance* (1397–1440), lines 3637–49

These framing speeches guide their audience as explicitly as devotional texts guide their readers towards the lessons they need to learn, and usually use a cleric or other figure of authority to pronounce that message. (We may note too the extent to which the need to engage the audience as a congregation overrides any notion of consistency of character. In *The Castle of Perseverance* it is the actor playing God the Father who here addresses that same God as 'you' in the Latin words of the '*Te Deum*'.) A teaching figure is routinely added to plays at the end where no speaker within the fiction is appropriate to speak with such authority, and some plays introduce a teacher who appears more frequently at strategic points to instruct the audience. The Expositor in the Chester cycle, Contemplacio in the N-Town cycle and Mercy in *Mankind*, for example, all perform this function.

Quite apart from the explicit moralising of early dramatic scripts, however, drama had the advantage of striking the heart and mind very directly through living and moving images; and contemporary eyewitness reports throughout the period of this book testify to the power of the stage picture.

> The machines of Paradise and of Hell were absolutely prodigious and capable of being taken by the populace for magic. For there one saw Truth, the Angels and other characters descend from on high, sometimes visibly and sometimes invisibly and then without warning. Lucifer arose out of Hell, riding on a dragon, without anyone being able to see how it was achieved. Moses' dry and sterile rod suddenly sprouted flowers and fruit; the souls of Herod and Judas were carried up into the air by devils.
>   Henri d'Outreman recounting a performance at Valenciennes in 1547
>   (translated from the French)[8]

in public theatres, when any notable show passeth over the stage, the people arise out of their seats, and stand upright with delight and eagerness to view it.

Stephen Gosson, sermon preached at St Paul's Cross, 7 May 1598

In *Macbeth* at the Globe [1611] the 20 of April, Saturday, there was to be observed first how Macbeth and Banquo, two noblemen of Scotland, riding through a wood, there stood before them three women fairies or nymphs and saluted Macbeth ... And when Macbeth had murdered the King the blood on his hands could not be washed off by any means, nor from his wife's hands, which handled the bloody daggers in hiding them.

Simon Forman, *Book of Plays and Notes* (1611)

This sight [of two old men, representing the end of the world and the last judgement, striking the cradle] took such impression in me that when I came towards man's estate, it was as fresh in my memory as if I had seen it newly acted.

Robert Willis, *Mount Tabor* (1639)

One day an old man (about sixty), sensible enough in other things, . . . coming to me about some business, I told him that he belonged to my care and charge, and I desired to be informed in his knowledge of religion. I asked him how many gods there were. He said he knew not; I, informing him, asked him again how he thought to be saved. He answered, he could not tell, yet thought that was a harder question than the other. I told him that the way to salvation was by Jesus Christ, God-Man, Who, as He was man, shed His blood for us on the cross, etc. 'Oh sir', said he, 'I think I heard of that man you spake of once, in a play at Kendal, called Corpus Christi play, where there was a man on a tree and blood ran down' etc. And after that he professed that though he was a good churchman, that is, he constantly went to common-prayer at their chapel, yet he could not remember that ever he heard of salvation by Jesus Christ, but in that play.

John Shaw, Yorkshire clergyman, writing about an encounter in 1644

In all the observations above the visual images have produced very powerful effects on the spectators, so remarkably in the last instance that the only thing the speaker can call to mind in response to the name 'Jesus Christ' is a stage picture of the crucified Christ (and he probably recalled this image from decades earlier, since performances of Corpus Christ plays had ceased by about 1603). In this case, one might argue, the power of the image has overwhelmed the teaching rather than served as a vehicle for it, since the spectator has not retained the lesson inherent in the image. And certainly the author of the *Treatise of Miracles Playing* distrusts plays on precisely these grounds.

He argues strongly against the defence of plays as living books which he cites above.

> miracles playing . . . been made more to delighten men bodily than to been books to lewd [ignorant] men. And therefore, if they been quick books, they been quick books to shrewdness [villainy] more than to goodness.
> *Treatise of Miracles Playing* (1380–1414)

This argument was to run through the whole debate about theatre which is the subject of chapter 3. Stephen Gosson worried about every form of appeal to the eye as a form of spiritual death.

> For the eye, beside the beauty of the houses and the stages, [the devil] sendeth in garish apparel, masks, vaunting, tumbling, dancing of jigs, galliards, morrises, hobby-horses; showing of juggling casts [throws], nothing forgot, that might serve to set out the matter with pomp, or ravish the beholders with variety of pleasure. To seek this is to spend our studies in things that are merely natural [instinctive]; to spend our time so is to be carnally minded, but to be carnally minded is death.
> Stephen Gosson, *Plays Confuted in Five Actions* (1582)

Yet there can surely be no single broad answer to the question of how images work on audiences: playhouses and juggling are not really to be equated either with each other or with other forms of imagery, however well the rhetorical manoeuvre of linking them may work for Gosson's purposes. Ultimately we can only seek to analyse the functioning of specific images in relation to individual plays and perhaps even individual spectators. It is thus worth looking closely at how images operate in several different early performance texts to see how they seem to address and position the spectators. We may look first at one of the earliest royal entries recorded in England, Richard II's entry into London in 1392.[9] Earlier records of royal entries include various kinds of decoration and mechanical devices, but do not supply enough information for us to know whether these earliest pageants sought only to amaze and impress or also to communicate meanings. The 1392 pageants are important because the records are detailed enough to convey their intention to communicate meaning within a specific context: the reconciliation of the King and the city of London following the city's refusal to furnish a loan to the King which he considered due to him by feudal right.

There were four pageants, set up at four important points along the cere-monial route and all four were, as Gordon Kipling has shown, 'co-ordinated in theme', depicting, respectively: a choir of angels singing and scattering gold pieces; two angels in clouds descending from a tower to offer a golden chalice and two golden crowns to the King and Queen; God enthroned, surrounded by three circles of angels singing and playing instruments; and John the Baptist preaching in a wilderness of wild beasts, announcing the descent of an angel bringing two altarpieces bearing images of the crucifixion to the King and Queen.[10] The unifying concepts are London as the New Jerusalem and King Richard himself as a type of Christ:

> As Saviour, Richard redeems and pardons – first a banished murderer
> who throws himself before his horse as the procession is about to enter
> the city, later the city itself as the mayor and sheriffs stand before his
> judgment throne repenting their offences . . . Like Christ at the Second
> Coming to the New Jerusalem, Richard comes to his kingdom for the
> second time. Forgiving bridegroom of an errant but penitent spouse, he
> takes his now faithful city to himself again. They shall henceforth be his
> people, he shall be their King, and he will dwell with them.[11]

The pageants no doubt impressed and entertained the King, but they also worked to affirm the city's gesture of renewed loyalty. As Richard Maidstone, the monk whose description of the occasion is the main source of our information about it, writes, 'If there was aught of anger in the King, it was immediately extinguished to nothing with the contemplation of this exhibit.'[12] Though the King presumably understood the meaning of the pageantry, however, that is no guarantee that a majority of spectators did so. Maidstone, describing the third pageant, says that the spectators were ravished by its beauty, an observation which points towards the possible overwhelming of the communicative dimension by the sensory appeal of the spectacle. Sydney Anglo, discussing the very sophisticated pageantry for the royal entry of Katherine of Aragon in 1501, notes that 'not one of the three surviving eyewitness observers (all of them otherwise competent and circumstantial) even hints at having an inkling as to what it was all about'.[13] On the other hand, some visual emblems were so familiar as to need no introduction. Thomas Dekker, scripting the figure of Justice into one of his pageants for the entry of King James in 1604, chooses not to offer a full description on the grounds that his audience will be familiar with its iconography;

> Having told you that her name was Justice, I hope you will not put me to describe
> what properties she held in her hands, sithence [since] every painted cloth can
> inform you.
>> Thomas Dekker, description of the pageant at the Fleet Street Conduit for
>> the coronation of James I, *The Magnificent Entertainment* (1604)

and Ben Jonson defends his refusal to make the witches in the *Masque of Queens* (1609) announce their own identities and characteristics by insisting on the need to 'trust . . . to the capacity of the spectator' most especially in the genre of masque, performed before a social and educated elite.

> For to have made themselves their own decipherers and each one to have told upon their entrance what they were, and whether they would, had been a most piteous hearing and utterly unworthy any quality of a poem, wherein a writer should always trust somewhat to the capacity of the spectator, especially at these spectacles, where men, beside enquiring eyes, are understood to bring quick ears, and not those sluggish ones of porters and mechanics, that must be bored through at every act with narrations.
> *The Masque of Queens* (1609), lines 89–96

Thomas Heywood echoes Jonson's social snobbery by dismissing some of his visual and sensory display as knowingly 'low', aimed at satisfying an appetite for spectacle amongst the least competent of potential spectators rather than communicating any subtlety of meaning.

> *The third Pageant or Show merely consisteth of antic gesticulations, dances, and other mimic postures, devised only for the vulgar, who are better delighted with that which pleaseth the eye, than contenteth the ear.*
> Thomas Heywood, *Londini Speculum* (1637)

Issues of spectatorial competence and social context (where known and understood) need to be kept in mind in discussing the way images function.

If we turn to look at scripted plays rather than pageantry we can observe images functioning in different ways. The stolen sheep in the Towneley *Second Shepherds' Play* offers a notable example of a subtly developed image which, while very different from the images of this civic pageant of 1392, is also producing different responses from different kinds of spectators, depending on their spectatorial competence. The play shows the shepherds who hear the news of Christ's birth from the angel and culminates in their visit to the Christ-child in the stable. Though all the extant cycles have at least one shepherds' play, this one is the best-known now because of its comic daring. It invents a shepherd called Mak, who is a sheep-stealer, and the centrepiece of the play is the moment when the other shepherds, noticing that one of their sheep is missing, come to call on Mak. In a moment of inspired deceit, Mak's wife, Gill, wraps the sheep in swaddling clothes, lays it in a cradle and pretends she has just given birth. The humour, anticipating and parodying the stable scene that is to follow, becomes increasingly outrageous. Mak demands sympathy and respect for his wife's postnatal condition:

Wist [knew] ye how she had farn [suffered], your hearts would be sore.
Ye do wrong, I you warn, that thus comes before
To a woman that has farn, but I say no more;

(531–3)

while Gill swears her honesty with an oath that goes right to the heart of the
mass, the liturgical ritual in which the body of Christ is eaten:

> I pray to God so mild,
> If ever I you beguiled,
> That I eat this child
> That lies in this cradle.
>
> (535–8)

The shepherds leave the house, unable to find their sheep, and then realise they
have not given the new baby any gift. They return to give the 'little day-star'
(577) the few pennies that they have. Mak tries to keep the shepherds back from
the cradle, and the humour turns to open farce as the third shepherd draws near:

> Give me leave him to kiss, and lift up the clout [cloth].
> What the Devil is this? He has a long snout.
>
> (584–5)

The dawning recognition is extended to milk every drop out of the comic
situation, as the shepherds in turn note his likeness to their sheep, his four feet
protruding either side of the swaddling bands, and so on, while Mak and Gill
first try to hush their insults, then claim that his nose was broken and he was
taken by an elf. This part of the play concludes quickly as the shepherds toss
Mak in a blanket as punishment and then lie down to sleep.

The play then abruptly moves into a different register as an angel appears
to them singing the familiar announcement of the birth of Christ: '*Gloria in
excelsis deo*'. Humour accompanies this epiphanic moment too, as the shepherds
talk about the strange song and one even tries to copy it. Yet within a few short
lines the play is cutting across this realist mode, in which the shepherds reveal
the limits of their understanding, with a sacred and celebratory mode which
reshapes the shepherds as possessing understanding beyond their station, able
to quote biblical prophecy in Latin and affirm for the audience the significance
of this birth. The two modes can be seen in tension in the first line of the
following stanza, which then moves wholly into the second mode

> We find by the prophecy . . . let be your din!
> Of David and Isay [Isaiah], and more than I min [remember],
> They prophesied by clergy that in a virgin
> Should he alight and lie, to sloken [relieve] our sin

. . .
For Isay said so,
Ecce virgo
Concipiet [behold a virgin shall conceive] a child that is naked.

(674–82)

This is not a matter of the three shepherds being characterised differently from one another, since all three now begin to speak a more formal and less 'characterful' verse. That verse becomes lyrical as they come to the stable and produce their gifts for the baby, addressing him in the same term of endearment as they used to describe Mak's baby: 'little day-star' (727). The tableau of the shepherds hailing the Saviour is an iconic representation of the coming of the Lamb of God. In echoing the earlier comic tableau of the stolen sheep the image now holds within it the dramatic trace of the very sinfulness that the true Lamb comes to redeem. It functions differently as a result of the earlier image, touching the sacred with the profane and giving the audience a sense that the coming of Christ is truly for them, sinners as they are.

Images function differently in the Croxton *Play of the Sacrament*. In addition to having a parodic dimension, they also appeal to, or perhaps produce, an appetite for the spectacular which is potentially in conflict with the Christian response they seek to evoke. As in the *Second Shepherds' Play* and elsewhere in the Corpus Christi plays, the image of the body of Christ is theologically central and dramatically climactic. The story centres upon a group of Jews who decide to test the Christian claim that the host is the body of Christ. They do so by stealing it from the church and subjecting it to physical torments dramatised as reminiscent of the torture and crucifixion of Christ. The sequence begins as the Jews plunge their daggers into the host. This is powerful and shocking enough, but it is merely the start of an escalating sequence of horrific images. As the host begins to bleed, Jonathas the Jew picks it up to throw it into a cauldron of boiling oil, but it sticks to his hand. He runs mad with the host sticking to his hand, and his fellow Jews nail it to a post, but as they then try to pull him away from it, his arm comes off.[14] One of the Jews plucks the nails out of the crucified hand, wraps it in a cloth and shakes it into the cauldron. The cauldron boils with blood. The Jews then heat an oven, take the hand and host together out of the cauldron with pincers and throw them into the oven. The oven promptly bursts open, blood seeps from the cracks and an image of Christ with bleeding wounds appears and speaks to the Jews, who fall on their knees and repent. Jonathas, on Christ's instruction, puts his hand back into the cauldron and is made whole again. When Jonathas finally kneels to the bishop in repentance, the image of Jesus turns back into bread and is reverently laid back on the altar.

The didactic intention of these images, leading as they do from the outrage of human blasphemy, through the fearful power of God, to repentance, reverence and conversion, is self-evident; and the recognition of these meanings positions the audience to respect and adore the sacred host and the power of God both to punish and to redeem sinners. But how is this audience position complicated by the fact that these same images are also wonderfully and desirably spectacular? The stabbing of the host, the nailing of it to the post, the throwing of it into the oven and its bursting out in an image of the living Christ, though they undoubtedly function as analogies for the wounding, crucifixion, burial and resurrection of Christ, also excite and satisfy the audience in and for their own sake, as images of piercing and bleeding still do now in contemporary body art. The technical sophistication of such special effects, furthermore, highlights the fact that this is theatre at its most tricksy and fraudulent, theatre parading its own capacity to manufacture illusion.

The effects, then, are almost certainly in excess of the dramatist's intention, though it is possible too that the dramatist was aware of the secular appeal of the spectacle, and may even have been cultivating it as a way of attracting spectators to engage with the piece through their eyes so that they might then be unwittingly drawn into the devotion the play wishes to inspire. This, of course, is precisely the kind of argument that the author of the *Treatise of Miracles Playing*, with his innate distrust of any shows that worked by delighting men 'bodily', would have treated with contempt. Even if we discard the idea of intention as neither provable nor very helpful here, however, we are still left with an excess. The images are, put simply, excessive in themselves; they are more exciting, more powerful, more risky, than they need to be in the interests of piety. And this is not unusual in late medieval drama. One only has to look at the sequence of stage directions in *Wisdom* (c. 1460–70), for example, to see how a very abstract, allegorical text could be animated through visual spectacle; and many plays of the period contain spectacular sieges, ascents and descents, irruptions of devils with fireworks and extended depictions of physical torments. When images of sacred truths become so material as to come close to violating the very sacredness of those truths, it is easy to see how the Catholic church's practice of using images to inspire devotion might seem to be a step too far. Thus it becomes easy too to see why images were to be one of the things Protestantism fastened on in attacking Catholic forms of worship.

Reformation and propaganda

Protestantism, however, was not always or only about attacking images and theatre. The early Reformers were very aware of the potential usefulness of theatre as a way of reaching a popular audience with their message. Sir Richard Morison wrote to Thomas Cromwell *c.* 1538 advising him to learn precisely this lesson from the medieval Catholic church, and Cromwell's heeding of this advice is evident in his sponsorship of John Bale and his players and in his deliberate use of drama to spread the new message of Reform (see chapter 1 above).

> Expedient and very necessary it is, that unto the time he [the Pope] be destroyed of all princes, banished out of all christendom, the ungodliness, hurts and evils that have come and may come through him to every Christian realm were [i.e. should be] daily by all means opened [revealed], inculked [inculcated] and driven into the people's heads, taught in schools to children, played in plays before the ignorant people, sung in minstrels' songs and books in English purposely to be devised to declare the same at large.
>
>   Richard Morison, 'A Discourse Touching the Reformation of the Laws of England' (*c.* 1538)

Protestant awareness of the power of theatre, however, is as evident in the suppression as it is in the patronage of plays, and it is partly the widespread evidence of suppression that has given rise to the view that Protestants were unilaterally antitheatrical. As Harold Gardiner and others have shown, one reason for the decline of the cycle plays was the hostility of some local authorities, as well as the central government, to their religious content, which came to seem increasingly controversial under Henry VIII, Edward VI and Elizabeth I (though not, of course, under the Catholic Queen Mary).[15] From the late 1530s to the end of the 1570s civic playbooks were being called in for inspection and revision, and the account of the York Creed Play in chapter 3 shows in some detail how this process might gradually lead to the end of the play's performance. Censoring of texts was another way in which the Reformation made its impact on the earlier drama. Thus the Early Banns at Chester (1539–40) erase a reference to the Virgin Mary, very much a focus of Catholic worship, and omit lines announcing the procession that carried the blessed sacrament, since Reformation thinking saw such ritual practices and reverence towards sacred objects as idolatrous. The text was altered and whole pages torn out at York; and missing leaves in the Towneley manuscript suggest the excision of an entire play or two, probably on the Coronation and Assumption of the Virgin. Sometimes the playbooks were simply returned to their owners too late for performance to take place, as at York and Chester.

While the Reformation was a major factor in bringing the performance of cycle drama to an end, the morality form proved more adaptable. From the time of Cromwell and Bale onwards it was frequently shaped towards Reformation ends. Where before the Reformation it had been used to teach a broad doctrine of salvation emphasising good works and mercy, now it became more polemically partisan, and virtues and vices became respectively Reformists and Catholics. Thus Treason in Bale's *King John* is a priest, Sedition swears to hold with the Pope 'so long as I have a hole within my breech' (lines 90–1) and Dissimulation is recognised as a 'religious man' (line 2093) (that is, a monk or a friar) because he is heard in the distance singing a drinking song.

> Let Idolatry be decked like an old witch, Sodomy like a monk of all sects, Ambition like a bishop, Covetousness like a Pharisee or spiritual lawyer, False Doctrine like a popish doctor, and Hypocrisy like a grey friar. The rest of the parts are easy enough to conjecture.
>
> John Bale, directions for costuming in *The Three Laws* (c. 1538)

Reformists in early and mid-Tudor plays go by names such as Good Counsel, Knowledge and Discipline (*Lusty Juventus*, c. 1550–3, *The Longer Thou Livest the More Fool Thou Art*, c. 1568) and often carry a Bible to signify their virtue. The Bible became a specifically Protestant prop, as opposed to a generally religious one, because one of the major points at issue between the two churches was the translation of the Bible. When Elizabeth was handed a Bible at one of the pageants in her coronation procession, the gesture was a political one: she was being invited to confirm her support for the Protestant faith; and she did so by kissing the book.

Elements of morality style survive into the seventeenth century in Protestant propagandist plays such as Heywood's *If You Know Not Me* (1604–5) and Dekker's *The Whore of Babylon* (c. 1606–7), both of which replay versions of the heavily invested moment when the new Queen kissed the Bible in her coronation procession. But Protestantism also created new dramatic forms and new modes of viewing. Peter Lake has described how his investigation of relations between 'the protestant and the popular' through murder pamphlets led him to look at the stage dramatisations of pamphlet literature, and in particular the performance of the repentant sinner on the scaffold.[16] What he found, comparing pamphlets with plays, was that the titillating features of the pamphlets became 'even more graphic and immediate once these features were transferred to the stage'.[17] The problem of the visual image and its intense power to titillate is not, as examination of the Croxton Play showed above, peculiar to Protestantism; but Lake's exploration of it in Protestant plays leads him to some suggestive conclusions. The elements of moralisation and titillation, he argues, are structurally necessary to each other as part of a tendency to see the world in terms of a binary opposition between order and disorder. Either element, the moral or the 'festive' (as Lake calls it), can be played up at the expense of the other, but the dialogic form of drama, he argues, puts particular strain on the relationship between the moralising frame and the titillating content, making it more likely that one element will outweigh and invalidate the other.

Huston Diehl's study, *Staging Reform*, examines how Reformist ways of thinking and seeing influenced theatre more widely, not just in its explicitly Protestant form. Arguing, with Lake and others, that reformed religion is not inherently antitheatrical, she identifies the 'intense interest in images and acts of seeing' manifested in Elizabethan and Jacobean tragedy as a specifically Reformation configuration, arising out of 'the reformers' struggle to suppress a persistent iconophilia among the English people'.[18] One problem with this argument is that the briefest look at medieval theatre will show it to be as intensely interested in images and acts of seeing as later theatre (as indeed the pre-existence of that 'persistent iconophilia' that the Reformers wanted to suppress already supposes). But the details of Diehl's case are more persuasive than the broad thesis, and some of the dramatic preoccupations she examines, including the concerns with representation itself, with indeterminate meaning and with false and demonic signs, do seem likely to be related to the deep uncertainties aroused by a century of religious upheaval. The particular targets of Protestant hostility to Catholicism, including its supposedly idolatrous tendency to represent the mysteries of religious doctrine in material images and its insistence that the bread and wine of the mass do not merely represent, but truly become, the body and blood of Christ, certainly indicate a focus on issues of representation.

Ruth Lunney, by contrast (in *Marlowe and the Popular Tradition*), has examined the changing nature of stage images and the changing ways in which audiences learned to view them from the late medieval period to the later sixteenth century, without particular recourse to the Reformation as the cause. Whatever one takes the cause or causes to be, it is undoubtedly the case that the nature of stage images and audiences' responses to them change over the period of this book, as demonstrated in the case studies of chapter 2 above and as discussion in the next section below explores further.

It would be distorting, however, to close this discussion of explicitly Reformist drama without some consideration of the stage Puritan. Whatever the true nuances and subtleties of Puritanism and its supposed hostility to the stage, the stage Puritan is usually a comic caricature created in response to the attacks that many Puritans did mount upon the stage (see chapter 3 above).[19] Some of the most memorable comic moments of the post-Reformation stage centre on such figures (though stage Puritans are not always comic, as Shakespeare's Angelo in *Measure for Measure* (1603) may remind us). It is Malvolio's hostility to revelry, for example, an attitude typical of the stereotyped Puritan, that sets in motion the comic plot against him in *Twelfth Night* (1601). Sir Andrew Aguecheek's response to Maria's suspicion of his Puritanism always raises a laugh in the theatre.

> MARIA Marry, sir, sometimes he is a kind of puritan.
> SIR ANDREW O, if I thought that, I'd beat him like a dog!
>
> William Shakespeare, *Twelfth Night* (1600–1), II.3.140–2

Ben Jonson and Thomas Middleton were two dramatists who satirised Puritans on several occasions in their plays. Middleton, who had strong Puritan connections himself, returned to mock Puritans in play after play, although, as Margot Heinemann has pointed out, his 'characteristic tone . . . is a rough irreverence towards arrogance, hypocrisy and greed, in whatever rank it is found'.[20] One of his greatest scenes, in *A Mad World, My Masters* (1604–7), involves the exposure of the wonderfully named Puritan, Penitent Brothel, as the victim of his own lust. At this point in the play Brothel's hypocrisy is already evident. He inveighs against harlots, but is himself sexually involved with Mistress Harebrain, another man's wife. As Act IV, scene 1 opens, he is anticipating his second encounter with her, and enters reading a morally improving book that underlines the extent to which he is endangering his soul by embracing the pleasures of the flesh. At precisely the moment when he resolves to end his affair with Mistress Harebrain, a devil enters to him in her shape. Since it is only a stage direction that reveals at this point that this is the devil, however, the audience is as yet unable to distinguish that this is not the real Mistress Harebrain, though they may be taken aback by her new boldness: 'What, at a stand? The fitter for my company' (30). ('At a stand' means both 'idle' and 'erect'.) The suspicion that she is a succubus (a devil in female form supposed to lead men astray in their sleep) is immediately voiced by Penitent Brothel, but the succubus responds to his suspicion with more pressing sexual advances and false logic: 'Feel, feel, man; has a devil flesh and bone?' (36).

As the scene develops, a regular theatre-going audience of the time would begin to recognise it as a parody of another very famous scene, that of Helen of Troy's appearance in Marlowe's *Dr Faustus*. Helen's first appearance has both distance and dignity. The scholars beg Faustus to let them see the woman renowned as 'the beautifull'st in all the world' (xii.3); '*music sounds*', according to the stage direction, '*and Helen passeth over the stage*' (19). But that brief visionary moment begins to descend into corporeality and even banality as Faustus begs for 'heavenly Helen' (79) as his paramour and embraces her. Faustus, in some of the most famous lines ever spoken in the early modern theatre, seeks to construct the moment of embrace as the fulfilment of all his desires:

Was this the face that launched a thousand ships
And burned the topless towers of Ilium?
Sweet Helen, make me immortal with a kiss.
> [*They kiss.*]

Her lips sucks forth my soul. See where it flies!
Come, Helen, come, give me my soul again.
> [*They kiss again.*]

Here will I dwell, for Heaven be in these lips,
And all is dross that is not Helena.

> (85–91)

Faustus' expression of extreme pleasure in terms of the image of having his soul sucked out gives ironic voice to the possibility that Helen is a succubus. Helen herself never speaks, but the Old Man utters the judgement that Faustus is damned, leaving the audience to infer that the seeming Helen was indeed a devil.

The insistent corporeality of the succubus who pursues Penitent Brothel, with her incessant commentary on the visibly changing level of his physical desire and her mocking song and dance around him, leads to a deliberately parodic climax that takes the carefully nuanced banalisation of sexual desire developed in Marlowe's *Faustus* into the realm of the comic grotesque:

SUCCUBUS Once so firm and now so hollow?
> When was place and season sweeter?
> Thy bliss in sight, and dar'st not meet her?
> Where's thy courage, youth, and vigour?
> Love's best pleased, when 't's seared with rigour;
> Sear me then with veins most cheerful,
> Women love no flesh that's fearful.
> 'Tis but a fit, come, drink't away,
> And dance and sing and kiss and play.
> > [*She sings and dances around him*]

> Fa le la, le la, fa le la, le la la,
> Fal le la, fa la le, la le la!

PENITENT Torment me not!
SUCCUBUS Fal le la, fa le la, fa la la loh!
PENITENT Fury!
SUCCUBUS Fa le la, fa le la, fa la la loh!
PENITENT Devil! I do conjure thee once again
> By that soul-quaking thunder to depart
> And leave this chamber freed from thy damned art.

Succubus stamps and exit, [descending through the trap-door]
> (54–71)

Penitent's questioning of his servant and the servant's insistence that Mistress Harebrain has not been there give the audience all the confirmation they need that the seeming woman was indeed a succubus and that Penitent is twice a joke, once as the object of a woman's taunting, and once as the dupe of the devil.

The different tonalities of the two plays, moreover, are highlighted by the different spaces in which they were performed and the different audiences they addressed. *Dr Faustus* was certainly performed by the Admiral's Men at the Rose from 1594 and later at the Fortune, though quite where it was first performed and by whom is not clear. It may have toured with the older company of Admiral's Men.[21] Accounts of early performances of *Faustus* make clear that it was especially notable for its special effects and that many spectators and even some actors were sometimes overwhelmed by its impact across a range of different venues.

> . . . a head of hair like one of my devils in Doctor Faustus, when the old Theatre cracked and frighted the audience.
>   Thomas Middleton, *The Black Book* (1604)

> [Prophecies are made] of lightning and thunder that shall happen such a day when there are no such inflammations seen, except men go to the Fortune in Golding Lane to see the tragedy of *Doctor Faustus*. There indeed a man may behold shag-haired devils run roaring over the stage with squibs in their mouths, while drummers make thunder in the tiring-house and the twelve-penny hirelings make artificial lightning in their heavens.
>   John Melton, *Astrologaster* (1620)

> Certain players at Exeter, acting upon the stage the tragical story of Dr Faustus the conjurer; as a certain number of devils kept every one his circle there, and as Faustus was busy in his magical invocations, on a sudden they were all dashed, every one harkening other in the ear, for they were all persuaded there was one devil too many amongst them; and so after a little pause desired the people to pardon them, they could go no further with this matter; the people also understanding the thing as it was, every man hastened to be first out of doors. The players (as I heard it) contrary to their custom spending the night in reading and in prayer got then out of the town the next morning.
>   Manuscript note of uncertain date[22]

> The visible apparition of the devil on the stage at the Bel Savage playhouse in Queen Elizabeth's days (to the great amazement both of the actors and

spectators), whiles they were there profanely playing the *History of Faustus*, the truth of which I have heard from many now alive who well remember it, there being some distracted with that fearful sight.
William Prynne, *Histriomastix* (1633)

Alleyn played the part in a surplice with a cross stitched on it.

Mad World, by contrast, was written for performance at the tiny, indoor Paul's Theatre by Paul's Boys, a children's company who built a reputation for satiric performance. Where the Admiral's Men were offering the thrills of horror and terror with *Faustus*, Paul's Boys were cultivating a relatively intimate and knowing relationship with a clientele who enjoyed in-jokes both about the theatre and about London life. Though the Paul's repertoire, Andrew Gurr argues, moved away from a somewhat elite satiric perspective towards an increasing alignment with a citizen viewpoint, the relationship between the company and the audience remained more playful and self-aware than that which obtained in the amphitheatres.[23] Boy-actors stood by definition in a different relation to predominantly adult audiences from adult male companies, and the parodic element was never far away. It would have been much more difficult for one of Paul's Boys to play a seductive succubus without parody than for him to mock his more famous and serious predecessor.

Vying with Penitent Brothel for the position of most memorably comic Puritan on the early modern stage is Jonson's Zeal-of-the-Land Busy in *Bartholomew Fair* (1614), a play which was performed on consecutive days (31 October and 1 November) in two venues that were culturally poles apart: the Hope, also used as a bearbaiting arena and stinking of the animals, according to the play's induction, and the court of King James at Whitehall the next. Named, like Middleton's Penitent Brothel, with a name that simultaneously apes the Puritan practice of abstract naming and chooses qualities that mock the actual attributes of the Puritan in question, Zeal-of-the-Land Busy from the outset condemns the sinful pleasures of the fair while at the same time seeking a way of enjoying its pleasures himself. His lengthy justification in Act I of why he should go to the fair is a triumph of absurdity, uttered in a language that parodies the language of Puritan 'prophesying' (preaching) and culminating in the argument that he will profess his 'hatred and loathing of Judaism' by publicly eating pork. 'I will therefore eat, yea, I will eat exceedingly' (I.6.114–5), he ends his ridiculously strained and inflated diatribe.

But he is at his most comic when he bursts in on the puppet-show at the fair, denouncing it as idolatry: 'Down with Dagon, down with Dagon; 'tis I, will no longer endure your profanations' (V.5.1–2). Initially Leatherhead, the puppet-master, responds to Busy in his own person, claiming to have a licence from the Master of the Revels; but his next move is to speak through the Puppet Dionysius, thus making Busy look a fool as he attempts to argue seriously with a puppet. Busy rehearses most of the standard anti-theatrical arguments illustrated in chapter 3 above: that it is idolatrous, licentious, profane, an idle occupation, and one that depends on male players wearing female clothing. In this last argument lies his downfall, as the Puppet Dionysius has the perfect, irrefutable response:

> It is your old stale argument against the players, but it will not hold against the puppets; for we have neither male nor female among us. And that thou may'st see, if thou wilt, like a malicious purblind zeal as thou art!
> *The Puppet takes up his garment.* (121–5)

Busy is completely confounded, and is reduced not only to admitting it, but to instant conversion, so that the positions of preacher and convert are comically reversed:

> BUSY I am confuted, the cause hath failed me.
> PUPPET DIONYSIUS Then be converted, be converted.
> LEATHERHEAD Be converted, I pray you, and let the play go on!
> BUSY Let it go on. For I am changed, and will become a beholder with you. (133–8)

Both Jonson's and Middleton's scenes, it could be argued, put pleasure well above instruction and aim above all to make the audience laugh. Yet they also instruct. In making a mockery of those who seek to preach on virtuous behaviour while failing to practise what they preach they make a didactic point about hypocrisy; and in the Jonsonian scene the attack on hypocrisy also turns into a defence of the stage. Though both scenes offer exquisite comic pleasure, they also make their audiences think. They use theatre instrumentally as well as for fun.

Changing images in playhouse drama

A sequence of chronologically organised quotations in the opening section of this chapter aimed to show how strongly rooted and enduring throughout the period of this book was the view that theatre aimed to teach and to improve its audiences. This aim, I have argued, was often in tension with the power of the visual images staged in different plays, though those images changed radically between the beginning and the end of the period, as did attitudes towards them. Some discussion of medieval stage images, and of the influence of the Reformation on changing stage images, has already been offered; and it is appropriate now to look from a wider perspective at the way stage images and attitudes towards them changed between the time just preceding the professionalisation of the stage and the closure of the theatres in 1642. I propose to do this by again selecting a chronological sequence of examples, in the first instance to allow the reader to make his or her own comparison between examples selected, but also as a resource for beginning a fuller analysis of how stage images function.

> APIUS But out, I am wounded, how am I divided?
> Two states of my life, from me are now glided.
> *Here let him [Apius] make as though he went out and let Conscience and*
>   *Justice come out of him, and let Conscience hold in his hand a lamp*
>   *burning and let Justice have a sword and hold it before Apius' breast.*
> R. B., *Apius and Virginia* (c. 1567)

> *Christianity must enter with a sword, with a title of Policy, but on the other side*
> *of the title, must be written God's Word; also a shield, whereon must be written*
> *Riches, but on the other side of the shield must be Faith.*
> George Wapull, *The Tide Tarrieth No Man* (c. 1571–5)

> *Enter first Shealty the Herald; then Pride, bearing his shield himself, his impresa*
> *[emblem with motto] a peacock, the word* Non parilli; *his page Shame after him*
> *with a lance, having a pendant gilt, with this word in it,* Sur le Ciel; *Ambition, his*
> *impresa a black horse salient [leaping], with one hinder foot upon the globe of*
> *the earth, one fore foot stretching towards the clouds, his word,* Non sufficit
> orbis; *his page Treachery after him, his pendant argent [silver] and azure, an*
> *armed arm catching at the sunbeams, the word in it,* Et gloriam Phoebi; *last,*
> *Tyranny, his impresa a naked child on a spear's point bleeding, his word* Pour
> sangue; *his page, Terror, his pendant gules [red]; in it, a tiger's head out of a*
> *cloud, licking a bloody heart, the word in it,* Cura Cruor. *March once about the*
> *stage, then stand and view the Lords of London, who shall march towards them,*
> *and they give back; then the Lords of London wheel about to their standing, and*
> *the other come again into their place; then Policy sends Fealty; their herald's coat*
> *must have the arms of Spain before and a burning ship behind.*
> Robert Wilson, *Three Lords and Three Ladies of London* (1588–90)

Enter in a chariot Muly Mahamet and Callipolis, on each side a page . . .

Muly Mahamet . . . with raw flesh . . . [*In the margin*:] raw flesh

Enter Nemesis above . . . to her three Furies bringing in the scales . . . three devils . . . three ghosts . . . The Furies first fetch in Sebastian and carry him out again, which done they fetch in Stukley and carry him out, then bring in the Moor and carry him out. Exeunt. [*In the margin*:] Three vials of blood and a sheep's gather [heart, liver and lungs].

Enter at one door the Portingall army with drum and colours . . . at another door Governor of Tangier . . . from behind the curtains to them Muly Mahamet and Callipolis in their chariot with Moors, one on each side.

Enter a banquet . . . one with blood to dip lights [lungs], one with dead men's heads in dishes, another with dead men's bones. [*In the margin*:] Dead men's heads and bones; banquet; blood
    Extracts from the 'plot' of *The Battle of Alcazar* (1588–9)

Enter the Presenter before the last dumb show, and speaketh.
Ill be to him that so much ill bethinks,
And ill betide this foul, ambitious Moor,
Whose wily trains with smoothest course of speech,
Hath tied and tangled in a dangerous war,
The fierce and manly king of Portugal.
                    Lightning and thunder.
Now throw the heavens forth their lightning flames,
And thunder over Afric's fatal fields,
Blood will have blood, foul murder scape no scourge.
 Enter Fame like an angel, and hangs the crowns upon a tree.
At last descendeth fame as Iris,
To finish fainting Dido's dying life,
Fame from her stately bower doth descend,
And on the tree as fruit new ripe to fall,
Placeth the crowns of these unhappy kings,
That erst she kept in eye of all the world.
                    Here the blazing star.
Now fiery stars and streaming comets blaze,
That threat the earth and princes of the same.
                    Fireworks.
Fire, fire about the axletree of heaven,
Whirls round, and from the foot of Cassiopa
In fatal hour consumes these fatal crowns.
                    One falls.
Down falls the diadem of Portugal.
                    The other falls.
The crowns of Barbary and kingdoms fall.
    George Peele, *The Battle of Alcazar* (1588–9), lines 1255–86

TAMORA   I am Revenge, sent from th'infernal kingdom
         To ease the gnawing vulture of thy mind,
         By working wreakful vengeance on thy foes.
                    . . .
TITUS   Do me some service ere I come to thee.
         Lo by thy side where Rape and Murder stands;
         Now give some surance that thou art Revenge –
         Stab them, or tear them on thy chariot-wheels,
         And then I'll come and be thy waggoner,
         And whirl along with thee about the globes.
         William Shakespeare, *Titus Andronicus* (1592),V.2.30–49

The Furies go to the door and meet them. First the Furies enter before, leading them, dancing a soft dance to the solemn music; next comes Lust before Brown, leading Mistress Sanders covered with a black veil; Chastity all in white, pulling her back softly by the arm; then Drury, thrusting away Chastity, Roger following. They march about, and then sit to the table. The Furies fill wine; Lust drinks to Brown, he to Mistress Sanders; she pledgeth him. Lust embraceth her; she thrusteth Chastity from her; Chastity wrings her hands, and departs. Drury and Roger embrace one another; the Furies leap and embrace one another.
      A Warning for Fair Women (1596–1600), stage direction

Enter Vindice [holding a skull; he watches as] the Duke, Duchess, Lussurioso [her] son, Spurio the bastard, with a train, pass over the stage with torch-light.
      Thomas Middleton/Cyril Tourneur, *The Revenger's Tragedy* (1605–6),
      opening stage direction

Enter Vindice, with the skull of his love dressed up in tires [headdress, veil, wig and mask].
      Thomas Middleton/Cyril Tourneur, *The Revenger's Tragedy* (1605–6),
      III.5.42

FERDINAND   I come to seal my peace with you. Here's a hand
                         Gives her a dead man's hand.
            To which you have vowed much love; the ring upon't
            You gave.
DUCHESS   I affectionately kiss it.
FERDINAND   Pray do and bury the print of it in your heart.
            I will leave this ring with you for a love-token;
            And the hand, as sure as the ring; and do not doubt

> But you shall have the heart too; when you need a friend
> Send it to him that owed [owned] it; you shall see
> Whether he can aid you.

DUCHESS   You are very cold.
> I fear you are not well after your travel.
> Hah! lights! Oh, horrible!

FERDINAND   Let her have lights enough.

                                                    Exit.

DUCHESS   What witchcraft doth he practise that he hath left
> A dead man's hand here?

Here is discovered, behind a traverse [a free-standing curtained structure], the artificial figures of Antonio and his children, appearing as if they were dead.

John Webster, *The Duchess of Malfi* (1612–14), IV.1.43–55

Enter Dog.

ELIZABETH SAWYER   My dear Tom-boy, welcome!
> I am torn in pieces by a pack of curs
> Clapped all upon me, and for want of thee.
> Comfort me; thou shalt have the teat anon.

DOG   Bow wow! I'll have it now.

ELIZABETH SAWYER   . . .
> Stand on thy hind-legs up. Kiss me, my Tommy,
> And rub away some wrinkles on my brow
> By making my old ribs to shrug for joy
> Of thy fine tricks. What hast thou done? Let's tickle.

William Rowley, Thomas Dekker and John Ford, *The Witch of Edmonton* (1621), IV.1.163–73

Enter Giovanni with a heart upon his dagger . . .

GIOVANNI   'Tis Annabella's heart, 'tis; why d'ee startle?
> I vow 'tis hers: this dagger's point ploughed up
> Her fruitful womb and left to me the fame
> Of a most glorious executioner.

John Ford, *'Tis Pity She's a Whore* (1630?), V.6.9, 30–3

The first thing to emphasise is that this laying out of examples in chronological order is not intended to illustrate a relentless progress towards change. On the contrary, one of the things that chronological sequence makes visible is the extraordinary persistence of certain kinds of image-making. Yet alongside that degree of continuity there is also an immense range and diversity, not methodically moving year by year along a simple evolutionary ladder of theatrical development but rather illustrating the crammed and complex ways in which theatre really does develop, accreting, modifying, extending and discarding in a rich and uneven swivelling between the radical and the familiar. Several of the quotations above, naturally enough in a consideration of stage images, are stage directions; others mix stage directions with speech; and one is a 'plot' (in the early sense of 'groundplan'), a quick key to casting, sound effects and sometimes props.[24]

The plot represents the barest indication of what took place on stage. Reducing the action to entrances, exits and special effects in this way reveals the strong affinity between plays and pageantry. Several modes of performance in the early period, notably royal entries and civic processions, as in the Midsummer Watch or the Lord Mayor's Show, routinely privileged moving tableaux; and processions bearing tableaux were sometimes associated with performances of fully scripted plays, as in York at the Festival of Corpus Christi. Many of the same writers, notably Middleton, Dekker and Jonson, wrote civic pageants as well as plays, and the same guilds mounted civic shows as mounted mystery plays. Court performance, including masques and disguisings, were equally steeped in the tendency to privilege pictorial spectacle, and again there was an overlap between writers of masque and writers of plays for the public theatre. With picture and spectacle so prominent in both popular and elite tradition, it should come as no surprise to find that public playhouse drama also constructs its stage pictures with care. Symmetry is visible at once as an aspect of this construction, as three Furies are matched by three devils and three ghosts, opposing armies enter one at each door, and Muly Mahamet's chariot is flanked by one Moor on each side. Such symmetrical arrangements are also a routine part of static pageantry, as are the emblematic aspects of the picture, such as the symbolic colours distinguishing the armies of Portugal and Tangier. The resemblance to pageant is even more marked in some of the fuller examples, most notably of all in the extract from Wilson's *Three Lords and Three Ladies of London*, which scripts a straightforward procession, at a level of detail which makes clear how insistently emblematic it is. Much more briefly and allusively, in atmospheric torchlight, Middleton too directs a processional entrance across the stage of characters whose names reveal their emblematic quality (Vindice means 'revenger', 'Lussurioso' means 'lustful', while 'Spurio' is explicitly glossed as 'bastard' within the direction).

The pleasure of the image goes beyond that of the static pageant, however, in the way movement animates its functioning. In Wilson's stage direction, the march of the procession about the stage gives way to a balletic representation of battle movement, while in the plot of *The Battle of Alcazar*, the repeated entrances and exits, together with the opposition between 'one door' and 'another door' creates a rhythmic symmetry that groups and balances characters meaningfully and gives the audience the repeated pleasure of responding to the action through the senses as well as the intellect. Not only does the filling and emptying of the stage give satisfactions of a purely visual and sensual kind, but that sequence of filling and emptying instructs the spectator in how to understand the units of action. As numerous commentators have rightly remarked, the basic unit of construction in early theatre is the scene, not the act. The clearing of the stage marks the end of one scene, as the entrance of a new character or characters marks the beginning of another. The audience thus learns to process meaning through the assimilation of the basic scenic unit, responding to the single actor in soliloquy differently from the way it responds to two characters in dialogue, or to two armies entering and leaving by opposite doors, or to the gradual mass filling of the stage typical of so many closing scenes.

Audiences are deeply aware of stage picture in ways that they tend now to be less than fully conscious or analytical about. But audiences in the early theatre were almost certainly more alert than modern audiences to the meanings of stage picture, accustomed as they were to pictures so consciously and carefully constructed. The sensational appeal of certain kinds of spectacle, however, is something that modern audiences still respond to, in film and television as well as theatre. The props listed in the margins of the *Alcazar* plot extracts above (three vials of blood and a sheep's gather; dead men's heads and bones) speak volumes about the kind of appeal that Peele and the Admiral's Men were cultivating with this play and are in some ways directly comparable with effects in recent popular films such as *Gladiator* or *The Silence of the Lambs*. In this respect, both are unlike the Croxton Play, where the gory excess is in tension with a didactic aim. *The Battle of Alcazar*, with no similarly didactic aim, is content to capitalise quite openly on an audience's desire for images of horror. The costumed skull in *The Revenger's Tragedy*, the dead hand in *The Duchess of Malfi*, the witch's dog sucking her teat in *The Witch of Edmonton* and Giovanni holding up his sister's heart on his dagger in *'Tis Pity She's a Whore* all show sensational appeal continuing through to the end of the period. The tendency, however, is towards ever more risky and excessive thrills, fetishising particular body parts and breaking particular taboos: incest or implied incest in *'Tis Pity* and *The Duchess of Malfi*, necrophilia in *The Revenger's Tragedy*, bestiality in *The Witch of Edmonton*. But the appeal to sensation is not only a matter of grotesque, titillating or horrific effects. The extract from the text of *The Battle of Alcazar* incorporates every kind of special effect that might showcase the richness and magic of spectacle: thunder and lightning bring excitement into both sound and picture; fireworks and a blazing star amaze the eye and the understanding; and the fall of the crowns shows in silent, moving and memorable pictures what the shape of the play as a whole has demonstrated. These effects function as a reminder that the advancing technical trickery of theatre is always part of an appeal that it shares with magic and miracles. It is no accident that playwrights turned so often to contemporary witchcraft and conjuring scandals for material for their plays.

But this is not to say that spectacle in secular drama is always or only sensationalist. Though the skull in *The Revenger's Tragedy* functions primarily to evoke pure frisson, with a vein of black comedy, it could be used emblematically elsewhere, as in *Hamlet*, to speak to an audience of human mortality, thus showing the inheritance of medieval dramaturgy (and preaching) very clearly (cf. pp. 31 and 92 above). The sequence of the first four images cited above shows a very clear development from the pre-professional through the professional theatre in this respect. *Apius and Virginia* has moved far enough away from morality play to make its protagonists named individuals from ancient times rather than abstract virtues and vices, but allegory is still intermittently very powerfully present in the mode of representation. In the extract cited above, two allegorical characters, Conscience and Justice, are called into being to represent Apius' state of mind, and each of them, in classic pageant mode, carries props that mark his quality, a lamp for Conscience and a sword for Justice. Apius, furthermore, presents and comments on his own state of mind in a way familiar from the self-announcement of morality characters and very far from the more realist representation that becomes familiar in the plays of Shakespeare and some of his contemporaries. *The Tide Tarrieth No Man*, by contrast, embodies the trail of that same older style of dramaturgy differently and more fully, being still dominated by allegorical characters called by names such as Hurtful Help, Faithful Few, Greediness and Despair. Christianity, accoutred, like Conscience and Justice, with props whose meaning is more explicitly spelled out in the stage direction, is typical of the way the play as a whole works, rather than at odds with its overall register, as Conscience and Justice are in *Apius and Virginia*. Thus the old tradition persists almost unaltered alongside a dramaturgical mode that registers change and continuity together in a juxtaposition that now looks awkward. Even as late as 1596–1600, *A Warning for Fair Women* is still incorporating an allegorical dumbshow to make explicit a moral judgement on the action of its more individualised protagonists.

We must recognise, however, that in naming this juxtaposition of allegory and realism awkward, we are judging from within a specific and historically situated field of vision, determined by preconceptions about the desirability of unity discussed more fully in chapter 4 above. The conjunction of different dramatic styles is not only widespread in the early modern period generally, but also, to a degree, inherent in the dramatic technique of Shakespeare and other later dramatists whom we now tend to view and perform from a perspective that quite falsely privileges realism. The discussion of *King Lear* in chapter 4 above shows how this persists in a play now widely considered to be one of the jewels of the Jacobean theatre; but the extract from *Titus Andronicus* cited above in this section shows pageant and allegory functioning much more explicitly and at greater length in a Shakespearean play (possibly a collaboration) of earlier date.

What does more or less disappear from plays after about 1600, however, is the figure of the presenter who reappears throughout the play to instruct the audience on how to view the play from a moral standpoint. Prologues and epilogues continue, and occasional choruses punctuate the acts in later drama, but the Presenter in *Alcazar* is one of the last explicit and formal guides to the moral dimension of the action. The chorus in Shakespeare's *Henry V* (1598–9), for example, far from explicating dumbshows, updates the audience on changes of scene and developments in narrative and teases their fancy with rhetorical descriptions of images not present, like the English navy approaching France ('A city on th' inconstant billows dancing', III. Chorus, 15); he does not invite them to see the fall of monarchs in partnership with images of that fall emblematically displayed. Nor does he instruct the audience in how to view and judge the action. On the contrary, as the range of modern critical opinions on that play demonstrates, *Henry V* offers no clear or consistent guidance on how to read its central protagonist and his actions.

A point well made by Ruth Lunney in her study of innovation in English drama before 1595 is precisely that audiences are invited to see differently with the arrival of Marlowe's drama in the 1590s. As the sure moral framework of choric guidance is increasingly withdrawn, audiences have to learn to deal with problematic, open-ended viewing. There is a shift from 'messages of general validity to individual moments of non-representative experience' and audience attention is newly focused on watching particular moments in the experience of an individual figure on the stage, a figure whose reactions are presented as 'fragmentary and confused'.[25] Such moments of uncertainty may be spliced in with references to the more traditional and didactic perspective, but the certainty provided by an overarching moral commentary disappears. Though a good and a bad angel, for example, counsel Marlowe's Faustus within the old structure of morality play, we engage with Faustus, as we never do with Mankind or Everyman, through his own radical uncertainty:

> FAUSTUS   Is't not too late?
> EVIL ANGEL   Too late.
> GOOD ANGEL Never too late, if Faustus can repent.
>   . . .
> FAUSTUS   Ah, Christ, my Savior,
>   Seek to save distressed Faustus' soul!
>   . . .
>   Pardon me in this,

And Faustus vows never to look to Heaven,
Never to name God or to pray to him,
To burn his Scriptures, slay his ministers,
And make my spirits pull his churches down.
                    (*Dr Faustus* (1588?), V.270–90)

A further feature that characterises many more of the images of commercial secular drama than those of earlier religious drama, is excess. Most of the images in the shaded examples above are excessive in one way or another. The sheer length of Wilson's stage direction for *Three Lords*, its crammed detail and exhaustive specificity, the multitude of effects in Peele's *Alcazar*, as thunder and lightning are followed by an angel hanging crowns upon a tree, a blazing star, fireworks and the sequential falling of the crowns, are part of a plenitude that puts the pleasure of theatrical spectacle higher on the agenda than it has ever been. The Croxton Play, as we saw, contains a similar abundance of images which are also excessive in themselves, but its concern to teach complicates its aim to entertain. When Muly Mahamet enters with lion's flesh upon his sword, or Giovanni with his sister-lover's heart upon his dagger, or when Ferdinand places a dead hand in his sister's hand, there is no tension between the excess of the images and a moral agenda that seeks to excite spectators in the interests of a 'higher' aim, namely saving their souls. The thrills of blood, violence and illicit sexual desires are there to be consumed in and for themselves. In the newly professionalised (hence more commercialised) and predominantly secular drama of the late sixteenth century onwards, the aim to pull in large audiences, to excite and satisfy their desires, is much more dominant than in earlier drama.

Even where that more secular drama aims to teach a moral lesson, as it does in *A Warning for Fair Women*, for example, the images are still in excess of the teaching agenda. If we compare the moral dumbshow of *A Warning* with the two earliest examples boxed above, instructive differences are evident. George Wapull's image is basically a description of emblematic costume, where the written word participates in the image in order to instruct the audience clearly; the moment when Conscience and Justice come out of Apius goes beyond Wapull both in animating the image into a moving dumbshow and in trying to represent one man through three actors; but the lengthy stage direction in *A Warning* not only splices the classical Furies in as well as named individuals and allegorical figures, it also prolongs and revels in that excessive moment, piling up effects. It scripts symbolic costume (a black veil for Mistress Sanders, white for Chastity), music and three kinds of stage movement, including dance, realistic action (sitting to table) and symbolic action (Lust leading Mistress

Sanders, Chastity pulling her back, etc.), and then caps that with a climax in which symbolic action echoes, exaggerates and comments on realistic action (Drury and Roger embrace, then the Furies leap into their embrace). The sheer number of jostling characters on stage at once, leading, pulling, pushing, thrusting, marching, drinking, leaping and embracing, gives some idea of how far the dumbshow is in excess of the point it seeks to make. But that very excess was part of the pleasure it offered to its audience.

Spectacle and play

There was risk attendant on that excess. It could all too easily become ridiculous; and whether the audience saw a spectacle of thrilling excess or a cheap and tawdry illusion was almost entirely a matter of point of view. When *The White Devil* (1612–13) succeeded at the indoor Phoenix after failing at the open-air Red Bull it may have been partly because of the different spatial conditions in outdoor and indoor playhouses and partly too because audiences were more easily distracted and less easily absorbed into the world of the play's darkness and excess when open-air conditions allowed them to see the stage illusions and each other more clearly. The danger of seeking to thrill an audience through the power of spectacle was always that they would see the picture as the sum of its constructed parts rather than being overwhelmed by it as illusion. Stephen Gosson, an antitheatrical writer who had been a playwright himself (quoted above condemning all forms of visual appeal as spiritual death), knew exactly how to focus on this Achilles' heel of theatre when he wanted to expose it to ridicule and repeatedly singled it out for attack. His trademark rhetorical device is to reduce spectacles to the paper they are made of.

> Sometime you shall see nothing but the adventures of an amorous knight, passing from country to country for the love of his lady, encountering many a terrible monster made of brown paper, and at his return is so wonderfully changed that he cannot be known but by some posy [motto] in his tablet [a flat piece of jewellery that could be inscribed], or by a broken ring, or a handkerchief, or a piece of a cockle shell. What learn you by that? When the soul of your plays is either mere trifles, or Italian bawdry, or wooing of gentlewomen, what are we taught?
>
> . . .
>
> The waste of expenses in these spectacles that scarce last, like shoes of brown paper, the pulling on, and this study to prank up themselves to please our eyes, was long ago condemned by the heathen Cato, whose opinion is registered to be this, that such carefulness of our bodies is a carelessness of our virtues.
>
> Stephen Gosson, *Plays Confuted in Five Actions* (1582)

More casually, we hear of how a spectator experienced this reduction of spectacle to absurdity at a performance of Shakespeare's *All is True*, or *Henry VIII* (1613).

> I will entertain you . . . with what has happened this week at the Bankside. The King's players had a new play, called *All Is True*, representing some principal pieces of the reign of Henry VIII, which was set forth with many extraordinary circumstances of pomp and majesty, even to the matting of the stage: the Knights of the Order with their Georges and garters, the guards with their embroidered coats and the like – sufficient in truth within a while to make greatness very familiar, if not ridiculous. Now King Henry making a masque at the Cardinal Wolsey's house, and certain chambers being shot off at his entry, some of the paper, or other stuff wherewith one of them was stopped did light on the thatch, where being thought at first but an idle smoke, and their eyes more attentive to the show, it kindled inwardly, and ran round like a train [i.e. of powder], consuming within less than an hour the whole house to the very grounds. This was the fatal period of that virtuous fabric wherein yet nothing did perish but wood and straw, and a few forsaken cloaks. Only one man had his breeches set on fire that would perhaps have broiled him if he had not by the benefit of a provident wit put it out with bottle ale.
>
> Letter from Sir Henry Wotton to Sir Edmund Bacon, 29 June, 1613

It seems here to be precisely the excess of the spectacle which is the problem. Its excess directs attention too emphatically towards the detail of stage and costume, resulting in a focus on the materiality of the show that detracts from the possibility of absorption into the illusion, leaving the spectator dissatisfied with what he has seen. Instead of seeing greatness on show, as Wotton suspects the company wanted him to see in this play, he sees how the illusion of greatness has been put together and is thereby cheated of the thrill that comes from immersion in the illusion. Since, by unlucky accident on this occasion, an especially risky special effect, namely the shooting of a cannon, causes the theatre to burn down, Wotton has a rare opportunity to turn his disappointing spectatorial experience into a comic anecdote, and the materials of the theatre, which have so let him down on this occasion, can become the fodder for his wit. Like Gosson, he reduces theatre to its material form, and thereby dismisses it. The things that perish in the fire are mere 'wood and straw, and a few forsaken cloaks'. In a final satiric thrust, Wotton wryly notes that real injury is avoided by the provident if ignominious upturning of a bottle of ale.

Spectacular excess was even more endemic to court masque than to popular theatre, and equally open to the risk of being perceived as the mere sum of its material parts. As the case study of *The Masque of Blackness* (1605) in chapter 1 showed, its aims in terms of spectacle, specifically Inigo Jones' advancement of perspective staging, large moving props and new forms of lighting, were hugely ambitious, and the expense underpinning it was enormous. The ambition of its designs, however, made it even more absurd when it fell short of that ambition, as numerous anecdotes, including Harington's account of the masque for the King of Denmark in 1606 (p. 63 above), testify. The tensions between Jones and Jonson, briefly referred to at the end of that study, were the result of increasingly divergent views of the role of spectacle in masque. We can observe the change from Jonson's early aim of arousing the reader's awe for spectacle, to his later object of arousing the reader to share his contempt for it.

> This throne, as the whole island moved forward on the water, had a circular motion of it own, imitating that which we call *motum mundi*, from the east to the west, or the right to the left side . . . The steps, whereon the Cupids sat, had a motion contrary, with analogy *ad motum planetarum*, from the west to the east; both which turned with their several lights. And with these three varied motions at once, the whole scene shot itself to the land.
>
> Above which, the moon was seen in a silver chariot, drawn by virgins, to ride in the clouds and hold them greater light, with the sign Scorpio, and the character, placed before her.
>
> Ben Jonson, *The Masque of Beauty* (1608), lines 225–33

> O shows! Shows! Mighty shows!
> The eloquence of masques! What need of prose,
> Or verse, or sense t'express immortal you?
> You are the spectacles of state!
> . . .
> O, to make boards to speak! There is a task!
> Painting and carpentry are the soul of masque.
>
> Ben Jonson, 'Expostulation with Inigo Jones' (1631)

When Jonson uses the term 'spectacle' in the texts of his early masques, it has no negative connotations. He uses it several times in *The Masque of Queens* (1609), including twice in the preliminary summary of the masque, first when he says that the Queen understood that 'a principal part of life in these spectacles lay in their variety' and secondly when he goes on to describe the notion of an anti-masque as 'a spectacle of strangeness' (lines 9–10, 17). When the anti-masque gives way to the masque proper, bringing the twelve queens in on a triumphal throne encircled with light, the figure of Perseus, embodying heroic virtue, presents it to the King as 'a spectacle so full of love, and grace / Unto your court' (lines 406–7) that he cannot fail to embrace it. And Jonson's detailed description of the scene uses the word again, in an effort to give full credit to Inigo Jones for 'the strangeness and beauty of the spectacle' (lines 638–9). But as the rivalry with Jones developed, and Jones himself gave expression to the view that masques were 'nothing else but pictures with light and motion', Jonson developed an increasing antipathy to the pictorial spectacle and resorted to the same strategy as Gosson to evacuate it of dignity.[26]

Masque, as a genre aimed at a powerful and elite audience, including the King himself, had to take itself and be taken seriously. It could only survive the attempt to reduce it to painting and carpentry by simply ignoring the attack and continuing on its path, as it did for a few more years up to 1640; but when the professional theatres reopened in 1660, with the restoration of the monarchy, masque was not revived as a form of court theatre. Public-theatre plays, however, had more varied and robust resources for survival than masque, including the ability not to take themselves wholly seriously. This chapter opened by arguing that neither medieval nor early modern dramatists were seeking to offer the mere replication of real life on stage. One of the ways in which the drama they offered avoided such replication was by aiming to teach, or to inspire to devotion, and this is visible in its text, its images and its structures. Another way in which it went beyond the boundaries of reality was in the excesses of its fancies, its fantasies and its spectacles and in this respect, as we have seen, early modern secular drama went further than medieval religious drama. But one strategy that theatre retains from the beginning to the end of the period studied in this book is the capacity to play. Plays, we may think, are playful by definition; but some kinds of theatre are more strongly characterised by a desire to play than others, and it is the case that the popular theatre of this period is generally more playful than elite theatre designed only for the court.

The tendency to play may in fact be viewed as another aspect of the very excess examined in terms of spectacle and mixed dramaturgy up to now. As the last two chapters have sought to demonstrate, early English drama is very often more interested in proliferation, extremity and abundance than it is in strict unity or what we would now consider 'coherence'. Instead it tends to multiply effects, to privilege local colour and to play on the edge of whatever boundaries it semi-recognises, rather than to keep strictly within the limits of the forms within which it broadly functions. Just as clowns thrust in amongst kings, to Sidney's dismay (p. 155 above), so a whole range of metadramatic moments bring a different kind of edginess and critical distance to bear on the theatrical experience itself. We have noted one or two such moments already in earlier chapters: the moment, for example, when the devil puts a board under the earth where Mankind is digging and the audience momentarily sees that there is no material difference between the board and the earth as far as staging is concerned (pp. 57–8); or the exposure of Cleopatra as a character who performs herself as 'tragic queen' (p. 91).

Directly comparable with the exposure of the stage as wooden boards in *Mankind*, but very different in its effect, is the scene in *King Lear* where Edgar, disguised as a madman, seemingly leads his father, Gloucester, to the edge of the cliff at Dover. It begins with an exchange between Gloucester and Edgar that signals to the audience that they are climbing up a hill.

> GLOUCESTER When shall I come to th'top of that same hill?
> EDGAR You do climb up it now; look how we labour.
> GLOUCESTER Methinks the ground is even.
> EDGAR Horrible steep.
> Hark, do you hear the sea?
> GLOUCESTER No, truly.
> EDGAR Why then your other senses grow imperfect
> By your eyes' anguish. (IV.5.1–6)

Gloucester is old and blind, and Edgar is leading him, so both actors' movements would be awkward and slow. When Edgar says 'look how we labour', it should be evident to the audience that they are indeed labouring. Thus, though Gloucester voices doubts about the fact that they are climbing uphill, Edgar's assurance that they are doing so functions to confuse the audience. When a play staged on a relatively bare and totally flat stage without a set needs to signal to an audience that there is a hill, it has two ways of doing so: by having the actors say that there is, as Edgar does here, and by having the actors demonstrate its presence by their movements, as they both do here.

Gloucester goes on to express doubts about the changes he hears in Edgar's voice, but Edgar's extended set-piece speech setting the scene distracts the attention of both Gloucester and the audience with a powerful evocation of place:

> How fearful
> And dizzy 'tis to cast one's eyes so low!
> The crows and choughs that wing the midway air
> Show scarce so gross as beetles. Halfway down
> Hangs one that gathers samphire, dreadful trade!
> Methinks he seems no bigger than his head.
> The fishermen that walk upon the beach
> Appear like mice, and yond tall anchoring bark
> Diminished to her cock, her cock a buoy
> Almost too small for sight. The murmuring surge
> That on th'unnumbered idle pebble chafes
> Cannot be heard so high. I'll look no more,
> Lest my brain turn and the deficient sight
> Toppled down headlong. (11–24)

Again, this is how the early modern stage characteristically indicated place. With only a few large props for particular settings, such as rocks and arbours, a location as huge and all-embracing as a cliff-edge would have to be evoked by words alone. So the audience is being given all the classic signals that this stage could muster to point to a cliff-setting, yet has also to process the fact that one character has doubts about whether or not it is; and because this character is blind, the audience has no way of knowing whether his hesitation is, as Edgar says it is, the result of his recent blinding and its jarring of his other senses, or something that should make them seriously doubt the indices of place that the script and the actors are otherwise providing.

It is not until Edgar leads his father to the very edge of the supposed cliff so that he can jump off it, that the audience is given clear reason to doubt the location:

> EDGAR Why I do trifle thus with his despair
> Is done to cure it. (33–4)

Thus, when Gloucester 'jumps' from a kneeling position on a totally flat stage, the audience almost knows that the flat stage in fact represents flat ground rather than an ascent. But if the scene had been set on rising ground towards a cliff edge, how would that have been represented? The disturbing answer is: exactly the same way. The only element that might have been absent was any expression of doubt; but a blind man's doubt could have been read, and perhaps was read, by contemporary audiences seeing the play for the first time as an evocation of Gloucester's fragile state of being, as part of the emotional aspect of the scene rather than as a signal to the audience to doubt the evidence of all the other stage signs. As this realisation dawns, the audience becomes aware that the preceding part of the scene has been being performed in a kind of bad faith, and this in turn heightens their awareness of the distance between the fictional world of the play and the bare boards of the theatre. They can scarcely avoid letting their minds run on the mechanics of theatre and the nature of the contract between actors and spectators: how does imaginary place come into being on a bare stage? How could they have been as mistaken as the deluded Gloucester? Where did the play betray them? And yet, at the same time as being a kind of joke played on the audience, this is also a shared joke *between* the play and the audience. In having the mechanics of the fiction offered up to them for contemplation, the audience are being treated as grown-ups, as thinking beings who know that theatre is play and can be expected to take pleasure in seeing how cleverly that play sets up its illusions. The play focuses the inappropriateness of yet another favoured modern binary that seeks to drive a wedge between illusion and anti-illusion; instead it encourages a viewing position that maintains a serious engagement with illusion in tension with a recognition of its constructedness.

The most striking difference between this moment and the moment when the audience is asked to think about the stage-boards in *Mankind* is that in *Mankind* the effect is primarily comic. The audience does its thinking about how theatre functions at the same time as it laughs at the particular cleverness of that tricksy moment. In *King Lear*, by contrast, the audience is given this moment of reflection on the tricksiness of theatre at a point of tragic climax. Just as Edgar trifles with Gloucester's despair, so Shakespeare trifles with the audience's emotional engagement with Gloucester's despair. But this 'trifling' is part of what makes early English drama distinctive, marking its difference from later, realist drama. And it is also what takes the best early drama beyond the risk of absurdity that some other aspects of its liking for excess point it towards. It is this very self-awareness about its own practices, and the invitation to the audience to become part of that awareness, that can defend it from the charge of being 'merely' spectacular, 'merely' grotesque, or 'merely' excessive in some other way. Where it is excessive, its excesses may be wonderful or ridiculous in and of themselves. But where it is also knowing and playful, its excesses cannot be dismissed as simple folly.

The spectacularity of theatre and its explicit pursuit of pleasure nevertheless become the grounds on which the authorities found their order of closure in 1642.

> And whereas public sports do not well agree with public calamities, nor public stage plays with the seasons of humiliation, this being an exercise of sad and pious solemnity, and the other being spectacles of pleasure, too commonly expressing lascivious mirth and levity: it is therefore thought fit and ordained by the Lords and Commons in this Parliament assembled, that while these sad causes and set-times of humiliation do continue, public stage plays shall cease and be foreborne.
>
> Ordinance of the Lords and Commons, 2 September 1642

The wording of this order, issued eleven days after the King had raised his standard at Nottingham, signalling the start of civil war, implies a temporary closure only. As 'spectacles of pleasure', plays are seen as an unseemly pastime in time of war. The later ordinances of 1647 and 1648, however, return to the discourse so familiar from the 1570s onwards, and widely quoted in chapter 3. Once again, plays are 'the occasion of many and sundry great vices and disorders', not to be tolerated in a Christian commonwealth; all players, 'notwithstanding any licence whatsoever from the King or any person or persons' are to be punished as rogues; playhouses are to be demolished; and even spectators are to be liable to penalties.[27] Plays, according to this discourse, are not merely potentially and occasionally excessive; they are in and of themselves in excess of a godly state.

Appendix 1

Select chronology of plays and other performances

This chronology has been put together using a number of sources, including *DTRB*; Andrew Gurr, *Shakespearean Stage*; Harbage, *Annals of English Drama*; Lancashire, *London Civic Theatre*; McGee/Meagher, 'Checklists'; Wells and Taylor, *Shakespeare Textual Companion*; and the *Revels History of Drama in English*, with occasional further modification.

Note that it is too select for readers to make any deductions about the number of plays by any given author, the point at which any author started writing, the concentration of plays in any given stretch of time, etc. It includes coronation pageants and a selection of masques and entertainments, but few other court ceremonials or tournaments and virtually no regular annual events (Accession Day tilts, Midsummer festivities, Lord Mayors' Shows) apart from some Christmas and Twelfth Night masques. Most court entertainments took place more frequently than indicated here.

965–75	*Regularis Concordia* (Winchester)
c. 1146–74	*The Play of Adam* (*Le Jeu d'Adam*)
c. 1300–25	*Interludium de Clerico et Puella* (first extant secular play)
c. 1350	*The Pride of Life*
c. 1375	Cornish Cycle
1376–1580	York Cycle
1377	Coronation of Richard II; first mention of Corpus Christi play at Beverley (now lost); first reference to the lost Paternoster play of York
1392	Richard II's entry into London
1397–1440	*The Castle of Perseverance*
1400	Entry into London of Emperor Manuel II
1403	Coronation of Queen Joan
1413	Coronation of Henry V
1415	Welcome into London of Henry V
1416	Entry into London of Emperor Sigismund
1421	Coronation of Queen Catherine of Valois

1421–1575	Chester Cycle
1424	Lydgate, *Mumming at Eltham*
*c.*1425	*Dux Moraud*
1427	Lydgate, *Mumming at Hertford*
c. 1427	Lydgate, *Mumming at London*
1429	Coronation of Henry VI
1429–30	Lydgate, *Mumming at Bishopswood*
1430	Lydgate, *Mumming for the Mercers, Mumming for the Goldsmiths*
c. 1430	Lydgate, *Mumming at Windsor*
1432	Welcome into London of Henry VI
1445	Coronation of Queen Margaret
1446	York Creed Play (first mentioned)
c. 1450–75	N-Town plays
c. 1450–?1576	Towneley Cycle (Wakefield)
c. 1454–99	Brome Play of *Abraham and Isaac*
c. 1460–70	*Wisdom*
1461	Coronation of Edward IV
1461–1520	Croxton *Play of the Sacrament*
1465	Coronation of Queen Elizabeth
1465–70	*Mankind*
1480–1520	*The Conversion of St Paul*
1480–1520	Digby *Mary Magdalene*
1483	Coronation of Richard III
1485	Coronation of Henry VII
1487	Entertainment of Henry VII in Coventry; Welcome into London of Henry VII; Coronation of Elizabeth of York
1489	Creation of Arthur Prince of Wales
c. 1490–1500	Medwall, *Nature*
1494	Creation of Henry Duke of York
1496	Entry into London of Pope's emissary
c. 1496–7	Medwall, *Fulgens and Lucres*
1498	Welcome into London of Prince Arthur; Reception of Prince Arthur at Coventry
1501	Entry into London of Katherine of Aragon
1502	Betrothal celebrations for Princess Margaret
c. 1507–8	*Mundus et Infans*
1509	Coronation of Henry VIII
1510	Entertainment for ambassadors of several countries
c. 1510–19?	*Everyman*

1511	Westminster Tournament and *Golden Arbour* disguising
1512	Digby *Killing of the Children*; *Le Fortresse Dangerous* disguising
1512–16	[Rastell prints *Fulgens and Lucres*, first printed English play]
c. 1513	*Youth*; *The Rich Mount*
c. 1513–21	John Heywood, *The Pardoner and the Friar*
c. 1514	*Hick Scorner*
1517	*The Garden of Esperance*
1517–20	Rastell, *The Nature of the Four Elements*; *The Pavilion in the Place Parlous*
1518	Entry into London of Cardinal Campeggio; Entertainment for French Ambassadors
1519	Entertainment for French hostages
c. 1519–20	Skelton, *Magnificence*
c. 1519–28	Rastell/John Heywood, *Gentleness and Nobility*; John Heywood, *The Play of the Weather*
1520	Field of the Cloth of Gold
c. 1520–2	John Heywood, *The Four Ps*
c. 1520–33	John Heywood, *Witty and Witless*
1522	*Chateau Vert* (entertainment for Imperial Ambassadors); Entry of Emperor Charles V into London
c. 1523–5?	?Rastell, *Calisto and Melebea*
1524	*Castle of Loyalty*
1525	Creation of Henry Fitzroy (illegitimate son of Henry VIII) Duke of Richmond
1527	Greenwich entertainments for French Ambassadors (including *Love and Riches*)
1528–33	John Heywood, *John John the Husband*, *A Play of Love*
1529–30	*Godly Queen Hester*
1533	Coronation of Anne Boleyn
1537	*Thersites*
c. 1538	Bale, *Three Laws*, *God's Promises*, *John Baptist's Preaching*, *The Temptation of our Lord*, *King John*
1540	Lindsay, *A Satire of the Three Estates*[1]; Entry into London of Anne of Cleves
c. 1544–7	Redford, *Wit and Science*
1546	Entry into London of Great Admiral of France; Entertainment of French Ambassadors
1547	Coronation of Edward VI
*c.*1547–8	Udall, *Ralph Roister Doister*

1547–53	*Nice Wanton*
1547–66	Lewis Wager, *The Life and Repentance of Mary Magdalen*
c. 1550?	Ingelend, *The Disobedient Child*
c. 1550–3	Wever, *Lusty Juventus*
c. 1551–4	?Stevenson, *Gammer Gurton's Needle*
1552–4	Lindsay, *A Satire of the Three Estates* [1]
1553	Udall, *Respublica;* Coronation of Mary I
1553–8	*Impatient Poverty*
1553–8	*Jack Juggler*
c. 1554–5	*The Interlude of Wealth and Health*
1554	Entry of Philip and Mary into London
1557	*A Sackful of News* (suppressed)
c. 1557–8	*Jacob and Esau*
c. 1558–69	Preston, *King Cambyses*
1559	Coronation of Elizabeth I
c. 1560	*Robin Hood and the Friar, Robin Hood and the Potter*
1562	*Gorboduc*
c. 1562	Garter, *The Most Virtuous and Godly Susanna*
c. 1563	*Tom Tyler and His Wife*
1564–5	Richard Edwards, *Damon and Pythias*
c. 1564–5	Phillip, *Patient Grissell; King Darius*
1565	Gray's Inn *Mask of Diana and Juno*
1566	Royal entry to Coventry
c. 1566	?William Wager, *The Trial of Treasure*
c. 1567	R. B., *Apius and Virginia*
1567?	Pickering, *Orestes*
c. 1567–8	Fulwell, *Like Will to Like; The Contention between Liberality* and Prodigality; *The Marriage of Wit and Science*
c. 1568	William Wager, *Enough is as Good as a Feast, The Longer Thou Livest the More Fool Thou Art*
c. 1570–3	*New Custom*
1571	*Challenge of Four Knights Errant*
c. 1571–5	Wapull, *The Tide Tarrieth No Man*
c. 1571–7	Merbury, *The Marriage between Wit and Wisdom*
1572	Entertainment of Elizabeth I and Duke of Montmorency
c. 1572–7	Lupton, *All for Money*
c. 1572–80	Woodes, *The Conflict of Conscience*
1574	Royal entry and entertainments at Bristol
1575	Royal entries to Shrewsbury and Worcester; entertainments for Elizabeth I at Kenilworth and Woodstock

1576	*Common Conditions*
1578	Whetstone, *Promos and Cassandra*; Norwich entertainments for Elizabeth I
1578–9	Sidney, *The Lady of May*
1579	*The Knight of the Burning Rock*
1579–84	?Munday, *Fedele and Fortunio*
1581	Sidney, *The Four Foster Children of Desire*
c. 1581	Wilson, *The Three Ladies of London*
1582	?Munday, *The Rare Triumphs of Love and Fortune*
1583–4	Lyly, *Campaspe*; *Sappho and Phao*; Peele, *The Arraignment of Paris*
1583–8	*The Famous Victories of Henry V*
1584	Westminster Tournament
1585	Lyly, *Gallathea*
1585–6	Marlowe and Nashe, *Dido, Queen of Carthage*
1585–9	Kyd, *The Spanish Tragedy*
1586–91	Lodge, *The Wounds of Civil War*
1587–8	Greene, *Alphonsus, King of Aragon*; Marlowe, *1* and *2 Tamburlaine*
1587–90	Lyly, *Mother Bombie*
1588	Lyly, *Endymion*; Elizabeth I's visit to Tilbury
1588?	Marlowe, *Dr Faustus*
1588–9	Peele, *The Battle of Alcazar*
1588–90	Wilson, *Three Lords and Three Ladies of London*
1588–94	*The True Tragedy of Richard III*
1588–98	*Mucedorus*
c. 1588–94	*The True Chronicle History of King Leir*
1589	Lyly, *Midas*
1589–90	Greene, *Friar Bacon and Friar Bungay*
c. 1589–90	Marlowe, *The Jew of Malta*
c. 1589–91	*Fair Em*
1590	Lee, Peele and ?Lyly, *Polyhymnia*
1590–91	Shakespeare, *The Taming of the Shrew*, *The Two Gentlemen of Verona*
1590–3	Peele, *Edward I*; *Jack Straw*
1590–4	Greene?, *John of Bordeaux*
1591	Greene, *Orlando Furioso*; Shakespeare, *2* and *3 Henry VI*; *The Troublesome Reign of King John*; Entertainments for Elizabeth I at Theobalds, Cowdray and Elvetham
1591–3	Marlowe, *Edward II*

1592	Shakespeare (? and Nashe), *1 Henry VI*; Shakespeare, *Titus Andronicus*; *A Knack to Know a Knave*; Entertainments for Elizabeth I at Bisham, Sudeley, Rycote, Ditchley and Ramsbury
1592–3	Munday et al., *Sir Thomas More*; Shakespeare, *Richard III*; *1* and *2 Tamar Cham*
1593	Marlowe, *The Massacre at Paris*
1594	Shakespeare, *The Comedy of Errors*; Entertainment for Elizabeth I at Theobalds
c. 1594?	Heywood, *The Four Prentices of London*
1594–5	Shakespeare, *Love's Labour's Lost*; *Gesta Grayorum*; Entertainment for Elizabeth I at Cecil House
c. 1594–1600	*A Larum for London*
1595	Shakespeare, *Richard II*; *Romeo and Juliet*; *Midsummer Night's Dream*; *Proteus and the Adamantine Rock*
1596	Bacon, *Love and Self-Love* (entertainment for Elizabeth I at Essex House); Chapman, *The Blind Beggar of Alexandria*; Shakespeare, *King John*; *Captain Thomas Stukeley*
1596–7	Shakespeare, *The Merchant of Venice*, *1 Henry IV*
1596–1600	*A Warning for Fair Women*
1597	Chapman, *An Humorous Day's Mirth*; Jonson and Nashe, *The Isle of Dogs*
1597–8	Jonson, *The Case Is Altered*; Shakespeare, *The Merry Wives of Windsor*, *2 Henry IV*
c. 1597–9	*Look About You*
1598	Chettle and Munday, *1* and *2 Robert Earl of Huntingdon*; Haughton, *Englishmen for my Money*; Jonson, *Every Man In His Humour*; Lyly? Entertainment for Elizabeth I at Mitcham; Rudyerd, *Le Prince d'Amour* (Middle Temple Christmas Revels); Shakespeare, *Much Ado About Nothing*
1598–9	Porter, *Two Angry Women of Abingdon*; Shakespeare, *Henry V*
1599	Dekker, *Old Fortunatus*, *The Shoemaker's Holiday*; Drayton, Hathway, Munday and Wilson, *1* and *2 Sir John Oldcastle*; Jonson, *Every Man Out of His Humour*; Shakespeare, *Julius Caesar*
1599–1600	Marston, *Antonio and Mellida*; Shakespeare, *As You Like It*
1599–1604	*The Merry Devil of Edmonton*

1600	Chettle, Day (and Haughton?), *The Blind Beggar of Bethnal Green*; Chettle, Dekker and Haughton, *Patient Grissil*; Marston, *Antonio's Revenge*; *The Wisdom of Doctor Dodypoll*
1600–1	Jonson, *Cynthia's Revels*; Shakespeare, *Hamlet, Twelfth Night*
1601	Chapman, *All Fools*; Dekker, *Satiromastix*; Dekker? *Blurt, Master Constable*; Jonson, *Poetaster*; Marston, *What You Will*
1602	Chapman, *Sir Giles Goosecap*; Chettle, *Hoffman*; Davies (and Lyly?), Entertainment for Elizabeth I at Harefield; Shakespeare, *Troilus and Cressida*; Entertainment for Elizabeth I at Chiswick
c. 1602–3	Chapman, *The Gentleman Usher*
1602–4	Marston, *The Malcontent*
1603	Jonson, *Sejanus*; Shakespeare, *Measure for Measure*; Heywood, *A Woman Killed with Kindness*; James VI and I's progress from Edinburgh to London; Entertainment of the Queen and Prince at Althorp
1603–4	Shakespeare, *Othello*; *The Fair Maid of Bristow*
1603–5	Marston, *The Dutch Courtesan*; *The London Prodigal*
1603–6	*Nobody and Somebody*
1604	Daniel, *Philotas, Vision of the Twelve Goddesses*; Dekker and Middleton, *1 The Honest Whore*; Dekker and Webster, *Westward Ho*; Jonson, *Entertainment at Highgate*; Middleton, *The Phoenix*; Rowley, *When You See Me, You Know Me*; *Gowry*; Coronation of James I
1604–5	Chapman, *Bussy D'Ambois, The Widow's Tears*; Dekker and Middleton, *2 The Honest Whore*; Heywood, *If You Know Not Me, You Know Nobody*; Shakespeare, *All's Well That Ends Well*
1604–7	Middleton, *A Mad World, My Masters*
1605	Chapman, *Monsieur D'Olive*; Chapman, Jonson and Marston, *Eastward Ho*; Dekker and Webster, *Northward Ho*; Jonson, *The Masque of Blackness*; Marston, *The Fawn*; Middleton, *A Trick to Catch the Old One*; Shakespeare and Middleton, *Timon of Athens*
1605–6	Marston, *Sophonisba*; Middleton/Tourneur, *The Revenger's Tragedy*; Shakespeare, *King Lear*; Wilkins, *The Miseries of Enforced Marriage*

1605–8	*The Yorkshire Tragedy*
1606	Barnes, *The Devil's Charter*; Beaumont, *The Woman Hater*; Day, *The Isle of Gulls*; Jonson, *Barriers at a Marriage, Hymenaei, Volpone*; Jonson, Roberts and Marston, *Entertainment of Christian IV*; Middleton, *Michaelmas Term*, *The Puritan*; Shakespeare, *Macbeth, Antony and Cleopatra*; Sharpham, *The Fleer*, *Challenge of the Four Knights Errant of the Fortunate Island*
c. 1606–7	Dekker, *The Whore of Babylon*
1606–8	Heywood, *The Rape of Lucrece*
c. 1606–8	Armin, *The Two Maids of Moreclacke*
1607	Beaumont, *The Knight of the Burning Pestle*; Campion, *Lord Hay's Masque*; Day, Rowley and Wilkins, *The Travels of Three English Brothers*; Jonson, *Entertainment at Theobalds, Entertainment at Merchant Taylors*; Marston, *Entertainment at Ashby*; Middleton, *Your Five Gallants*; Shakespeare and Wilkins, *Pericles*; Sharpham, *Cupid's Whirligig*
1607–8	Chapman, *The Conspiracy and Tragedy of Biron*; Marston and Barkstead, *The Insatiate Countess*; Sansbury et al., *The Christmas Prince* (St John's College, Oxford Christmas Revels)
c. 1607–8	Beaumont and Fletcher, *Cupid's Revenge*
1607–11	Tourneur, *The Atheist's Tragedy*
1608	Jonson, *The Masque of Beauty, Lord Haddington's Masque, Entertainment at Salisbury House*; Shakespeare, *Coriolanus*
1608–9	Beaumont and Fletcher, *The Coxcomb*; Fletcher, *The Faithful Shepherdess*
1608–?1610	Barry, *Ram-Alley*
1609	Beaumont and Fletcher, *Philaster*; Jonson, *Entertainment at Britain's Burse, Epicoene, The Masque of Queens*; Shakespeare, *The Winter's Tale*; *St Christopher*
1609?	Shakespeare, *Cymbeline*
1609–10	Field, *A Woman is a Weathercock*
1609–11	Heywood, *The Golden Age*
1609–12	Fletcher, *The Captain*
1610	Daniel, *Tethys' Festival*; Jonson, *The Alchemist, Prince Henry's Barriers*; Munday and Price, *London's Love to Prince Henry*; Shakespeare, *The Tempest*; Royal entertainment at Chester
1610–11	Heywood, *The Brazen Age*

c. 1610–11	Beaumont and Fletcher, *The Maid's Tragedy*; Chapman, *The Revenge of Bussy*; Field, *Amends for Ladies*
1610–12	Heywood, *The Silver Age*
1610–14	Fletcher, *Valentinian*
1611	Beaumont and Fletcher, *A King and No King*; Cooke, *Greene's Tu Quoque*; Dekker and Middleton, *The Roaring Girl*; Fletcher, *The Woman's Prize*; Jonson, *Catiline*, *Oberon*, *Love Freed from Ignorance and Folly*; Middleton? *The Second Maiden's Tragedy*
1611–12	Dekker, *If It Be Not Good, the Devil Is In It*
1611–14	Fletcher, *Bonduca*
1612	Jonson, *Love Restored*; *The Prince's Entertainment of the King at Woodstock*
1612–13	Heywood, *The Iron Age*; Webster, *The White Devil*
1612–14	Webster, *The Duchess of Malfi*
1613	Campion, *Entertainment at Caversham*; Chapman, *The Memorable Masque*; Middleton, *A Chaste Maid in Cheapside*, *New River Entertainment*; Shakespeare and Fletcher, *All Is True* (*Henry VIII*); Tailor, *The Hog Hath Lost His Pearl*; Marriage of Princess Elizabeth and Elector Palatine (royal entry, fireworks, masques including Campion, *The Lords' Masque*, and Inns of Court masques); Royal entries into Bristol and Wells
1613–14	Shakespeare and Fletcher, *Two Noble Kinsmen*
c. 1613–16	Middleton, *The Witch*
1614	Jonson, *Bartholomew Fair*; Middleton, *The Masque of Cupid*
1615	Jonson, *Mercury Vindicated from the Alchemists at Court*
c. 1615–17	Middleton and Rowley, *A Fair Quarrel*
1615–?20	Middleton, *Hengist*
c. 1615–22	Fletcher (and Massinger?), *The Beggar's Bush*
1616	Jonson, *The Devil Is an Ass*, *The Golden Age Restored*; Middleton, *Civitatis Amor* (royal entry and entertainments)
c. 1616	Middleton, *The Widow*
1616–*c.* 18	Fletcher (and Massinger and Field?), *The Queen of Corinth*
1617	Campion (?) et al., *Entertainment at Brougham Castle*; Fletcher, *The Bloody Brother*; Jonson, *The Vision of Delight*, *Lovers Made Men*; White, *Cupid's Banishment*; *Masque for the Queen at Somerset House*; Progress of James I to Edinburgh
1617–19	*Swetnam the Woman Hater*

1617–21	Webster, *The Devil's Law-Case*
1618	Jonson, *Pleasure Reconciled to Virtue, For the Honour of Wales*; Jonson (?) and Brome (?), *Coleoverton Masque*
1619	Fletcher and Massinger, *Sir John Van Olden Barnavelt*; Middleton, *Masque of Heroes*
1619–20	I. C., *The Two Merry Milkmaids*; Fletcher and Massinger, *The Custom of the Country*
c. 1619–20(?)	Middleton and Rowley, *All's Lost by Lust*
1619–21	Fletcher, *The Island Princess*
c. 1619–22	Markham and Sampson, *Herod and Antipater*
1619–23	*The Two Noble Ladies*
1620	Dekker and Massinger, *The Virgin Martyr*; Jonson, *News from the New World*; Middleton, *Entertainment at the Conduit Head, Prince Charles' First Tilt, The 'Running' Masque*
1620–7	Middleton, *Women Beware Women*
1621	Dekker, Ford and Rowley, *The Witch of Edmonton*; Jonson, *The Gypsies Metamorphosed*
1621–2	Massinger, *The Maid of Honour*; Entertainment of the French Ambassadors; *The Prince's Masque*
1621–3	Massinger, *The Duke of Milan*
1622	Fletcher, *The Spanish Curate*; Jonson, *Masque of Augurs*; Middleton and Rowley, *The Changeling*
1623	Dekker and Ford, *The Spanish Gypsy*; Jonson, *Time Vindicated*; Massinger, *The Bondman*; Maynard, *Masque at York House*
1624	Drue, *The Duchess of Suffolk*; Heywood, *The Captives*; Middleton, A *Game at Chess*
1625	Massinger, A *New Way to Pay Old Debts*
1626	De Bueil, *Artenice*; Jonson, *The Staple of News*; Massinger, *The Roman Actor*; Shirley, *The Brothers, The Maid's Revenge, The Wedding*; Entertainments for French Ambassador
1627	Davenant, *The Cruel Brother*; Massinger, *The Great Duke of Florence*; Buckingham's entertainment for King and Queen
c. 1627	Heywood, *The English Traveller*
1628	Ford, *The Lover's Melancholy*
1629	Brome, *The Northern Lass*; Carlell, *The Deserving Favourite*; Jonson, *The New Inn*; Shirley, *The Grateful Servant*
c. 1630	Ford, *The Broken Heart*

1630?	Ford, *'Tis Pity She's a Whore*
c. 1630–1	Heywood, *The Fair Maid of the West*
1631	Jonson, *Chloridia, Love's Triumph through Callipolis*; Marmion, *Holland's Leaguer*; Massinger, *Believe as You List*; Shirley, *The Humorous Courtier, The Traitor*; Wilson, *The Swisser*
1632	Brome, *the Weeding of Covent Garden*; Ford, *Perkin Warbeck*; Jonson, *The Magnetic Lady*; Massinger, *The City Madam*; Shirley, *The Ball, Hyde Park*; Townshend, *Albion's Triumph*; *Tempe Restored*; Queen's Country Village Masque
1632–3	Ford, *Love's Sacrifice*
1632–8	Glapthorne, *Argalus and Parthenia*
1633	Jonson, *A Tale of a Tub*, Entertainment for Charles I at Welbeck; Montagu, *The Shepherds' Paradise*; Nabbes, *Covent Garden*; Shirley, *The Bird in a Cage, The Gamester*; Mountfort, *The Launching of the Mary, or the Seaman's Honest Wife*; Entry of Charles I into Edinburgh
1634	Brome and Heywood, *The Late Lancashire Witches*; Carew, *Coelum Britannicum*; Davenant, *The Wits*; Jonson, *Love's Welcome at Bolsover*; Milton, *Masque Presented at Ludlow Castle (Comus)*; Salusbury, Entertainment at Chirke Castle, Denbighshire; Shirley, *The Triumph of Peace*
1634–9	Glapthorne, *Albertus Wallenstein*
1635	Brome, *The Sparagus Garden*; Davenant, *The Platonic Lovers, The Temple of Love*; Glapthorne, *The Lady Mother*; Shirley, *The Lady of Pleasure*; Townshend, *Florimène Anti-Masques*
c. 1635	Cavendish, *The Masque of Ladies at Welbeck Abbey*
1636	Two *Skipton Castle Masques*; *Lady Hatton's Masque*; Entertainment of King and Queen at Richmond
1636–8	Brome, *The Antipodes*
1637	Heywood, *Masque at Hunsdon*; Suckling, *Aglaura*
c. 1637–8	Nabbes, *The Spring's Glory*
1637–41	Suckling, *The Goblins*
1638	Carlell, *1* and *2 The Passionate Lovers*; Davenant, *Britannia Triumphans, Luminalia*; Massinger, *The King and the Subject*; Nabbes, *The Bride*
1639	Drue? *The Bloody Banquet*; Entry into York of Charles I (no pageants)
1639–40	Brome, *The Court Beggar*

c. 1639–*c.* 1640	Cavendish and Shirley, *The Country Captain*
1640	Cokain, *A Masque at Bretbie*; Davenant, *Salmacida Spolia*; Sadler, *Masquerade du Ciel*; Shirley, *The Impostor*; Entry into York of Charles I (no pageants)
1641	Cavendish (and Shirley?), *The Variety*; Killigrew, *The Parson's Wedding*; Salusbury, *A Masque at Knowsley, Anti-Masque of Gypsies*; Shirley, *The Brothers, The Cardinal*; Entry into London of Charles I (no pageants)
c. 1641	Salusbury, *A Citizen and his Wife*
1641–2	Brome, *A Jovial Crew*
1642	Shirley, *The Sisters*

Note

1. See chapter 4, n. 44 above.

Chronology of events

Note that this table becomes more detailed for later years. This is partly a matter of the survival of records and partly a matter of the proliferation of records produced by the growth and professionalisation of theatre. Year entries are organised by subject rather than chronology, with theatre-related events listed last.

1337–1453	Hundred Years' War with France.
1377	Death of Edward III. Accession of Richard II (under protectorate of John of Gaunt). First poll tax.
1378–1417	Papal Schism.
1378	Second poll tax.
1379	Third poll tax.
1381	English Rising (Peasants' Revolt)
1382	Blackfriars Council condemns ten of Wyclif's propositions as heretical. Earthquake.
	Richard II marries Anne of Bohemia.
1384	Death of Wyclif.
c. 1385	Wyclifite translation of the Bible.
	Campaign in Scotland.
1386	Wonderful Parliament impeaches Chancellor.
1387	Lords Appellant restrict authority of Richard II.
1388	Merciless Parliament; execution of King's supporters remaining in England.
	Scots defeat English at Otterburn.
1389	Richard reasserts personal authority.
1393	Revolt in Cheshire.
1394–5	Irish campaign.
1396	Richard II marries Isabella of France.
	28-year truce with France.

1399	Death of John of Gaunt.
	Richard's second Irish campaign. Deposition of Richard II; accession of Henry IV.
1400	Murder of Richard II.
	Scottish campaign.
	Glendower's revolt in Wales.
1401	Statute *De Heretico Comburendo* (providing for burning of Lollard heretics).
	Execution of William Sawtry for heresy.
1402	Scots defeated at Homildon Hill.
1403	Defeat of Percy rebellion at Shrewsbury.
1405	Northern revolt; execution of Archbishop Scrope.
1408	Earl of Northumberland defeated at Bramham Moor.
1410	Civil war in France.
	Execution of John Badby for heresy.
1411	England sends aid to Burgundy.
1413	Death of Henry IV; accession of Henry V.
	Trial of Sir John Oldcastle for heresy.
1414	Oldcastle Revolt.
1414–18	Council of Constance (to resolve papal schism and suppress heresy).
1415	England defeats France at Agincourt.
1417	Capture and execution of Oldcastle.
1419	Fall of Rouen.
1420	Treaty of Troyes: Henry V recognised as heir to France.
1421	Birth of Prince Henry (future Henry VI).
1422	Death of Henry V; accession of Henry VI (under protectorate of Duke of Gloucester).
1423	Triple alliance of England, Burgundy and Brittany.
1428	Arrest of Lollards in Kent.
1428–31	Heresy proceedings in Norfolk.
1429	Joan of Arc appears; siege of Orleans raised.
	Charles VII crowned King of France.
1430	Capture of Joan of Arc.
1431	Execution of Joan of Arc.
	Henry VI of England crowned King of France.
	Rising at Abingdon, Berks (possibly Lollard).
1438–9	Bad harvest and food shortages.
1444	Truce of Tours; marriage of Henry VI to Margaret of Anjou.
1448	English surrender Maine to France.

1449	Rouen falls to French.
1450	Impeachment of Duke of Suffolk – later exiled and killed.
	Jack Cade's rebellion.
	Loss of Normandy.
1451	Fall of Bordeaux; loss of Gascony.
1453	Final expulsion of England from France.
	Henry VI's first attack of insanity.
	Birth of Edward, Prince of Wales.
	Disorder in Northern England between Nevilles and Percies.
	Fall of Constantinople.
1454	Duke of York appointed Protector (subsequently relieved and reappointed depending on Henry VI's condition).
1455–85	Wars of the Roses
1455	Conflict in Devon between Courtenays and Bonvilles.
1461	Battles at Mortimer's Cross, St Alban's and Towton; defeat and escape to Scotland of Henry VI; accession of Edward IV (Yorkist).
1462–4	Heresy proceedings in Chilterns.
1463	Statute of apparel.
1464	Edward IV marries Elizabeth Woodville. Defeat of last Lancastrian force at Hexham.
1465	Capture and imprisonment of Henry VI.
1469	Rebellion in northern England.
	Edward IV defeated at Edgecote and captured, but later released.
1470	Restoration of Henry VI; escape of Edward IV.
	Lincolnshire rebellion.
1471	Restoration of Edward IV; murder of Henry VI.
	Death of Prince of Wales. Rising in Kent.
1475	Edward IV's expedition to France; Treaty of Picquigny.
1476	Caxton's printing press established at Westminster.
1477	Duke of Burgundy dies, giving rise to struggles over his lands.
1478	Execution of Duke of Clarence.
1482	War with Scotland.
	Statute of apparel.
1483	Death of Edward IV; accession of Edward V under protectorate of Richard III. Richard usurps the crown and confines the young princes, Edward V and Richard, Duke of York, in the Tower.
	Revolt and execution of Duke of Buckingham.

1485	Henry Tudor invades England; battle of Bosworth; death of Richard III; accession of Henry VII.
1486	Henry VII marries Elizabeth of York, daughter of Edward IV, to secure the crown and succession. Birth of Prince Arthur.
1487	Lambert Simnel is crowned Edward VI in Dublin. His forces invade England. Battle of Stoke the last battle of the Wars of the Roses; Simnel defeated and captured.
1489	Tax revolt in Yorkshire.
	Treaty of Medina del Campo with Spanish kingdoms.
1491	Birth of Prince Henry (later Henry VIII).
	Perkin Warbeck in Ireland claims to be Richard, Duke of York, the younger of the two princes imprisoned in the Tower by Richard III.
1492	Siege of Boulogne; Treaty of Étaples with France.
1493	Burgundy and Habsburgs support Warbeck.
1494	Henry VII makes Sir Edward Poynings Deputy of Ireland in place of the Earl of Kildare, who had offered assistance to Simnel and Warbeck.
1495	French invade Italy; start of Italian wars.
	Warbeck's invasion of England fails; he flees to Scotland, where he is accepted as King Richard IV of England and marries the cousin of the King of Scotland.
	Act regulating wages, fixing maximum rates of pay.
1496	Scottish attack on Northern England, in support of Warbeck.
	Kildare reinstated as Deputy of Ireland.
	John Cabot's voyage to the Americas.
1497	Cornish Rebellion in protest against taxes for war on Scotland.
	Warbeck captured. Cabot returns, having discovered Nova Scotia.
1498	Warbeck escapes, is recaptured and imprisoned.
1499	Execution of Perkin Warbeck and Edward, Earl of Warwick (last heir to York line).
	Peace treaty with Scotland.
1501	Marriage of Prince Arthur, heir to English throne, and Katherine of Aragon.
	Earl of Suffolk's conspiracy.
1502	Treaty of Perpetual Peace between Scotland and England; marriage between James IV of Scotland and Princess

Margaret, daughter of Henry VII, agreed.

Death of Prince Arthur.

1503   Betrothal of Prince Henry (future Henry VIII) to Katherine,
        Prince Arthur's widow. James IV marries Princess Margaret.

1504   Statute of Liveries reinforces existing legislation against
        keeping retainers.

1509   Death of Henry VII; accession of Henry VIII. Henry VIII
        marries Katherine of Aragon, Arthur's widow.

1510   Statute of apparel.

1511   Birth and death of Prince Henry.

        England joins Holy League, allying with Spain, the Pope and
        the Venetian Republic against France.

        Heresy trials in Kent and Chilterns.

1511–12 Heresy trials in Coventry.

1512   James IV refuses to join Holy League and renews 1492
        alliance with France.

        Henry VIII declares war on France. Statute consolidates
        Henry VII's attacks on clerical privileges.

1513   English victories in France (Thérouanne, Tournai) and
        Scotland (Flodden). Death of James IV at Flodden; accession
        of infant James V under regency of Margaret, sister of Henry
        VIII.

1514   Peace treaty between England and France; betrothal and
        marriage of Henry VIII's younger sister, Mary, to Louis XII
        of France.

        Thomas Wolsey becomes Archbishop of York and Henry's
        chief minister.

1514–15 Richard Hunne case (struggle between lay and clerical
        rights). Hunne imprisoned, then found dead in his cell.

1515   Death of Louis XII and secret marriage of Princess Mary to
        Charles Brandon, Duke of Suffolk. Deteriorating relations
        with France again following refusal of Francis I to repay
        Mary's dowry.

        Act fixing hours and wages of laboureres and artisans. Acts
        ordering reconversion of pasture to arable land and
        rebuilding of decayed houses. Statutes of apparel.

1516   Birth of Princess Mary (later Mary I).

1517   Luther publishes his '95 theses' at Wittenberg, calling for
        debate within the church. Evil May Day (riot against
        foreigners in London).

	Pope proclaims a five-year universal peace amongst Christian countries to enable them to unite in a crusade to win back Constantinople from the Turks.
	First circumnavigation of the globe.
1518	Treaty of London: peace between England, France, Empire, Pope, Spain, Burgundy and Netherlands; also separate peace between England and France.
1520	English army goes to Ireland to suppress rebellion.
	Meeting between Henry VIII and Francis I of France at Field of Cloth of Gold. Meeting between Henry VIII and Emperor Charles V at Calais.
	Cambridge group sympathetic to church reform begins regular meetings at White Horse tavern.
1521	Diet of Worms condemns Luther for heresy.
	Wolsey takes action against import of Lutheran books; books burned in London.
	Heretics persecuted and burned in London.
	Henry VIII publishes *The Assertion of the Seven Sacraments*, a condemnation of Luther; Pope confers title of *Fidei Defensor* (Defender of the Faith) on him.
	Secret Treaty of Bruges arranges alliance between England and Empire in event of war with France.
	Duke of Buckingham executed for treason.
1521–2	Heresy trials in Chilterns.
1522	Emperor Charles V visits England; Treaty of Windsor between England and Empire.
	England declares war on France; a truce quickly follows.
	Anglo-Scottish truce.
1524	Renewal of war with France.
	William Tyndale flees to Germany.
1525	Resistance to the 'Amicable Grant', a forced loan to raise money for the war with France.
	Wolsey suppresses many religious houses.
	Emperor Charles V defeats and captures Francis I at Pavia.
	Tyndale's English Bible is printed in Cologne.
1526	Treaty of Madrid; Francis I liberated.
	England helps to negotiate League of Cognac with France, Milan, Florence, Venice and the Pope against the Empire.
	Copies of Tyndale's Bible seized and burned in London.
	Debasement of coinage.

1527	Treaty of Westminster: peace between England and France. Emperor invades Rome and takes Pope captive; Pope later escapes. Henry VIII begins proceedings for divorce. Lollards persecuted in Essex and Buckinghamshire.
1528	England declares war against the Empire.
1529	Reformation Parliament opens. Cardinal Wolsey dismissed from position as Lord Chancellor; Thomas More replaces him. Emperor defeats France, takes control of Italy and is crowned Holy Roman Emperor by the Pope. Peace of Cambrai leaves England diplomatically isolated.
1530	Death of Wolsey.
1531	Thomas Bilney, Lutheran preacher, burned for heresy in Norwich. Act concerning the Punishment of Beggars and Vagabonds (beginnings of state poor relief).
1532	Commons 'Supplication of the Ordinaries' against legislative power of the clergy; leads to 'Submission of the Clergy' ending independent legislative power of church in England. Thomas Cromwell becomes King's chief minister.
1533	Act in Restraint of Appeals to Rome severs English ecclesiastical courts from Rome. Thomas Cranmer becomes Archbishop of Canterbury and pronounces Aragon marriage invalid. Henry VIII marries Anne Boleyn; birth of Princess Elizabeth (later Elizabeth I). Henry excommunicated. Statute of apparel.
1534	Acts of Succession and Supremacy mark formal breach with Rome and establishment of King as head of the Church of England. Treason Act (now defined to include verbal acts of treason). Elizabeth Barton ('Holy Maid of Kent') and others hanged for speaking against the divorce. Anglo-Scottish peace treaty.
1535	Thomas Cromwell appointed Vice-gerent in spiritual matters to the King, as supreme head of the English church. Execution of Sir Thomas More and Bishop John Fisher.
1536–9	Dissolution of the monasteries.

1536	Execution of Anne Boleyn; Henry VIII marries Jane Seymour.
	Ten Articles issued (pro-Lutheran); Cromwell issues the first Royal Injunctions to the clergy.
	Second Succession Act.
	Beggars Act (first statute accepting state responsibility for poor relief).
	Execution of William Tyndale.
	Lincolnshire rising;
	Pilgrimage of Grace (rebellion against religious Reform).
	Act of Union with Wales.
1537	Birth of Prince Edward; death of Jane Seymour.
	Robert Aske, leader of the Pilgrimage of Grace, executed for treason.
	First licensed English Bible (the 'Mathew Bible' based on Tyndale).
1538	Henry VIII excommunicated.
	Royal Injunctions to clergy include provision for an English bible in all parish churches.
1539	Act of Six Articles restores a more conservative doctrine.
	Fears of invasion by French, Emperor and Scots.
	Coverdale's 'Great Bible' published.
1540	Henry VIII marries Anne of Cleves; marriage is annulled; he marries Catherine Howard.
	English Bible ordered in every parish church. Execution of Thomas Cromwell. Robert Barnes and two other radical Reformers burned for heresy.
	Three Catholics executed for treason.
1541	Catherine Howard arrested, her lovers executed.
	Catholic conspiracy to incite rebellion in the North fails; Countess of Salisbury executed.
	Abolition of all shrines ordered.
1542	Catherine Howard executed.
	War with Scotland: English defeat Scots at Solway Moss.
	James V of Scotland dies; accession of infant Mary.
	Marriage negotiated between Prince Edward and infant Queen Mary of Scotland.
	Beginning of the 'great debasement' of the coinage.
1543	Henry VIII marries Catherine Parr.
	Statute extending English law to Wales.

Anglo-Scottish Treaty of Greenwich signed, agreeing
marriage between Prince Edward and Queen Mary, but
rejected by Scottish parliament.
Act for the Advancement of True Religion forbids lower
social ranks and women below the rank of gentlewomen
from reading the Bible; forbids plays to contravene centrally
promoted religious doctrine.

1544   War with France; England captures Boulogne.
English liturgy introduced into churches.

1545   Scots defeat English at Ancrum Moor.
First permanent appointment to post of Master of the Revels

1545–63   Council of Trent meets to define Roman Catholic doctrine
and look at church reform.

1546   Treaty of Camp: peace between England and France.
Fall of the Howards: Duke of Norfolk and Earl of Surrey
arrested and imprisoned in Tower.
Anne Askew burned for heresy.

1547   Death of Henry VIII; accession of Edward VI under
protectorate of Edward Seymour, Earl of Hertford (later
Somerset).
Execution of Earl of Surrey.
Treasons Act repeals much repressive legislation.
Repeal of 1543 Act for the Advancement of True Religion.
Act for Dissolution of Chantries.
Corpus Christi procession suppressed.

1547–9   Western rebellion.

1548   Hall's Chronicle published.

1549   Act of Uniformity imposes First Protestant Prayer Book;
forbids interludes containing matter 'depraving and
despising' the new Book of Common Prayer. Western
Rebellion against Prayer Book and religious reform. Kett's
rebellion (following the assembly of a large crowd at
Wymondham, Norfolk, to see a play); proclamation warning
against performances in English for a period of three months.
Protectorate dissolved: Somerset imprisoned in the Tower.
Parliament passes a poll tax on sheep to discourage
enclosure. Bad harvest.

1550   John Dudley, Earl of Warwick (later Northumberland)
becomes chief power in the state as Lord President of the
Council; Somerset released.

	Ango-French Treaty of Boulogne; English withdraw from Boulogne.
	Injunctions order the removal of altars and screens from parish churches.
	Burning of Joan Bocher and other Anabaptists in London.
	Further bad harvest and further local risings.
1551	Anglo-Scottish peace treaty.
	Somerset rearrested; tried for treason.
	Further bad harvest; further local risings; widespread epidemic of 'sweating sickness'.
	Proclamation enforcing statutes against players and forbidding performances in English without special licence.
1552	Somerset executed.
	Second Act of Uniformity.
	Second Book of Common Prayer.
1553	Death of Edward VI; accession of Catholic Mary I. (Lady Jane Grey, married to Northumberland's son, briefly proclaimed Queen). Northumberland executed.
	Forty-Two Articles of religion. Repeal of Edwardian religious laws: return to Catholicism; Mary relinquishes title of Supreme Head of the English church. Proclamation forbidding books and interludes on matters of religious doctrine.
1553–4	Sir Thomas Wyatt's rebellion against Mary I.
1554	Wyatt executed; Lady Jane Grey executed.
	Mary marries Philip II of Spain.
	Protestants begin to flee abroad.
1555	Act restoring papal supremacy; heresy laws revived.
	Beginning of Marian persecutions: John Rogers, John Hooper, Hugh Latimer and Nicholas Ridley burned for heresy.
	Peace of Augsburg allows Protestant domination of most of Germany.
	Statute of apparel.
1556	Charles V abdicates; Philip II becomes King of Spain and Netherlands and Charles' brother, Ferdinand, becomes Emperor.
	Dudley conspiracy aimed at deposing Mary for Elizabeth.
	Thomas Cranmer and many others burned for heresy.

Refoundation of religious houses begins.

Worst harvest of the century.

1557 War with France: English-Spanish victory over French at St Quentin.

Stafford conspiracy.

Tottel's *Miscellany* published.

1558 Death of Mary I; accession of Elizabeth I.

Surrender of Calais to France.

Proclamation outlining fundamentals of Elizabethan censorship.

1559 Acts of Uniformity and Supremacy (Elizabethan Church Settlement); papal authority renounced in England and Elizabeth becomes Supreme Governor of the Church of England; repeated 1549 order against anything 'depraving and despising' the Book of Common Prayer.

Peace with France: Treaty of Câteau-Cambrésis.

Death of Henry II of France; accession of Francis II, husband of Mary Queen of Scots.

Protestant revolt in Scotland against Catholic Queen Regent.

Proclamation ordering licensing of all performances.

1560 Treaty of Berwick: English send military aid to Scots rebels.

Treaty of Edinburgh: England and France withdraw from Scotland.

Presbyterianism established in Scotland: papal jurisdiction and the mass abolished. Geneva Bible printed.

1561 Rebellion in Ireland.

1562 French wars of religion begin; English troops sent to help Protestants but withdrawn the following year.

Shane O'Neill campaigning to take Ulster.

John Hawkins' first voyage to West Indies.

Statute of apparel.

1563 Thirty-nine Articles established by the Church of England.

Statute of Artificers, regulating and fixing maximum wages.

Differences between Queen and parliament over the succession.

English campaign against O'Neill in Ireland; O'Neill submits.

Publication of John Foxe's *Acts and Monuments* (*Book of Martyrs*).

1564	Earl of Sussex recalled from Ireland. Irish riots against English plantation in Ireland.
	Discussions of possible marriage between Queen and Robert Dudley, Earl of Leicester.
	Clergymen refusing to wear vestments (surplices) are deprived.
1566	Vestiarian controversy (over wearing of surplices) continues. Differences between Queen and parliament over succession continue; parliament asks Queen to marry.
	Birth of James (future James VI and I) to Mary Queen of Scots.
1567	Rebellion in Ireland; O'Neill defeated and murdered.
	Murder of Henry Stuart, Lord Darnley, husband of Mary Queen of Scots; Mary marries Earl of Bothwell; is imprisoned for complicity in Darnley's murder; abdicates in favour of her one-year-old son, James VI (later James I of England).
	Red Lion in Stepney built (first purpose-built playhouse).
1567–8	First revolt of the Netherlands against Spanish rule suppressed by Spanish troops under Duke of Alva.
1568	English College founded at Douai for the training of Jesuits.
	Mary Queen of Scots escapes, is defeated at Langside, flees to England.
	Bishops' Bible printed.
1569	Thomas Howard, Duke of Norfolk arrested for involvement in plot to marry Mary Queen of Scots.
	Northern Rebellion in support of Mary Queen of Scots, led by Catholic earls (of Northumberland and Westmorland), with papal support.
1570	Elizabeth excommunicated by Pope Pius V.
	Elizabeth considering marriage with either Archduke Charles or Henry, Duke of Anjou (later Henry III).
	Duke of Norfolk released into house arrest.
1571	Ridolfi plot with Spanish against the life of Queen Elizabeth; Norfolk again arrested for his involvement and imprisoned in Tower.
	Treasons Act; Act against Papal Bulls; Act against Fugitives over the Sea.
	More difficulties with parliament over succession. Battle of Lepanto (victory against the Turks).

Foxe's *Book of Martyrs* ordered to be made available in every cathedral and collegiate church in England.

1572   St Bartholomew massacre of French Protestant leaders.

Duke of Norfolk executed for his part in the Ridolfi plot.

Act against unlawful retaining.

Act against Vagabonds. Letter from Leicester's Men to Leicester asking to be retained but not asking for 'any further stipend or benefit . . . but our liveries, as we have had'.

Pater Noster play the last production of religious drama in York.

1574   Rebellion against Earl of Essex in Ireland.

Convention of Bristol between England and Spain.

Statute of apparel.

Patent issued to Leicester's Men, constraining their plays to be allowed by the Master of the Revels.

Act of Common Council of London forbidding performance of plays 'within the house, yard or any other place within the liberties of this city'.

1575   Poor law.

Two Dutch Anabaptists burned.

Queen's progress to Kenilworth.

1576   Spanish sack Antwerp and Netherlands unite against Spain (Treaty of Ghent).

Earl of Essex made Marshal of Ireland; later poisoned by supporters of Brian O'Neill.

Priests from Douai arrive in England.

Peter Wentworth, Puritan MP, attacks clerical abuses and claims that there should be freedom of speech in parliament; imprisoned in the Tower. Queen orders 'prophesyings' (Puritan preaching exercises) suppressed; Archbishop Grindal refuses.

The Theatre built. Newington Butts opens around this time. Children of Chapel Royal begin playing at 1st Blackfriars theatre.

1577   Grindal suspended.

Curtain Theatre opens. Strange's Men become active.

Northbrooke's *Treatise Against Dicing, Dancing, Plays and Interludes* published.

1577–80   Sir Francis Drake sails round the world.

1578	Elizabeth reconsiders proposals for marriage to the Duke of Alençon.
	Douai priest and Catholic layman hanged.
	Elizabeth's progress to Norwich.
1579	Protestant northern provinces of Netherlands unite (Union of Utrecht). England's military involvement with Dutch rebellion against Spain begins.
	Elizabeth's plans to marry the French Roman Catholic Duke of Alençon provoke strong responses: Philip Sidney banished from court for his letter advising the Queen against the marriage and John Stubbes has his right hand cut off for publishing a pamphlet against it.
	English College at Rome founded by Jesuits.
	Edmund Tilney appointed Master of the Revels; full document giving him new powers to license and suppress plays at his discretion and to imprison players or playwrights who disregarded his authority.
	Gosson's *School of Abuse* and *Apology of the School of Abuse* published. Lodge's *Reply to Stephen Gosson's School of Abuse, in Defence of Poetry, Music and Stage Plays* published.
1579–83	Desmond rebellion in Ireland.
1580	Jesuit missionaries, Edmund Campion and Robert Parsons, land in England.
	First treaty between England and Ottoman Empire.
	Privy Council investigating breaches of the peace at the Theatre.
	Final performance of the Coventry Corpus Christi cycle.
	Munday's *Second and Third Blast of Retreat from Plays and Theatres* published.
1581	Strengthening of laws against Catholic recusancy (refusal to attend services of the Church of England) and increase of fines to £20 per month.
	Act 'against seditious words and rumours uttered against the Queen's most excellent Majesty': circulation of any slander or incitement punishable by death.
	Campion arrested for treason and executed.
	Alençon arrives in London to finalise marriage plans with Elizabeth.
	Full powers of censorship (performance only) invested in the Master of the Revels.

1582	Alençon leaves London after failure of marriage negotiations. Protestant earls capture James VI.
	Gosson's *Plays Confuted in Five Actions* published.
1583	Throckmorton plot to overthrow Elizabeth, implicating Jesuits and Spanish.
	Assassination of William of Orange at Delft.
	Giordano Bruno visits England.
	Archbishop Whitgift begins to press Puritan ministers to subscribe to the Prayer Book.
	Collapse of Paris Garden; Sunday playing forbidden from this date (though continued in practice for some time).
	Queen's Men founded.
	Stubbes' *Anatomy of Abuses* published.
1583–5	Fluidity around office of Lord Chamberlain following death of Sussex in this year.
1584	Expulsion of Spanish ambassador for complicity in Throckmorton plot; execution of Throckmorton.
	More differences between Queen and parliament over succession.
	Scottish parliament declares James VI head of the church and ends Presbyterian system.
	Assassination of William of Orange at Delft.
	New proposal for plantation of Ulster.
1585	Leicester's expedition to Netherlands (inaugurates undeclared war with Spain).
	Act against Jesuits, seminary priests and others disobedient to the Queen.
	First English colony founded in Virginia.
1586	Philip II of Spain assembling armada; Anglo-Scottish treaty of mutual defence. Babington plot to free Mary Queen of Scots; Babington executed; trial of Mary; declared guilty of treason.
	Treaty of Berwick: defensive alliance between England and Scotland.
	Star Chamber decree consolidates church control over printed matter.
	Severe famine; food riots in three counties, Gloucs., Somersetshire and Hants.
1587	Execution of Mary Queen of Scots.
	Pope declares crusade against England.

Leicester's troops surrender to Duke of Parma in Netherlands.

Raid on Spanish at Cadiz. Wentworth speaks on free speech again.

Second English colony in Virginia founded.

Privy Council goes over heads of licensers to halt circulation of second edition of Holinshed's Chronicles.

Rose Theatre built.

1588	Defeat of the Spanish Armada; renewed fears of Spanish invasion.
1588–9	Marprelate tracts (against the bishops).
1589	Catholic Henry III of France assassinated; Henry of Navarre proclaimed King.
	Victory over Spanish in Netherlands. James VI travels to Denmark to marry Princess Anna of Denmark.
1590	Virginia colony of 1587 found abandoned.
	Paul's Boys cease playing.
1591	England sends forces to defend Brittany against Spain and French Catholic League.
1592	Riots in London amongst apprentices and masterless men and against foreigners living in London.
	Fears of Spanish invasion.
	Plague in London; may have dispersed the companies.
	Theatres closed for almost two years (1592–4). Pembroke's Men become active.
	Queen's progress to Oxford University.
1593	Jesuit plot to kill Elizabeth discovered.
	Severe acts against recusants and members of religious sects.
	Wentworth raises issue of succession in parliament; is arrested and dies in Tower in 1597.
	Two radical Protestants hanged for sedition.
	Execution of Samuel family for witchcraft.
	Marlowe murdered.
1593–7	Period of poor harvests, famine, rising prices, plague.
1594	Execution of Roderigo Lopez, Queen's physician, on charges of treason.
	Henry of Navarre crowned Henry IV of France.
	Consolidation of Admiral's Men (Alleyn leading actor) and assembling of Lord Chamberlain's Men (Burbage leading

actor, Shakespeare a sharer); both companies played briefly
at Newington Butts, but Admiral's moved to Rose by
mid-June 1594. (These two companies played all the court
performances over Christmas 1594–5 and regularly until the
death of Elizabeth, with rare exceptions.)
Request from Lord Hunsdon to Lord Mayor Oct 1594 asking
permission for his men to play at Cross Keys in Gracious
(Gracechurch) St. London theatres move from 4pm to 2pm
start.
Henslowe's Diary covers 1592–1603.

1595	Sir Walter Ralegh sails to Guiana.

Execution of the Jesuit Robert Southwell.
More riots in London; proclamation against unlawful
assemblies follows.
Last English troops leave France.
Hugh O'Neill, Earl of Tyrone, leads rebellion in Ireland.
Dublin government makes peace with Tyrone and
Tyrconnell.
Sidney's *Apology for Poetry* printed.
Swan Theatre built.

1596   League of Amity between England and France.
Spanish raid near Plymouth.
Cadiz expedition: Cadiz itself and many Spanish ships
burned.
Tyrone receives royal pardon; incites rebellion in Munster
again.
Food riots in Oxon and Kent.
Second Blackfriars built in Upper Frater of former
Dominican Priory (but performances forbidden by Privy
Council; first in use 1600).
Death of Lord Chamberlain, Lord Hunsdon; William
Brooke, Lord Cobham, becomes Lord Chamberlain.

1597   Edict of Nantes ends French civil war, with toleration
granted to Protestants.
Defence preparation for expected Spanish invasion.
Tyrone submits to Earl of Ormond.
Grain riots in Kent, Sussex and Norfolk.
Male witch hanged at Lancaster.
Statute of apparel.

George Carey, 2nd Lord Hunsdon, becomes Lord Chamberlain.

Full investigation of Bankside playhouses following more riotous behaviour among audiences and *Isle of Dogs* furore. Order that playhouses be demolished and playing prohibited for three months.

1597–8   Boar's Head in Whitechapel undergoing conversion into theatre.

Alleyn retires (lured back for a while, but permanently retired by 1604).

1598   Edict of Nantes ends wars of religion in France: partial toleration granted to Protestants. English defeated in Ulster. Poor Law.

Legislation restoring recently enclosed land to tillage.

Victory for Tyrone over English forces.

Materials from Theatre transported for reconstruction as Globe.

1599   Earl of Essex takes army to Ireland; is defeated; negotiates a truce and returns to England without Queen's permission; is put under house arrest.

Anne Kerke hanged for witchcraft.

Burning of satires and epigrams in Stationers' Hall (by order of Whitgift and Bancroft, bishops of Canterbury and London).

Injunction against printing of English histories unless licensed by Privy Council; Hayward, *First part of Life and Raigne of King Henrie IIII* suppressed.

Opening of Globe Theatre. Paul's Boys resume playing.

Amalgam of Worcester's and Derby's Men established at Boar's Head.

1600   Essex tried and placed again under house arrest; released but barred from court.

Gowrie plot against James VI of Scotland.

Birth of Charles, son of James VI (future Charles I).

Grain riots in Somerset.

Fortune Theatre built. Order permitting only the two new playhouses, the Globe and the Fortune, to operate.

Innyard performance prohibited and playing restricted to two performances a week.

Chapel Children begin playing at Blackfriars.

Will Kemp dances from London to Norwich.

East India Company founded.

1601   Essex rebellion (fails); Sir Gelly Meyrick and other members of Essex faction visit Globe to commission *Richard II* the next Saturday (7 Feb). Essex rides into London on 8 Feb. Executed 25 February.

Proclamation offering reward of £100 for information about libels 'tending to the slander of our royal person and state, and stirring up of rebellion and sedition within this our realm'.

New Poor Law codifies 1598 law and places responsibility for poor relief on local parish.

Debate in parliament on monopolies.

Fear of Spanish invasion. Spanish fleet arrives in Ireland to help Tyrconnell and Tyrone against English; Irish defeat at Kinsale.

First East India Company voyage from London.

1602   Tyrone submits to Elizabeth.

Worcester's Men established in London, playing at the Boar's Head and perhaps the Rose (having played the provinces through 1590s up to this date).

1603   Death of Elizabeth; names James VI as her successor; accession of James I. (Elizabeth died 24 March 1603; James delayed arrival in London.)

Maine and Bye plots against the King.

Tyrone surrenders and is pardoned; ends Irish war.

Puritan Millenary Petition presented to King on his journey south.

Letters patent announcing King's Men issued 19 May.

Chamberlain's Men become King's; Admiral's become Prince Henry's.

Plague closure 1603–4. Proclamation forbidding all forms of entertainment on Sundays.

1604   Peace with Spain (Treaty of London).

Hampton Court Conference establishes a moderate line for the English church, disappointing the Puritans.

Act against Recusants confirms anti-Catholic statutes, but James promises to delay enforcing it.

Negotiations for union with Scotland begin, continuing until 1607.

James VI adopts title 'King of Great Britain, France and Ireland'.

Worcester's Men become Queen Anna's; Children of the Chapel Royal become Children of the Queen's Revels.

1605   Gunpowder Plot.

Red Bull built.

1606   Recusancy laws made more severe; new oath of allegiance imposed on Catholics. Parliament dominated by the question of union with Scotland.

Power to license plays for print transferred to Revels Office.

Act to Restrain Abuses of Players forbids use of names of God, Jesus, Holy Ghost or Trinity (i.e. oaths; but also the kind of material familiar from Catholic drama such as mystery plays).

?Whitefriars Theatre built in Great Hall of former Carmelite priory (not in use until 1609).

1607   Midlands Rising against enclosures.

Flight abroad of Tyrone and other Ulster lords; confiscation of much Ulster land leading to plantation of Ulster by English and Scottish settlers.

John Smith settles Jamestown, Virginia.

New Banqueting House built.

Paul's Boys cease playing.

1608   Case of the *post nati*: decision that Scots born after James' succession to English throne are his natural-born subjects in both England and Scotland.

Treaty of mutual defence between England and United Provinces (Netherlands).

New Charter to City of London: Whitefriars and Blackfriars move into city jurisdiction.

Biron plays crisis: Blackfriars children have to move out to Whitefriars, leaving Blackfriars Theatre open to King's Men to reclaim.

1609   King and Edward Coke (Lord Chief Justice) clash over boundary between common law and ecclesiastical jurisdiction.

Twelve-year truce between Spain and United Provinces begins.

	?King's Men begin playing at Second Blackfriars.
	Cockpit (or Phoenix) built as cockpit (used as theatre from 1616).
1610	Petition of Right.
	Great Contract (Robert Cecil's plan to provide King with more money) fails to get parliamentary consent.
	Prince Henry created Prince of Wales.
	Imprisonment of Arbella Stuart, claimant to throne, for marrying William Seymour, a claimant of the Suffolk line.
	Assassination of Henry IV of France.
	Plantation of Ulster.
	George Buc becomes Master of the Revels.
1611	Arbella Stuart escapes, is recaptured and reimprisoned.
	Title of baronet created and openly sold.
	Authorised Version of the Bible printed.
	Lady Elizabeth's Men become active.
1612	Death of Henry, Prince of Wales.
	Execution of Lancashire witches.
	Two English heretics burned for Aryan and Anabaptist beliefs (the last heretics burned in England).
	Heywood's *Apology for Actors* published.
1613	Princess Elizabeth marries Frederick, Elector Palatine (later King of Bohemia).
	Countess of Essex's divorce; Overbury murder.
	Fears of a Spanish invasion.
	Globe Theatre burns down.
	Amalgamation of Children of the Revels and Lady Elizabeth's Men.
	Prince Henry's Men become Palatine's (Palsgrave's) Men.
1614	'Addled' Parliament.
	Cockayne's scheme leads to a crisis in the cloth industry.
	Walter Ralegh's *History of the World* called in for suspected 'application' to the King.
	Hope built. Second Globe built.
1615	Inigo Jones appointed Surveyor of the King's Works.
	Porter's Hall built.
1615–16	Earl and Countess of Somerset tried for Overbury murder.
1616	Charles created Prince of Wales.
	Pocahontas is brought to England.

Ralegh released from Tower to prepare for voyage to Guiana.

Jonson's *Works* published in folio.

Death of Shakespeare.

1617   James I visits Scotland.

Ralegh leaves for Guiana.

Phoenix damaged in Shrove Tuesday riots.

1618   Bohemian Revolt begins Thirty Years War.

Synod of Dort opens in United Provinces, discussing theological differences between Calvinists and Arminians.

Ralegh executed following his return to England.

1619   Death of Queen Anna.

Frederick accepts the elective crown of Bohemia.

Sir John van Olden Barnavelt executed.

First colonial parliament meets at Jamestown, Virginia.

Queen Anna's company becomes Red Bull (Revels) Company. Banqueting House at Whitehall burns down; Inigo Jones begins work on the new one (completed 1622).

1620   Mayflower arrives in Massachusetts.

Secret treaty between England and Spain for marriage of Prince Charles and Infanta Maria of Spain.

Growing economic depression.

1621   Attack on monopolies; impeachment revived.

War between Spanish and Dutch resumes.

Fortune Theatre burns down.

1622   Negotiations for marriage between Prince Charles and Infanta of Spain.

John Astley becomes Master of the Revels.

1622–3 Fortune Theatre rebuilt.

1623   Charles and Buckingham make abortive expedition to negotiate Spanish marriage; return offended and resolved on war.

Frederick expelled from Palatinate by imperial troops.

Henry Herbert becomes Master of the Revels.

Shakespeare's plays published in folio.

1624   Clamour for war with Spain.

Marriage agreed between Prince Charles and Henrietta Maria of France.

Statute against monopolies.

1625   Death of James I; accession of Charles I. Charles' marriage to Henrietta Maria.

	Beginnings of war with Spain: English defeat by Spanish at Cadiz.
	Plague in London; theatres remain closed following death of James in March until November.
	Queen Henrietta's Men become active.
1626	Forced Loan controversy over loan raised to support the war with Spain.
	York House debate on religious doctrine. Prince's Men become Red Bull Company.
1627	English intervention on behalf of French Huguenots: beginnings of war with France; siege of La Rochelle.
	Darnel's case: judges rule that the King's 'special command' is sufficient cause for imprisonment.
1628	Petition of Right condemns extra-parliamentary taxation.
	Assassination of Buckingham.
	La Rochelle falls to Louis XIII of France.
1629	Charles dissolves parliament: beginning of eleven-year period of 'personal rule' without parliament.
	Treaty of Susa: peace with France.
	Salisbury Court Theatre built.
1629–31	Trade slump.
1630	Treaty of Madrid: peace with Spain.
	Birth of Prince Charles (later Charles II).
	Beginning of large-scale emigration to New England.
1631	Prince Charles's Men become active.
1632	Thomas Wentworth appointed Lord Deputy of Ireland.
	Cockpit-in-Court converted.
	Prynne's *Histriomastix* published.
1633	Charles I visits Scotland for his coronation.
	William Laud becomes Archbishop of Canterbury.
	Crown imposes large fines on city of London.
1634	First collection of ship money (a defence tax levied without parliamentary consent).
	Obsolete forest laws enforced to secure large fines for the crown.
	Charles negotiates with Spain for treaty against the Dutch.
	Prynne fined £5000 and condemned to lose his ears and remain in perpetual imprisonment.
1635	Second levy of ship money.
	Formal declaration of war between France and Spain.

1636	Third levy of ship money.
1637	Hampden's case: controversy over legality of ship money.
	Bishop Williams sent to the Tower for opposing Laudian ideas.
	New Prayer Book imposed on Scotland.
	Star Chamber decree imposing severe restrictions on printing.
	Beeston's Boys and Queen's Men become active.
1638	National Covenant signed in Scotland (legal establishment of Reformation in Scotland in opposition to Charles I).
	Ship money pronounced legal.
1639	First Bishops' War (between King and Scots, determined to abolish episcopacy).
	Wentworth returns from Ireland and becomes one of the King's chief advisers.
	Beginning of the 'taxpayers' strike'; royal control of local government breaks down.
	Battle of the Downs: Spanish fleet defeated by Dutch in English waters.
1640	Wentworth created Earl of Strafford and Lord Lieutenant of Ireland.
	Second Bishops' War: Scots defeat English; Treaty of Ripon: Charles agrees to pay the Scots until settlement is reached.
	Short Parliament dissolved without voting supply. Long Parliament: impeachment of Laud and Strafford; Commons condemn new Arminian canons.
	'Root and Branch' Petition against episcopacy submitted to Commons by London citizens.
	Beeston imprisoned for Beeston's Boys' play at Cockpit; William Davenant takes over the company until 1641.
	Plague closes theatres July–Oct.
1641	Act dissolving Long Parliament without its own consent.
	Earl of Strafford attainted and executed.
	Star Chamber abolished.
	Commons leaders demand that appointments of royal ministers should be subject to parliamentary approval.
	Second session of Long Parliament: Grand Remonstrance (a parliamentary petition listing the alleged misdeeds of Charles I).
	Supporters of parliamentary opposition gain control of the

government of the city of London.
Catholic rebellion in Ireland.
Plague closes theatres July–Dec.

1642   King leaves London; gradual beginning of hostilities between supporters of the crown and supporters of parliamentary opposition (Civil War).
Theatres closed by parliamentary ordinance.

Appendix 3

Known dimensions of playing spaces

The table only includes those venues where something is known about the dimensions. Useful short summaries of what is known about each theatre, together with the surviving documents that form the basis of that knowledge, are provided in *EPT*.

Venue	Approx. dimensions, if known	Approx. stage dimensions where relevant, if known
1st Blackfriars	*c.* 46'6" × 26'	
2nd Blackfriars	66' × 46'	
Boar's Head		39'7" × 25'
Cockpit, Drury Lane		24' × 15'
Christ Church Hall, Oxford	115' × 40'	40' × 18–20'
Fortune	80' × 80'	43' × 27'6"
Globe	99' diameter	49'6" wide
Hampton Court Hall	106' × 40'	
Hope	99' diameter	
St Paul's	*c.* 29' wide	
Queen's Hall, Cambridge	44' × 27'	
Red Lion		40' × 30'
Richmond Great Chamber	14' × 14'	
Rose	*c.* 72' diameter	36'9" (tapering to 26'10") × 16'5" (later extended)
Swan	99' diameter	
Theatre	99' diameter	
Trinity College Hall, Cambridge	85' × 40'	
Trinity Hall, Holborn	35' × 15'	
Whitefriars	*c.* 94' × 17'	
Whitehall Great Chamber	60' × 30'	
Whitehall Hall	*c.* 90' × *c.* 40'	

Notes

1 Places of performance

1 The earliest recorded use of the term 'Protestant' for the broad grouping that rejected Catholic doctrine and papal authority, according to the *OED*, is in 1553. Opposition to the Catholic church within the period of this book began with the Lollards in the late fourteenth century, and pockets of heresy remained across England through the fifteenth century. Early sixteenth-century opponents of Catholicism are now usually known broadly as Reformers or Reformists, though there are of course distinct strands within the Reforming movement, such as Lutheranism and Calvinism. Scholars disagree about the degree of continuity between these different reforming groups.

2 Wasson, 'The English Church', 25.

3 I use the spelling 'mask' for Tudor shows and 'masque' for the Jacobean revival of the form (though they are not separately indexed). Generic differences between these and between both of these and disguisings, mummings, interludes and so on are further discussed in chapter 4 below.

4 On the size of troupes and length of plays see further Bevington, *From Mankind to Marlowe*, ch.5.

5 Siobhan Keenan's *Travelling Players* is especially helpful in providing numerous detailed examples illustrating the range of designs and dimensions of available performance spaces.

6 Weimann first set out his analysis in these terms in *Shakespeare and the Popular Tradition* and has since developed it further, notably in *Author's Pen and Actor's Voice*.

7 David Bevington offers a suggested reconstruction for the play's staging based on the extant *Castle of Perseverance* and Cornish *Ordinalia* diagrams, putting Magdalene's castle at the centre and most of the other scaffolds in a circular arrangement around it (*Medieval Drama*, 688). John McKinnell discusses staging more fully and provides an illustration of the plan used for a performance at Durham in 1982 ('Staging the Digby *Mary Magdalen*'). Glynne Wickham, somewhat surprisingly, states that Hell is the only scaffold required ('Staging of Saint Plays'). It seems highly unlikely that so ambitious a play would restrict itself to only one scaffold.

8 Wickham, *Medieval Theatre*, plate 33.

9 Though Hall's Chronicle was first published in 1548, much of it was written considerably earlier, and quotations throughout this book are from my edition of extracts from the 1550 print.

10 Meredith, 'Putting on Plays', 23.

11 For a brief description of processional staging see Twycross, 'Theatricality of Medieval English Plays', 39–41. There is some debate, however, about whether in some locations, where a procession of static pageants took place separately from the plays, the plays were in fact performed only once, following this procession. Alexandra Johnston cites work by Alan Nelson, Martin Stevens and Margaret Dorrell on this question ('The Plays of the Religious Guilds', 55–6). See further p. 19 below. The N-town plays were not conceived as a cycle, and it is doubtful whether all the plays in the manuscript were ever performed as a single cycle.

12 Glynne Wickham offers a useful brief outline of the guild as 'a social unit formed for a particular purpose which could be religious, charitable, artistic or commercial' (*Medieval Theatre*, 67). In practice these functions often overlapped within a given guild. See also pp. 130–1 below.

13 Lancashire, ed., *Two Tudor Interludes*, 33, 200.

14 Walker, *Plays of Persuasion*, 173.

15 On this company's touring practice, see White, *Theatre and Reformation*, ch.1, where a map of their conjectured touring routes is included on p. 24.

16 References to passion plays, as at Leicester and at New Romney in Kent, further complicate the question of what kinds of drama were played in different places. Barbara Palmer summarises the doubts about whether Towneley is either a cycle or attributable to Wakefield and notes continuing investigation of the manuscript by Alexandra Johnston and Malcolm Parkes ('Recycling "The Wakefield Cycle"').

17 See Fletcher, 'N-Town Plays', 164–7 and Gibson, 'Bury St Edmunds'. Fletcher makes the point that the banns, which make the reference to touring (p. 70 below), apply only to some of the plays in the cycle.

18 On East Anglian culture, including its theatrical culture, see further Gibson, *Theater of Devotion* and Coldewey, 'Non-cycle plays'.

19 See further Keenan, *Travelling Players*, ch.8.

20 *REED: Cambridge*, I.348.

21 For a fascinating account and analysis of three performances of Shakespeare on board Captain Keeling's ship while anchored off the coast of Sierra Leone, see Taylor, 'Hamlet in Africa'.

22 Acts of Uniformity from 1552 onwards (repealed by Mary, but confirmed by subsequent monarchs) required all parishioners to attend their parish church on Sundays and holy days under threat of punishment.

23 Rubin, *Corpus Christi*, 61–2. Shaded citations immediately above and below are also taken from Rubin.

24 The text has 'graces', but William Hamilton, editor of the Chronicle, notes that it is probably an error for 'vices'.

25 Wilson, *Early Middle English Literature*, 255.

26 *Tractatus de Abundantia Exemplorum*, cited Owst, *Preaching*, 351.

27 *REED: York*, II.728.

28 *Acts and Monuments*, VI.57.

29 Gascoigne, *Complete Works*, II.91, 107, 120. This account of the Kenilworth entertainments is also printed in Nichols, *Progresses of Queen Elizabeth*, vol. I. Carter
Daniel argues that the content of the show, with its implicit advice to the Queen
to marry, was the more probable reason for its non-performance ('Patterns and
Traditions', 314).

30 Hall's Chronicle, in Dillon, *Performance and Spectacle*, 97.

31 Nichols, *Progresses of Elizabeth*, II.327.

32 Monarchs and some noblemen had their own private Chapel personnel, just as they
might have their own players. The primary function of the Chapel was to provide
music for the lord's worship, and since this was a daily requirement, the Chapel
personnel were fully supported members of the household. They consisted of two
groups of choristers: the Gentlemen and the Children. As practised performers with
highly developed musical skills, they were often called upon to participate in dramatic entertainments, sometimes alongside household players, where they were part
of the same household, and sometimes in place of them. Sometimes this dramatic
role became more formalised under particular Chapel Masters: the Gentlemen of
the Chapel Royal, for example, became the 'Players of the Chapel' under William
Cornish in the reign of Henry VII, and the children's acting companies of the late
sixteenth and early seventeenth centuries had their roots in the Chapels of St Paul's
and the Queen. See further below, p. 66 and ch. 2 n.3; and for a fuller picture, see
Westfall, *Patrons and Performance*.

33 I have written elsewhere, however, on the very particular circumstances of a masque
staged at the New Exchange on its opening in 1609 (see Dillon, *Theatre, Court and
City*, ch. 6).

34 Anne Lancashire brings together the known facts about Lydgate's mummings and
discusses them more fully in *London Civic Theatre*. Derek Pearsall notes how exceptional Lydgate's position was, as a monk apparently within the royal household
(*John Lydgate: Bio-Bibliography*, 30).

35 The manuscripts were all written by one scribe, John Shirley, Lydgate's contemporary, who struggles to find a term with each new heading.

36 Quotations from the *Mumming at Hertford* are from *The Minor Poems of John
Lydgate*, ed. MacCracken.

37 It is not absolutely clear from the documents that Rastell had the stage built outdoors
rather than indoors. The details of the lawsuit and its implications are discussed more
fully in Dillon, 'John Rastell's Stage'.

38 Twycross, 'Felsted of London'.

39 Stow's *Survey of London* contains several references to these plays. See also *DTRB*,
112–13.

40 On Trinity Hall, see further Prouty, 'An Early Elizabethan Playhouse' and Hosley,
'Three Renaissance English Indoor Playhouses'. They discuss the likely layout of the

stage and an estimated audience capacity of 200. Other references are given in more detail in *DTRB*.

41 *EPT*, no. 295.

42 As mentioned above, the early reference to the Boar's Head concerns a play stopped rather than performed, and it is not certain that the inn was fully converted to a playhouse before 1598.

43 Most hall screens before 1660 had two doors, but on the variety of possible models see Hosley, 'Three Renaissance English Indoor Playhouses'. In addition, we must remember that the hall space could be very differently adapted for different performances. Edward Hall's description of the Greenwich revels of May 1527, for example (cited on p. 37 above) shows different areas of the hall in use for different parts of the entertainment.

44 For reproduction and discussion of these illustrations see Foakes, *Illustrations*, nos. 31 and 70. Andrew Gurr, in private correspondence, has also pointed out that Inigo Jones depicts fourth-wall seating in the design for an indoor theatre which may have been Beeston's Cockpit (Foakes, *Illustrations*, no. 29, though the reproduction of the drawing there and elsewhere is not sharp enough to show the lines drawn across the stage gallery).

45 Beckerman, *Shakespeare at the Globe 1599–1609*, 106.

46 Philip Henslowe was a notable theatre entrepreneur of the period, owner of the Rose Theatre. His so-called '*Diary*', compiled over the period 1592–1603, is actually a mixture of different kinds of records, including accounts, lists of properties and costumes and more miscellaneous and personal items. It remains our best guide to the day-to-day workings of an Elizabethan playhouse.

47 For a commentary on these items, see Foakes, ed., *Henslowe's Diary*, 319–21.

48 This modernised text is taken from Peter Meredith, 'Putting on a Play', where a full list is given and the terminology and implications of the list are more fully discussed, together with reconstructive diagrams of the Mercers' staging of the Last Judgement at York.

49 For further discussion of the drawing and its implications, see Foakes, *Illustrations*, and Schlueter, 'Rereading the Peacham Drawing'. Schlueter argues that the drawing depicts a sequence from a different play about Titus Andronicus performed by English actors in Germany.

50 Dutton, *Jacobean and Caroline Masques*, 15. Though this was Jonson's first court masque, it was the second masque to be performed at the Jacobean court. The first was Samuel Daniel's *Vision of Twelve Goddesses*, performed the previous year, in 1604.

51 Orgel and Strong, *Theatre of the Stuart Court*, I. 7.

52 These quotations from contemporary documents are taken from R. A. Foakes, *Illustrations*, 56–61, which reproduces the seating plan and directions and discusses the details more fully.

53 Dutton, *Jacobean and Caroline Masques*, 15–16.

54 Dutton, *Jacobean and Caroline Masques*, ix.

55 'Of Masques and Triumphs', quoted in Orgel, ed., *Ben Jonson*, 2.

2 Actors and audiences

1 Wasson, 'Professional Actors', 3. As Peter Greenfield points out, the wording of Latin records makes it frequently impossible to distinguish minstrel troupes from players ('Touring'). The distinction is of course slightly distorting, since most travelling player-troupes would also have had some musical skills. A new *REED* Patrons and Performances website, under development at the time of writing, will offer the facility to search for patrons, troupes and venues using both text and interactive maps: see http://eir.library.utoronto.ca/reed.

2 For records of their places of performance, see *DTR*, 387–92. From 1515 the King's Players were split into two groups, only one of which toured (Streitberger, 'Court Performances by the King's Players', 98–9).

3 The Chapel Royal under William Cornish became very active in the performance of court disguisings, so much so that some of them emerged as the 'Players of the Chapel', active 1505–12. The royal Chapel Children first appeared as an acting company in 1517. See further Streitberger, 'William Cornish'.

4 David Bevington suggests four to six players as commonest (*From Mankind to Marlowe*, 71), while John Wasson gives three or four as the standard, noting that two is also quite common ('Professional Actors', 4).

5 On the sharing system see Gurr, *King's Men*, ch. 3. Boys might be apprenticed to some of the sharers, but because theatre companies were not formally constituted as trade guilds, the apprenticeships were technically to actors who were also formal members of other occupational guilds: goldsmiths, cobblers or the like. For a table of actors who were also affiliated to other livery companies, see Forse, *Art Imitates Business*, p. 8.

6 Legislation attempting to deal with the problem of masterless men went back to 1285, and had been renewed at intervals between then and 1572.

7 Relevant contemporary documents here include *EPT*, nos. 152, 154, 66. On relations between patrons and players see further Greg Walker, *Plays of Persuasion*; Suzanne Westfall, *Patrons and Performance*; Paul White and Suzanne Westfall, eds., *Shakespeare and Theatrical Patronage*, especially Leeds Barroll, 'Shakespeare, Noble Patrons, and the Pleasures of "Common" Playing'.

8 Meredith and Tailby, *Staging of Religious Drama*, 58. Clerical acting is harder to be sure of in English contexts. Grace Frank (cited by John R. Elliott, 'Medieval Acting', 245), reads a petition presented to Richard II in 1378 by the choristers of St Paul's asking him to 'prohibit some inexpert people from presenting the history of the Old and New Testament, to the great prejudice of the clergy, who had been at great expense, in order to represent it publicly at Christmas' as evidence of rivalry between regular clergy and parish clerks over the right to perform, but the clergy's involvement in

mounting that performance cannot be tied down with complete certainty to include acting. William Tydeman's examples of clerical acting are similarly impossible to tie down ('Agreable to his Pageaunt', 35).

9 William Ingram has also noted the effect of the 1550 decree against players performing in London without a licence, which made it more difficult for 'loose and informal associations of players' to continue inside the city of London (*Business of Playing*, 84).

10 *EPT*, no. 339, and *ES* IV, 269.

11 *EPT*, no. 153.

12 For a contemporary account of the 'Turk', a tightrope perfomer with the company, see Gurr, *Shakespearian Playing Companies*, 205.

13 On the innovativeness of shared ownership of the playhouse and the circumstances that led to it, see further Gurr, 'Money or Audiences'.

14 The Chamberlain's Men were taken on under the King's name within two months, but the other two companies had to wait for some months longer before coming under royal protection.

15 As Roslyn Knutson notes, entries in Henslowe's Diary show continuous playing across Sundays. Some earlier scholars 'corrected' these entries to eliminate Sunday performances on the basis of Privy Council bans on them, but it seems more likely that the Privy Council had to keep issuing such restraints because they continued to be contravened ('The Repertory', 465). Peter Thomson discusses rehearsal practices in *Shakespeare's Theatre*, 59–60.

16 Beckerman, *Shakespeare at the Globe*, 9.

17 Gurr (citing Harbage), *Shakespearean Stage*, 213.

18 The level of deaths deemed 'normal' by the authorities was not fixed, but varied between 30 and 50 per week.

19 *EPT*, no. 418(c).

20 Keenan, *Travelling Players*, 49–50.

21 Ingram, 'The Globe Playhouse and its Neighbors in 1600'.

22 Gurr, *Shakespearian Playing Companies*, 218. On the ages of the boys, see further Lin, 'How Old Were the Children of Paul's?'

23 Knutson gives an account of the rise of the rivalry narrative in *Playing Companies and Commerce*, 5–7. She discusses the *Hamlet* passage, which is much longer and more interesting than the extract quoted above, in 'Falconer to the Little Eyases'.

24 Tables of payments to licensed players on tour between 1560–1639, indicating the frequency of recorded visits to different areas, are supplied in Keenan, *Travelling Players*, 166–71.

25 Strange's Men are recorded visiting Bath and Bristol in August, Norwich in September and Coventry in December. Alleyn was an Admiral's Man before and after his time with Lord Strange's Men, during which period, unusually, he retained the Admiral's livery (Gurr, *Shakespearian Playing Companies*, 234–5). On friendship

and kinship ties between players see e.g. Cerasano, 'Patronage Network' and 'The Chamberlain's-King's Men', in Kastan, ed., *Companion*, 334.

26 Keenan, *Travelling Players*, 71.

27 Coldewey, 'That Enterprising Property Player'. Coldewey discusses other instances of small rural towns consulting London 'directors' to oversee their plays. 'Felsted of London' (see p. 42) and Richard Gibson, who was involved in the production of most of the entertainments at Henry VIII's court between 1510 and 1534, crop up in the records of Maldon in Essex and Lydd and New Romney in Kent in this capacity.

28 For an excellent brief summary of the jig and its stage life, see Gurr, *Shakespeare Company*, 69–77.

29 Thomas Dekker, *Gull's Hornbook*, ch. 6; cf. the first-person account of a gallant's visit to the theatre in the 1620s cited from *The Life of a Satirical Puppy called Nim* in Gurr, *Shakespeare Company*, 37–40.

30 See e.g. *EPT*, nos. 264, 266, 272.

31 In 1566 there was such a crush of spectators outside Christ Church hall in Oxford, hoping for admission to a performance of *Palamon and Arcite*, that a wall collapsed, killing three people and injuring five more.

32 *EPT*, nos. 413(a), 192, 400(b). Cf. the incident recounted of a play presented in the churchyard at Beverley *c.* 1220, when two boys who had climbed the the tower to see the play, fell to the ground but were miraculously saved (Clopper, *Drama, Play, and Game*, 72, n.29).

33 *Historia Histrionica* (1699), quoted in Bentley, *Jacobean and Caroline Stage*, II.693.

34 Kinney, *Shakespeare by Stages*, 91. Forman's notes on the Shakespearean plays he saw are reproduced in full in the *Riverside Shakespeare*, 1966–8. Kinney's whole chapter on 'Playgoers' is excellent, though Andrew Gurr's full-length study of *Playgoing in Shakespeare's London* has become the classic account of Renaissance theatre audiences.

35 Knutson, *Playing Companies and Commerce*, 145–6.

36 Beckerman *Shakespeare at the Globe*, 164.

37 Robert Weimann quotes Julian Hilton and discusses this concept further in *Author's Pen*, ch. 3.

38 Douglas Bruster further develops the observation that so many of our memories of early plays 'involve images of characters holding things', noting a 'fluidity between person and thing' except when there is 'some breach of decorum', making objects seem to 'stand out' from their surroundings ('The Dramatic Life of Objects', 67, 89). Bruster provides a table listing the frequency of props in non-Shakespearean plays between 1587 and 1636 (84). A detailed property list for Shakespearean plays is provided as an appendix to Frances Teague's study, *Shakespeare's Speaking Properties*.

39 In using the capital letter in 'Naturalist' here I am distinguishing 'Naturalism' as a movement in theatre beginning in the late nineteenth century from 'naturalism' as

a broader term for the realistic mode of performance deriving from that nineteenth-century style.

40 *Play of Adam*, 101–3.

41 See further Twycross and Carpenter, 'Masks' and *Masks and Masking*.

42 G. K. Hunter explores these aspects of early dramaturgy illuminatingly in 'Flatcaps and Bluecoats'.

43 Beckerman, *Shakespeare at the Globe*, 162 and ch. 4.

44 Quotations from *King Lear* are not taken from the *Riverside Shakespeare* in this instance, which prints a composite text of two versions now usually recognised as separate states of the play. I cite the Folio text from René Weis' parallel-text edition.

45 For fuller documentation of these two styles of acting, see Gurr, 'Who Strutted and Bellowed', which brings together several of the quotations that follow here.

46 For an exploration of the excess implicit in this kind of performance see Shepherd, 'Voice'.

47 Thomas Carew, quoted by Gurr, 'Who Strutted and Bellowed', 95.

48 Heywood, *Apology for Actors*, 29–30. The *OED* cites Massinger's *Believe as You List* (1631) as first to use the term 'overact' in this sense, but Heywood clearly predates this.

49 McKellen is quoted in White, *Renaissance Drama*, 77.

50 Quoted in Kiernan, *Staging Shakespeare*, 133, 155.

51 For easy access to relevant extracts from one such proclamation, see Rutter, *Documents*, 233–4; and for excellent introductions to costume in early drama see Craik, *Tudor Interlude*; MacIntyre and Epp, '"Cloathes worth all the rest"'; and MacIntyre, *Costumes and Scripts*.

52 Nelson, 'Contexts for Early English Drama: The Universities', in Briscoe and Coldewey, *Contexts for Early English Drama*, 143; Dillon, 'John Rastell v. Henry Walton' and 'John Rastell's Stage'.

53 Westfall, *Patrons and Performance*, 138.

54 Different systems of colour symbolism were in use, deriving respectively from religious iconography (made daily visible in church vestments, which changed for different ecclesiastical feasts) and heraldry. For tables of the meanings assigned to different colours under these systems see Wickham, *Early English Stages*, I. 47–8.

55 Stephen Spector, editor of the Early English Text Society edition of the N-Town cycle, gives the play a double title: *The Slaughter of the Innocents; The Death of Herod*. On genre, see further chapter 4 below.

56 The Coventry and Chester Herods, unlike other tyrant-figures, were masked (MacIntyre and Epp, '"Cloathes worth all the rest"'). Death too was usually masked (see Twycross and Carpenter, *Masks and Masking*, 247–50, and plates 26 and 27).

57 For the inventory of props see p. 51 above, and for the inventory of costumes see *EPT*, no. 167. Though *Tamburlaine* was certainly performed at the Rose from 1594, it is not certain where it was first performed. Gurr suggests the Theatre as the most likely venue (*Shakespearian Playing Companies*, 232).

3 Writers, controllers and the place of theatre

1 See Minnis, *Medieval Theory of Authorship*.
2 For an excellent, brief account of printers' practices and attitudes, see Blayney, 'Publication of Playbooks'.
3 Seven of these, furthermore, 'advertise the authority of the text as theatrical rather than authorial, by insisting that it is published "As it was played"' (Kastan, *Shakespeare and the Book*, 31).
4 Erne, *Shakespeare as Literary Dramatist*. The 1590s and the plays of Marlowe, especially *Tamburlaine*, have been noted as a key time of change in other contexts. See e.g. numerous studies of Marlowe; and McMillin and MacLean, *Queen's Men*, who put the argument in terms of a contrast between the kinds of plays the Queen's Men were staging and Marlowe's *Tamburlaine* (ch. 6).
5 Kastan, *Shakespeare and the Book*, 48; Peters, *Theatre of the Book*, 136.
6 For a more detailed description of how such collaboration might work, see McMillin, 'Professional Playwrighting', in *A Companion to Shakespeare*, esp. 229–31; and for a lengthy list of some of the collaborative groupings of authors, see Masten, 'Playwrighting', 357.
7 Orgel, *Imagining Shakespeare*, 4–8.
8 Richard Dutton proposes this theory in 'Birth of the Author', suggesting that Shakespeare circulated his plays in manuscript as well as giving them to his company for performance.
9 Epistle to the Reader, *The English Traveller* (1633).
10 See *EPT*, no. 512.
11 Wheeler, ed., *Letters of Sir Thomas Bodley*, 219. Erne, however, argues that Bodley's attitude was the exception rather than the norm, though he admits that 'the composition of libraries in Shakespeare's time was in a state of flux' (*Shakespeare as Literary Dramatist*, 13). Erne certainly demonstrates that some educated contemporaries of Bodley's collected playbooks, sometimes in considerable numbers, but it is more difficult to demonstrate that their ownership of playbooks necessarily points to their perception of plays as literary compositions.
12 Kastan, *Shakespeare and the Book*, 71.
13 The city authorities had been forbidding performances on Sundays and other holy days since at least 1557 (*EPT*, no. 20(c)), and these orders were renewed in the 1570s and 1580s.
14 Peter Lake provides a fairly detailed, but brief, survey of religious positions in his essay on 'Religious Identities' in Kastan's *Companion to Shakespeare*. See also Collinson, *The Religion of Protestants* and Lake, *The Antichrist's Lewd Hat*.
15 Johnston, 'What if No Texts Survived?', 3.
16 For useful collections of such documents see Chambers, *ES*, IV, Appendix C; Pollard, *Shakespeare's Theater*; and for a full discussion see Barish, *Antitheatrical Prejudice*.
17 Stephen Orgel cites contemporary accounts of the Blackfriars incident more fully, besides bringing together a number of references to female performance in England

(*Impersonations*, 1–9), implying that it was more widespread than is commonly thought.

18 See *EPT*, nos. 29–33. Performances of Corpus Christi plays are documented as late as 1603 in Preston and Lancaster.

19 'Reforming Mysteries' End', 125. See also Bills, '"Suppression Theory"'.

20 For copies of documents cited see *EPT*, nos. 8, 14, 15, 16, 19, 20(b), 22, 24, 29, 153, 34, 54, 65, 66, 73(b); and for a detailed chronological narrative and discussion see Gildersleeve, *Government Regulation*. Both also cover city, provincial and church edicts, not included in this table. Amongst the many moves by the city of London authorities to control theatrical activity, the 1574 Act of Common Council was especially important (see *ES*, IV. 273–6; Gildersleeve, *Government Regulation*, 156–9).

21 Though the play was first performed in 1606, the Epistle is internally dated 'From my house in the Blackfriars this 11 of February 1607'. Richard Dutton examines the position from which it was written in 'Jonson: the Epistle to *Volpone*', *Licensing* 114–31.

22 For the text of the French Ambassador's account of his complaint about the *Biron* plays and the King's response, see Dutton, *Mastering the Revels*, 182–3.

23 See especially Walker, *Plays of Persuasion* (*passim*) and *Politics of Performance*, ch. 2.

24 See further Pearl, *London*, ch. 3 and Foster, *Politics of Stability*.

25 For fuller discussion and citation of the documents see *EPT*, nos. 53–5; Wickham, 'Privy Council Order'; and Dutton, *Licensing*, ch. 2.

26 De Feria, the Ambassador, wrote to King Philip of Spain in April 1559 saying that the Queen had 'partly admitted' to him that William Cecil, the most prominent member of her Privy Council, 'had given the arguments to construct these comedies' (White, *Theatre and Reformation*, 58–9).

27 Minute of the City Court of Aldermen, 20 May 1572, in *ES*, IV. 269.

28 Gildersleeve, *Government Regulation*, 169.

29 Gurr, *Shakespearian Playing Companies*, 278. Lord Hunsdon also wrote to the mayor to ask for his players to be allowed to use the Cross Keys through the winter of 1594–5 (*EPT*, no. 218).

30 Rutter, *Documents*, 44.

31 On the Revels Office, the Master of the Revels and the organisation of the court see Streitberger, *Court Revels*; Introduction to *Malone Society Collections* XIII; Astington, *English Court Theatre*; Chambers, *ES*, I; and Dutton, *Mastering the Revels*.

32 The patent is extracted and summarised in *EPT*, no. 34, and printed in full in Chambers, *ES*, IV. 285–6.

33 Dutton, 'Censorship', 299.

34 The documentation of the history of the York Creed Play can be found in *REED: York*, and is also given in Johnson, 'Plays of the Religious Guilds', from which subsequent quotations from the documents are taken.

35 Though medieval works rarely have titles in quite the fixed sense we now understand, this play is referred to in the vernacular as 'le Crede Play' within the Latin text of Revetour's will: '*quemdam librum vocatum le Crede Play cum libris et vexillis eidem pertinentibus*' [a certain book called the Creed Play with the books and banners belonging to it'] (Johnson, 'Plays of the Religious Guilds', 81).

36 York had two guild plays in addition to the Corpus Christi cycle: the Creed Play and the Pater Noster Play. Despite Dean Hutton's warning of the dangers of performing the Creed Play in 1568, the Pater Noster Play was still being performed up to 1572, and the volatility of religious thinking discussed earlier in this chapter needs to be borne in mind. The last recorded performance of the Corpus Christi Play was in 1569.

37 Marie Axton ('Tudor Mask', 37–8) has brought forward good evidence for dating the visit to 1578, which Edward Berry supports with additional evidence ('Sidney's May Game', n.4).

38 Kimbrough and Murphy argue that the epilogue, which begs the Queen, probably on Leicester's behalf, 'to love me much better than you were wont', was omitted from the printed version 'not simply because the allusions were dated, private, and slightly damaging to the name of Leicester but mainly because Rombus' speech is an anticlimax' ('Sidney's *The Lady of May*', 107).

39 'Sidney's Experiment in Pastoral', rpt in *Jonsonian Masque*.

40 Gondomar had an anal fistula, hence the opening in the chair for comfort.

41 The full text of the letter is printed in Gurr, *Shakespeare Company*, Appendix 2.

42 See e.g. Limon, *Dangerous Matter*, ch. 4; Howard-Hill, 'Political Interpretations'; *Middleton's 'Vulgar Pasquin'*; Heinemann, *Puritanism and Theatre*, ch.10; Dutton, 'Receiving Offence'.

43 Quoted in Dutton, 'Receiving Offence', 54. Margot Heinemann, however, argues that the attack was 'not merely flogging a dead horse', but symptomatic of an ongoing fear of increasing Catholic influence at court, with another Catholic marriage planned for Prince Charles and high-church practices in the English church growing (*Puritanism and Theatre*, 154–5).

44 Dutton, 'Receiving Offence', 55. Dutton goes on to argue that there were particular reasons for this beyond the mere fact of the play's attack on Spain.

45 Dudley Carleton to Ralph Winwood, January 1605, cited in Dutton, ed., *Jacobean and Caroline Masques*, 15.

46 Quoted in Butler, *Theatre and Crisis*, 26.

47 Veevers, *Images of Love and Religion*, 6.

48 Orgel and Strong, *Inigo Jones*, I. 384–5.

49 See further Dillon, 'Theatre and Controversy', 378–9.

50 'Powerless Theatre', 50, rpt in *Stage-Wrights*, 3.

51 Andrew Hadfield's introduction to *Literature and Censorship* outlines the different positions critics have taken on the degree to which censorship was either an organised mechanism for state control or a series of ad hoc responses to particular events. Janet Clare, in that same volume, argues strongly against Yachnin.

52 Gardiner, *Documents*, 16.
53 Richard Dutton, however, argues that the conspirators did not intend the play as incendiary, though the actors could hardly have failed to realise its significance in the context (*Mastering the Revels*, 123).
54 Yachnin, 'Powerless Theater', 59, rpt in *Stage-Wrights*, 12.
55 Gurr, *Shakespearean Stage*, 213.

4 Genre and tradition

1 John Orrell argues in *The Human Stage* that theatre design is underpinned from the start by a classical model.
2 See e.g. Davidson, Clopper and Baldwin, 'Saint Plays'. On the Latin terms for performance see further Young, 'Plays and Players'.
3 There are several discrepancies between Hall's and Spinelli's account of this event, further discussed in Dillon, *Performance and Spectacle*, 244–6. On the prominence of 'as if' in early liturgical drama, and the question of how far this constitutes a definition of drama, see further Wickham, *Medieval Theatre*, 32–41. Wickham himself emphasises the introduction of an element of entertainment into the act of worship.
4 Dillon, *Performance and Spectacle*, 246.
5 Hall, in Dillon, *Performance and Spectacle*, 126.
6 Hall, in Dillon, *Performance and Spectacle*, 43.
7 See, for example, Ros King's reconstruction of Elizabeth's visit to the University of Oxford in 1566 (*Works of Richard Edwards*, 70–9) or George Gascoigne's contemporary account of her progress to the Earl of Leicester's Kenilworth estate in 1575 (*Complete Works of George Gascoigne*, vol. II).
8 On the elements of the N-town compilation see further Fletcher, 'N-Town Plays'; and on Towneley as a sixteenth-century compilation see Palmer, 'Recycling "The Wakefield Cycle"'.
9 *DTRB*, nos. 616, 878.
10 Lawrence Clopper argues, against the drift of the *Treatise*, it seems to me, that the term *miracle*, as used by this writer, should be understood in its primary Latin sense to mean 'horror', and is not a reference to a kind of drama at all (*Drama, Play and Game*, ch. 2). Clopper supplies, however, a very useful appendix listing medieval and early modern references to '*miracula*', 'miracles' and the much rarer 'steracles' [spectacles].
11 Alan Dessen collects and discusses some very interesting early modern uses of the term (*Shakespeare and the Late Moral Plays*, 11–14).
12 For a list of uses and discussion of the term 'interlude', see Davis, 'Meaning' and 'Allusions'.
13 For transcription and discussion of the documents see further Dillon, 'John Rastell v. Henry Walton' and 'John Rastell's Stage'.

14 Walker, *Plays of Persuasion*, 25.

15 Hall, in Dillon, *Performance and Spectacle*, 41.

16 For a useful collection of essays on the subject of humanism, see Kraye, ed., *Cambridge Companion to Humanism*.

17 Hall, in Dillon, *Performance and Spectacle*, 67.

18 For a list of early productions of Greek and Latin comedies at Oxford and Cambridge, see Smith, *Ancient Scripts*, 138.

19 *Intermezzi* were extra entertainments inserted at intervals during the play. They were first used in comedies and only much later in tragedies. On *intermezzi*, see further Welsford, *Court Masque*, 44–6, 91–2; and for illustrations of *intermezzi* see also Strong, *Art and Power*.

20 On Wolsey's influence see further Streitberger, *Court Revels*, 121–36.

21 This extract is cited by Smith (*Ancient Scripts*, 135), who notes that the entry echoes Petrarch's *Triumph of Love*.

22 Happé, *English Drama*, 99.

23 Smith, *Ancient Scripts*, ch. 5.

24 Smith, *Ancient Scripts*, 6; cf. Cartwright, *Theatre and Humanism*.

25 It is not clear whether the Thomas Preston who wrote *King Cambyses* is to be identified with the Thomas Preston whose Latin orations earned Elizabeth's favour on her visit to Cambridge University in 1564.

26 Though these lines are usually printed as two- and three-syllable lines, the rhythm is actually the same as that of a seven-beat line with internal rhyme. *Cambyses* does include some other metres, but the fourteener is heavily dominant.

27 King, ed. *Works of Richard Edwards*, 87–92.

28 My discussion here is indebted to Smith, *Ancient Scripts*, who provides much fuller information on this subject.

29 Geoffrey Shepherd, in the introduction to his edition of the *Apology*, says: 'We cannot be sure that Sidney had read much in the commentaries on Aristotle's *Poetics* (he was more interested in Aristotle's *Ethics* and *Rhetoric*) but he had acquired some knowledge of what Italian critics thought were Aristotelian principles' (Sidney, *Apology* (1965), 43). He does not, however, suggest how Sidney might have acquired such knowledge other than through the commentaries.

30 This and the following quotations from Sidney below are cited from pp. 110–12 of his *Apology* in Maslen's revised version of Shepherd's edition.

31 Sidney may have been influenced too by George Whetstone, whose Epistle Dedicatory to *Promos and Cassandra*, published in 1578, praised classical principles of decorum and denounced English popular practice thus: 'I divided the whole history into two comedies for that, decorum used, it would not be conveyed in one. The effects of both are both good and bad: virtue intermixed with vice, unlawful desires (if it were possible) quenched with chaste denials: all needful actions, I think, for public view . . . [The typical English writer of comedy] grounds his work on impossibilities; then in three hours runs he through the world, marries, gets children, makes children men, men to conquer kingdoms, murder monsters,

and bringeth gods from heaven, and fetcheth devils from hell. And, that which is worst, their ground is not so unperfect as their working indiscreet ... Many times, to make mirth, they make a clown [peasant] companion with a king ... to work a comedy kindly [appropriately], grave old men should instruct, young men should show the imperfections of youth, strumpets should be lascivious, boys unhappy, and clowns should speak disorderly; intermingling all these actions in such sort as the grave matter may instruct, and the pleasant delight.' Whereas the word 'clown' probably carries the early sense of a low-class, rustic character in Whetstone, Sidney seems to mean something closer to the more modern sense of 'fool' or comic character.

32 The date of Sidney's *Apology*, as noted above (p.112), cannot be determined (though could be as early as 1579), so Lyly's borrowing from Sidney cannot be certain either, but this passage strongly suggests borrowing in one direction or the other.

33 McMillin and MacLean offer illuminating discussion of 'medley' style, adopting the term preferred by Robert Wilson, a Queen's Man himself, to discuss the characteristic acting and dramaturgy of the Queen's Men (*Queen's Men*, especially 124–7, 143–6).

34 *Dr Faustus* is not the first play to disrupt the expectation of salvation; indeed the Protestant adaptation and remaking of morality form was ongoing throughout most of the sixteenth century.

35 We may note, however, that some of these more specific terms appear in earlier documents. See, for example, the Act of Common Council of 1574 quoted on p. 72 above.

36 Jean Howard considers the generic problems of the First Folio in more detail in 'Shakespeare and Genre'. See also Snyder, 'The Genres of Shakespeare's Plays'.

37 Woudhuysen (ed.), *Samuel Johnson on Shakespeare*, 127.

38 The quotation is from Chaucer's translation of Boethius.

39 Salingar, *Shakespeare and the Traditions of Comedy*, 257. 'Comedy' is in earlier use in English, but without specifically dramatic application.

40 See Griffin, *Playing the Past*, Appendix B and cf. Kewes, 'Elizabethan History Play', esp. 170–1. I argue elsewhere that the broad consensus is overdependent on Shakespeare and excludes plays that might usefully be considered under such a heading ('The Early Tudor History Play', forthcoming in *English Historical Drama 1500–1660: Forms Outside the Canon*, ed. Teresa Grant and Barbara Ravelhofer (Palgrave)).

41 Snyder, 'The Genres of Shakespeare's Plays', 95.

42 The existence of two versions of *King Lear* does not substantially affect the argument of this section. As elsewhere in this book, I cite the Folio text in Weis's edition.

43 The term 'horizon of expectations' is coined by Hans Robert Jauss, *Toward an Aesthetic of Reception*.

44 Writers who discuss these effects include Dessen, *Shakespeare and the Late Moral Plays*; Craik, *Tudor Interlude*, ch. 5; and Jones, *Scenic Form*, 188–9. The dating

of *A Satire of the Three Estates* to 1552 is based on the first performance date for which any evidence of the script survives. The textual and performance history of the play is very complex, since the text exists in two versions and there are three performances on record, for the first of which (in 1540) no script survives.

45 'In the present case', writes Johnson in the notes to his edition of *King Lear*, 'the public has decided [about the ending of the play]. Cordelia from the time of Tate has always retired with victory and felicity. And if my sensations could add anything to the general suffrage, I might relate that I was many years ago so shocked by Cordelia's death that I know not whether I ever endured to read again the last scenes of the play till I undertook to revise them as an editor' (Woudhuysen, *Samuel Johnson on Shakespeare*, 222–3).

46 The source play has no subplot and no fool. Such disguise as there is is merely passing and does not include any Poor Tom equivalent, and there is no real equivalent of the heath scenes in Shakespeare's *Lear*. Lear and Perillus (Kent) stay briefly in a thicket, where Ragan has sent them with a view to murder, and sail to France, but there is no attempt to produce the sense of an consistent alternative world. On the comic elements in *Lear* see further Snyder, *Comic Matrix*, ch. 4.

5 Instruction and spectacle

1 Shepherd and Wallis include an illuminating and informative brief discussion of the term in *Drama/Theatre/Performance*, 212–9.

2 Several of the examples following are taken from Rosemary Woolf's excellent discussion of 'Attitudes to Drama and Dramatic Theory' in *English Mystery Plays*, ch. 5. Cf. also the extract from *Dives and Pauper* quoted on p. 115 above.

3 Heywood, *Apology*, 57–60.

4 This is not the author's own view in the *Treatise*. His practice is to cite the possible lines of defence and then argue against them. Here he is citing a line of defence; his own attitude is made clear in the boxed quotation on p. 183 below.

5 Owst, *Preaching*, 490, 486–7.

6 Jeffrey, 'English Saints' Plays', 83. The sermon is cited in the shaded text below.

7 The *Meditations on the Life of Christ*, attributed to St Bonaventure, was translated and adapted by Nicholas Love in the first decade of the fifteenth century as the *Mirror of the Blessed Life of Jesus Christ*, and this became a very widely circulated text. Its influence on the N-town cycle is well established.

8 Peter Meredith and John Tailby have collected and translated a large number of records of early European performance, and those gathered together in the sections on machinery and special effects (*Staging of Religious Drama*, 94–116) indicate something of the range and prominence of spectacle in early drama.

9 Royal entries in England are recorded from 1255, but accounts do not become very detailed until the later fourteenth century. See further Lancashire, *London Civic*

Theatre, 43–50; Wickham, *Early English Stages*; Kipling, 'Sumptuous Pageants'; and Kipling, *Enter the King*, ch. 1, to which the following account is especially indebted.

10 The probability that earlier pageantry also communicated meanings is implied by the fact that its devices recall the 1377 pageant, which in turn recalls earlier pageants (see Lancashire, *London Civic Theatre*, 45). The scattering of gold coins, however, though echoing the 1377 pageant, may have had an additional and very material significance in the context of the city's willingness now to supply the loan to Richard it had earlier offended him by refusing.

11 Kipling, *Enter the King*, 12, 17–19.

12 Quoted in Kipling, *Enter the King*, 20.

13 *Images of Tudor Kingship*, 109.

14 At this point the images of torment are interrupted by an episode in which a quack doctor comes looking for patients and looking at Jonathas as a prospective patient, but the Jews beat him away. I have discussed the relevance of this episode elsewhere (in 'What Sacrament?').

15 This broad statement should not be taken to occlude the conflicted and contradictory way that attitudes developed in different parts of the country at different dates. Important qualifications of Gardiner's view are briefly discussed in ch. 3 above (pp. 117–18).

16 Lake's emphasis on the relationship between Protestantism and popular culture arises out of a wish to refute the emphasis of some scholars' insistence that Protestantism was imposed from above upon an unwilling people. His own agenda was 'to complicate this starkly adversarial revisionist account of the relations between the protestant and the popular' (*Antichrist's Lewd Hat*, xvi).

17 Lake, xx.

18 *Staging Reform*, 4.

19 Berger, Bradford and Sondergard's *Index of Characters* lists 60 plays containing Puritans, beginning with *New Custom* (*c.* 1570–3) and ending with *The Parson's Wedding* (1641).

20 Heinemann, *Puritanism and Theatre*, 55.

21 Gurr, *Shakespearian Playing Companies*, 237.

22 See *ES*, III. 424.

23 Gurr, *Shakespearian Playing Companies*, 341–2. See also ch. 2 above.

24 Plots (or 'plats', as the Elizabethans sometimes spelled it) were pasted on to thin board and pierced at the top for hanging up, probably in the tiring house. Six of them survive, in varying conditions of preservation, excluding one extant only in a later transcript. They are reproduced and discussed in Bradley, *From Text to Performance*, where it is evident that their use is far from clear. Bradley, opposing the earlier views of W. W. Greg, summarises their purpose as 'not, as Greg supposed, to direct performances, but to count the actors, to construct a framework for the correct making-out of their acting scrolls, to create a mutual accommodation between the cast and the text, and to direct rehearsals in the absence of the Book' (*From Text*

to Performance, 126). *The Battle of Alcazar* is the only play for which the plot and the play both survive, which makes it uniquely important as a source for comparison of the two. For reproduction and discussion of the plot, see Bradley, *Text and Performance.*

25 Lunney, *Marlowe and the Popular Tradition*, 56–63.
26 Jones is cited in Orgel, *Court Masque*, 3.
27 *EPT*, no. 74 (c).

Bibliography

Plays and entertainments

All For Money, in *CHD*.

Apius and Virginia, in *CHD*.

Axton, Marie, ed., *Three Tudor Classical Interludes* (Cambridge: D. S. Brewer, 1982).

Bale, John, *The Complete Plays of*, ed. Peter Happé, 2 vols. (Cambridge: D. S. Brewer, 1985–6).

Bevington, David, ed., *Medieval Drama* (Boston: Houghton Mifflin, 1975).
  English Renaissance Drama: a Norton Anthology (New York: W. W. Norton, 2002).

Cambyses in Manly, ed., *Specimens*.

The Castle of Perseverance, in Bevington, ed., *Medieval Drama*.

[*CHD*] *Chadwyck-Healy database of English Drama*,
    http://lion.chadwyck.co.uk/marketing/index.jsp

The Chester Mystery Cycle, ed. R. M. Lumiansky and David Mills, EETS, Special Series, 3 (London: EETS, 1974).

Croxton *Play of the Sacrament*, in Walker, ed, *Medieval Drama*.

Death of Herod, in Bevington, ed., *Medieval Drama* and Happé, ed., *English Mystery Plays*.

Dekker, Thomas, and Ben Jonson, *The Magnificent Entertainment*, in Dutton, ed. *Jacobean Civic Pageants*.

[Digby Plays], *The Late Medieval Religious Plays of Bodleian MSS. Digby 133 and E Mus. 160*, ed. Donald C. Baker, John L. Murphy and Louis B. Hall Jr (Oxford: Oxford University Press, 1982).

Dodsley, Robert, ed., *A Select Collection of Old English Plays*, 4th edn, ed. W. Carew Hazlitt, 15 vols. (London: Reeves and Turner, 1874–6).

Dutton, Richard, ed., *Jacobean and Caroline Masques* (Nottingham: Nottingham Drama Texts, 1981).
  ed., *Jacobean Civic Pageants* (Keele University: Ryburn Publishing, 1995).

Edwards, Richard, *The Works of: Politics, Poetry and Performance in Sixteenth-Century England*, ed. Ros King (Manchester and New York: Manchester University Press, 2001).

[*EEBO*] *Early English Books Online*, http://eebo.chadwyck.com/

Fletcher, John, *The Faithful Shepherdess*, in *CHD*.
Ford, John, *'Tis Pity She's a Whore*, in Kinney, ed., *Renaissance Drama*.
Gascoigne, George, *The Complete Works of*, ed. John W. Cunliffe, 2 vols. (Cambridge: Cambridge University Press, 1907–10).
Godly Queen Hester, in Walker, ed., *Medieval Drama*.
Happé, Peter, ed., *English Mystery Plays* (Harmondsworth: Penguin, 1975).
Heywood, Thomas, *A Woman Killed with Kindness*, in Kinney, ed., *Renaissance Drama*.
  The English Traveller, in *EEBO*.
Heywood, Thomas, *The Dramatic Works of Thomas Heywood* [ed. Richard Herne Shepherd], 6 vols. (London: John Pearson, 1874).
Hick Scorner, in *Two Tudor Interludes: the Interlude of Youth, Hick Scorner*, ed. Ian Lancashire (Manchester: Johns Hopkins University Press, 1980).
Jeu d'Adam, see *Play of Adam*.
Jonson, Ben, *Bartholomew Fair*, in Kinney, ed., *Renaissance Drama*.
  Barriers at a Marriage, Masque of Blackness, Masque of Queens, Pleasure Reconciled to Virtue in Lindley, ed. *Court Masques*.
  Masque of Beauty, in Dutton, ed., *Jacobean and Caroline Masques*.
Jonson, Ben: The Complete Masques, ed. Stephen Orgel (New Haven and London: Yale University Press), 1969.
Jonson, Ben, ed. C. H. Herford and Percy Simpson, 12 vols. (Oxford: Clarendon Press, 1925–52).
King Cambyses, see *Cambyses*.
Kinney, Arthur, ed., *Renaissance Drama: an Anthology of Plays and Entertainments* (Malden, Mass.: Blackwell, 1999).
Kyd, Thomas, *The Spanish Tragedy*, in Kinney, ed., *Renaissance Drama*.
Lindley, David, ed., *Court Masques: Jacobean and Caroline Entertainments 1605–1640* (Oxford and New York: Oxford University Press, 1995).
Lydgate, John, *The Minor Poems of*, ed. Henry Noble MacCracken, vol.II., EETS, Original Series, 192 (Oxford: EETS, 1934).
Lyly, John, *Campaspe* and *Sappho and Phao*, ed. G. K. Hunter and David Bevington (Manchester and New York: Manchester University Press, 1991).
  Gallathea and *Midas*, ed. Anne Begor Lancashire (London: Arnold, 1969).
Mankind, in Walker, ed., *Medieval Drama*.
Manly, John Matthews, ed., *Specimens of Pre-Shakespearean Drama*, 2 vols. (Boston: Ginn, 1897).
Marlowe, Christopher, *Dr Faustus*, in Kinney, ed., *Renaissance Drama*.
  Tamburlaine the Great, ed. J. S. Cunningham and Eithne Henson (Manchester and New York: Manchester University Press, 1981).
Mary Magdalene, in Bevington, ed., *Medieval Drama*.
Medwall, Henry, *Fulgens and Lucres*, in Walker, ed., *Medieval Drama*.
Middleton, Thomas, *A Game at Chess*, ed. T. H. Howard-Hill (Manchester and New York: Manchester University Press, 1993).

Middleton, Thomas, *A Mad World, My Masters and Other Plays*, ed. Michael
    Taylor (Oxford and New York: Oxford University Press, 1995).
Middleton, Thomas, and Cyril Tourneur, *The Revenger's Tragedy*, ed. R. A.
    Foakes (Manchester and New York: Manchester University Press,
    1996).
Munday, Antony, et al., *Sir Thomas More*, ed. Vittorio Gabrieli and Giorgio
    Melchiori (Manchester and New York: Manchester University Press,
    1990).
Nichols, John, ed., *The Progresses and Public Processions of Queen Elizabeth*, 3 vols.
    (London: Society of Antiquaries, 1823).
Nichols, John, ed. *The Progresses, Processions, and Magnificent Festivities of King
    James I*, 3 vols. (London: Society of Antiquaries, 1828).
The N-Town Play, ed. Stephen Spector, 2 vols, EETS, Special Series, 11 (Oxford:
    EETS, 1991).
N-Town, Death of Herod, see *Death of Herod*.
N-Town, The Shepherds, in *The N-Town Play*, ed. Spector.
Orgel, Stephen, and Roy Strong, eds., *Inigo Jones: the Theatre of the Stuart Court*,
    2 vols. (London, 1973).
Peele, George, *The Battle of Alcazar*, Malone Society Reprints (Oxford: Oxford
    University Press, 1907).
The Play of Adam (Ordo Representacionis Ade), trans. Carl J. Odenkirchen
    (Brookline, Mass. and Leyden: Classical Folia Editions, 1976).
[Rastell, John], *Three Rastell Plays,* ed. Richard Axton (Cambridge: D. S. Brewer,
    Rowman and Littlefield, 1979).
The Revenger's Tragedy, see Middleton, Thomas.
Rowley, William, Thomas Dekker and John Ford, *The Witch of Edmonton*, ed.
    Peter Corbin and Douglas Sedge (Manchester and New York:
    Manchester University Press, 1999).
Second Shepherds' Play, in Walker, ed., *Medieval Drama*.
Shakespeare, William, *The Riverside Shakespeare*, gen. ed. G. Blakemore Evans,
    2nd edn (Boston: Houghton Mifflin, 1997).
    King Lear: a Parallel Text Edition, ed. René Weis (London: Longman, 1993).
Shirley, James, *The Bird in a Cage*, ed. Frances Frazier Senescu (New York and
    London: Garland, 1980).
Sidney, Philip, *The Lady of May*, in *Sir Philip Sidney*, ed. Katherine Duncan-Jones
    (Oxford and New York: Oxford University Press, 1989).
The Towneley Plays, ed. Martin Stevens and A. C. Cawley, 2 vols., EETS, Special
    Series, 13, 14 (Oxford: EETS, 1994).
Walker, Greg, ed., *Medieval Drama* (Oxford: Blackwell, 2000).
Wapull, George, *The Tide Tarrieth No Man*, in *CHD*.
A Warning for Fair Women, in *CHD*.
Webster, John, *The Duchess of Malfi*, in Kinney, ed., *Renaissance Drama*.
Webster, John, The Works of: An Old-Spelling Critical Edition, ed. David Gunby,
    David Carnegie, Antony Hammond and Doreen Del Vecchio, vol. I
    (Cambridge: Cambridge University Press, 1995).

Whetstone, George, *Promos and Cassandra*, in *CHD*.

Wilson, Robert, *Three Lords and Three Ladies of London*, in CHD.

The York Cycle, ed. Richard Beadle, York Medieval Texts (London: Edward Arnold, 1982).

Non-dramatic and secondary sources

Agnew, Jean-Christophe, *Worlds Apart: The Market and the Theater in Anglo-American Thought 1550–1750* (Cambridge: Cambridge University Press, 1986).

Anglo, Sydney, 'An Early Tudor Programme for Plays and Other Demonstrations Against the Pope', *Journal of the Warburg and Courtauld Insititutes*, 20 (1957), 176–9.

    Images of Tudor Kingship (London: Seaby, 1992).

    Spectacle, Pageantry and Early Tudor Policy, 2nd edn (Oxford: Clarendon Press, 1997).

Astington, John H., *English Court Theatre 1558–1642* (Cambridge: Cambridge University Press, 1999).

Axton, Marie, *The Queen's Two Bodies: Drama and the Elizabethan Succession* (London: Royal Historical Society, 1977).

    'The Tudor Mask and Elizabethan Court Drama', in *English Drama: Forms and Development*, ed., Marie Axton and Raymond Williams (Cambridge: Cambridge University Press, 1977), 24–47.

Barish, Jonas A., *The Antitheatrical Prejudice* (Berkeley: University of California Press, 1981).

Barroll, Leeds, *Politics, Plague, and Shakespeare's Theater* (Ithaca and London: Cornell University Press, 1991).

    'Shakespeare, Noble Patrons, and the Pleasures of "Common" Playing', in White and Westfall, eds., *Shakespeare and Theatrical Patronage*, 90–121.

Baskervill, Charles Read, *The Elizabethan Jig and Related Song Drama* (1929; rpt New York: Dover Publications, 1965).

Bawcutt, N. W., ed., *The Control and Censorship of Caroline Drama: The Records of Sir Henry Herbert, Master of the Revels, 1623–73* (Oxford: Clarendon Press, 1996).

Beadle, Richard, ed., *The Cambridge Companion to Medieval Theatre* (Cambridge: Cambridge University Press, 1994).

Beckerman, Bernard, *Shakespeare at the Globe, 1599–1609* (New York: Macmillan, 1962).

Beier, A. L., *Masterless Men: The Vagrancy Problem in England 1560–1640* (London and New York: Methuen, 1985).

Bentley, Gerald Eades, *The Jacobean and Caroline Stage*, 7 vols. (Oxford: Clarendon Press, 1941–68).

    The Profession of Dramatist in Shakespeare's Time (Princeton: Princeton University Press, 1971).

The Profession of Player in Shakespeare's Time (Princeton: Princeton University Press, 1984).

Berger, Thomas, William C. Bradford and Sidney L. Sondergard, *An Index of Characters in Early Modern English Drama: Printed Plays, 1500–1660*, revised edn (Cambridge: Cambridge University Press, 1998).

Bergeron, David M., *English Civic Pageantry, 1558–1642* (London: Edward Arnold, 1971).

ed., *Pageantry in the Shakespearean Theater* (Athens, Ga.: University of Georgia Press, 1985).

Berry, Edward, 'Sidney's May Game for the Queen', *Modern Philology*, 86 (1989), 252–64.

Berry, Herbert, *Shakespeare's Playhouses* (New York: AMS Press, 1987).

Bevington, David M., *From Mankind to Marlowe: The Growth of Structure in the Popular Drama of Tudor England* (Cambridge, Mass.: Harvard University Press, 1962).

Tudor Drama and Politics: A Critical Approach to Topical Meaning (Cambridge, Mass.: Harvard University Press, 1968).

Bills, Bing D., 'The "Suppression Theory"and the English Corpus Christi Play: A Re-Examination', *Theatre Journal*, 32 (1980), 157–68.

Blayney, Peter, 'The Publication of Playbooks', in Cox and Kastan, eds., *New History*, 383–422.

Bonaventure, St [attributed to], *Meditations on the Life of Christ*, trans. Isa Ragusa, eds. Isa Ragusa and Rosalie B. Green (Princeton and Guildford: Princeton University Press, 1977).

Bradley, David, *From Text to Performance in the Elizabethan Theatre: Preparing the Play for the Stage* (Cambridge: Cambridge University Press, 1992).

Braunmuller, A. R., and Michael Hattaway, eds., *The Cambridge Companion to English Renaissance Drama*, 2nd edn (Cambridge: Cambridge University Press, 2003).

Briscoe, Marianne G., and John C. Coldewey, eds., *Contexts for Early English Drama* (Bloomington, In.: Indiana University Press, 1989).

Bruster, Douglas, 'The Dramatic Life of Objects in the Early Modern Theatre', in Harris and Korda, eds. *Staged Properties*, 67–96.

Butler, Martin, *Theatre and Crisis, 1632–1642* (Cambridge: Cambridge University Press, 1984).

Cartwright, Kent, *Theatre and Humanism: English Drama in the Sixteenth Century* (Cambridge: Cambridge University Press, 1999).

Cavendish, George, *The Life and Death of Cardinal Wolsey*, ed. Richard S. Sylvester, EETS, Original Series, 243 (London: EETS, 1959).

Cerasano, S. P., 'The Chamberlain's-King's Men', in Kastan, ed., *Companion*, 328–45.

'The Patronage Network of Philip Henslowe and Edward Alleyn', *Medieval and Renaissance Drama in England*, 13 (2001), 82–92.

Chambers, E. K., *The Medieval Stage*, 2 vols. (Oxford: Clarendon Press, 1903).

The Elizabethan Stage, 4 vols. (Oxford: Clarendon Press, 1923).

Clopper, Lawrence M., *Drama, Play, and Game: English Festive Culture in the Medieval and Early Modern Period* (Chicago and London: University of Chicago Press, 2001).

Coldewey, John C., 'The Non-Cycle Plays and the East Anglian Tradition', in Beadle, ed. *Companion*, 189–210.

Collinson, Patrick, *The Religion of Protestants: The Church in English Society, 1559–1625* (Oxford: Clarendon Press, 1982).

Cox, John D., and David Scott Kastan, eds., *A New History of Early English Drama* (New York: Columbia University Press, 1997).

Craik, T. W., *The Tudor Interlude* (Leicester: Leicester University Press, 1958).

Cunliffe, J W., *The Influence of Seneca on Elizabethan Tragedy* (London: Macmillan, [1893] 1965).

Daniel, Carter Anderson, 'Patterns and Traditions of the Elizabethan Court Play to 1590', PhD dissertation, University of Virginia, 1965.

Davidson, Clifford, *Illustrations of the Stage and Acting in England to 1580* (Kalamazoo, Michigan: Medieval Institute Publications, 1991).

  ed., *A Tretise of Miraclis Pleyinge* (Kalamazoo, Michigan: Medieval Institute Publications, 1993).

Davidson, Clifford, Lawrence Clopper and Elizabeth Baldwin, 'Saint Plays', *Early Theatre*, 1 (1998), 97–116.

Davis, Nicholas, 'The Meaning of the Word "Interlude": A Discussion'; 'Allusions to Medieval Drama in Britain (4): Interludes', *Medieval English Theatre*, 6 (1984), 5–27, 61–91.

  'The *Tretise of Myraclis Pleyinge*: On Milieu and Authorship', *Medieval English Theatre*, 12 (1990), 124–51.

Dawson, Antony B., and Paul Yachnin, *The Culture of Playgoing in Shakespeare's England* (Cambridge: Cambridge University Press, 2001).

De Grazia, Margreta, and Stanley Wells, eds., *The Cambridge Companion to Shakespeare* (Cambridge: Cambridge University Press, 2001).

Dekker, Thomas, *The Wonderful Year, The Gull's Hornbook, Penny-Wise, Pound-Foolish, English Villainies Discovered by Lantern and Candlelight and Selected Writings*, ed. E. D. Pendry (London: Edward Arnold, 1967).

Dessen, Alan C., *Elizabethan Stage Conventions and Modern Interpreters* (Cambridge: Cambridge University Press, 1984).

  Shakespeare and the Late Moral Plays (Lincoln and London: University of Nebraska Press, 1986).

  Recovering Shakespeare's Theatrical Vocabulary (Cambridge: Cambridge University Press, 1995).

  and Leslie Thomson, *A Dictionary of Stage Directions in English Drama, 1580–1642* (Cambridge: Cambridge University Press, 1999).

Diehl, Huston, *Staging Reform, Reforming the Stage: Protestantism and Popular Theater in Early Modern England* (Ithaca: Cornell University Press, 1997).

Dillon, Janette, *Language and Stage in Medieval and Renaissance England* (Cambridge: Cambridge University Press, 1998).

Theatre, Court and City, 1595–1610: Drama and Social Space in London (Cambridge: Cambridge University Press, 2000).

Performance and Spectacle in Hall's Chronicle (London: Society for Theatre Research, 2002).

'John Rastell's Stage', *Medieval English Theatre*, 18 (1996), 15–45.

'John Rastell v. Henry Walton', *Leeds Studies in English*, 28 (1997), 57–75.

'What Sacrament? Excess, Taboo and Truth in the *Croxton Play of the Sacrament* and Twentieth-Century Body Art', in *European Medieval Drama 4 (2000)*, ed. André Lascombes and Sydney Higgins (Turnhout, Belgium: Brepols, 2001), 169–79.

'Theatre and Controversy 1603–1642', in Milling and Thomson, eds., *Cambridge History of British Theatre*, 364–82.

'Chariots and Cloud Machines: Gods and Goddesses on Early English Stages', in Kermode, Scott-Warren and van Elk, eds., *Tudor Drama*, 111–29.

Dives and Pauper, ed. Priscilla Heath Barnum, EETS, Original Series, 275 (London: EETS, 1976).

Duncan-Jones, Katherine, *Sir Philip Sidney: Courtier Poet* (New Haven and London: Yale University Press, 1991).

Dutton, Richard, *Mastering the Revels: The Regulation and Censorship of English Renaissance Drama* (London and Basingstoke: Macmillan, 1991).

Licensing, Censorship and Authorship in Early Modern England: Buggeswords (Basingstoke: Palgrave, 2000).

and Jean E. Howard, eds., *A Companion to Shakespeare's Works*, 4 vols. (Oxford: Blackwell, 2003).

'The Birth of the Author', in *Texts and Cultural Change in Early Modern England*, ed. Cedric C. Brown and Arthur F. Marotti (Basingstoke and New York: Macmillan, St Martin's Press, 1997), 153–78.

'Receiving Offence: *A Game at Chess* Again', in Hadfield, ed., *Literature and Censorship*, 50–71.

'Censorship', in Cox and Kastan, eds. *A New History*, 287–304.

Eccles, Christine, *The Rose Theatre* (London: Nick Hern, 1990).

Erne, Lukas, *Shakespeare as Literary Dramatist* (Cambridge: Cambridge University Press, 2003).

Farnham, Willard, *The Medieval Heritage of Elizabethan Tragedy* (Oxford: Blackwell, 1936).

Fletcher, Alan, 'The N-Town Plays', in Beadle, ed., *Companion*, 163–88.

Feuillerat, Albert, ed., *Documents Relating to the Revels at Court in the Time of Queen Elizabeth* (1908; rpt Vaduz: Kraus Reprint Ltd, 1963).

Documents Relating to the Revels at Court in the Time of King Edward VI and Queen Mary (1914; rpt Vaduz: Kraus Reprint Ltd, 1963).

Foakes, R. A., *Illustrations of the English Stage, 1580–1642* (Stanford, California: Stanford University Press, 1985).

and R. T. Rickert, *Henslowe's Diary*, 2nd edn (Cambridge: Cambridge University Press, 2002).

Forse, James H., *Art Imitates Business: Commercial and Political Influences in Elizabethan Theatre* (Bowling Green, Ohio: Bowling Green State University Press, 1993).

Foster, Frank Freeman, *The Politics of Stability: A Portrait of the Rulers in Elizabethan London* (London: Royal Historical Society: 1977).

[Foxe, John], *The Acts and Monuments of John Foxe*, ed. George Townsend, 8 vols. (New York: AMS Press, 1965).

Gair, Reavley, *The Children of Paul's: The Story of a Theatre Company, 1553–1608* (Cambridge: Cambridge University Press, 1982).

Galloway, David, ed., *Records of Early English Drama: Norwich 1540–1642* (Toronto, Buffalo and London: University of Toronto Press, 1984).

Gardiner, Harold C., *Mysteries' End: An Investigation of the Last Days of the Medieval Religious Stage* (Hamden, Conn.: Archon Books, 1967).

Gibson, Gail McMurray, 'Bury St Edmunds, Lydgate, and the N-Town Cycle', *Speculum*, 56 (1981), 56–90.

　　The Theater of Devotion: East Anglian Drama and Society in the Late Middle Ages (Chicago: University of Chicago Press, 1989).

Gildersleeve, Virginia Crocheron, *Government Regulation of the Elizabethan Drama* (1908; rpt New York: Burt Franklin, 1961).

Gosson, Stephen, *Plays Confuted in Five Actions*, in *EEBO*.

Graves, R. B., *Lighting the Shakespearean Stage, 1567–1642* (Carbondale, Ill.: Southern Illinois University Press, 1999).

Greenfield, Peter H., 'Touring', in Cox and Kastan, eds., *New History*, 251–68.

Griffin, Benjamin, *Playing the Past: Approaches to English Historical Drama, 1385–1600* (Woodbridge: D. S. Brewer, 2001).

Gurr, Andrew, *Playgoing in Shakespeare's London*, 3rd edn (Cambridge: Cambridge University Press, 1987).

　　The Shakespearean Stage, 1574–1642, 3rd edn (Cambridge: Cambridge University Press, 1992).

　　The Shakespearian Playing Companies (Oxford: Clarendon Press, 1996).

　　The Shakespeare Company, 1594–1642 (Cambridge: Cambridge University Press, 2004).

　　and M. Ichikawa, *Staging in Shakespeare's Theatres* (Oxford: Oxford University Press, 2000).

　　'Money or Audiences: The Impact of Shakespeare's Globe', *Theatre Notebook*, 18 (1988), 3–14.

Hadfield, Andrew, ed., *Literature and Censorship in Renaissance England* (Houndmills, Basingstoke: Palgrave, 2001).

Hager, Alan, 'Rhomboid Logic: Anti-Idealism and a Cure for Recusancy in Sidney's *Lady of May*', *ELH*, 57 (1990), 485–502.

Happé, Peter, *English Drama Before Shakespeare* (London and New York: Longman, 1999).

　　Cyclic Form and the English Mystery Plays: A Comparative Study of the English Biblical Cycles and their Continental and Iconographic Counterparts (Amsterdam: Rodopi, 2004).

Harbage, Alfred., ed., *Annals of English Drama, 975–1700*, revised S. Schoenbaum and Sylvia Stoler Wagonheim, 3rd edn (London and New York: Routledge, 1989).

Harris, Jonathan Gil, and Natasha Korda, eds., *Staged Properties in Early Modern English Drama* (Cambridge: Cambridge University Press, 2002).

Harrison, William, *The Description of England*, ed. Georges Edelen (Ithaca, N.Y.: Cornell University Press, 1968).

Haynes, Alan, *The White Bear* (London: Peter Owen, 1987).

Heinemann, Margot, *Puritanism and Theatre: Thomas Middleton and Opposition Drama under the Early Stuarts* (Cambridge: Cambridge University Press, 1980).

Herbert, Henry, *see* Bawcutt (ed.).

Heywood, Thomas, *An Apology for Actors from the edition of 1612*, with introduction and notes by J. P. Collier, Shakespeare Society Publications, 3 (London: Shakespeare Society, 1841).

Hosley, R., 'Three Renaissance Indoor Playhouses', *ELR*, 3 (1973), 166–82.

Howard, Jean E., 'Shakespeare and Genre', in Kastan, ed., *Companion*, 297–309.

Howard-Hill, T. H., 'Political Interpretations of Middleton's *A Game at Chess*', *Yearbook of English Studies*, 21 (1991), 274–85.

   Middleton's 'Vulgar Pasquin': Essays on 'A Game at Chess' (Newark: University of Delaware Press, 1995).

Hughes, Paul L., and James F. Larkin, *Tudor Royal Proclamations*, 3 vols. (New Haven and London: Yale University Press, 1964–9). (See also Larkin and Hughes.)

Hunter, G. K., 'Flatcaps and Bluecoats: Visual Signals on the Elizabethan Stage', in *Essays and Studies*, 33 (1980), 16–47.

Ingram, William, *The Business of Playing: The Beginnings of Adult Professional Theater in Elizabethan London* (Ithaca and London: Cornell University Press, 1992).

   'The Globe Playhouse and its Neighbors in 1600', *Essays in Theatre*, 2 (1984), 63–72.

James, Mervyn, 'Ritual, Drama and Social Body in the Late Medieval English Town', *Past and Present*, 98 (1983), 3–29.

Jauss, Hans Robert, *Toward an Aesthetic of Reception*, trans. Timothy Bahti (Brighton, Sussex: Harvester, 1982).

Jeffrey, David L., 'English Saints' Plays', in *Medieval Drama*, ed. Neville Denny (London: Edward Arnold, 1973), 68–89.

[Johnson, Samuel], *Samuel Johnson on Shakespeare*, ed. H. R. Woudhuysen (London: Penguin, 1989).

Johnston, Alexandra F., and Margaret Rogerson, eds., *Records of Early English Drama: York*, 2 vols. (Manchester: Manchester University Press, 1979).

   and Wim Hüsken, eds., *English Parish Drama* (Amsterdam and Atlanta: Rodopi, 1996).

'The Plays of the Religious Guilds of York: the Creed Play and the Pater Noster Play', *Speculum*, 50 (1975), 55–90.

'What If No Texts Survived?', in Briscoe and Coldewey, eds., *Contexts for Early English Drama*, 1–19.

Jones, Emrys, *Scenic Form in Shakespeare* (Oxford: Clarendon Press, 1971).

Jones, Norman, and Paul Whitfield White, 'Gorboduc and Royal Marriage Politics: an Elizabethan Playgoer's Report of the Premiere Performance', *ELR*, 26 (1996), 3–16.

Kastan, David Scott, *Shakespeare and the Book* (Cambridge: Cambridge University Press, 2001).

ed., *A Companion to Shakespeare* (Oxford: Blackwell, 1999).

Kathman, David, *Biographical Index of English Drama Before 1660*, http://shakespeareauthorship.com/bd/

Keenan, Siobhan, *Travelling Players in Shakespeare's England* (Houndmills, Basingstoke: Palgrave, 2002).

Kermode, Lloyd Edward, Jason Scott-Warren and Martine van Elk, eds., *Tudor Drama Before Shakespeare, 1485–1590: New Directions for Research, Criticism, and Pedagogy* (Houndmills, Basingstoke: Palgrave, 2004).

Kernan, Alvin, *Shakespeare, the King's Playwright: Theater in the Stuart Court, 1603–1613* (New Haven and London: Yale University Press, 1995).

Kewes, Paulina, 'The Elizabethan History Play: A True Genre?', in Dutton and Howard, ed., *Companion*, Vol. II, 170–93.

Kimbrough, Robert, and Philip Murphy, 'The Helmingham Hall Manuscript of Sidney's *The Lady of May*: A Commentary and Transcription', *Renaissance Drama*, 1 (1968), 103–19.

King, T. J., *Shakespearean Staging, 1599–1642* (Cambridge, Mass.: Harvard University Press, 1971).

Casting Shakespeare's Plays: London Actors and their Roles, 1590–1642 (New York and Cambridge: Cambridge University Press, 1992).

Kinney, Arthur, *Shakespeare by Stages: An Historical Introduction* (Oxford: Blackwell, 2003).

Kipling, Gordon, *Enter the King: Theatre, Liturgy, and Ritual in the Medieval Civic Triumph* (Oxford: Clarendon Press, 1998).

Knutson, Roslyn Lander, *The Repertory of Shakespeare's Company, 1594–1613* (Fayetteville: University of Arkansas Press, 1991).

Playing Companies and Commerce in Shakespeare's Time (Cambridge: Cambridge University Press, 2001).

'The Repertory', in Cox and Kastan, eds., *New History*, 461–80.

Kraye, Jill, ed., *The Cambridge Companion to Renaissance Humanism* (Cambridge: Cambridge University Press, 1996).

Lake, Peter, 'Religious Identities' in Kastan, ed., *Companion*, 57–84.

with Michael Questier, *The Antichrist's Lewd Hat: Protestants, Papists and Players in Post-Reformation England* (New Haven and London: Yale University Press, 2002).

Lancashire, Anne, *London Civic Theatre: City Drama and Pageantry from Roman Times to 1558* (Cambridge: Cambridge University Press, 2002).

Lancashire, Ian, *Dramatic Texts and Records of Britain: A Chronological Topography to 1558* (Cambridge: Cambridge University Press, 1984).

Larkin, James F., and Paul L. Hughes, *Stuart Royal Proclamations*, vol. I (Oxford: Clarendon Press, 1973).

Laroque, François, *Shakespeare's Festive World: Elizabethan Seasonal Entertainment and the Professional Stage*, trans. Janet Lloyd (Cambridge: Cambridge University Press, 1991).

Leacroft, Richard, and Helen Leacroft, *Theatre and Playhouse: an Illustrated Survey of Theatre Building from Ancient Greece to the Present Day* (London: Methuen, 1988).

Leech, Clifford, and T. W. Craik, *Revels History of Drama in English*, 8 vols. (London: Routledge, 1996).

Leggatt, Alexander, *Jacobean Public Theatre* (London and New York: Routledge, 1992).

Limon, Jerzy, *Dangerous Matter: English Drama and Politics in 1623–4* (Cambridge: Cambridge University Press, 1986).

Loengard, Janet S., 'An Elizabethan Lawsuit: John Brayne, his Carpenter, and the Building of the Red Lion Theatre', *Shakespeare Quarterly*, 34 (1983), 298–310.

Love, Nicholas, *Nicholas Love's Mirror of the Blessed Life of Jesus Christ*, ed. Michael G. Sargent (New York: Garland, 1992).

Lunney, Ruth, *Marlowe and the Popular Tradition: Innovation in the English Drama Before 1595* (Manchester and New York: Manchester University Press, 2002).

Malone Society Collections, vol. III, *Calendar of Dramatic Records in the Books of the Livery Companies of London, 1485–1640*, ed. Jean Robertson and D. J. Gordon (Oxford: Malone Society, 1954).

    vol. VII, *Records of Plays and Players in Kent, 1450–1642*, ed. Giles E. Dawson (Oxford: Malone Society, 1965).

    vol. VIII, *Records of Plays and Players in Lincolnshire, 1300–1585*, ed. Stanley J. Kahrl (Oxford: Malone Society, 1974).

    vol. XI, *Records of Plays and Players in Norfolk and Suffolk, 1330–1642*, ed. David Galloway (Oxford: Malone Society, 1980/1).

Mann, D. *The Elizabethan Player: Contemporary Stage Representations* (London: Routledge, 1991).

Masten, Jeffrey, *Textual Intercourse: Collaboration, Authorship, and Sexualities in Renaissance Drama* (Cambridge: Cambridge University Press, 1997).

    'Playwrighting: Authorship and Collaboration', in Cox and Kastan, eds., *New History*, 357–82.

McGee, C. E., and John C. Meagher, 'Preliminary Checklist of Tudor and Stuart Entertainments: 1558–1603', *Research Opportunities in Renaissance Drama*, 24 (1981), 51–155.

'Preliminary Checklist of Tudor and Stuart Entertainments: 1485–1558', *Research Opportunities in Renaissance Drama* 25 (1982), 31–114.

'Preliminary Checklist of Tudor and Stuart Entertainments: 1603–1613', *Research Opportunities in Renaissance Drama*, 27 (1984), 47–126.

'Preliminary Checklist of Tudor and Stuart Entertainments: 1614–1625', *Research Opportunities in Renaissance Drama*, 30 (1988), 17–128.

'Preliminary Checklist of Tudor and Stuart Entertainments: 1625–1634', *Research Opportunities in Renaissance Drama*, 36 (1997), 23–95.

'Preliminary Checklist of Tudor and Stuart Entertainments: 1634–1642', *Research Opportunities in Renaissance Drama*, 38 (1999), 23–85.

MacIntyre, Jean, *Costumes and Scripts in the Elizabethan Theatres* (Edmonton: University of Alberta Press, 1992).

MacIntyre, Jean, and Garrett P. J. Epp, '"Cloathes worth all the rest": Costumes and Properties', in Cox and Kastan, eds., *New History*, 269–85.

McKinnell, John, 'Staging the Digby *Mary Magdalen*', *Medieval English Theatre*, 6 (1984), 127–52.

McLuskie, Kathleen, *Dekker and Heywood* (Basingstoke and London: Macmillan, 1994).

McManus, Clare, *Women on the Renaissance Stage: Anna of Denmark and Female Masquing in the Stuart Court, 1590–1619* (Manchester and New York: Manchester University Press, 2002).

McMillin, Scott, 'Professional Playwrighting', in Kastan, ed., *Companion*, 225–38.

McMillin, Scott, and Sally-Beth MacLean, *The Queen's Men and their Plays* (Cambridge: Cambridge University Press, 1998).

Mehl, Dieter, *The Elizabethan Dumb Show: The History of a Dramatic Convention* (London: Methuen, 1965).

Meredith, Peter, 'Putting on Plays in the Fifteenth Century', in Peter Meredith, William Tydeman and Keith Ramsay, *Acting Medieval Plays* (Lincoln Cathedral Library: Honywood Press, 1985), 1–26.

Meredith, Peter, and John Tailby, *The Staging of Religious Drama in Europe in the Later Middle Ages: Texts and Documents in English Translation* (Kalamazoo: Medieval Institute Publications, 1983).

Milling, Jane, and Peter Thomson, eds., *The Cambridge History of British Theatre*, vol. I (Cambridge: Cambridge University Press, 2004).

Minnis, Alastair J., *Medieval Theory of Authorship: Scholastic Literary Attitudes in the Later Middle Ages*, 2nd edn (London: Scolar Press, 1988).

Montrose, Louis, *The Purpose of Playing: Shakespeare and the Cultural Politics of the Elizabethan Theatre* (Chicago and London: Chicago University Press, 1996).

Nelson, Alan H., *Early Cambridge Theatres* (Cambridge: Cambridge University Press, 1994).

'Contexts for Early English Drama: The Universities', in Briscoe and Coldewey, eds., *Contexts for Early English Drama*, 138–49.

ed., *Records of Early English Drama: Cambridge*, 2 vols. (Toronto, Buffalo and London: University of Toronto Press, 1989).

Orgel, Stephen, *The Jonsonian Masque* (New York: Columbia University Press, 1981).

Impersonations: The Performance of Gender in Shakespeare's England (Cambridge: Cambridge University Press, 1996).

Imagining Shakespeare: A History of Texts and Visions (Basingstoke: Palgrave, 2003).

'Sidney's Experiment in Pastoral: *The Lady of May*', *Journal of the Warburg and Courtauld Institutes*, 26 (1964), 198–203.

Orrell, John, *The Human Stage: English Theatre Design, 1567–1640* (Cambridge: Cambridge University Press, 1988).

Owst, G. R., *Preaching in Medieval England: An Introduction to Sermon Manuscripts of the Period c. 1350–1450* (Cambridge: Cambridge University Press, 1926).

Palmer, Barbara D., 'Recycling "The Wakefield Cycle": The Records', *Research Opportunities in Renaissance Drama*, 41 (2002), 88–130.

Patterson, Annabel, *Censorship and Interpretation: The Conditions of Writing and Reading in Early Modern England* (Madison, Wisconsin: University of Wisconsin Press, 1984).

Pearsall, Derek, *John Lydgate* (London: Routledge and Kegan Paul, 1970).

John Lydgate (1371–1449): A Bio-Bibliography (Victoria, B.C.: University of Victoria, 1997).

Peters, Julie Stone, *Theatre of the Book, 1480–1880: Print, Text, and Performance in Europe* (Oxford: Oxford University Press, 2000).

Phythian Adams, Charles, 'Ceremony and the Citizen: The Communal Year at Coventry 1450–1550', in *Crisis and Order in English Towns, 1500–1700: Essays in Urban History*, ed. Peter Clark and Paul Slack (Toronto: University of Toronto Press, 1972), 57–85.

Platter, Thomas, *Thomas Platter's Travels in England*, ed. Clare Williams (London: Jonathan Cape, 1937).

Pollard, Tanya, ed., *Shakespeare's Theater: A Sourcebook* (Oxford: Blackwell, 2004).

Prouty, Charles Tyler, 'An Early Elizabethan Playhouse', *Shakespeare Survey*, 6 (1953), 64–74.

REED [*Records of Early English Drama*] Patrons and Performances Website, http://eir.library.utoronto.ca/reed

Roach, Joseph, *The Player's Passion: Studies in the Science of Acting* (Ann Arbor: University of Michigan Press, 1993).

Roper, William, *The Life of Sir Thomas Moore, Knighte*, ed. Elsie Vaughan Hitchcock, EETS, Original Series, 197 (London: EETS, 1935).

Rubin, Miri, *Corpus Christi: The Eucharist in Late Medieval Culture* (Cambridge: Cambridge University Press, 1991).

Rutter, Carol Chillington, *Documents of the Rose Playhouse*, revised edn (Manchester: Manchester University Press, 1999).

Salingar, Leo, *Shakespeare and the Traditions of Comedy* (London: Cambridge University Press, 1974).

Schlueter, June, 'Rereading the Peacham Drawing', *Shakespeare Quarterly*, 50 (1999), 171–84.

Shapiro, Michael, *Children of the Revels: The Boy Companies of Shakespeare's Time and their Plays* (New York: Columbia University Press, 1977).

Shaw, John, *The Life of*, in *Yorkshire Diaries and Autobiographies in the Seventeenth and Eighteenth Centuries*, vol. I, Surtees Society, 65 (Durham: Andrews and co., 1877).

Shepherd, Simon, and Peter Womack, *English Drama: A Cultural History* (Oxford: Blackwell, 1996).

Sidney, Philip, *An Apology for Poetry*, ed. Geoffrey Shepherd (Manchester and New York: Manchester University Press, 1965).

   An Apology for Poetry, ed. Geoffrey Shepherd, revised and expanded R. W. Maslen (Manchester and New York: Manchester University Press, 2002).

Sidney, Philip, *Report on the Manuscripts of Lord De L'Isle and Dudley preserved at Penshurst Place*, vols. 1, 2, ed. C. L. Kingsford (London: Historical Manuscripts Commission, 1925).

Skura, Meredith Ann, *Shakespeare the Actor and the Purposes of Playing* (Chicago: University of Chicago Press, 1993).

Smith, Bruce R., *Ancient Scripts and Modern Experience on the English Stage, 1500–1700* (Princeton: Princeton University Press, 1988).

Snyder, Susan, *The Comic Matrix of Shakespeare's Tragedies: Romeo and Juliet, Hamlet, Othello and King Lear* (Princeton, New Jersey: Princeton University Press, 1979).

   'The Genres of Shakespeare's Plays', in De Grazia and Wells, eds., *Cambridge Companion to Shakespeare*, 83–97.

Southern, Richard, *The Staging of Plays Before Shakespeare* (London: Faber and Faber, 1973).

Stow, John, *A Survey of London*, ed. Charles Lethbridge Kingsford, 2 vols. (Oxford: Clarendon Press, 1908).

Strong, Roy, *Art and Power: Renaissance Festivals, 1450–1650* (Woodbridge: Boydell Press, 1984).

Taylor, Gary, 'Hamlet in Africa', in *Travel Knowledge: European "Discoveries" in the Early Modern Period*, ed. Ivo Kamps and Jyotsna G. Singh (New York: Palgrave, 2001), 223–48.

Teague, Frances, *Shakespeare's Speaking Properties* (Lewisburg: Bucknell University Press, 1991).

Thomson, Peter, *Shakespeare's Theatre*, 2nd edn (London: Routledge, 1992).

A Tretise of Miraclis Pleyinge, ed. Clifford Davidson (Kalamazoo, Michigan: Medieval Institute Publications, 1993). (*Also extracted in* Walker, ed., *Medieval Drama*).

Twycross, Meg, 'Playing the Resurrection', in *Medieval Studies for J. A. W. Bennett* (Oxford: Clarendon Press, 1981), 273–96.

'Felsted of London: Silk-Dyer and Theatrical Entrepreneur', *Medieval English Theatre*, 10 (1988), 4–16.

Twycross, Meg, and Sarah Carpenter, 'Masks in Medieval English Theatre: The Mystery Plays', *Medieval English Theatre*, 3 (1981), 7–44, 69–113.

Masks and Masking in Medieval and Early Tudor England (Aldershot: Ashgate, 2002).

Tydeman, William, *English Medieval Theatre, 1400–1500* (London: Routledge and Kegan Paul, 1986).

Veevers, Erica, *Images of Love and Religion* (Cambridge: Cambridge University Press, 1989).

Walker, Greg, *Plays of Persuasion: Drama and Politics at the Court of Henry VIII* (Cambridge: Cambridge University Press, 1991).

The Politics of Performance in Early Renaissance Drama (Cambridge: Cambridge University Press, 1998).

Wasson, John, 'Professional Actors in the Middle Ages and Early Renaissance', in *Medieval and Renaissance Drama in England*, 1 (1984), 1–11.

'The English Church as Theatrical Space', in Cox and Kastan, eds., *New History*, 25–37.

Weimann, R., *Shakespeare and the Popular Tradition in the Theatre: Studies in the Social Dimension of Dramatic Form and Function* (Baltimore: Johns Hopkins University Press, 1978).

Authority and Representation in Early Modern Discourse, ed. David Hillman (Baltimore and London: Johns Hopkins University Press, 1996).

Author's Pen and Actor's Voice: Playing and Writing in Shakespeare's Theatre (Cambridge: Cambridge University Press, 2000).

Wells, Stanley, and Gary Taylor, *William Shakespeare: A Textual Companion* (Oxford: Clarendon Press, 1987).

Welsford, Enid, *The Court Masque: A Study in the Relationship between Poetry and the Revels* (Cambridge: Cambridge University Press, 1927).

Westfall, Suzanne R., *Patrons and Performance: Early Tudor Household Revels* (Oxford: Clarendon Press, 1990).

Wheeler, G. W., ed., *Letters of Sir Thomas Bodley to Thomas James* (Oxford: Bodleian Library, 1926).

White, Martin, *Renaissance Drama in Action: An Introduction to Aspects of Theatre Practice and Performance* (London and New York: Routledge, 1998).

White, Paul Whitfield, *Theatre and Reformation: Protestantism, Patronage and Playing in Tudor England* (Cambridge: Cambridge University Press, 1993).

'Reforming Mysteries' End: A New Look at Protestant Intervention in English Provincial Drama', *Journal of Medieval and Early Modern Studies*, 29 (1999), 121–47.

and Suzanne Westfall, *Shakespeare and Theatrical Patronage in Early Modern England* (Cambridge: Cambridge University Press, 2002).

Wickham, Glynne, *The Medieval Theatre*, 3rd edn (Cambridge: Cambridge University Press, 1987).
  Early English Stages, 2nd edn, 4 vols. (London: Routledge 2002).
  Herbert Berry and William Ingram, eds., *English Professional Theatre, 1530–1660* (Cambridge: Cambridge University Press, 2000).
  'The Privy Council Order of 1597 for the Destruction of All London's Theatres', in *The Elizabethan Theatre*, I, ed. David Galloway (London: Macmillan, 1969), 21–44.
  'The Staging of Saint Plays in England', in *The Medieval Drama*, ed. Sandro Sticca (Albany: New York State University Press, 1972), 99–119.
Wiggins, Martin, *Shakespeare and the Drama of his Time* (Oxford: Oxford University Press, 2000).
Wiles, David, *Shakespeare's Clown: Actor and Text in the Elizabethan Playhouse* (Cambridge: Cambridge University Press, 1987).
Wilson, R. M., *Early Middle English Literature*, 3rd edn (London: Methuen, 1968).
Withington, Robert, *English Pageantry: An Historical Outline*, 2 vols. (1918, 1926; rpt New York: B. Blom, 1963).
Womack, Peter, *Ben Jonson* (Oxford: Blackwell, 1986).
  'Shakespeare and the Sea of Stories', *Journal of Medieval and Early Modern Studies*, 29 (1999), 169–87.
Woolf, Rosemary, *The English Mystery Plays* (London: Routledge and Kegan Paul, 1972).
Wriothesley, Charles, *A Chronicle of England During the Reigns of the Tudors*, ed. William Douglas Hamilton, Vol. I, Camden 2nd series, 11 (London: Camden Society, 1875).
Yachnin, Paul, *Stage-Wrights: Shakespeare, Jonson, Middleton, and the Making of Theatrical Value* (Philadelphia: University of Pennsylvania Press, 1997).
  'The Powerless Theater', *ELR*, 21 (1991), 49–74.
Young, Abigail, 'Plays and Players: the Latin Terms for Performance', *Records of Early English Drama*, 9 (1984), 56–62 and 10 (1985), 9–16.

Index

'property players' 84
props 50, 51–3, 59, 71, 89, 91, 94, 98–9, 103, 104–6, 201, 202, 203, 211
proscenium arch 38, 53, 58, 94
Protestantism, *see also* Reform 1, 18–19, 83, 101, 114, 115, 117, 118, 133, 136, 188
Proteus and the Adamantine Rock 52
Prynne, William 114, 117, 136–7, 138, 139; *Histriomastix* 113, 114, 136–7, 138, 194–5
public playhouses, *see* amphitheatres
Pudsey, Edward 88
Puritans 114, 116, 117, 191–4

Queen's (Elizabeth's) Men 21, 71, 74–5, 81, 90, 114
Queen's (Anna's) Men 76, 120
Queen's (Henrietta's) Men 124, 137

Ralph Roister Doister 148
Rastell, John 40–3, 99, 127, 146–7; *Calisto and Melibea* 43; *Four Elements* 43, 147, 175; *Gentleness and Nobility* 43–7, 146; *Love and Riches* 37, 38, 40, 143
realism 91, 92, 93, 98, 159–60, 171, 186, 203, 205, 209, 212
rebellion, *see* sedition
Records of Early English Drama 16
Red Bull Theatre 46, 47, 82, 83, 88, 206
Red Lion Theatre 40, 46, 72
Reform (*including* Reformation; (*see also* Protestantism) 1, 28–30, 32, 42, 69, 115, 117–19, 130–1, 149, 188, 197
regionalism 19–21
Regularis Concordia 172
rehearsal 71, 76, 125
repertories 56, 76, 81, 87–8, 195
Revels Office 40, 52, 71, 125, 126–9
Revenger's Tragedy 199, 201, 202, 203
Revetour, William 130

Richard II 53, 58, 183–4
Richard II 121, 138, 139, 165
Richard III 130
Richard III 164
Richmond 21
riots (*see also* sedition) 86, 122, 123, 128–9, 138
ritual 1, 24–33, 66, 91, 92, 141, 186
Robertello, Francesco 154
Rochester, Bishop of 30
Roman Actor 121
Rome 18, 28, 134
Rookwood, Edward 132
Roper, William, *Life of Sir Thomas More* 43
Rose Theatre 46, 47, 51, 75, 76, 80, 98, 104, 194
Rowley, William, *Witch of Edmonton* 200, 202
Roxana 49
royal entries 10, 39, 51, 53, 59, 127, 183–4, 201
Rubin, Miri 30
Russell, Willy 98

Sackful of News 44
Sackville Thomas, *Gorboduc* 104, 112, 122, 149, 154
sacraments 186
saint plays 142
Salisbury Court 49, 112
Salisbury, Earl of 82
Sappho and Phao 155
Saracen's Head 44
satire 81, 82, 111, 121, 134–5, 163, 195
Satire of the Three Estates 168
Scotland 75
Scott, Thomas, *Vox Regis* 122
Second Maiden's Tragedy 129
Second Shepherds' Play, see Towneley cycle
sedition 72, 75, 120, 121, 123, 138
Sejanus 121, 165
Seneca 149, 154; *Hippolytus* 149